The Medieval Chronicle 15

The Medieval Chronicle

VOLUME 15

The titles published in this series are listed at *brill.com/mc*

Erik Kooper

The Medieval Chronicle 15

Essays in Honour of Erik Kooper

Edited by

Sjoerd Levelt
Graeme Dunphy

BRILL

LEIDEN | BOSTON

The Library of Congress Cataloging-in-Publication Data is available online at https://catalog.loc.gov
LC record available at https://lccn.loc.gov/2006233263

Typeface for the Latin, Greek, and Cyrillic scripts: "Brill". See and download: brill.com/brill-typeface.

ISSN 1567-2336
ISBN 978-90-04-54590-8 (paperback)
ISBN 978-90-04-54712-4 (e-book)

Contents

Preface

In his preface to the booklet of abstracts to the second international conference on the Medieval Chronicle in 1999, Erik Kooper looked back at the first conference, which he had hosted in Utrecht in 1996, and stated: 'the chronicle was then, and still is, a little studied topic'. When in 2023 we come together for the tenth international conference, we will be able to say with confidence that the study of medieval chronicles is now firmly established as a focus of research in the whole range of disciplines which comprise Medieval Studies: medieval literature, history, art history, linguistics, book history, digital humanities, and so forth—and communicates productively with both Classical Studies on one side and Early Modern Studies on the other. This is due in no small part to the series of conferences instigated by Erik, the book series *The Medieval Chronicle* which originated as the conference proceedings, the Medieval Chronicle Society which Erik founded and over which he presided in its infancy, childhood and adolescence, and the *Encyclopedia of the Medieval Chronicle* which it produced. It is therefore with great indebtedness and gratitude that we, members of the Medieval Chronicle Society, present this volume of essays to Erik on the occasion of the 10th International Conference of the Medieval Chronicle Society, as a special issue within the series *The Medieval Chronicle*.

This volume, co-edited by Erik's successor as president of the Medieval Chronicle Society, Graeme Dunphy, and the co-editor with Erik of the series *The Medieval Chronicle*, Sjoerd Levelt, is a collection of essays written for Erik Kooper by members of the Medieval Chronicle Society—in particular those involved in the organization of the successive conferences of the Society, those who currently hold positions in the running of the Society, and those who have or have had roles on the advisory board of *The Medieval Chronicle*.

Contributors were asked to focus their chapters on the kinds of materials and arguments in chronicle studies that each author would like to talk with Erik about: a chronicle of interest, a remarkable manuscript, an aspect of a particular historiographical corpus, a particularly interesting stylistic issue, a small but significant historical discovery, etc. Each article presents a brief case study, balancing the particulars of the chosen materials with some more generalized conclusions about their significance. In line with this brief, contributions have been kept relatively short, in order to accommodate as many contributors as possible, for the number of scholars in Medieval Chronicle Studies indebted to Erik greatly surpasses the maximum number of papers that can be contained in a single volume. The resulting collection is an anthology of different approaches in Medieval Chronicle Studies, and while not aiming to be exhaustive presents a rich overview of the geographical, linguistic, chronological and methodological diversity of chronicle research as it has developed since the first Conference of the Medieval Chronicle in no small part thanks to Erik's rallying.

The diverse community which Erik sought to nurture with his instigation of the Medieval Chronicle Society, and which came into being through the series of conferences, the production of the *Encyclopedia of the Medieval Chronicle*, and the series of volumes of *The Medieval Chronicle*, is reflected in the list of contributors, which has a wide disciplinary spread: we include essays with a historical, a literary, a book-historical, a linguistic and an art-historical bent; a broad geographical sweep ranging from York to Byzantium and from Bohemia to Castile, including, in line with Erik's particular drive to seek connections with scholars from the former Eastern Bloc, a significant number of contributions focusing on Central and Eastern Europe; an extensive chronological scope from the ninth to the seventeenth century; and contributions by both established and independent scholars, including a number who have been encouraged and supported by Erik from a very early stage in their careers.

Some who would have been asked to contribute had already contributed to the earlier volume of studies presented to Erik, *People and Texts: Relationships in Medieval Literature: Studies Presented to Erik Kooper*, edited by Thea Summerfield and Keith Busby (Brill, 2007), on the occasion of his sixty-fifth birthday and retirement from the University of Utrecht, where he taught Old and Middle English. In this current volume, we update the previous volume's select bibliography of publications by Erik Kooper with his publications since 2007.

Others we were unable to reach, and the work of yet others has since their engagement with the Society moved away from chronicle studies to such an extent that they felt unable to contribute. Many other stalwarts of the Medieval Chronicle Society—regular attendees of its conferences, contributors of articles to the series *The Medieval Chronicle* and/or entries to the *Encyclopedia of the Medieval Chronicle*—would have been more than welcome, and no doubt eager, to contribute had there not been a page limit to the projected volume; they are with us in spirit. We have been able to include papers by twenty-eight authors, but this is a present to Erik Kooper from hundreds of friends and colleagues: the entire membership of the Medieval Chronicle Society.

The editors would like to thank Marie Bláhová, Peter Damian-Grint, Isabel Barros Dias, Márta Font, Chris Given-Wilson, Michael Hicks, David Hook, Carol Sweetenham and Jaclyn Rajsic for lending us their expertise in reviewing the contributions, Kate Hammond and Marcella Mulder of Brill for welcoming our volume as a special issue in the series *The Medieval Chronicle*, and finally the two anonymous readers for the press for their invaluable suggestions.

Sjoerd Levelt and Graeme Dunphy

Abbreviations

Af.X–XI	*De Afonso X a Afonso XI*
ANPB	Anglo-Norman Prose *Brut* chronicle
BUW	Biblioteka Uniwersytecka we Wrocławiu
Chron.	*Chronica Hungaro-Polonica*
ChronicleNov I.	*The Chronicle of Novgorod 1016–1471*, trans. Robert Michell
ChronikNov I.	*Die erste Novgoroder Chronik nach ihrer ältesten Redaktion*
Cr.1344	*Crónica Geral de Espanha de 1344*
CS	Camden Society / Series
CUL	Cambridge University Library
EETS OS	Early English Text Society, Original Series
EMC	*The Encyclopedia of the Medieval Chronicle*. Ed. Graeme Dunphy. Leiden & Boston: Brill, 2010. / referenceworks.brillonline.com/browse/encyclopedia-of-the-medieval-chronicle
Gallus	*Gesta principium Polonorum*
GS	*Gesta Stephani*
HN	William of Malmesbury, *Historia novella*
ISTC	Incunabula Short Title Catalogue, data.cerl.org/istc/
Kadłubek	*Magistri Vincenti dicti Kadłubek Chronica Polonorum*
KNM	Knihovna Národního muzea
KPMK	Knihovna pražské metropolitní kapituly
Legenda	*Sancti Stephani regis maior et minor, atque Legenda ab Hartvico episcopo conscripta*
Linhagens	Pedro Afonso de Barcelos, *Livro de Linhagens*
MEPB	Middle English Prose *Brut* chronicle
MGH, SS	Monumenta Germaniae Historica, Scriptores
MPH KHW	*Kronika Halicko-Wołyńska* (*Kronika Romanowiczów*)
NK ČR	Národní knihovna České republiky
NLR	Saint Petersburg, National Library of Russia
NPL	*Новгородская Первая летопись старшего и младшего изводов*
ODNB	*Oxford Dictionary of National Biography*. Oxford: Oxford University Press. / oxforddnb.com
ÖNB	Österreichische Nationalbibliothek Wien
Onceno	*Cronica de D. Alfonso el Onceno de este nombre*
Partidas	Alfonso el Sabio, *Las Siete Partidas*
PL	*Patrologiae cursus completus*. Series Latina, ed. J.P. Migne
PSRL I	*Лаврентьевская летопись*
PSRL II	*Ипатьевская летопись*

PSRL III	*Новгородская Первая летопись старшего и младшего изводов*
PV	Peculiar Version
RHC.Occ	*Recueil des Historiens des Croisades, Historiens Occidentaux*
RHGF	*Recueil des historiens des Gaules et de la France*
RIS	*Rerum Italicarum Scriptores*
SOA Třeboň	Státní oblastní archiv v Třeboní
STC	*Short Title Catalogue*, ed. A.W. Pollard and G.R. Redgrave (2nd edn, 1976–1991)
TCR-*Polychronicon*	Condensed version of Trevisa's *Polychronicon* I.2–24
Vyšší Brod	Knihovna cisterciáckého opatství Vyšší Brod
Wood	Oxford, Bodleian Libraries, MS Wood empt. 8

Notes on Contributors

Firuza Abdullaeva
Pembroke College—University of Cambridge (UK)

Marie Bláhová
Department of Auxiliary Historical Sciences and Archive Studies—Charles University, Prague (Czech Republic)

Cristian Bratu
Department of Modern Languages and Cultures—Baylor University (USA)

Elizabeth J. Bryan
Department of English—Brown University (USA)

Godfried Croenen
Department of Languages, Cultures and Film—University of Liverpool (UK)

Peter Damian-Grint
School of History—University of St Andrews (UK)

Kelly DeVries
Department of History—Loyola University Maryland (USA)

Isabel Barros Dias
Departamento de Humanidades—Universidade Aberta; IELT | IEM—FCSH-NOVA (Portugal)

Graeme Dunphy
Faculty of Applied Natural Sciences and Humanities—Technical University of Applied Sciences Würzburg-Schweinfurt (Germany)

Márta Font
Department of Medieval History—University of Pécs (Hungary)

Chris Given-Wilson
School of History—University of St Andrews (UK)

Ryszard Grzesik
Institute of Slavic Studies—Polish Academy of Sciences (Poland)

Isabelle Guyot-Bachy
Centre de Recherche Universitaire Lorrain d'Histoire—Université de Lorraine—Nancy (France)

Michael Hicks
Department of History—University of Winchester (UK)

David Hook
Faculty of Medieval & Modern Languages—University of Oxford (England)

Sjoerd Levelt
Department of English—University of Bristol (UK)

Alison Williams Lewin
History Department—Saint Joseph's University—Philadelphia PA (USA)

Julia Marvin
Program of Liberal Studies—University of Notre Dame (USA)

Charles Melville
Pembroke College—University of Cambridge (UK)

Martine Meuwese
Department of History and Art History—Utrecht University (the Netherlands)

Sarah L. Peverley
Department of English—University of Liverpool (UK)

Jaclyn Rajsic
School of English and Drama—Queen Mary University of London (UK)

Lisa M. Ruch
Liberal Studies Department—Bay Path University (USA)

Françoise Le Saux
Department of Languages and Cultures—University of Reading (UK)

Carol Sweetenham
University of Warwick / Royal Holloway College—London (UK)

Letty ten Harkel
Faculty of Archaeology—Leiden University (the Netherlands)

Grischa Vercamer
Institut für Europäische Studien und Geschichtswissenschaften—Technische Universität Chemnitz (Germany)

Jürgen Wolf
Institut für Deutsche Philologie des Mittelalters—Philipps-Universität Marburg (Germany)

1

Die ‚Geschichte in Daten' im mittelalterlichen Böhmen

Marie Bláhová

Zusammenfassung

This study analyzes concise historical compendia, or ‚histories in dates', in medieval Bohemia. These include the *Excerpta de diversarum chronicarum* (1330s), spanning the period 80–1314 with continuations to 1330; the so-called Beneš Minorit Chronicle, a brief history of Bohemia from its Christianisation until 1492; the Chronicle of Abbot Neplach of Opatovice (1360s), a brief compendium of universal and Bohemian history from the birth of Christ until 1365; and *Annales breves Bohemici saeculi XIV* (end of the 1390s or early fifteenth century) covering the period from 1310 to 1399, with a continuation to 1432. However, the work that received the greatest acclaim was a concise overview of Bohemian history from ‚the beginning' until the early fifteenth century, with a number of continuations, called *Chronicon Bohemorum ab ipsorum inicio conscripta*, also *Chronicon anonymi*, or ‚From Czech and Lech'. This has survived in nine versions which differ in their introductions, number of records, and continuations. The perspectives and significance of these little-studied texts are elucidated.

Die Geschichtsschreibung in den Böhmischen Ländern kopierte im Mittelalter mit gewisser Verspätung die Entwicklung der Historiographie des lateinischen Kulturkreises. Bis zum Spätmittelalter entstanden zwar weder in Böhmen noch in Mähren ursprüngliche Universalchroniken, auch wenn hier entsprechende Werke der lateinischen europäischen Kultur abgeschrieben und genutzt wurden.[1] Der Schwerpunkt der historiographischen Tätigkeit lag jedoch bei der Staatsvolksgeschichte, der Landesgeschichte sowie der institutionellen Geschichte.[2]

---

1 Bláhová (2007). Dieser Artikel ist Teil des Programms Cooperatio der Karlsuniversität Prag des Wissenschaftsbereichs ‚History'. Die Studie nutzte die Datenbank Czech Medieval Sources online, bereitgestellt von der Forschungsinfrastruktur LINDAT/CLARIAH-CZ (https://lindat.cz), die vom tschechischen Schulministerium gefördert wird (Projekt Nr. LM2018101).
2 Bláhová (1995: 90–161).

Eine detaillierte narrative Geschichte war zwar ein gutes Mittel zur Belehrung über die Vergangenheit sowie zur Formulierung der Ideologie und Propaganda, aber für jene Benutzer, die sich nur in der Reihenfolge der Herrscher oder kirchlichen Würdenträger, in den Ereignissen und historischen Daten orientieren wollten, war sie erheblich unpraktisch. Deshalb wurden seit den ältesten Zeiten Listen von Würdenträgern sowie Verzeichnisse von Daten und Ereignissen zusammengestellt, und es wurden kurze historische Handbücher und Lehrbücher verfasst.[3] Vor allem für Theologen erarbeitete man spezifische ‚Lehrbücher' der Universalgeschichte, wie das kurzgefasste theologisch-historische Handbuch von Hugo von Sankt Viktor (um 1097–1141) *Chronicon* oder *Liber de tribus maximis circumstantiis gestorum*, in dem der Verfasser von der biblischen Geschichte ausging und auch die profane Geschichte miteinbezog.[4] Peter von Poitiers dagegen bearbeitete tabellarisch die biblische Geschichte und die Geschichte des Altertums in der kurzen Schrift *Compendium historiae in genealogia Christi*.[5] Das klassische Beispiel eines praktisch orientierten Handbuchs ist die Chronik der Päpste und Kaiser des Martin von Troppau, die für (kirchliche) Rechtsgelehrte bestimmt ist und dazu dient, sich leichter im Dekret zu orientieren, und die auf 28 Folien die ‚Weltgeschichte' von Christi Geburt bis in die zweite Hälfte des 13. Jahrhunderts zusammenfasst,[6] oder die ähnlich konzipierte Schrift *Flores temporum*.[7] Vergleichbare übersichtliche Handbücher wurden für Universalgeschichte, Staatsvolksgeschichte und institutionelle Geschichte zusammengestellt.

Aus den böhmischen Ländern sind neben den Herrscherkatalogen und Katalogen kirchlicher Würdenträger[8] sowie kurzen Einführungen, die die Anfänge der tschechischen Geschichte in retrospektiven historischen Schriften reproduzieren, mehrere knapp gefasste Kompendien bekannt.

Eines von ihnen ist die kurze, in den dreißiger Jahren des 14. Jahrhunderts im Zisterzienserkloster Zbraslav (Königsaal) zusammengestellte annalistische Kompilation. Sie umfasst die Jahre 80–1314, mitunter mit einer Fortsetzung bis 1330. Von den modernen Historikern wird sie oft als eine Sammlung von Auszügen aus verschiedenen Chroniken – *Excerpta de diversarum chronicarum*

---

3 Joachimsen (1910: 3); Studt (1999: 305–321); Melville (1980: 61–77). Bemühungen um eine Anordnung des Stoffs in übersichtlichen Büchern und Kapiteln zeigten sich ab dem 13. Jahrhundert in Kompilationen auf allen Fachgebieten. Vgl. Parkes (1976: 130).

4 *Chronica quae dicitur Hugonis de Sancto Victore.* Vgl. Green (1943: 484–493); Rech (*EMC* 1, 817–818); Menzel (1998: 50–51).

5 Norbye (2010: 1205); Gauthier (2008).

6 Vgl. Martin von Troppau, Startseite.

7 Vgl. Mierau et al. (1996); Kümper (2010).

8 Bláhová (1999; 2003).

bezeichnet.[9] Sie enthält Berichte aus der Kirchengeschichte, wie die Sterbe-
daten von Heiligen und Kirchenvätern, die Entstehungsjahre von geistlichen
Orden, ferner Berichte über die österreichische und tschechische Geschichte
und ihre Herrscher sowie Berichte aus Zbraslav. Diese Kompilation wurde nach
der Chronik der Päpste und Kaiser des Martin von Troppau, nach österreichischen Annalen, böhmischen Annalen und Chroniken, Genealogien und Katalogen zusammengestellt.[10]

Eine ,Geschichte in Daten' stellt ebenfalls die als Chronik des sog. Benesch
Minorit bekannte Schrift dar. Diese kleine Schrift berichtet nach einem knap-
pen die alttestamentarischen Ereignisse zusammenfassenden *temporum ratio*
über die tschechische Geschichte ab der Taufe des ersten christlichen Fürsten, die traditionell mit dem fehlerhaften Jahreszahl 894 datiert wird.[11] In einigen Phasen und einschließlich verschiedener Fortsetzungen wurde die tschechische Geschichte bis zum Jahr 1492 weitergeführt.[12] Es ist dies eine Kompilation sowohl aus erhaltenen, als auch aus verschollenen, jedoch in anderen Quellen belegten Annalen und Chroniken, an die die eigenen zeitgenössischen Nachrichten des Kompilatoren angehängt wurden. Die Grundlagen dieser Geschichte in Daten wurden wohl im Lauf des 13. Jahrhunderts und wahrscheinlich im Prager Domkapitel gelegt. Man verlängerte sie schrittweise und
fügte auch weitere Berichte ein. Zur Wende der fünfziger und sechziger Jahre
des 14. Jahrhunderts gelangte diese Kompilation in ein Minoritenkloster, wahrscheinlich ins Sankt-Jakob-Kloster in der Prager Altstadt. Hier verband man
sie mit den Minoritenannalen. Dadurch entstand eine eigene Chronik des sog.
Benesch Minorit.[13] Dieser Text wurde bis 1416 durch Auszüge aus der Chronik
des Prager Domherren und Baudirektor der Kathedrale Benesch von Weitmühl
(† 1375), durch einen Teil des *Cronicon Bohemorum Anonymi* beziehungsweise
seiner Vorlage sowie durch weitere Aufzeichnungen des Prager Domkapitels

---

9   Auszüge aus verschiedensten Chroniken. Zur Datierung vor allem Novotný (1905: IX–X).
    Vgl. auch Müller (1983: 166–167); Bláhová (2017: 18–20).
10 Detailliert vgl. Bláhová (2017: 19).
11 Der Ursprung dieses Datums, das vom Dekan des Prager Domkapitels Kosmas in die tsche-
    chische Geschichtsschreibung eingeführt wurde, wird akzeptabel rekonstruiert von Wol-
    verton (2015: 56–58).
12 *Benedicti minoritae dicti Chronica*. Eine detaillierte Analyse der Chronik nahm Dušek
    (1990) vor.
13 Dieser zuerst von Palacký verliehene Werktitel (1869: 195–196, 301), wurde durch die vor-
    hergehende fehlerhafte Interpretation und das Zusammentreffen zufälliger Umstände
    beeinflusst, die zur irrtümlichen Identifizierung des Verfassers mit Benesch von Weitmühl
    führten. Vgl. Dušek (1990: 7–8).

verlängert.[14] Eine weitere Fortsetzung stellen die Aufzeichnungen eines pro-
hussitisch orientierten Prager Stadtbürgers (1419–1422, wohl auch einzelne Eintragungen bis 1438) dar. Die Ereignisse des Zeitraums 1438–1457 und die Interpolation in den vorhergehenden Text ab 1419 wurden von einem unbekannten
katholischen Bürger Prags eingetragen. An ihn knüpften dann im Gegenteil ein
Kalixtiner, Anhänger des böhmischen Königs Georg von Podiebrad (1458–1471)
und vielleicht auch andere Annalisten an.[15]

Systematischer konzipiert ist die Chronik des Abts Neplach von Opatovice
aus den sechziger Jahren des 14. Jahrhunderts. Sie stellte ein knapp gehaltenes
Kompendium der Universalgeschichte mit der anknüpfenden tschechischen
Geschichte von Christi Geburt bis zum Jahr 1365 dar. Die Universalgeschichte
ging von der Chronik des Martin von Troppau aus, die tschechische Geschichte
wird hier aufgrund des Katalogs der böhmischen Herrscher, älterer tschechi-
scher Chroniken und Legenden dargestellt.[16]

Wahrscheinlich gegen Ende der neunziger Jahre des 14. oder zu Beginn des
15. Jahrhunderts (vor dem 24. September 1405) wurden die kurzen Annalen
zusammengestellt, die die Geschichte des Hauses Luxemburg und die wichtigsten Ereignisse der luxemburgischen Regierungszeit erfassten. Sie beginnen
mit Johann von Luxemburgs Besteigung des böhmischen Throns im Jahr 1310
und enden 1399. Diese *Annales breves Bohemici saeculi XIV*. – Kurze böhmische
Annalen des 14. Jahrhunderts[17] – informieren über Geburten, Eheschließungen
und das Ableben von Mitgliedern des Luxemburgergeschlechts, über einige
Gründungstaten von Karl IV., ferner von Überschwemmungen und anderen
Katastrophen in Prag, schließlich über die Gefangennahme von Wenzel IV.
sowie über den Brand des Altstädter Rathauses im Jahr 1399. An diese Annalen knüpften später andere Kompilatoren an und führten sie bis 1432 weiter.

Einen weitaus größeren Anklang fand im Spätmittelalter jedoch der annalis-
tisch angeordnete kurze Überblick der tschechischen Geschichte vom ‚Anfang‘
bis zur zweiten Hälfte des zweiten Jahrzehnts des 15. Jahrhunderts, in der
modernen Geschichtsschreibung bekannt als *Chronicon Bohemorum ab ipsorum inicio conscripta* – ‚Chronik Böhmens, verfasst von seinen Anfängen an‘,
auch als *Chronicon anonymi* – ‚Anonyme Chronik‘, mitunter ebenfalls unter der
Bezeichnung ‚Von Čech und Lech an‘.[18]

---

14   Dušek (1990: 84–91). Das *Cronicon Bohemorum Anonymi* wird hier weiter unten behandelt.
15   Dušek (1990: 91–97, 98–99).
16   Bláhová (1987: 583–585, 594).
17   ÖNB 5483, fol. 210ʳ⁻ᵛ. Vgl. Bláhová (2009).
18   Die Chronik hat keine kritische Edition. 1774 gab Gelasius Dobner eine ihrer späteren

Der Text stellt in der Einleitung das Programm der Chronik vor: Der Verfasser konstatiert, dass die Chronik Böhmens von ihren Anfängen an aus vielen Chroniken dieses Landes exzerpiert wurde, und somit in gekürzter Form zur Erinnerung für die Nachwelt berichtet, wer die ‚Entdecker‘ (*inventores*) des böhmischen Landes, die Richter, Herzöge, Fürsten und Könige, Bischöfe und Erzbischöfe waren. Die Chronik beginnt mit einer Darlegung der ‚Entdeckung‘ oder ‚Gründung‘ Böhmens und der Nachbarländer. Sie setzt fort mit einer kurzen Schilderung der mythischen Geschichte. Es folgt eine Aufzählung der mythischen Fürsten mit ihren genealogischen Beziehungen (*x filius y*) bis zum letzten ‚heidnischen‘ Fürsten Hostivít und seinem Sohn Bořivoj, der *primo paganus, sed postea cristianus* (‚zunächst Heide, dann Christ‘) war und die ‚heilige‘ Ludmila zur Frau nahm. Getauft wurde er der Chronik zufolge im Jahr 895 vom mährischen Erzbischof Method. Die fehlerhafte Angabe 895 (in einigen Handschriften 896 oder 890), die wahrscheinlich durch ein fehlerhaftes Lesen oder durch die falsche Eintragung der römischen Ziffern der traditionellen, ebenfalls falschen Jahreszahl 894 entstand, ist das erste in der *Anonymen Chronik* genannte Datum. Das nächste Datum betrifft die Ermordung des heiligen Wenzels am 28. September, der Chronik zufolge im Jahr 929,[19] und seine Übertragung am 4. März 932. Danach sind die Ereignisse dann durchgehend datiert. Es folgen kurze Eintragungen über die Reihenfolge der böhmischen Herrscher beziehungsweise ihre wichtigen Taten. Zum Jahr 967 wird die Gründung des Bistums Prag erwähnt, wonach Berichte über die Wahl bzw. das Ableben der einzelnen Bischöfe folgen. Ab dem Jahr 999, für das der Tod von Fürst Boleslav II. (dem ‚Frommen‘) erwähnt wird, folgen in gemischter Reihenfolge Nachrichten über Antritt beziehungsweise Tod der Herrscher und Bischöfe, mitunter über Ereignisse in ihrer Regierungszeit. Dazu kommen Meldungen über die Gründung von Kirchen, Domen und Klöstern, über das Auffinden und die Erwerbung der sterblichen Überreste von Heiligen, die Krönung von Königen, die Kanonisation von Heiligen und weitere Ereignisse. Mit dem Jahr 1394 brechen die Berichte ab und werden erst mit den Jahren 1405, 1410, 1412, 1414, 1415 und 1416 fortgesetzt. Der Text endet also mit Berichten über die unruhigen Ereignisse der ersten beiden Jahrzehnte des 15. Jahrhunderts, über das Konzil von Konstanz und die Verbrennung von Johannes Hus am 6. Juli 1415 und von

---

Rezensionen heraus (*Chronicon Anonymi*). Vgl. Bláhová (2010a), Šimák (1918: 171–185); Čornej (2003: XXVI–XXVII).

19   Dieses offenbar fehlerhafte Datum gab Kosmas in seiner Chronik an, aus der es von anderen Autoren übernommen wurde. Zum Datum der Ermordung des heiligen Wenzel (richtig 28. September 935) vgl. Třeštík (1997: 209–260).

Hieronymus von Prag am 30. Mai 1416 sowie über die in dieser Zeit in Böhmen beobachteten Himmelserscheinungen.

Der Text der *Anonymen Chronik Böhmens* wurde zumeist aus bekannten Quellen zusammengestellt.[20] Die Hauptquelle für ihren Großteil war die zweite Rezension der *Böhmischen Chronik* von Přibík Pulkava von Radenín, einer offiziellen tschechischen Geschichte, verfasst im Auftrag von Karl IV. (1346–1378).[21] Ihren Text straffte der Kompilator der *Anonymen Chronik* erheblich. Nach den einleitenden Passagen, die narrative Form besitzen, wählte er aus ihr nur die nackten Tatsachen. Diese präsentierte er in kurzen und stichwortartigen Sätzen. Der Chronik des Pulkava folgte der unbekannte Autor bis zum Ende deren zweiter Rezension, also bis 1330.[22] Nur mit geringen Änderungen übernahm er aus ihr auch Pulkavas Paraphrase von Kosmas Anmerkung darüber, dass die Chronik vom Anfang bis 895 nicht nach den Jahren des Herren gegliedert ist, weil sie von Heiden handelt, während sie danach so gegliedert wird.[23] Im Bericht vom Amtsantritt des Prager Bischofs Andreas (1214–1224), in der auch dessen Tod und Bettung der sterblichen Überreste erwähnt wird, verweist der Kompilator auf eine ‚Chronik‘, aus der der Leser von den Ursachen für den Weggang des Bischofs aus Böhmen erfahre. Damit ist offenbar wiederum Pulkavas Chronik gemeint.[24]

In die aus Pulkavas Chronik übernommenen Nachrichten fügte der Kompilator Berichte aus der Kirchengeschichte ein, darunter Angaben über Ordensgründungen, über den Tod der Verfasser des Dekrets, über die Überführung der sterblichen Überreste der Heiligen Drei Könige von Mailand nach Köln sowie über die Ankunft der Flagellanten. Diese Berichte der *Anonymen Chronik* nähern sich entsprechenden Einträgen in den Auszügen aus verschiedenen Chroniken und stammen aus der Chronik des Martin von Troppau.[25]

---

20   Zu den Quellen der *Anonymen Chronik* vgl. Mareš (1866: 137–138). Hier sind einige Präzisierungen.

21   Bláhová (1987: 573–577, 590–593).

22   Zur Genesis von Pulkavas Chronik und zu ihren Rezensionen Bláhová (1987: 574–577; 590–592).

23   ‚Nota quod Cronica Boemorum ab inicio usque ad presens et huc per annos domini distincta non fuit, que narrat tamquam de paganis que in sequentibus distingwere prout melius poterit.‘ Diese Anmerkung findet sich in den meisten Handschriften vor dem Jahr 895 (vgl. z.B. ÖNB 3282, fol. 8ᵛ), in einigen ist sie stilistisch bearbeitet. Dazu *Kronika Pulkavova*, 15.

24   ‚Quare exulavit, patet in Cronica.‘ *Chronicon Anonymi*, 49; *Kronika Pulkavova*, 127–129.

25   *Výpisky z rozličných kronik*, 341–342; Martin von Troppau: *passim*.

Eine weitere Quelle des Kompilators der *Anonymen Chronik Böhmens* war die zweite Redaktion der Chronik des Franz von Prag,[26] ebenfalls verfasst in der Regierungszeit von Karl IV. und fertig gestellt in der ersten Hälfte der fünfziger Jahre des 14. Jahrhunderts. Der Kompilator nutzte die Quelle zur Erforschung der Ereignisse etwa von den achtziger Jahren des 13. Jahrhunderts bis 1353. Belegt wird ihre Nutzung durch den Bericht über die Ernennung des Kaplans des Prager Bischofs Johann IV. von Dražice Franz, ‚der zur Ehre des Bischofs diesen zweiten Teil der Chronik schrieb‘, und zwar nach dem Konflikt von 1334 zwischen den Pfarrern und den Bettelordensbrüdern in Prag.[27] Der Kompilator übernahm ihn Wort für Wort aus der Chronik des Franz von Prag, obwohl er für seinen Text keinerlei Bedeutung hatte. Die aus dieser Quelle übernommenen Nachrichten sind zu Beginn mit Berichten aus Pulkavas Chronik durchsetzt. Aufgrund der Kürze der ausgewählten Berichte kann nicht immer festgestellt werden, aus welcher dieser Quellen die Information übernommen wurde.

Der Kompilator verwendet ebenfalls die Chronik der Prager Kirche des Benesch von Weitmühl,[28] jenes Chronisten, der in seiner Schrift den längsten Abschnitt der Regierungszeit von Karl IV. schilderte (bis 1374). Aus ihr schöpfte der Kompilator Nachrichten bis zum Anfang der siebziger Jahre des 14. Jahrhunderts. Anhand der Eintragungen, in denen sich der Text des Benesch von Weitmühl mit dem des Franz von Prag deckt, der bis 1340 Beneschs Quelle war, kann die Vorlage wiederum nicht genau identifiziert werden. Daneben benutzte der Kompilator offenbar auch die Genealogie der Luxemburger sowie nicht näher bekannte annalistische Aufzeichnungen. Aus diesen entnahm er Angaben vor allem für die zweite Hälfte des 14. Jahrhunderts bis in die neunziger Jahre. Ähnliche Aufzeichnungen wie in der *Anonymen Chronik* erscheinen auch in der Fortsetzung der Chronik des sog. Benesch Minorit, deren Kompilator offenbar eine gemeinsame Vorlage mit dem Kompilator der *Anonymen Chronik* verwendete.[29] Einige lassen sich auch in anderen kurzen historischen Schriften des 15. Jahrhunderts finden, ohne dass jedoch zwischen diesen Schriften ein unmittelbarer Zusammenhang gefunden werden kann. Offenbar gingen diese Texte von einer gemeinsamen Vorlage aus, die jedoch von den

---

26 Bláhová (2016: 43–49).

27 ‚Eodem anno insurrexerunt plebani Ecclesiarum Pragensium contra ordines mendicancium, qui consveverant predicare in Eccleesia Pragensi. Sed postea Dominus Johannes Episcopus Pragensis XXVII. Franciscum capellanum suum predicatorem et penitenciarium scilicet Ecclesie Pragensis instituit, qui ob reverenciam Episcopi hanc secundam partem cronice conscripsit.‘ *Chronicon Anonymi*, 55; *Chronicon Francisci Pragensis*, 149.

28 Bláhová (2016: 50–64).

29 Dušek (1990: 85).

Schreibern ergänzt und verändert wurde. Durch häufiges Abschreiben der Vorlagen und des ‚fertigen' Textes sowie durch Verwendung von mehreren Quellen gelangten in die *Anonyme Chronik* zahlreiche Fehler bei den Daten und der Interpretation der Ereignisse. Einige Nachrichten werden wiederholt, oft mit unterschiedlichem Daten, manche werden weggelassen, die Chronologie ist oft falsch. Einige Fehler könnten auch dadurch verursacht werden, dass der Schreiber einen flüchtigen, möglicherweise auch beschädigten Text der Vorlage nicht richtig lesen konnte.

Die ursprüngliche Fassung der *Anonymen Chronik* ist nicht erhalten. Die Chronik ist aus neun Handschriften bekannt, die aus verschiedenen Zeiten des 15. Jahrhunderts stammen, deren Wortlaut allerdings nur ausnahmsweise übereinstimmt.[30] Unterschiede bestehen in der Anzahl und mitunter auch im Charakter der vorhandenen Eintragungen. In einigen Handschriften sind dem Grundtext individuelle Fortsetzungen beigefügt, die bis in verschiedene Zeiten des 15. Jahrhunderts führen.

Ein auffälliger Unterschied besteht bereits in den einleitenden Abschnitten der Chronik. Der Text beginnt bei den meisten Handschriften mit den Worten *Primus inventor terre Boemie* (eventuell *Boemorum*) *fuit Czech ...*, also ‚Der erste Entdecker des Landes Böhmen war Čech'. Dann folgt eine Erzählung über Čechs Bruder Lech, der der erste Entdecker des polnischen Landes war. Mitglieder seines Geschlechts bebauten und besiedelten die Länder Russland, Pommern, Kaschubei bis zum Königreich Dänemark und zu den Meeresgestaden. Ähnlich bearbeiteten und besiedelten die Menschen aus Čechs Stamm das Land Mähren, ferner Meißen, Bautzen und das Fürstentum Lausitz, also alle Länder, die im 14. Jahrhundert Teil der Böhmischen Krone waren. Die Beschreibung entspricht dem von Přibík Pulkava von Radenín in der offiziellen böhmischen Geschichte festgehaltene Territorium.[31] In einer der Handschriften (NK ČR XIX B 26) sind allerdings die von Lechs Stamm besiedelten Länder ausgelassen.[32]

30   Praha KNM VIII D 20, fol. 124ᵛ–129ᵛ; VIII F 49, fol. 186ᵛ–204ʳ; KPMK O III, fol. 144ʳ–150ᵛ; NK ČR XIX B 26, fol. 240ᵛ–248ᵛ; Wien ÖNB 3282, fol. 8ʳ–17ᵛ; Třeboň SOA A 7, fol. 7ᵛ–25ᵛ; A 10, fol. 1ʳ–16ᵛ; Vyšší Brod 101, fol. 182ᵛ–188ʳ; Wrocław BUW IV F 104, fol. 2ʳ–10ᵛ.

31   ‚Primus inventor terre Boemie fuit Czech, cuius frater Lech fuit primus inventor terre Polonie, De cuius genere coluerunt inhabitare ceperunt terras Russiam, Pomeriam, Cassubiam usque ad regnum Dacie et confinia maritima. Similiter de genere Czech excoluerunt inhabitare ceperunt terram Moravie, Misnam, Budissin, Luzaciam principatum, qui sunt primo ab ipsis inventi et ab ipsorum genere possessi.' KPMK O III, fol. 144ʳ; KNM VIII D 20, fol. 124ᵛ; ÖNB 3282, fol. 8ʳ; Vyšší Brod 101, fol. 182ᵛ; SOA Třeboň A7, fol. 7ᵛ; SOA Třeboň A 10, fol. 1ʳ. *Kronika Pulkavova*, 5. Vgl. Bláhová (2020:32–33).

32   NK XIX B 26, fol. 240ʳ.

In zwei Handschriften (KNM VIII F 49 und BUW IV F 104) hat der Text jedoch eine abweichende Einleitung. Er beginnt mit den Worten *Fuerunt tres fratres ...* – ,es waren drei Brüder ...‘ und führt mit der Mitteilung fort, dass der erste Čech hieß und Böhmen gegründet habe, der zweite sei Krok gewesen, der Krakau errichtet und Polen gegründet habe, der dritte war Lech, der Liegnitz (polnisch Legnica) gegründet und Schlesien besiedelt habe.[33] Die unterschiedliche Einleitung war offenbar eine durchdachte Absicht und wurde aus Propagandagründen gewählt, womit der Textbearbeiter die Zusammengehörigkeit von Polen, vor allem aber von Schlesien und Böhmen zum Ausdruck bringen wollte.[34]

Weitere wichtige Unterschiede bestehen bereits in der Beschreibung der ,historischen‘ Periode der tschechischen Geschichte in den einzelnen Handschriften. Außer offensichtlichen Schreibfehlern und fehlerhaften Jahreszahlen, zumeist von den Vorlagen übernommen, lassen einzelne Handschriften einige Berichte aus, anderswo fügen sie dagegen neue ein. Bis auf Ausnahmen gelang es jedoch nicht, in den Bearbeitungen des folgenden Textes eine bestimmte Absicht zu entdecken. Die ausgelassenen und die interpolierten Berichte wirken zumeist zufällig. Zu den wenigen Ausnahmen gehören die beiden bereits erwähnten Handschriften. Der Text der Chronik in der Handschrift KNM VIII F 49 wurde für Laien, insbesondere für das bürgerliche Publikum, angepasst. Programmatisch sind die meisten Berichte über die allgemeine und tschechische Kirchengeschichte sowie einige andere Berichte ausgelassen, die für das bürgerliche Publikum nicht von Interesse waren. In der Handschrift BUW IV F 104 wurde die Chronik für das schlesische Publikum angepasst. Zum Wortlaut der *Anonymen Chronik* wurden einige Wrocław betreffende Berichte hinzugefügt und eine Fortsetzung zur Geschichte Schlesiens beigefügt.[35]

Bei einem Vergleich der eingefügten und der fehlenden Eintragungen in den einzelnen Handschriften können die Genesis des Werks sowie seine einzelnen Rezensionen zumindest teilweise erfasst werden. Bei einer Analyse der Handschriften gelang es, neun Rezensionen der Chronik zu identifizieren, die sich voneinander außer in der Einleitung auch durch die Anzahl und Auswahl der Berichte sowie durch die beigefügte Fortsetzung unterscheiden.[36]

---

33 ,Fuerunt tres fratres, unus nomine Czech, qui fundavit Bohemiam, secundus Krok, qui construxit Cracoviam et originavit Poloniam, tercius Lech, qui fundavit Lechnicz que civitas dicitur Legnicz, et plantavit totam Silesiam.‘ KNM VIII F 49, fol. 186ᵛ; BUW IV F 104, fol. 2ʳ.

34 Bláhová (2005, 2008, 2011).

35 Bláhová (2005, 2008, 2011); Mrozowicz (2005).

36 Diesem Thema ist eine gesonderte Studie gewidmet.

Der Kompilator der *Anonymen Chronik* ist nicht bekannt und er verrät nirgends seine Identität. Sein Interesse ist auf Prag konzentriert. Die Verweise auf Agnes von Böhmen, die Gründerin des Ritterordens der Kreuzherren mit dem Roten Stern, als ‚unserer Gründerin' in einigen Handschriften sowie die Berichte vom Prager Kreuzherrenkloster und über mehrere weitere Kreuzherrenklöster und -spitäler deuten an, dass die Chronik im Prager Konvent der Kreuzherren mit dem Roten Stern entstanden ist. Die Entstehungszeit der Kompilation wird von den Erwähnungen der ältesten Rezension der Chronik, der Nennung von Wenzel IV. (1378–1419) als derzeitigem König (*modernus rex*) abgegrenzt, die Erwähnungen der lebenden mährischen Markgrafen sowie die Gestaltung des Endes der Chronik datieren dessen Entstehen in das Ende der neunziger Jahre des 14. Jahrhunderts. Zusätzlich wurden Eintragungen hinzugefügt, die Ereignisse der ersten beiden Jahrzehnte des 15. Jahrhunderts betreffen. Man nahm sie noch in der Regierungszeit von Wenzel IV. auf, wahrscheinlich im Jahr 1416 oder kurz danach.

Die *Anonyme Chronik* ist eine Kompilation nüchterner Aufzeichnungen, die wortwörtlich aus älteren, zumeist umfangreichen Quellen herauspräpariert sind. Sie erfasst lediglich die wichtigsten Tatsachen der überwiegend tschechischen Kirchengeschichte und politischen Geschichte ohne Einzelheiten, zudem häufig mit fehlerhaften Daten. Es handelt sich also um eine ‚Geschichte in Daten' ohne deutliches Konzept oder ausgeprägte Intention. Konzept und Absicht sind lediglich in der Einleitung der Chronik angedeutet, in der ihr Inhalt mitgeteilt und das von Tschechen und den verwandten Slawen besiedelte Gebiet umgrenzt wird. In der zweiten Version, die in die tschechische Geschichte auch die schlesische und polnische Geschichte einbezieht, bringt die Einleitung ebenfalls diesen Umstand zum Ausdruck. Mit einer solchen Einleitung rief die *Anonyme Chronik* auch eine gewisse Resonanz in Schlesien hervor. Wohl gerade der knappe Überblick von Daten und Ereignissen verhalf der Chronik allerdings zu erheblicher Popularität, belegt nicht nur durch die neun erhaltenen Handschriften, die zudem vom Bestehen weiterer Exemplare – ihrer Vorlagen – zeugen, sondern auch durch die Tatsache, dass die *Anonyme Chronik* zur Grundlage einer umfangreichen annalistischen Kompilation wurde, die die tschechische Geschichte von der zweiten Hälfte des 14. bis zur ersten Hälfte des 16. Jahrhunderts erfasst, also bis zu den Alten Böhmischen Annalen.[37]

In den spätmittelalterlichen Handschriften sind verschiedene knapp gehaltene Schriften meist aus dem 15. Jahrhundert erhalten, die ‚in Daten' über

---

37   Vgl. Čornej (2003: XXVIII–XXX); Bláhová (2010c).

die Geschichte kurzer Zeitabschnitte berichten. Es sind dies sämtlich chro-
nologisch geordnete, nüchterne Aufzeichnungen mit Daten, ohne erkennbare
Intention. Keine der spätmittelalterlichen Schriften dieses Typs erlangte
jedoch die Popularität der *Anonymen Chronik*.

Bibliographie

Handschriftenquellen
Praha
Knihovna Národního muzea (KNM)
VIII D 20; VIII F 49
Knihovna pražské metropolitní kapituly (KPMK)
O III
Národní knihovna České republiky (NK ČR)
XIX B 26

Wien
Österreichische Nationalbibliothek Wien (ÖNB)
3282
5483

Třeboň
Státní oblastní archiv v Třeboní (SOA Třeboň)
A 7
A 10

Vyšší Brod
Knihovna cisterciáckého opatství Vyšší Brod (*Vyšší Brod*)
101

Wrocław
Biblioteka Uniwersytecka we Wrocławiu (BUW)
IV F 104

Quelleneditionen
Benedicti minoritae dicti Chronica et eius continuatio. Ed. Dušek Ladislav, in: *Zakony
      Franciszkańskie w Polsce*, red. J. Kłoczowski, I, 2–3. Kraków, 1993. 323–434.
Bláhová, Marie, ‚*Annales historiam regni Bohemiae et urbis Pragensis ab anno 1278 usque
      ad 1399 illustrantes*.' *Studie o rukopisech* 39: 2009, 89–112.

Horčička Adalbert, ‚Ein „Chronicon breve regni Bohemiae saec. XV."' *Mitteilungen für die Geschichte der Deutschen in Böhmen* 37: 1899, 461–467.

Chronica quae dicitur Hugonis de Sancto Victore. Ed. Georg Waitz, MGH, SS XXIV, 1879, 90–97.

Chronicon Anonymi. In: *Monumenta historica Boemiae nusquam antehac edita*, Tomus III, ed. Gelasius Dobner. Pragae, 1774. 43–62.

Chronicon Francisci Pragensis. Ed. Jana Zachová, Fontes rerum Bohemicarum, Series nova, I. Praha, 1997.

Chronicon Treboniense. In: *Geschichtschreiber der husitischen Bewegung in Böhmen* I, ed. Konstantin Höfler. Wien, 1856. 50–65.

Kronika Pulkavova. Ed. Josef Emler, Jan Gebauer, *Fontes rerum Bohemicarum* V. Praha, 1893. 1–326.

Martin von Troppau, *Chronicon Pontificum et Imperatorum*, ed. Anna-Dorothee von den Brincken, MGH http://www.mgh.de/ext/epub/mt/index.htm.

Výpisky z rozličných kronik. Ed. Josef Emler, *Prameny dějin českých* IV. Praha, 1884. 341–344.

Sekundärliteratur

EMC – *Encyclopedia of the Medieval Chronicle*, 2 vols. Gen. ed. Graeme Dunphy. Leiden: Brill, 2010.

Bartoš, František Michálek (1937). ‚Úvod.' In: *Staré letopisy české*, ed. František Šimek, F.M. Bartoš. Praha: Historický spolek. I–XVII.

Bláhová, Marie (1987). ‚Kroniky doby Karla IV.' In: *Kroniky doby Karla IV.*, edd. Marie Bláhová, Jakub Pavel, Jana Zachová. Praha: Svoboda. 557–594.

Bláhová, Marie (1995). *Staročeská kronika tak řečeného Dalimila* 3. Praha: Academia. 90–16.

Bláhová, Marie (2005), ‚Mezi Čechami a Polskem. Poznámky k otázce historického vědomí slezských intelektuálů v pozdním středověku.' In: *Korunní země v dějinách českého státu II. Společné a rozdílné. Česká koruna v životě a vědomí jejích obyvatel ve 14.–16. století.* Praha: Albis international. 319–332.

Bláhová, Marie (2007), ‚Universalgeschichtsschreibung in den mittelalterlichen böhmischen Ländern. Ein Überblick.' In: *Wirtschaft – Gesellschaft – Mentalitäten im Mittelalter*, edd. Hans-Peter Baum, Rainer Leng, Joachim Schneider. Stuttgart: F. Steiner. 563–578.

Bláhová, Marie (2008), ‚Společné dějiny? Slezská redakce anonymní České kroniky 15. století.' In: *Slezsko – země Koruny české. Historie a kultura 1300–1740.* Ed. Helena Dáňová, Jan Klípa, Lenka Stolárová. Praha: Národní galerie. 233–243.

Bláhová, Marie (2009), ‚Annales historiam regni Bohemiae et urbis Pragensis ab anno 1278 usque ad 1399 illustrantes.' *Studie o rukopisech* 39: 89–112.

Bláhová, Marie (2010a), ‚Chronica Bohemorum [anonymi].' In: EMC, 308.

Bláhová, Marie (2010b), ‚Neplach of Opatovice.' In: *EMC*, 1139–1140.

Bláhová, Marie (2010c), ‚Staré letopisy české.' In: *EMC*, 1386–1387.

Bláhová, Marie (2011), ‚Tercius Lech ... plantavit totam Silesiam. Die Widerspiegelung des Wissens um die Zusammengehörigkeit der Schlesier zur Böhmischen Krone in der Historiographie des Spätmittelalters.' In: *Geschichte Erinnerung Selbstidentifikation. Die schriftliche Kultur in den Ländern der Böhmischen Krone im 14.–18. Jahrhundert*, edd. Lenka Bobková, Jan Zdichynec. Praha: Casablanca. 14–26.

Bláhová, Marie (2016), ‚Soudobé kroniky o Karlovi IV.' In: Marie Bláhová, Zuzana Lukšová, Martin Nodl, *Karel IV. v soudobých kronikách*. Praha: Argo. 31–64.

Bláhová, Marie (2017), ‚Cisterciáci a historická kultura ve středověku.' *Mediaevalia historica Bohemica* 20/1: 6–22.

Bláhová, Marie (2020), ‚Origo gentis v české středověké historiografii.' *Slavia antiqua* 61: 23–39.

Čornej, Petr (2003), ‚Původní vrstva Strarých letopisů českých.' In: *Staré letopisy české (texty nejstarší vrstvy)*, edd. Alena M. Černá, Petr Čornej, Markéta Klosová, Prameny dějin českých. Nová řada, II. Praha: Filosofia. VII–XLIII.

Dušek, Ladislav (1990), ‚Kronika tzv. Beneše Minority a její pokračování.' *Minulostí západočeského kraje* 26: 7–112.

Gauthier, Marc-Edouard (2008). *Mille ans d'histoire de l'arbre généalogique en France*. Rennes: Éd. Ouest-France.

Green, William M. (1943). ‚Hugo of St. Victor: De Tribus Maximis Circumstantiis Gestorum.' *Speculum* 18: 484–493.

Joachimsen, Paul (1910). *Geschichtsauffassung und Geschichtsschreibung in Deutschland unter dem Einfluss des Humanismus*, I. Leipzig und Berlin: Teubner.

Klebel, Ernst (1928). ‚Die Fassungen und Handschriften der österreichischen Annalistik.' *Jahrbuch für Landeskunde von Niederösterreich*, N.F. 21: 43–185.

Kümper, Hiram (2010). ‚Flores temporum (Blossoms of the times).' In: *EMC*, 625.

Mareš, František (1866). ‚Chronicon Treboniense.' *Český časopis historický* 5: 135–143.

Melville, Gert (1980). ‚Spätmittelalterliche Geschichtskompendien – eine Aufgabestellung.' *Römische Historische Mitteilungen* 22: 51–104.

Menzel, Michael (1998). *Predigt und Geschichte. Historische Exempel in der geistlichen Rhetorik des Mittelalters*. Köln – Weimar – Wien: Böhlau.

Mierau, Heike Johanna, Antje Sander-Berke, Birgit Studt (1996). *Studien zur Überlieferung der Flores temporum*. MGH, Studien und Texte, Bd. 14. Hannover: Hahnsche Buchhandlung.

Mrozowicz, Wojciech (2005). ‚Die Acta quedam notatu digna im Lichte einer neu entdeckten Handschrift. Plädoyer für eine Neuausgabe.' In: *Editionswisseschaftliche Kolloquien 2003/2004. Historiographie, Briefe und Korrespondenzen, Editorische Methoden*, hrsg. von Matthias Thumser und Janusz Tandecki. Toruń: Verlag der Nikolaus-Kopernikus-Universität Thorn. 85–98.

Müller Michael (1983). *Die Annalen und Chroniken im Herzogtum Bayern, 1250–1314*. München: C.H. Beck.

Norbye, Marigold Anne (2010). ‚Peter of Poitiers.' In: *EMC* 2, 1205.

Novotný, Václav (1905). ‚Úvod.' In: *Kronika zbraslavská*, transl. J.V. Novák. Praha: Nadání Františka Palackého.

Palacký, František (1830, ²1869). *Würdigung der alten böhmischen Geschichtsschreiber.* Prag: Borrosch.

Parkes, Malcolm B. (1976). ‚The Influence of the Concepts of Ordinatio and Compilatio on the Development of the Book.' In: *Medieval Learning and Literature*, edd. by J.J.G. Alexander, M.T. Gibson. Oxford: Clarendon Press. 115–141.

Rech, Régis (2010). ‚Hugh of St. Victor.' In: *EMC* 1, 817–818.

Spunar, Pavel (1966). ‚Drobné texty a zprávy z rukopisů. 3. Z historik vídeňského konvolutu ÖNB 3282.' *Sborník Národního muzea*, řada C, sv. XI, č. 2: 65–71.

Studt, Birgit (1999). ‚„Kleine Formen" der spätmittelalterlichen Geschichtsüberlieferung. Zu Vermittlungsweisen und Verbreitungsmustern von Fürstengeschichten.' In: *Die Geschichtsschreibung in Mitteleuropa. Projekte und Forschungsprobleme*, ed. Jaroslaw Wenta. Toruń: Uniwersytet Mikołaja Kopernika. 305–321.

Šimák, Josef Vítězslav (1918). ‚Studie ke Starým letopisům českým.' *Věstník České akademie věd a umění* 27: 171–185.

Třeštík, Dušan (1997). *Počátky Přemyslovců. Vstup Čechů do dějin (530–935)*. Praha: Lidové noviny.

Wolverton, Lisa (2015). *Cosmas of Prague. Narrative, Classicism, Politics*. Washington, DC: Catholic University of America Press.

2

Authorship in Medieval Breton Chronicles

Cristian Bratu

Abstract

Like elsewhere in medieval Europe, history-writing in Brittany was often anonymous. We do not know who authored the *Chronicon Namnetense* and the *Chronicon Briocense*. However, a number of medieval Breton historians did create fairly elaborate authorial personae for themselves. Such is the case with Guillaume de Saint-André, whose name appears in an acrostic at the end of his *Libvre du bon Jehan, duc de Bretaigne*, and Pierre le Baud, author of a *Compillation des cronicques et ystoires des Bretons*. This chapter focuses on the authorial images of late medieval Breton historians, with particular emphasis on Saint-André, Le Baud and Bouchart.

In a previous study, I discussed authorial self-representations and self-promotion strategies in the works of ancient and medieval historians, from Herodotus to Philippe de Commynes.[1] After describing the emergence of an author figure in the works of ancient Greek and Roman historians, I showed that, in spite of the emphasis placed by the nascent Christian civilization on humility, medieval historians were anything but self-effacing. Subsequently, I focused on the authorial figures of medieval French historians who wrote in the vernacular between the twelfth and fifteenth centuries. Obviously, it was impossible to discuss all French-language historians from that period, and in this chapter, I attempt to fill, albeit schematically, a geographic *lacuna* in the above-mentioned study, which is Breton historiography.[2] In so doing, I aim to assess authorial dynamics within a specific regional context, as well as give readers a fuller picture of authorship in medieval French history-writing.

---

1 Bratu (2019). There are also a several major studies focusing, at least in part, on the medieval historian's *persona*: Partner (1977), Blacker (1984), Beer (1989), Damian Grint (1999), Cheney and Armas (2002) and Greene (2006).
2 For an introduction to medieval Brittany, see Jones (1988), Cornette (2005) and Tourault (2005; 2009).

1   Anonymity and Low-Key Authorship

The founding text of Breton history-writing is the *Chronicon Namnetense*, written in Latin around 1060 and which covers the period between 570 and 1049. The *Chronicon Namnetense* itself is no longer extant but excerpts can be found in later texts, such as the *Chronicon Briocense* and the one penned by Pierre Le Baud.[3] The author of the text was a canon of Nantes who compiled various annals and other documents from the cathedral archives. The compiler had a clear interest in the ecclesiastical history of Brittany, its successive bishops, episcopal rights and possessions, as well as the history of Viking settlements in the wider Loire Valley. However, as is often the case with ecclesiastical and regional chronicles, the author does not reveal his identity.

At the other end of the Middle Ages stands another anonymous text, the fifteenth-century *Chronicon Briocense*. This unfinished Latin chronicle written between 1389 and 1416 covers the history of Brittany from its alleged Trojan origins all the way to the compiler's present. For the early history of Brittany, the compiler draws on the *Chronicle of Nantes* and Geoffrey of Monmouth, *chansons de geste* and hagiographies, as well as documentary sources. The presumed author of this otherwise anonymous text is Master Hervé Le Grant, archivist (1395–1416) and councillor of the dukes of Brittany. According to Michael Jones, '[r]ecent research confirms how closely what can be deduced about the writer from the *Chronicon* alone accords with the known facts of Le Grant's professional career, while also highlighting the contemporary role of the chancery in propagating views of Breton history (cf. Guillaume de Saint-André) to enhance the policies of the Montfort dynasty, thus strongly reinforcing this attribution'.[4]

Between the two chronological *termini* set by these two major anonymous Breton chronicles, the eleventh and the fifteenth centuries, there are a number of chroniclers who seem to be, to paraphrase Luigi Pirandelli, in search of an authorial *persona*. Such is the case, for instance, with Guillaume de la Penne, who does not reveal his name in his *Geste des Bretons en Italie sous le pontificat de Grégoire XI* (1378), which is *ipso facto* anonymous. It is only thanks to the scribe who copied his work that we know the identity of the author.[5] The text starts with the *topos* of melancholy, a *locus communis* in fourteenth-century French literature:

---

3 Jones (2007). For an introduction to the *Chronicon Namnetense*, see Jones' forthcoming entry in the *Encyclopedia of the Medieval Chronicle* (currently available online).

4 Jones (2010).

5 Pierre Courroux has done extensive research on the author and his family, and his forthcoming critical edition of La Penne's 'geste' will provide more information on this topic. My thanks to Dr Courroux for allowing me to view his critical edition prior to publication.

Une nuit en Italie,
Melancomoye en la vie
D'un Chevalier de bel estre
Que l'on clame Monsieur Selvestre,
Et comment, & en quelle maniere
Il a vescu ça en arriere.

La Penne, *Geste des Bretons*, ll. 1–6

(One night in Italy, I was rememorating the life of an excellent knight called Sir Silvestre, and about how and in what way he lived his life.)[6]

Later, the poet adds a light touch of colour to his authorial *persona* by saying he does not indulge in flattery or fiction ('Quar moy qui fait icest Romans / Ne fu onques mon temps usans / En songe ne en flatterie', ll. 232–234), but after this passage, Guillaume de la Penne does not substantively elaborate his otherwise fairly minimal self-sketch. As Pierre Courroux points out in the introduction to his critical edition, it is obvious that La Penne was familiar with epic material such as *La Chanson de Roland* and *Le Couronnement Louis*, as well as with elements of the *Roman de Renart*—all texts that possess a modest narrator figure, just like his own chronicle. Instead, he is much keener on portraying himself as an eyewitness to the events. The large number of eyewitness phrases and formulae used by La Penne in the text bear witness, as it were, to this intent. In verse 218, for instance, he says he was present at the events narrated ('De tout yce je suis temoing'), a claim reinforced farther in the text by countless other testimony formulae which all roughly translate as 'I assure you', such as 'Et de vray je vous affie', 'je vous creans' and 'je vous asseur'. Elsewhere, he provides the names of three people, cardinal Pierre d'Estaing, Hugues de la Roche and Guy de Pruynes, who agreed to pay Sylvestre Budes for his services, which seems to imply that La Penne personally witnessed the agreement (ll. 2376–2383). Finally, La Penne is obviously proud of his ability to remember the events he narrates, as formulae relating to memory and remembrance occur repeatedly ('je m'en recors', l. 356; 'je m'en recole', l. 1072). However, the *romans* ends abruptly after Pope Gregory XI's death, without a proper epilogue, aside from a few pious remarks by La Penne on the late pontiff's deeds and worthiness.

A similar text with regard to authorial self-depiction is Guillaume Gruel's *Chronique d'Arthur de Richemont* (1462–1466). Gruel was Arthur III's squire and

---

6 All translations are mine.

the value of his work resides mainly in the fact that he was an eyewitness to many of the events narrated in his *chronique*. His presence in the text, however, is relatively limited and his biography of Arthur III does not possess an elaborate prologue like other texts from the same period. In the epilogue, Gruel refers to himself simply as the person who dictated—or wrote—this book ('celuy qui a dictié ce livre', Gruel, *Chronique d'Arthur de Richemont*, 232). For the period prior to Arthur becoming *connétable*, Gruel suggests that he collected reliable information from the prince himself and his retinue, and concludes, in formulaic fashion, that he did not write anything untruthful. In the rest of the text, Gruel depicts himself several times as a character in the third person. He mentions, for instance, that together with Gilles de Saint-Simon, he was in charge of the captive Robert de Sarrebruck-Commercy (Gruel, *Chronique d'Arthur de Richemont*, 95). A bit later, we see him announcing the birth of Francis, future Francis II of Brittany, the son of Richard of Montfort-Étampes and Marguerite of Orléans, to his master, Arthur III (Gruel, *Chronique d'Arthur de Richemont*, 101). He reappears as a character during the siege of Meaux, in Formigny, and then again after the surrender of Caen and Cherbourg (Gruel, *Chronique d'Arthur de Richemont*, 153, 206 and 213–214). In an earlier passage, in which Gruel wrote that he had attended Arthur III's wedding with Jeanne d'Albret, he is mentioned as the person who dictated (or wrote) the book, 'named Guillaume Gruel' ('celui qui a dictié ceste cronique, nommé Guillaume Gruel', Gruel, *Chronique d'Arthur de Richemont*, 179). This is in essence the only passage that mentions Gruel's authorship of the text in a clear and unambiguous manner.[7]

2   Towards a Breton Pantheon

However, in late medieval Breton historiography there is also a category of historians who *did* try to assert themselves, in diverse manners and to different extents.[8] The first on this list is Guillaumé de Saint-André who is, in a sense, the connecting link between the less and the more self-assertive historians. As Jean-Michel Cauneau and Dominique Philippe have shown in the introduction

---

7   There are other works that belong to this category of texts with minimal authorial self-depictions, such as the *Chronique de Bretagne* (1470–1474) penned by Jean de Saint-Paul, chamberlain to duke Francis II of Brittany, which we cannot discuss here due to space limitations.

8   On late medieval Breton history-writing, see also Jones (1976), Kerhervé (1980) and Philippe (1997).

to their excellent critical edition of Saint-André's *Libvre du bon Jehan, duc de Bretaigne* (1381–1385), followed by the *Jeu des échecs*, the chronicler's identity is a tremendously complex issue. There are several candidates for the authorship of this text, and it is possible that some of these are the same person but for now, there is no definite answer. A likely candidate was one of John IV of Brittany's notaries called Guillaume de Saint-André, probably a layman, and whose name appears in over fifteen charters of the dukes of Brittany between 1382 and 1399. There is also a chaplain of Saint-Aubin in Guérande, mentioned as 'Guillermus de Sancto Andrea' in a papal document from 1371. Another possibility is the priest and rector of the Touches parish, in the diocese of Nantes, who might be identical to the Guillaume de Sainte-André mentioned slightly earlier (Saint-André, *Chronique de l'État breton*, 3–58, 191–200).

Whoever the actual author was, which is a matter of interest for this paper only insofar as it affects the authorial persona discernible in the text, he clearly intended to pose as a reflective, educated author, yet as one who does not attempt to parade his erudition. In the opening lines, the narrator claims to have read ('vi escript') in a prologue a maxim saying that he who remembers his life is short should be content with little. This might be a reference to a ballad by Eustache Deschamps, but it might simply be a savant-seeming reference to another, possibly fictional, prologue. The narrator then further elaborates the theme of the worthlessness of earthly possessions, which would be consistent with the hypothesis of an ecclesiastical author, although in truth, almost any writer with a modicum of education could have easily produced this trope. The following lines might contain autobiographical (or possibly pseudo-biographical) details, as the narrator claims to be an old man ('je suys ancien et vueill') who no longer wishes to live in this world, since death spares neither the strong nor the weak. The following sequence is also replete with clerkly overtones, as the historian decries the lack of empathy of the rich and powerful towards the less fortunate. However, the historian-*cum*-moralist argues, Fortune is always quick to correct these imbalances as she brings down the mighty and frustrates their dominion over the poor. Should readers not be convinced by Saint-André's words, they should reflect on the destiny of King Arthur who, though once a powerful and valiant ruler, vanished and died. The prologue ends with additional—and predictable—reflections on the fickleness of Fortune, which can just as easily bring honour or shame, make one rich or poor, generous or greedy, powerful or downtrodden (Saint-André, *Chronique de l'État breton*, 226–230).

Who if not Fortune, asks Saint-André rhetorically, could have brought the life of the good duke John III of Brittany to an abrupt end in April 1341? After the duke's death, the War of Succession started in Brittany between the duke's half-brother, John of Montfort, on the one hand, and Charles of Blois, count of Penthièvre, on the other. What interests us here is the argument in support of John of Montfort adduced by Saint-André, who quotes a passage from the Bible (Numbers 27.8–10) in which Moses instructs the daughters of Salphaad on an inheritance matter saying that if a man dies childless, his brother becomes his heir. Is this clerical knowledge? Perhaps, but it could also be legal expertise. Sadly, this passage does not further clarify the nature of the author's professional background.

Quite predictably, in the narrative part of the text, which focuses on the history of Brittany during John IV's reign, Guillaume de Saint-André makes himself rather discreet. He returns centre-stage in the epilogue with an *amplificatio* of the fickle Fortune theme (Saint-André, *Chronique de l'État breton*, 480–483). The chronicle is followed by a poem titled *Jeu des échecs*, which further elaborates the Fortune motif, as well as a few other themes such as the author's old age. Guillaume de Saint-André's name appears in reverse order in an elaborate acrostic at the very end of the *Jeu*, in which he also asks the 'son' to whom the poem is dedicated, and whose identity remains a mystery, to pray for his soul (Saint-André, *Chronique de l'État breton*, 550). Although a veil of mystery still shrouds the identity of the individual(s) who penned this text, we have here what I believe is the first elaborate authorial *persona* in Breton historiography.

Saint-André is thus, in a sense, a path opener for other self-assertive Breton historians from the autumn of the Middle Ages and beginning of the Renaissance, such as Pierre le Baud and Alain Bouchart. Between 1470 and 1473, Pierre le Baud authored a *Compillation des cronicques et ystoires des Bretons*, which he dedicated to Jean de Derval. Around 1486, he composed the *Chroniques de Vitré* for Jeanne de Laval, as well as a *Bréviaire des Bretons*. Between 1498 and 1505, he wrote a history of Brittany at the request of Anne of Brittany, whose advisor he was, although he was not officially a court historiographer. His work served as a source of inspiration for Alain Bouchart's chronicle, as well as the work of Bernard d'Argentré, the grandson of Pierre le Baud's sister.

Le Baud's prose chronicles contain elaborate authorial prologues (and sometimes epilogues as well), many of which share a large number of themes and *topoi*. The prologue to the *Compillation*, for instance, starts with a beautiful, classicizing allegory of life—and Breton history—as a form of maritime travel. When the traveller reaches the safety of a harbour, Le Baud notes, one cannot fully recreate the itinerary followed by the ship because of the fluid and ever-changing nature of the waves (Le Baud, *Compillation*, 57). Citing Petrarch's *Triumphs*, Le Baud argues that Renown alone is able to save one from death and oblivion. As I have argued in my recent monograph, the *topos* of the historian's duty to prevent historical events from falling into oblivion is not only very common in late medieval historiography, but it is also a very efficient means to claim a place in the Pantheon of Fame for oneself without appearing to do so. Had anyone called the author using this *topos* presumptuous, the historian could have easily retorted that he simply intended to preserve the memory of the princes and heroes mentioned in his work. Unsurprisingly, after this passage focusing on the necessity of preserving the past through writing, Le Baud writes that he meant to 'escripre les gestes de nos souverains' ('write down the deeds of our sovereigns') so that they can serve as an *exemplum* to future leaders. Immediately thereafter, though, the historian introduces himself as 'je, Pierre le Baud, secretaire de hault et puissant Jehan, sire de Derval, de Combour, de Chateaugiron, de Rogé et de Saint Mars (...)' ('I, Pierre le Baud, secretary of the noble and powerful Jehan, lord of Derval, Combour, Rogé and Saint Mars', Le Baud, *Compillation*, 57). Considering the close textual proximity between the passages focusing on fame (*Renommée*) and the historian's own name, it would be difficult to dismiss the notion that Le Baud *did* intend his name to be associated with the much desired *Renommée*.

By revealing his identity in this formulaic manner (the first-person pronoun, the historian's name and position, as well the historian's patron) that had become customary in Anglo-Norman texts since the twelfth century, Le Baud seemingly attempts to bridge the gap between Breton and other regional French-language historiographies. We might note in passing that Le Baud's intent to elevate Breton historiography to a level similar to that of other regional Francophone historiographies is obvious in more ways than one. For instance, the classicizing, neologism-heavy style practiced by Le Baud is in a sense comparable to the style of Georges Chastelain, Jean Molinet and other *indiciaires*. That said, Le Baud never explicitly mentions the Burgundian historians; instead, he emphasizes his debt to classical and Italian authors, such as Petrarch and Leonardo Bruni ('Leonard Aretin'). In the rest of the text, there are abundant references to classical authors such as Homer, Dictys of Crete, Aristotle, Cornelius Nepos, Lucan, Livy, Flavius Josephus, Apuleius, as well as later classics such as Eusebius of Caesarea, Orosius and Isidore of Seville. Thus, Le Baud attempts to both 'classicize' and modernize Breton historiography; his authorial persona, too, combines classical erudition and modernist style.

In the rest of the text, Le Baud attempts to enhance his *auctoritas* through a number of textual strategies. One of the most interesting and effective techniques is the relative thoroughness of his quotations. Whereas most medieval writers tend to refer to other texts in rather vague terms, which often creates a sense that the cited 'sources' are, to use a phrase coined by Roger Dragonetti, a mere 'mirage', Le Baud references his sources in a relatively scrupulous manner. Of course, one can find brief and vague references to various writers such as Flavius Josephus, Isidore of Seville or Alcuin in Le Baud's work as well (Le Baud, *Compillation*, 64–65). Oftentimes, though, the Breton writer tends to quote specific chapters or books from an author's work, such as the fourth book of Ovid's *Fasti* or the thirteenth chapter of the first book of Laurent de Premierfait's French translation of Boccaccio's *Fates of Illustrious Men and Women* (Le Baud, *Compillation*, 66). By constantly citing other 'aucteurs', Le Baud subtly suggests that he belongs in that esteemed company. Moreover, attention to detail is one of the elements that Le Baud hoped would support his claim to notoriety, as he lists, for instance, thirty-one of Priam and Hecuba's sons and their seven daughters (Le Baud, *Compillation*, 70). In so doing, Le Baud clearly attempts to bolster his scholarly credentials and thus distinguish himself from other, supposedly less thorough historians.[9]

In spite of Le Baud's constant professions of humility, such as in the epilogue where he mentions his 'faible engin' ('weak abilities'), 'obscur entendement' ('darkness of the mind') and 'rudesse de [mon] gros et confus langage' ('the coarseness of [my] unpolished and jumbled language'), which incidentally seem to echo Christine de Pizan's rhetoric of humility, it is nevertheless quite obvious that he was fascinated by the idea of authorial fame. His constant references to *Renommée, sapience,* to other 'cronicques autentiques' and *acteurs* (Le Baud, *Compillation*, 545–546) that inspired his own work and to which, as he points out, he added his own materials ('augmentation des choses'), in conjunction with his emphasis on 'mon labeur' ('my hard work'), are all part of the arsenal of historians who wish to assert themselves *qua* authors without appearing to do so. Le Baud also mentions, quite explicitly, the 'paresse de nos escripvains' ('the idleness of our writers') who had allegedly not written more extensively on Breton history. Such criticism is unjustified since Le Baud was aware of the existence of other Breton chronicles, such as the *Chronicles of Nantes*, and the only point of this criticism is, quite clearly, to highlight the author's own contribution to Breton historiography.

In later texts, Pierre Le Baud uses a different type of *incipit*, in which he mentions the name of the dedicatee, followed by his own name and title. In the dedication to Jeanne de Laval from the *Chroniques de Vitré et de Laval* (ca. 1486), for instance, Pierre le Baud describes himself as a priest, cantor and canon of the church of Notre Dame de Laval. In the prologue we find, once again, references to Leonardo Bruni as well as various 'autheurs' and charters that are intended to prove Le Baud's extensive knowledge of Breton history and historiography

---

9   Although, of course, in this particular context his sources, Ovid and Boccaccio, are not exactly historical in nature.

(Le Baud, *Chroniques de Vitré et de Laval*, 1–2). We find a similar authorial self-depiction in Le Baud's *Livre des cronicques des roys, ducs et princes de Bretagne* (1498–1505). In this book, dedicated to Anne of Brittany, Le Baud describes himself as treasurer of the Church Sainte-Madeleine of Vitré, as well as the French queen's 'humble servant' and 'chaplain' ('Pierre Le Baud, Tresorier de l'Eglise Collegiale de la Magdelene de Vitré … Orateur et Aumosnier'). Farther in the prologue, in which he mentions once again Leonardo Bruni, Petrarch and several unspecified historical texts, Le Baud describes himself not as an author, but as 'je nouvel Escripvain', who will narrate the history of Brittany in a chronologically accurate manner (Le Baud, *Livre des cronicques des roys, ducs et princes de Bretagne*, 1–5). In this passage from the end of the prologue, Le Baud points out that historiographers generally narrate history with ample detail, whereas the works of chronographers like himself tend to be more succinct and chronologically accurate.

A third Breton writer belonging to the group of the more self-assertive historians is Alain Bouchart, secretary to Francis II, duke of Brittany. In 1491, he followed duchess Anne of Brittany to Paris, as a result of her marriage to Charles VIII of France. In 1494, he became an advisor to the king and member of the Grand Council. This writer is intriguing on more than one count. On the one hand, in his *Grandes chroniques de Bretagne*, printed in 1514, Bouchart does not mention his name. In the prologue, he suggests that he belonged to or worked for the Breton court because he mentions that Anne of Brittany listened to his work ('a veu et fait lire en sa presence ce que ja en avions fait') and then asked him, both orally and in writing, to complete it as soon as possible ('et puis aprés nous a expressement enchargé et commandé, tant de bouche que par ses lettres missives, iceluy ouvrage parfaire en toute diligence', Bouchart, *Grandes chroniques de Bretagne*, 66). We can therefore infer that he was a secretary at the ducal and/or royal court, but there is no mention whatsoever of the author's name in the 1514 edition. The only element that suggests his identity is the heraldic shield, *d'argent à trois dauphins pâmés de sable*, printed on the first folio. Bouchart's name will appear in print only in the 1531 edition. But on the other hand, just like Pierre Le Baud, on whose work Bouchart draws heavily without ever admitting his debt, he clearly aimed to create an elaborate and erudite authorial persona for himself. Bouchart does not mention other Breton historians, which allows him to claim in the prologue, quite deceitfully, that he has not yet read a single book on the history of the noble land of Brittany or on the kings and princes who ruled over Brittany ('encores n'ay je veu aucun traicté qui ait esté entierement composé du noble pays de Bretaigne … ne des noms des roys et princes qui ont occupé et possidé celuy pays depuis qu'il fut appellé Bretaigne', Bouchart, *Grandes chroniques de Bretagne*, 64). In fact,

Bouchart rarely mentions contemporary historians, except for Robert Gaguin, author of a *Compendium de Francorum origine et gestis*. Like Le Baud, Bouchart has a marked preference for classical authors and works. Erudite references to Gregory the Great's *Moralia*, Cicero, Macrobius's *Somnium Scipionis*, Augustine and other *acteurs* help bolster his erudite persona. In fact, Bouchart names himself 'acteur' on four occasions in the epilogue. In spite of Bouchart's rhetorical humility and claims that his French is less elaborate due to his Breton origins, his references to many classical authors and texts highlight the historian's extensive knowledge; if we consider his emphasis on the fact that Anne of Brittany herself had authorized his work, it becomes quite clear that, like Le Baud and possibly Guillaume de Saint-André before him, Alain Bouchart did everything in his power to suggest that he belonged in the nascent Pantheon of Breton *auteurs*.

In conclusion, in spite of a certain delay with regard to the rise of authorial assertiveness compared to other areas of the medieval French-speaking world, such as the Anglo-Norman and Burgundian realms, there are also a number of Breton historians who seem eager to enter the Pantheon of French-speaking historians-*cum*-authors. I have shown that these late medieval Breton authors often use similar tactics to assert themselves, such as suggesting that they are either the first to have ever written about the history of Brittany or that they are more thorough and accurate than their unnamed predecessors; they sometimes mention the *potestates* who commissioned or 'authorized' their work; they often mention other authors whose work they purport to emulate and in some cases, they suggest that they, too, deserve to be called 'acteurs'.

Bibliography

Primary Sources

Bouchart, Alain. *Grandes chroniques de Bretagne*. Ed. Marie-Louise Auger. Paris: CNRS Éditions, 2013.

Gruel, Guillaume. *Chronique d'Arthur de Richemont, connétable de France, duc de Bretagne (1393–1458)*. Ed. Achille Le Vavasseur. Paris: Renouard, 1890.

La Penne, Guillaume de. *Geste des Bretons en Italie*. In *Mémoires pour servir de preuves à l'histoire ecclésiastique et civile de Bretagne*. Ed. Dom Morice. 3 vols. Paris: Osmont, 1742–1746. II, 132–172.

Le Baud, Pierre. *Histoire de Bretagne avec les Chroniques de Vitré et de Laval*. Ed. Pierre d'Hozier. Paris: Alliot, 1638.

Le Baud, Pierre. *Compillation des cronicques et ystoires des Bretons*. Ed. Karine Abélard. Rennes: Presses Universitaires de Rennes, 2018.

Saint-André, Guillaume de. *Le bon Jehan & Le jeu des échecs (XIVe siècle): Chronique de l'État breton*. Rennes: Presses Universitaires de Rennes, 2005.

Secondary Sources

Beer, Jeanette, ed. (1989). *Medieval Translators and Their Craft*. Kalamazoo: Western Michigan University Press.

Blacker, Jean (1984). 'Wace's Craft and His Audience: Historical Truth, Bias, and Patronage in the *Roman de Rou*'. *Kentucky Romance Quarterly* 31: 355–362.

Bratu, Cristian (2019). *'Je, auteur de ce livre': l'affirmation de soi chez les historiens, de l'Antiquité à la fin du Moyen Âge*. Leiden/Boston: Brill.

Cheney, Patrick G., and Frederick A. de Armas, eds. (2002). *European Literary Careers: The Author from Antiquity to the Renaissance*. Toronto/Buffalo, NY: University of Toronto Press.

Cornette, Joël (2005). *Histoire de la Bretagne et des Bretons: Tome 1, Des âges obscurs au règne de Louis XIV*. Paris: Seuil.

Damian Grint, Peter (1999). *The New Historians of the Twelfth-Century Renaissance: Inventing Vernacular Authority*. Rochester, NY: Boydell Press.

Greene, Virginie, ed. (2006). *The Medieval Author in Medieval French Literature*. New York: Palgrave MacMillan.

Jones, Michael (2010). 'Chronicon Briocense'. *Encyclopedia of the Medieval Chronicle*. Ed. Graeme Dunphy. Leiden/Boston: Brill. I, 312.

Jones, Michael (2007). *Le Premier Inventaire du Trésor des chartes des ducs de Bretagne (1395): Hérve Le Grant et les origines du* Chronicon Briocense. Rennes: Société d'histoire et d'archéologie de Bretagne.

Jones, Michael (1988). *The Creation of Brittany: A Late Medieval State*. London: Hambledon Press.

Jones, Michael (1976). '"Mon pais et ma nation": Breton Identity in the Fourteenth Century'. In *War, Literature and Politics in the Late Middle Ages. Essays in Honour of G.W. Coopland*. Ed. Christopher Allmand. Liverpool: Liverpool University Press. 144–168.

Kerhervé, Jean (1980). 'Aux origines d'un sentiment national. Les chroniqueurs bretons de la fin du Moyen Âge'. *Bulletin de la Société archéologique du Finistère* 108: 165–206.

Minnis, Alastair (1984). *Medieval Theory of Authorship: Scholastic Literary Attitudes in the Later Middle Ages*. London: Scolar Press.

Partner, Nancy (1977). *Serious Entertainments: The Writing of History in Twelfth-Century England*. Chicago: University of Chicago Press.

Philippe, Dominique (1997). 'L'élaboration d'une méthode historique: la chronique bretonne aux XIVe et XVe siècles'. *Annales de Bretagne et des pays de l'Ouest* 104.2: 47–58.

Tourault, Philippe (2005). *Les rois de Bretagne (IVe–Xe siècle)*. Paris: Perrin.

Tourault, Philippe (2009). *Les ducs et duchesses de Bretagne*. Paris: Perrin.

3

A Peculiar *Polychronicon* for a Peculiar Prose *Brut*: The Trevisa Abridgement in Cleveland, Dublin, and Oxford Manuscripts

Elizabeth J. Bryan

Abstract

The anonymous Middle English Prose *Brut* and John Trevisa's Middle English translation of Higden's *Polychronicon* were both influential chronicles of England, but they
understood historical comprehensiveness very differently. The Prose *Brut* was a linear foundation narrative and dynastic series with no authorial attribution, whereas the
Polychronicon was a universal history that cited scholarly authorities as it synchronized
English history with world history. This article examines two manuscripts that pair an
abbreviated *Polychronicon* excerpt with an abbreviated Prose *Brut* chronicle. It offers
textual evidence that this pairing was a manuscript program that was once transmitted
beyond these two surviving manuscripts, and it asks how and why these two chronicles
could possibly work together in a manuscript program.

1 Introduction

Dublin, Trinity College Library MS 489 (MS T) and Cleveland Public Library,
White Collection MS Wq091.92-C468 (MS C) include the only two known cop-
ies of one of the Peculiar Versions (PV) of the Middle English Prose *Brut*
(MEPB).[1] Interestingly, the two manuscripts share more than that single text.
Both manuscripts feature what appears to be (up to a point) the same planned,
sequenced program of historical texts in Middle English, several of them

---

[1] This MEPB-PV has not been edited. For manuscript descriptions, see Scattergood et al. (2021:
247–256) for T and Moe, Phyllis, ed. (1977: 9–13), 'Introduction' to D'Argenteuil *Middle English Bible en François* for C. For classification, see Kennedy (1989: 2820.129,160); Matheson
(1998: 259–263) classified C as 'Peculiar Version to 1419: Group A' (PV-1419:A) and T as 'Peculiar
Version to 1460' (PV-1451/1460). He paired T and C for discussion because they are the same
MEPB-PV text to 1333, but he assigned different PV insignia based on the *Brut* histories' end
dates. For an edition of MEPB based on manuscripts of the Common Version et al., see *The
Brut or The Chronicles of England*.

abridgements: 1. an abridged *Polychronicon* excerpt of book 1, chapters 2–24, of John Trevisa's Middle English translation from Higden, which was edited by Julia Boffey in 2019 as 'The Description of the World', and which I will call the TCR-*Polychronicon* or Trevisa abridgement; 2. the narrative of Albina of Syria that usually introduces the Middle English Prose *Brut* but here is separated from the MEPB by an interpolation; 3. a genealogy from Adam to Aeneas and Brutus; and 4. the MEPB-PV.[2] The first history in this sequence, the TCR-*Polychronicon*, is also found as a stand-alone text in a third manuscript witness copied s. xv^{ex}–xvi^{in}, Oxford, Bodleian Library, MS. Rawl. C. 86, ff. 31^v–49^v (MS R), a well-known anthology of Middle English literary texts.[3] Suggestively, R also includes fragments of two other texts contained in T and C, about which more below. Closer comparative study of the manuscript packaging of abridged Middle English histories in T and C can potentially tell us something about how history was transmitted to the late fifteenth-century Middle-English-reading public. What concepts of history and realities of readership motivated this abridging and this grouping of histories in the vernacular? What can the methods of abbreviation tell us? How did this *Polychronicon* abridgement and this Peculiar Prose *Brut* relate to each other? In this article, I will consider these questions with a focus on the TCR-*Polychronicon* introduction and the Peculiar Version Prose *Brut* chronicle that travel together in MSS T and C.

2   The Prose *Brut* in Manuscripts C and T

The shared sequence of texts in C and T is justification enough for examining the textual *group* as the object of study, but it must be acknowledged that there are discontinuities in the manuscripts' later contents, as well as uncertainties caused by the loss of early folios of MS T, so the claim of a program of histories being transmitted does have some limits.[4] The two manuscripts' syn-

---

2   [Trevisa], 'Description of the World,' 93–121 edited by Boffey (2019: 91–92). Kennedy (1989: 2662 [25]) first identified R, T, and C as containing the same 'Policronica Fragment.' I have used Boffey's manuscript symbols C, T, and R for continuity. For an edition of the MEPB-CV including the Albina prologue, see *The Brut or The Chronicles of England*. Scattergood et al. (2021: 247–256) and Moe, Phyllis, ed. (1977: 9–13) treat the Albina text and the genealogy from Adam to Aeneas as part of the Prose *Brut* in T and C respectively, but the genealogy of Adam is not part of the Common Version of MEPB, and I treat its insertion between the narratives of Albina's landing and Brutus's landing as a manuscript interpolation. MS C also contains D'Argenteuil, *Middle English Bible en François*.

3   Boffey (2019: 91–92) uses R as her base text.

4   Manuscript T lacks pages at the beginning, probably 4 folio leaves (equivalent to Trevisa

chronicity ends within their respective Prose *Brut* texts, around the year 1333. From that point the *Brut* **texts** of T and C continue, but their *Brut* **versions** diverge.[5] After 1333, their ending points and their wording are quite different. The *Brut* history in T extends to the 1450s and concludes with the 1460 Act of Accord between Henry VI and Richard, duke of York, beyond which no pages of T survive. The *Brut* history in C ends earlier, at 1419. C contains an additional final text not in T, chapters 5–24 of Roger D'Argenteuil's *Bible en François* translated into Middle English prose (yet another abridgement) which summarizes biblical Creation through the crucifixion of Christ and concludes with Roman Vespasian's retaliatory destruction of Jerusalem and its Jews.[6] This alignment and divergence of the contents of C and T are not in dispute, and it may be, as Matheson suggests, that T and C had access to different exemplars after the divergence point of 1333, but at present there is insufficient evidence of the conditions of copying to explain the divergence or to assign textual priority (see stemma discussion below). Whereas the alternate *Brut* endings account for a discordant one-fourth of what I am calling a manuscript program, what we see in T and C is that about three-fourths of the abridged TCR-*Polychronicon* to Prose *Brut* program is shared.[7]

Book I, chapters 2–7 and beginning of 8; T p. 1 begins '**Exherses** þe kynge made a **Bridge** be crafte ... .'); lacks 1 folio between pages 12 and 13, (missing text equivalent to Trevisa Book I, mid-chapter 14, from Jerusalem's cisterns to the Dead Sea); lacks 1 folio between pages 34 and 35 (the very end of the TCR-*Polychronicon* and the first half of the Albina story); and lacks 1 folio between pages 56 and 57 (MEPB-PV, Cassibelan, Julius Caesar, Kinbelyn). My estimates are based on average wordcounts per page in T and textual comparisons with C and R, following an (unprovable) assumption that T originally had the complete text. (T does have relatively complete text elsewhere in the TCR-*Polychronicon* when C or R have sizable silent lacunae. See notes 12, 13.) Scattergood et al. (2021: 247–256 esp. 251) think that only 2 leaves are missing from the first quire of T and do not account for a leaf missing between pages 12 and 13 but acknowledge the difficulties of codicological collation of this manuscript, as do I. Boffey (2019: 91–92, 96, 104–105) in her edition of TCR-*Polychronicon* gives major variants and notes accurately that T begins "imperfectly in the middle of chapter 8." See 'Description of the World,' 91–121.

5   See discussion in Matheson (1998: 259–263).
6   D'Argenteuil, *Middle English Bible en François*. Moe (1977: 9–13) describes the contents of C, including a 34-line poem on folios 76^{r-v} 'Cur mundus militat' beginning 'Why is this world loved þat is false and vayne.' This poem, written on a single leaf between the *Brut* and *Bible* texts, is not the hand that writes the historical works in the rest of the manuscript, and I do not consider it part of the primary manuscript plan.
7   Shared text is T pages 1–165 (out of total 213 pages in the manuscript), and C folios 1–55^{r} (out of a total 75 folios to the end of MEPB on folio 75, and a total of 99 folios to the end of the manuscript). The divergent post-1333 Brut text occupies T pages 165–213 and C folios 55^{r}–75^{v}. C has additional texts on folios 76^{r}–99^{v}, so the portion of shared texts in relation to that whole manuscript is smaller (56%), but still over half.

It is worth observing that both T and C are crafted to link their assemblage of texts visually. There is no appearance of random compiling of texts in these two manuscripts. Manuscript C achieves a continuous mise-en-page by regular use of blue and red inks for decorated initials, headings, line fillers, and paraph marks. Blue initials (2 to 4 lines high) mark the locations of chapters (though without numbers or captions) in the TCR-*Polychronicon*, mark selected kings' reigns through the *Brut*, and mark rubricated topical headings (about one per page) in the Middle English *Bible en François*.[8] Three prominent red-ink headings divide the *Brut* material of C into large sections (without ever using the term 'Brut'): 'Here folowith the Cronicles of Englond shortly abreggid' (fol. 13^{1}v); 'The genologie of Adam' (fol. 13^{2}v); and 'The lyne of Normandye' (fol. 40^r). Collectively, these attentive red- and blue-ink features create a clear and consistent *ordinatio* across the various histories of manuscript C.

Manuscript T has an artistic program of coloured drawings across the manuscript: thirty-six large decorated polychrome initials, most of them historiated with royal portraits or grotesque faces in profile, and a series of miniatures of which only one survives intact.[9] The first pages of the *Polychronicon* abridgement and then of the Albina narrative are physically missing from manuscript T, so any first-page decoration has been lost from those two texts in T, but a decorated initial is found once in the interior of the *Polychronicon* text (historiated G introducing Greece on page 27), and coloured initials occur at the beginning of the Genealogy of Adam (decorated A on page 35), and at the birth of Brutus (historiated B on page 38) that opens the *Brut* matter proper. The *Brut* continues with 31 decorated, usually historiated, initials that mark selected kings'

---

8   Note that despite its *litterae notabiliore*, the *Polychronicon* text in C does not have 'chapters'— no numbers, no headings—and its *ordinatio* does not thus explain or call attention to its intellectual organization as a geographical description of the world.

9   For description of the 36 decorated initials, see Scattergood et al. (2021: 248–251), where the number of decorated initials has been misidentified as 37. Additional decorated initials or miniatures could have existed in pages now missing from T, especially the lost opening pages of the *Polychronicon* abridgement and of the Albina narrative. According to my textual collation of T with C, if one assumes hypothetically that T and C originally contained the same or similar text, then T has 4 missing folios at the beginning (TCR-*Polychronicon* ch. 2–7, partial 8), 1 missing folio between pages 12 and 13 (TCR-*Polychronicon* ch. 14 partial), 1 missing folio between pages 34 and 35 (end of TCR-*Polychronicon* and beginning of Albina), and 1 missing folio between pages 56 and 57 (MEPB-PV, from Julius Caesar's defeat of Cassibellaunus through King Kinbelyn). My physical examination of T bears out the likelihood that at least some of these are missing folios, rather than silent lacunae. (If so, the collation of the manuscript is further vexed.) For contrast to these physical lacunae, see T page 47 for a silent lacuna, plausibly the result of scribal eyeskip, at the beginning of King Leir's reign in the MEPB-PV, such that Leir's name is, confusingly, never mentioned in T.

reigns, all but one accompanied by rubricated headings that announce these kings' reigns. The final two historiated initials in T (one royal portrait and one grotesque in profile, on pages 207 and 210) introduce the 1460 document at the conclusion of the *Brut* text, the *Act of Accord between Henry VI and Richard, duke of York*, which includes the Duke of York's genealogical claim to the throne.

The art in these decorated initials of T is sometimes cartoonish yet surprisingly fetching. Of the miniatures, only one scene (Augustine of Canterbury at King Athelbry3t's court, T page 91) survives of the series that once existed in at least the Prose *Brut* section of this manuscript. Cutouts from the paper leaves show that similar miniatures likely existed on pages 65 or 66 (in text about Armorica, Saints Ursula and Alban, and Constantine of Little Britain); pages 101 or 102 (in text about St Edmund or King Alfred); pages 113 or 114 (in text about the disemboweling of Alfred, the brother of Edward the Confessor, or about King Edward the Confessor's reign); pages 131 or 132 (in text about Henry II and Thomas Becket); and pages 155 or 156 (in text about Edward II's reign). The artistic program of historiated initials and miniatures in T have a sometimes ambiguous relation to historical interpretation. In particular, the selection of kings in the *Brut* who are graced with portraits (or grotesques) is unusual, to say the least. Even if slightly unconventional, however, the images form an unmistakable pictorial linkage among these Middle English histories in manuscript T. In their different ways, C and T both give this same group of Middle English abridged histories (through 1333) the look of a unified book.

3   The Trevisa Abridgement in Three Manuscripts

Another piece of evidence for transmission of these history texts as a program concerns manuscript R, its value for stemmatic analysis as a third manuscript witness of the TCR-*Polychronicon*, and the presence of fragments of these history texts among its folios. Here, it is necessary to clarify what can be known about the textual, stemmatic relationship of T and C. My textual collation of the *Polychronicon* introduction and the Prose *Brut* (to 1333) text in manuscripts T and C reveals both resilient textual agreement—these are the same texts— and the presence of many textual variants.[10] For the Prose *Brut* text to 1333, with only the two manuscript witnesses T and C, neither manuscript can hold textual authority over the other as to which is closer to the original *Brut*

---

10   Boffey records the most important textual variants of the TCR-*Polychronicon*, using R as base text.

abridger's version. For the TCR-*Polychronicon*, however, we have both the third manuscript, R, and a decent critical edition (though not specific manuscript) of the work from which this introduction was demonstrably condensed (by an unidentified abridger), John Trevisa's Middle English translation of Ranulph Higden's *Polychronicon*.[11] With three manuscript witnesses and an identified remote textual source, it is possible to know more about the textual genealogy of this Trevisa introduction than we can know at present about the Peculiar *Bruts* in T and C.

With regard to the TCR-*Polychronicon* text only, each of the three manuscript witnesses should be viewed as a distinct recension. Collation of the Trevisa abridgement in manuscripts T, C, and R shows that no one of these three manuscript witnesses of the Trevisa abridgement can possibly have been a single direct exemplar of either of the other two. Each one features a number of silent lacunae that while relatively brief would make it impossible for a scribe of one of the other two manuscripts to generate necessary details. In addition, C features two larger silent lacunae, so it is quite impossible for it to be a sole exemplar of T or R (C omits text that corresponds to the concluding section of Trevisa's chapter 18, concerning Amazons and Alexander the Great, and it omits the entirety of Trevisa's chapter 20 on Numidia).[12] Manuscript R, likewise, silently omits text equivalent to the final section of Trevisa's chapter 22, on the Greek province of Boeotia.[13] R cannot, therefore, be a sole exemplar for either C or T, with regard to the TCR-*Polychronicon*. Their common textual ancestry but stemmatic independence of each other speak to a complex transmission history for this Trevisa abridgement in T, C, and R and heighten the probability that a greater number of manuscripts of this TCR-*Polychronicon* must have once existed and circulated.

In R, the presence of a very brief fragment of the Peculiar *Brut* encourages speculation that the TCR-*Polychronicon* might have been bundled with the genealogy of Adam and Peculiar abridged *Brut* in at least one other manuscript that does not survive. On folio 49ᵛ of R, beneath the *Explicit* to the TCR-

---

11   Higden, *Polychronicon*, I.21–221.

12   For Trevisa I.18 lacuna in Manuscript C, see folio 9ᵛ–10ʳ, cf. R folio 44ʳ8–44ʳ16 and T page 22 line 18 to page 23 line 1; cf. 'Description of the World,' 111: 'Isodre telleth that kyng Alexaunder [...] Gallea and many grete iles.' For Trevisa I.20 lacuna in Manuscript C, see folio 10ᵛ11, cf. R folios 45ʳ13 to 45ᵛ11, and T page 24 line 23 to page 25; cf. 'Description of the World,' 113–114: 'Numedia that londe hath [...] Dydo was a comelyng of Fenys' and Boffey (2019:113n468 and 114n480).

13   For Trevisa I.22 lacuna in Manuscript R, see folio 47ᵛ17, cf. C folio 12ʳ22–12ʳ34 and T page 30 line 22 to page 31 line 8; cf. Boffey (2019: 118 note 587).

Polychronicon, the *Polychronicon* scribe writes four lines that have exact counterparts in the Peculiar Prose *Brut* abridgement text of T (page 42) and C (folio 16ʳ):

> After þᵉ begynnyng of þᵉ worlde iij Mˡ iiijˣˣ vj yere Brute |
> landyd in Albian and afore þᵉ Incarnac[i]on I Mˡ ix yere |
> Gogmagog kyng of Albian gave many harde assautes |
> to the Trog[e]auns &cˡ⁴ [*The R scribe's pen flourish indicates stopping point.*]

These lines, about the date of Trojan Brutus' landing in Albion where Gogmagog had been 'kyng', are an excerpt that comes from an advanced point in the abridged Peculiar Prose *Brut* narrative of Brutus (after his exile to Greece and his leading of the flotilla of Trojan war slaves, now freed by his leadership, to Albion), a text that—apart from these four lines—is not contained in R at all, at least as R is now bound.

The lines were plausibly copied from a manuscript that, like T and C (but not T or C), contained *both* the abridged TCR-*Polychronicon* and the abridged Peculiar Prose *Brut* text. These scribal lines written beneath the Trevisa abridgement in R make a connection between the TCR-*Polychronicon* text present in R and the Peculiar *Brut* absent from R. Manuscript R (folios 50ʳ⁻ᵛ) does contain a fragment of the Genealogy of Adam to Aeneas and Brutus (on a single leaf that directly follows the TCR-*Polychronicon*), the text that in T (pages 35–38) and C (fol. 13²v–14ʳ) comes between the Albina narrative and the Brut material proper. Of the four texts shared by T and C, that is, the anthology R contains the TCR-*Polychronicon* in total (R fols 31ᵛ–49ᵛ), the genealogy of Adam to Aeneas and Brutus in a fragment on a single folio that directly follows the TCR-*Polychronicon* (R fol. 50ʳ⁻ᵛ), and a scribal appendage of four lines about Brutus derived from this Peculiar Version of the Prose *Brut* (R fol. 49ᵛ), written beneath the conclusion of the TCR-*Polychronicon* by the same hand on the same page. R does not contain the Albina episode. The scribe of TCR-*Polychronicon* on R folios 31ᵛ–50ᵛ almost certainly had access to a manuscript exemplar that contained at least three of the four texts found in T and C, but that postulated exemplar could not have been T or C itself for the stemmatic reasons detailed above. These textual traces strongly suggest that at least one more manuscript with this bundle of Middle English histories likely existed in the late fifteenth or early sixteenth centuries, when R would have been copied from it.

---

14   My transcription from R fol. 49ᵛ.

Apart from manuscript evidence, the historical matter in the T and C sequence of texts makes sense as a sort of program. This sequence suggests a historiographic organization of Britain within the world, shaped through recapitulating foundation narratives. The *Polychronicon* abridgement, the initial text in both C and T, is not just a geographic description. It starts from the widest of temporal and spatial perspectives—Creation and the world—and moves forward in time and westward in space from Eden to the City of Rome before being interrupted. This geography embeds biblical events (Paradise and the fall, the Flood, generations of Noah and Abraham) in its spatial demarcations of lands and peoples from east to west, and it includes as well Euhemeristic understandings of the Greek pantheon in its repertoire of founders of provinces and cities.

The second narrative in C and T backtracks eastward to Syria, a land already described in the *Polychronicon* abridgement, and tells of Albina's exile from Syria and voyage to the extreme west of the world to populate Albion with degenerate giants. The third text (Genealogy of Adam to Aeneas) begins again temporally at Adam and traces biblical and pagan genealogies to arrive at Aeneas, whose epic voyages from Troy westward to Tuscany will result in future generations' foundation of Rome (the city of empire where the TCR-*Polychronicon* left off) and the foundation of Britain through Aeneas' grandson Brutus.

The career and voyages of Brutus—exile from his birthplace of Italy, conqueror of Greeks and liberator of their Trojan war-slaves, founder of Britain (with his Greek queen)—culminate in the west, in Britain, where begins the conventional historical matter of the *Brut* tradition. Once the Peculiar Version Prose *Brut*—the fourth text in C and T—is underway, the dynastic organization of ancient British, then English, then Norman kings prevails, and this lengthiest text in the manuscript focuses on the history of Britain and England (a history shared by T and C until the year 1333, then continued variously). The sequence of texts shared by C and T—the abridged *Polychronicon*, the revised and repositioned Albina, the Genealogy of Adam, and the peculiar Prose *Brut* (to 1333)—has a clear organization in which a recapitulating East-to-West structure of space and time, at times suggestive of *translatio studii et imperii*, operates as setting for the long history of Britain.

4   Clash of the Titans, *Polychronicon* vs. *Brut*: Final Contemplations

And yet, there are tensions built into this manuscript collocation of *Poly-chronicon* and Prose *Brut* as a historical program, although it is easy to see why these two histories would be, and were, brought into conversation with each other in the fifteenth century. Both the *Polychronicon* and Prose *Brut* texts were widely circulating, lengthy histories from ancient Britain to present-day England, and both laid claim to some concept of comprehensiveness. However, their historiographical forms differed architecturally: the structure of the *Polychronicon* as a universal history was encyclopedic whereas the form of the *Brut* was genealogical.

Emily Steiner's recent study of John Trevisa (d. 1402) argues persuasively that Trevisa's translations into Middle English of encyclopedic or 'compendious' works in Latin, including *De proprietatibus rerum* by Bartholomaeus Anglicus, Giles of Rome's *De regimine principum*, and Ranulph Higden's *Polychronicon*, contributed to an English age of information in the vernacular for an aristo-cratic elite audience across the second half of the fourteenth century.[15] Trevisa's reworking of the *Polychronicon* into Middle English gave its baronial reader-ship (Trevisa's patron Lord Thomas de Berkeley, in the first instance) access to multiple academic and religious authorities—previously available only to readers of Latin—assembled in a universal history that was both chronological and encyclopedic. Steiner describes Trevisa's fourteenth-century Middle English translation of Ranulph Higden's *Polychronicon* as 'compendious' in that it displays its principles to assemble multiple *auctores* whose names are juxta-posed side by side on any given point of world geography or history, on the page.

The Middle English Prose *Brut* (Common Version extant after 1400), on the other hand, follows insistently linear dynastic generations of kings from an ori-ginary founding by Trojan descendent Brutus, through British, Anglo-Saxon, Danish, Norman, and Plantagenet kings. This is Geoffrey of Monmouth's struc-ture carried on, become so generic after 250 years that no author's name is attached to this text at all, just the name of the traditional founder of Bri-tain, Brutus. Throughout its thirteenth- and fourteenth-century formations, the Anglo-Norman and Middle English Prose *Brut* texts resist naming their authors or revisers or translators and avoid citation of *auctores*. If the *Polychronicon* has a compendious informational structure, the *Brut* is genealogical, linear, and uninterested in authorities.

---

15   Steiner (2021).

What did the readers make of the joining of *Polychronicon* and Prose *Brut* in T and C, in the late fifteenth century? C and T with their program of abridged Middle English histories were made for a readership distinct from Ranulph Higden's scholarly monastic audience or John Trevisa's informed aristocracy. These manuscripts are less expensive, with shortened texts and folios of paper, yet are made with an eye to production values like *ordinatio* features and colourful drawings. They take less time to read than the full versions of either compendious or genealogical history.

If the owners of late fifteenth-century manuscripts C and T were reading comprehensive works made shorter and quicker, just how comprehensive could these histories be? The TCR-*Polychronicon* has certainly been condensed, by about half, from Trevisa's 19,187 words to the TCR Version's 9,819 words (approximate counts).[16] The abridger accomplished this shrinkage by omissions at all levels from single words to subsections of up to 100 words and by rewording and restructuring sentences and passages. Content is left out and sometimes distorted, although as Boffey notes the resulting description of the world has some value as geographic information. The abridgement is carried out pragmatically, and there is no obvious sign of any ideological or political censorship.

Most revealing for how the TCR-*Polychronicon* alters Trevisa's text and its compendious form is the abridger's reduction of authorial citations. Trevisa, following Higden, had listed the names of forty-one authors and translators with their book titles in *Polychronicon* book 1, chapter 2. The TCR-*Polychronicon* reduces that initial master list of 'auctores' to nine: Josephus Judeorum, Eusebius, Hieronymus, Theodorus episcopus, Orosius, Alfridus (Beverlacensis) (in C) *or* Galfridus (Monamutensis) (in R), Cassiodorus, Gregorius, and Beda. More significantly, the TCR-*Polychronicon* throughout the text removes many of the names of authors that Higden and Trevisa recorded.

These internal authorial citations constitute the compendious historical structure in Higden and Trevisa, to the extent that both 'Ranulph' and 'Trevisa' insert their own names—they cite themselves—when they are adding knowledge or commenting on the historical statements by their cited 'auctores'. Even

---

16   TCR is 52% the length of Trevisa, based on word counts of Trevisa's Middle English *Poly-chronicon* as edited in the Rolls edition, Book I chapters 2–24 (ends on page 221, line 12), compared to word counts from my transcribed texts of TCR, using the fullest text among manuscripts T, C, and R for each Trevisa chapter equivalent: by my count, Trevisa I.2–24 (to Rolls 1.p. 221, line 12) contains 19,187 words, and TCR contains 9,819 words. I counted actual words rather than relying on computer word counts, for consistency across the two texts, so actual numbers may be slightly off but not enough to change the significant statistic.

allowing for some collateral elimination of authors' names along with other omissions of text, the result is a sharp diminution of cited authors across TCR-*Polychronicon*. For example, in sections equivalent to Trevisa chapters 5, 7, 8, 11, 12, 15, and 24, which cite an average of seven 'auctores' apiece in Trevisa, TCR-*Polychronicon* cites only one author apiece ('Isodre' or Isidore of Seville, not included in the master list, is the single author cited in three of these chapters). Trevisa chapter 23 has seven citations, whereas the TCR-*Polychronicon* equivalent has none. Several Trevisa chapters contain larger numbers of authorial citations nested in extended arbitrations of multiple—sometimes competing—authorial claims on some point of history. When confronted by such a nest of argumentation, TCR-*Polychronicon* habitually selects for its abridged text only one or two of these points (and maybe its author) and deletes the rest without apparent regard to their relative importance in the extended argument. Trevisa chapters 14 (cites 23 authors), 16 (cites 5 authors), and 20 (cites 12 authors) contain such dense nests of authorial commentary; the equivalent passages in TCR-*Polychronicon* cite only 6 authors (compared to 23, in Trevisa chapter 14); 3 authors (compared to 5, in chapter 16); and 3 authors (compared to 12, in chapter 20). Trevisa's meticulously preserved display of historical controversy among authors is thus distorted and re-represented in TCR-*Polychronicon* as simple recitation of 'the facts'. Blind authority, not epistemological engagement, is the effect achieved by the TCR-*Polychronicon* abridger's elimination of authorial citations.

There is also no way for a reader of the TCR-*Polychronicon* to consult any of the authorities that do survive into the abridgement, because not a single author's name in TCR-*Polychronicon* is accompanied by a book reference. Higden and Trevisa cite book and chapter number for most of the *auctores* they named, reminding us that another aspect of 'compendious' history is that its references can be checked. The closing lines of the TCR-*Polychronicon* show awareness of that limitation when they advise the reader to consult the full-length *Polychronicon*, from which this abridgement is 'more shortly drawen':

> Aucto(u)rs and maistirs of histories afferme bi scripture alle the discripc(i)ons of p(ro)uincis / landis / citees / hillis Sees and alle othir merueils that ben~ tofor~ rehercid / which ben~ here more shortly drawen~ out of Pollicronicon~ / which is witnessid p(re)ued / & autorisid bi scriptur~ bi many right notable maistirs of Stories Doctours and auctours / Whos names beth in the begynnyng of the first book of policronicon~ more pleinly rehercid And the Scriptur~ and Chapit(er)s accordyng to the same./
>
> MS C, fol. 13¹v

One wonders, practically speaking, how easy it could have been to get access to the full *Polychronicon*, if one were reading this abridgement in the first place.

In manuscripts C and T, the abridged *Polychronicon* excerpt and the Peculiar Version *Brut* configure an introduction to world geography that *appears* compendious (but is not truly), to be the setting for a linear history of Britain and England, the MEPB-PV, which in fact abridges many things but never omits the genealogies essential to regnal succession. Analysis of the MEPB-PV in T and C is outside the scope of this article, but let me observe that it features a few interpolations that provide alternative versions of points of history (Mordred gets two different treatments, for one thing). The MEPB-PV, I suggest, shows limited pressure in late fifteenth-century book culture to represent comparative authorities. Let me suggest that identifying this manuscript program in T and C helps make visible a dynamic in which two ideas of historical comprehensiveness—'compendiousness' and genealogy—are putting pressure on each other in this time and for a new set of readers. There seems to be no expectation, however, that these readers will consult or verify or critique the 'Auctores' in any scholarly way.

Bibliography

Abbreviations

C	Cleveland Public Library MS Wq091.92-C468 (formerly Aldenham)
EETS, OS	Early English Text Society, Original Series
R	Oxford, Bodleian Library, Rawlinson C.86
T	Dublin, Trinity College Library MS 489
MEPB	Middle English Prose *Brut*
PV	Peculiar Version
TCR-*Polychronicon*	Condensed version of Trevisa's *Polychronicon* I.2–24 in T, C, and R

Primary Sources—Manuscripts
Cleveland, Ohio
Cleveland Public Library
White Collection MS Wq091.92-C468 [Referred to as C.]

Dublin
Trinity College Library
MS 489 [Referred to as T.]

Oxford

Bodleian Library

MS. Rawl. C. 86, ff. 31ᵛ–49ᵛ. [Referred to as R.]

Primary Sources—Editions

[D'Argenteuil, Roger]. *The M(iddle) E(nglish) Prose Translation of Roger D'Argenteuil's Bible en François, edited from Cleveland Public Library, MS W q 091.92—C 468*. Ed. Phyllis Moe. Heidelberg: Carl Winter, Universitätsverlag, 1977.

The Brut or The Chronicles of England. 2 vols. Ed. Friedrich W.D. Brie. EETS OS 131, 136. 1906, 1908: Reprint as one volume London: Oxford University Press for EETS, 2000.

Higden, Ranulph, and John Trevisa. *Polychronicon Ranulphi Higden Monachi Cestrensis; together with the English Translations of John Trevisa and of an Unknown Writer of the Fifteenth Century*. Ed. Churchill Babington. Rolls Series 41, 1–2. Rerum Britannicarum Medii Ævi Scriptores, or Chronicles and Memorials of Great Britain and Ireland during the Middle Ages. London: Longman, Green, and Co.: 1865, 1869.

Trevisa, John. *John Trevisa's Translation of the **Polychronicon** of Ranulph Higden, Book VI: An Edition Based on British Library MS Cotton Tiberius D.VIII*. Ed. Ronald Waldron. Middle English Text Series 35. Heidelberg: Universitätsverlag Winter, 2004.

[Trevisa, John]. 'The Description of the World.' Ed. Julia Boffey. *Medieval English Travel: An Anthology*. Ed. Anthony Bale and Sebastian Sobecki. New York: Oxford University Press, 2019, 91–121.

Secondary Sources

Boffey, Julia, ed. (2019). 'Introduction.' In [Trevisa], 'Description of the World.' 91–92.

Brie, Friedrich W.D. (1905). *Geschichte und Quellen der mittelenglischen Prosachronik: The Brute of England oder The Chronicles of England*. Marburg: N.G. Elwert'sche Verlagsbuchhandlung.

Edwards, A.S.G. (1973). 'A Sixteenth-Century Version of Trevisa's Polychronicon.' *English Language Notes* 11: 34–38.

Edwards, A.S.G. (1980). 'The Influence and Audience of the *Polychronicon*: Some Observations.' *Proceedings of the Leeds Philosophical and Literary Society*, 17: 113–119.

Edwards, A.S.G. (2004a). 'John Trevisa.' In Edwards, ed. (2004b). 117–126.

Edwards, A.S.G., ed. (2004b). *A Companion to Middle English Prose*. Cambridge: D.S. Brewer.

Kennedy, Edward Donald (1989). *Chronicles and Other Historical Writing*. Vol. 8 of *A Manual of the Writings in Middle English, 1050–1500*. Gen. ed. Albert E. Hartung. New Haven CT: The Connecticut Academy of Arts and Sciences.

Matheson, Lister M. (1998). *The Prose **Brut**: The Development of a Middle English Chronicle*. MRTS 180. Tempe, Arizona: Medieval & Renaissance Texts & Studies.

Moe, Phyllis, ed. (1977). 'Introduction.' In D'Argenteuil, *Middle English Bible en François*. 8–43.

Scattergood, John, with Niamh Pattwell and Emma Williams (2021). *Trinity College Library Dublin: A Descriptive Catalogue of Manuscripts Containing Middle English and Some Old English*. Dublin: Four Courts Press.

Steiner, Emily. (2021). *John Trevisa's Information Age: Knowledge and the Pursuit of Literature, c. 1400*. Oxford: Oxford University Press.

Waldron, Ronald, ed. (2004). 'Introduction.' In Trevisa, *Polychronicon VI*.

4

The Bruges Manuscript and Book III of Jean Froissart's *Chroniques*

Godfried Croenen

Abstract

Jean Froissart wrote and rewrote his *Chroniques* over a period of several decades. We can reconstruct the genesis and development of the text from the surviving manuscript versions of each of the first three books of the *Chroniques*, although the chronology of these versions and their relationships to each other and to the underlying authorial texts are not yet fully understood. The recent identification of a manuscript containing Books II and III of the *Chroniques* in the library of the Seminary in Bruges (MS 468) now further complements this picture. Codicologically the Bruges manuscript is related to the famous 'Rome' manuscript, which contains the latest authorial version of Book I, and it may therefore belong to the same authorial revision campaign of the *Chroniques*. MS 468 contains versions of the *Chroniques* that have not been transmitted elsewhere, including an unrecorded version of Book II. While the text of Book III in MS 468 clearly represents the 'second' authorial redaction of Book III, comparison with the only other known witness of that version (Paris, BnF, fr. 2650) suggests that the state of the text in the latter reflects a further authorial revision of the text as it is recorded in Bruges 468.

1   The *Chroniques*

The best-known medieval historian of the Hundred Years' War is undoubtedly Jean Froissart.[1] This writer from the Southern Low Countries practised various literary genres but is remembered in particular for his extensive *Chroniques*, which deal with the Anglo-French conflict up to c. 1400 and situate the various interrelated conflicts in their wider political, social and cultural context. Despite Froissart at times giving the impression of being superficially and naively enthralled by chivalry and courtly life, scholarly work on the *Chroniques* since

---

1   I am grateful to Sjoerd Levelt, Hartley Miller, Jaclyn Rajsic and Dirk Schoenaers, who generously gave feedback on earlier versions of this essay, which helped me to improve it.

the 1970s has shown him to be a shrewd and intelligent observer of the Western political and military elite of his time.[2] In his prologue Froissart recommends his work to the aristocratic reader as a means of acquiring useful insight and knowledge. Dependent as he was on aristocratic patronage on both sides of the Channel, Froissart rarely formulated direct critiques of the actions and behaviours he witnessed, especially if the actors involved were still alive. Instead he used literary strategies and techniques to create a level of complexity and ambiguity in his narratives, leaving it ultimately to the readers to draw their own conclusions.

Froissart's preoccupation with making his *Chroniques* a useful and entertaining text is probably part of the reason why he not only wrote successive continuations to his text—the most complete form of which is conventionally divided into four Books—but also why he kept rewriting the *Chroniques*, adding or removing details and story lines and refashioning what he had already written. The result of this process can be seen in the manuscript transmission of the *Chroniques*, with more than 160 often incomplete or imperfect manuscripts representing a number of substantially different versions of the text, several of which scholars have recognized as being authorial.[3]

The textual situation is the most complex in relation to the first part of the *Chroniques*—traditionally referred to as Book I—which deals with the Hundred Years' War up to 1377. At least seven authorial versions of this part of the text have been transmitted in about 60 manuscripts. Earlier scholarship, starting from Kervyn de Lettenhove's and Luce's text editions, disagreed fundamentally on the relative chronology of some of these versions. Only recently has it been possible to establish a more convincing and acceptable chronology.[4]

The continuation of Book I up to 1385—the part of the *Chroniques* normally referred to as Book II—exists in at least three or four authorial versions and their relative chronology has been better understood than that of Book I. The situation of Book III, which covers the years 1386 to 1389, but which contains several excursions about earlier events, is also less complex than Book I. Only 24 manuscripts and one incunable edition containing this part of the *Chroniques* are known. They represent two authorial versions of Book III.[5]

---

2 Amongst the extensive secondary literature, see in particular the monographs by Diller (1984), Ainsworth (1990), Zink (1998), Schwarze (2003), Guenée (2008), Varvaro (2011), and Soupoukova (2021).

3 Ainsworth and Croenen (2013).

4 In their likely chronological order these versions are the 'A', 'Amiens', 'Valenciennes', Abridgment, 'B', 'C' and 'Rome' versions. See Croenen (2018).

5 Kervyn de Lettenhove (1873); Mirot (1931); Croenen (2007); Croenen (2009).

2   The Bruges Manuscript of Froissart's *Chroniques*

In 2020, while checking the collection of the Seminary in Bruges for a cata-
loguing project of medieval manuscripts,[6] I was able to identify an unrecorded
manuscript containing Books II and III of Froissart's *Chroniques* kept there
under the shelfmark MS 468. After some initial research it became clear that
this manuscript was none other than the long-lost Froissart manuscript which
in the nineteenth century had been part of the collection of Jean-Jacques
Lambin (d. 1841), archivist of the city of Ypres. After Lambin's death his collection had been auctioned. The Froissart manuscript is briefly described in
the auction catalogue, under no. 5, as an in-quarto manuscript of 304 paper
leaves (it is actually in-folio), without title, containing part of Froissart's *Chroniques*. The manuscript's whereabouts after 1841 were unknown and it was consequently ignored by later scholars like Kervyn, Luce and Raynaud, who do not
even mention it in their discussions of the manuscripts.[7]

The discovery of the manuscript in the Bruges Seminary has now shown
that Lambin's manuscript was acquired, probably at the auction in 1841, by
the Leuven professor Jan Baptist Malou (d. 1864). Malou, also from Ypres, later
become bishop of Bruges. After his death his collection, including the Froissart codex, remained in the episcopal palace in Bruges. Nearly a century later,
in 1955, the Malou books were transferred to the Seminary, where they are still
kept today. Although there is a brief reference to the manuscript in the printed
subject index to the Seminary's manuscript collection, it has until now entirely
escaped the attention of Froissart scholarship.[8]

While it is always interesting to find an unrecorded manuscript of a well-
known medieval vernacular text, the discovery of the Bruges Froissart is particularly exciting for Froissart scholars, and this for several reasons. First, unlike
the many Parisian illuminated manuscripts of the *Chroniques*, the Bruges
manuscript was probably copied in the Southern Low Countries by a scribe
who wrote a Middle French Picard that must have been very similar to Froissart's own language. While not necessarily a guarantee for the correctness of
the manuscript's readings, the linguistic proximity between author and scribe
means that it is less likely that the Picard exemplar would have been misunderstood and that the scribe would have introduced changes to the copied text to
remedy real or perceived textual problems, a phenomenon that can be readily
observed in the manuscripts copied in Paris. The Bruges volume can there-

6   Wuyts and Coppoolse (2018).
7   Kervyn de Lettenhove (1867–1877); Luce (1869–1888); Raynaud (1894–1899).
8   Vander Plaetse (1984: 131).

fore be added to a small group of late fourteenth- or early fifteenth-century manuscript of the *Chroniques* from the Low Countries, which include Città del Vaticano, Reg. Lat. 869 (Book I), Kortrijk Cod. 329 (Book I), Leiden, MS VGGF 9 II (Book II) and Paris, BnF, fr. 6477–6479 (Book I).

Second, the Bruges manuscript is older than most manuscripts of the *Chroniques* and may date to Froissart's own lifetime. An indication is that it is copied by the scribe of the so-called 'Rome' manuscript of Book I of the *Chroniques*, now kept in the Vatican Library (Reg. Lat. 869) and the only witness of the last authorial version of Book I, composed c. 1404 shortly before the 'Rome' manuscript itself was written. The scribe of these two manuscripts wrote a low grade version of a Northern textualis script in brown ink. However, the writing of the Bruges manuscript is less consistent than that of the 'Rome' manuscript. While the 'mise-en-page' of most of the codex resembles very much the 'Rome' manuscript, some sections are slightly different and may have been copied at a different time, in a different, darker ink. In these sections the writing is less careful, with the letters more slanting to the right and the writing not always parallel to the page's edge. The text block is often also slightly larger, with longer lines and more lines per page. Finally, in these sections initials have been executed in red ink, whereas elsewhere, as in the 'Rome' manuscript, there are only guide letters with spaces left for two-line initials that have not been executed.

Third, like the manuscript now in the Vatican Library, the Bruges manuscript is incomplete but both codices nevertheless contain a significant amount of text. Reg. Lat. 869 breaks off after fol. 152, before the midpoint of the text of Book I. The Bruges manuscript, with its 304 leaves, is twice as long as the 'Rome' manuscript. It does not include Book I and it lacks the beginning of Book II but it still has about 80% of the text of Book II (starting at §100) and all of Book III. Moreover, the Bruges manuscript is exceptional in bringing together in one volume the text of both Books II and III (Besançon MS 865 is the only other manuscript to do so).

Fourth, in addition to the scribal hand shared between the Vatican and Bruges manuscripts, there are several other codicological similarities. Bruges 468 is copied on paper like the Vatican manuscript. It uses the same one-column layout with frame ruling and has similar low-grade decoration, which consists of simple two-line initials that have been planned but mostly not executed, although in Bruges 468 the initials were executed as plain initials in red ink in some sections (fol. 2^r–45bis v, 47bis r–55^v, 57^r–100^v). In the Vatican manuscript two-line initials were planned but never executed. Both manuscripts contain some marginal rubrics in brown ink added by contemporary cursive hands that are very similar. On the basis of these elements, and given that there is no textual overlap between the Bruges and Vatican manuscripts, one could hypothesize that they are both the remnants of a larger manuscript volume or set of manuscripts which originally contained the last authorial revision of the *Chroniques* for Books I–III, possibly even for Books I–IV. In order to evaluate this hypothesis more work is needed but the codicological similarities nevertheless strongly suggest close connections between the two volumes. Finally, like Reg. Lat. 869, Bruges MS 468 also contains versions of parts of the *Chroniques* that are not found in other witnesses and that have all the hallmarks of authorial rewriting. The version of Book III in the Bruges manuscript seems at first sight to be identical to the 'second' redaction identified by Kervyn de Lettenhove and Léon Mirot, and preserved otherwise only in Paris, BnF, fr. 2650 (which only contains Book III).[9] The text of Book II in the Bruges codex, however, is very different from the two versions known to the authors of the standard editions of Book II, Kervyn de Lettenhove and Gaston Raynaud. It comes closest to the version of Book II found in the manuscript of the *Chroniques* now in the Newberry Library in Chicago (MS f.37), a version that I have identified as a later reworking of the so-called 'revised redaction' found in the manuscript of Book II in the University Library at Leiden (VGGF 9 II).[10]

3   The Bruges Manuscript and Book III of the *Chroniques*

In order to assess the full significance of the Bruges manuscript a wide-ranging comparative textual investigation will be necessary. The text of Book II (fol. 1ʳ– 108ᵛ, Figure 1) should be carefully compared to the versions of Book II edited by Kervyn de Lettenhove and Gaston Raynaud but also, in particular, to the unedited Newberry version.[11] This analysis should furthermore try to establish if there are any textual or historical connections between the Bruges text and the 'Rome' version of Book I transmitted in Reg. Lat. 869. It would be crucial to develop a better understanding of their relative chronology, in particular to see whether the Bruges text and the Vatican manuscript of Book I belong to the same authorial rewriting campaign and could therefore have been part of the same manuscript set.

---

9   Kervyn de Lettenhove (1867–1877); Mirot and Mirot (1933–1975).
10   Croenen (2010a).
11   A partial transcription is already available in Ainsworth and Croenen (2013).

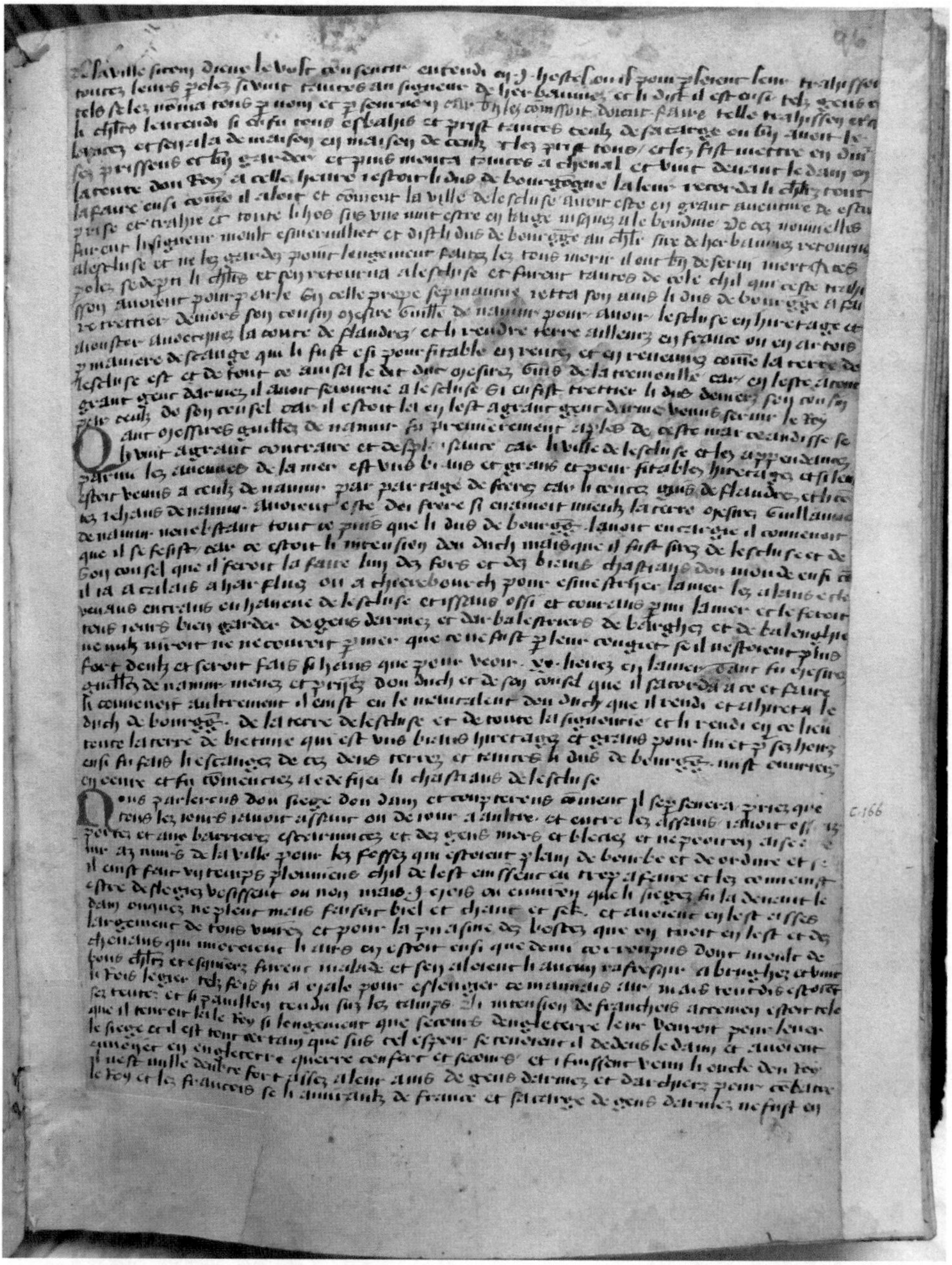

FIGURE 1   Archief Grootseminarie Brugge (AGSB), MS 468, fol. 96ʳ (Jean Froissart, *Chroniques*, Book II)
PHOTOGRAPH BY THE AUTHOR, REPRODUCED WITH KIND PERMISSION OF THE
ARCHIEF GROOTSEMINARIE BRUGGE

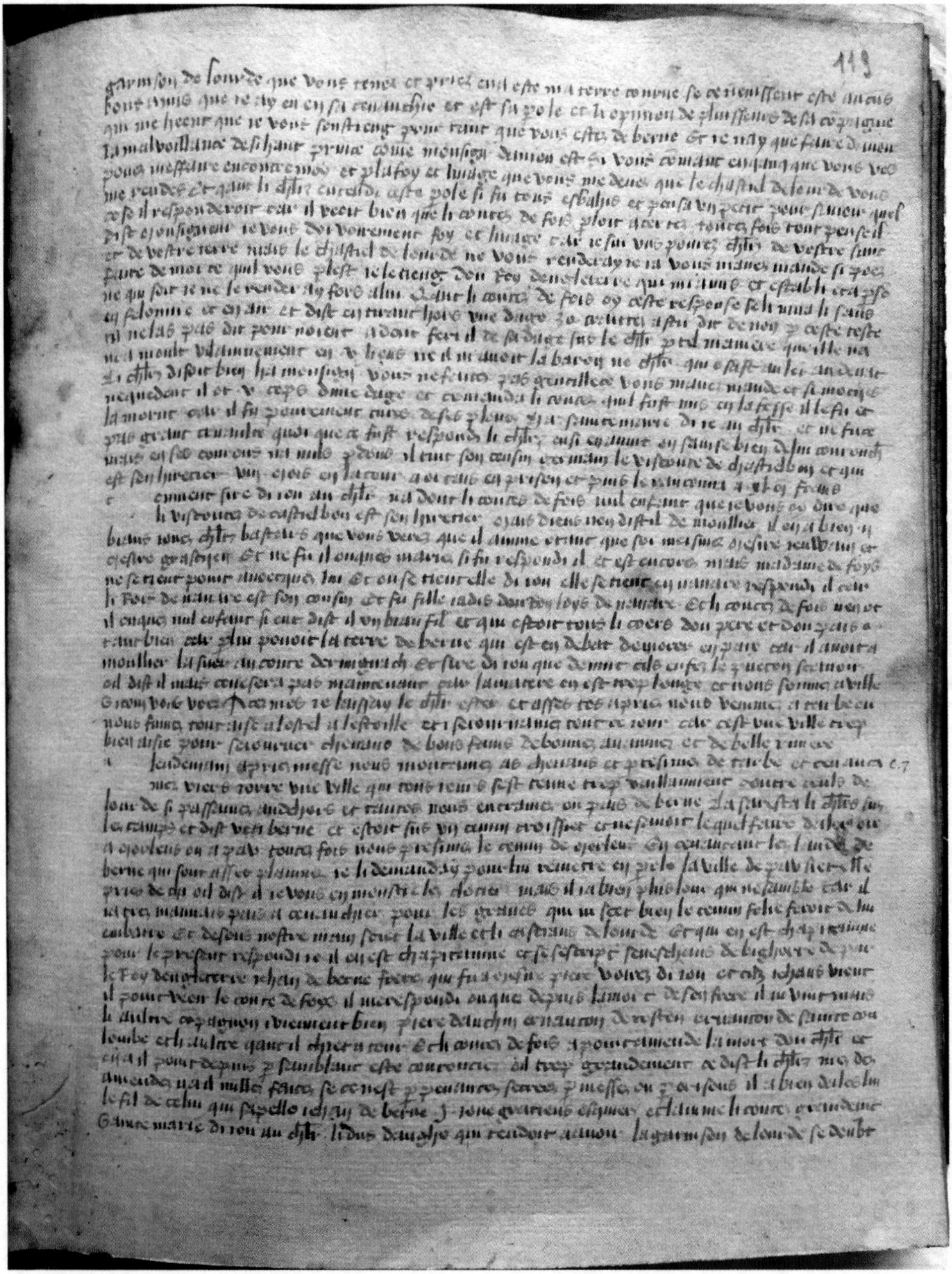

FIGURE 2 Archief Grootseminarie Brugge (AGSB), MS 468, fol. 119ʳ (Jean Froissart, *Chroniques*, beginning of Book III)

PHOTOGRAPH BY THE AUTHOR, REPRODUCED WITH KIND PERMISSION OF THE ARCHIEF GROOTSEMINARIE BRUGGE

Trying to answer these important questions surrounding the version of Book II preserved in the Bruges manuscript would far exceed the limits of this essay. I will therefore limit myself instead to the text of Book III and briefly consider what we can already learn from it regarding the textual development and transmission of Book III of the *Chroniques*. As indicated above, the Book III part of Bruges 468 (Figure 2) is to a very large extent identical to the 'second' redaction as it was edited by Léon and Albert Mirot from fr. 2650. This 'second' redaction text is a reworked version of the earlier 'first' redaction, which is found in all the other witnesses. Given that the reworked text contains unmistakeable autobiographical elements not present in the 'first' redaction, Froissart himself must have been the agent responsible for the rewriting resulting in the 'second' redaction.

The authorial text of the 'first' redaction can be reconstructed using the best and earliest witnesses of this version (Besançon 865; Arundel 67; Arsenal 5189; fr. 2653 and fr. 6475). Comparison between the 'first' redaction and the readings of fr. 2650 and Bruges 468 shows that the authorial text of most chapters in both redactions is identical or nearly identical. There are small differences in the wording of the witnesses throughout the text but most of these probably result from the mechanics of scribal transmission. The substantial differences between the two versions are limited to a relatively small set of fifteen chapters, out of a total of 306, that have been partly or completely rewritten by the author in the 'second' redaction as represented by fr. 2650 and Bruges 468 (§ 109, 111, 120–122, 261, 275–278, 288–290, 306–307 and possibly also 70).[12] Apart from these rewritten chapters there are two chapters that are present in one version only: § 308 is found in the 'first' redaction but has been omitted from the 'second'; and § 110 is only found in the 'second' redaction and has no counterpart in the 'first' redaction.

Although the authorial rewriting of Book III is on a smaller scale than can be observed between the known versions of Book I, the differences in the rewritten chapters justify the conclusion that the text of Book III in fr. 2650 and Bruges 468 represents a 'second' authorial version, which was the result of an

---

12   It should be pointed out that the chapter divisions of Book III, as indicated in Mirot and Mirot's edition for the Societé de l'Histoire de France, do not take into account the chapter divisions present in the edition's base manuscript fr. 2650. This is an unfortunate editorial decision, because the segmentation of fr. 2650 is probably authorial, as it largely agrees with what is found in Bruges MS 468 as well as in the early witnesses of the 'first' redaction. The chapters of Mirot's edition are usually longer than in the manuscripts. In contrast the editions of the preceding Books I and II published by Societé de l'Histoire de France do follow the manuscript segmentation of the text.

authorial revision of the 'first' version. The rewriting often aligns with Froissart's apparent increasing interests in certain aspects of contemporary history
that have also been detected in the later versions of Book I, such as the 'Rome'
version, and in Book IV, composed at the same time as the latter.[13] Froissart's
interests in ideology, good leadership and the processes of political and military
decision making, for example, seem to have been the reason for the inclusion of
several detailed literary representations of discussions between kings, princes,
military leaders and their advisors, using the narrative device of realistic—but
invented—dialogues in which different points of view are formulated or represented by different interlocutors.

The chronicler also included more, and more detailed and realistic (but not
necessarily historically accurate), accounts of military operations (including
tournaments and duels) and details of the role played by exemplary soldiers
and knights in these events. This concern with the realities of warfare corresponds to Froissart's stated principal aim to provide his readers with useful
information to help them to develop a better understanding of military matters.[14] In the rewriting of Book III, as in the rewritten versions of other parts
of the *Chroniques*, Froissart also shows an increasing interest in the characteristics of different national or ethnic groups.[15] Finally, the 'second' version of
Book III includes a number of vignettes recording actions of certain historical
actors in particular contexts, like the count of Foix in relation to his son's acci-
dental death or the duke of Berry in the pursuit of his second marriage. These
allow the author to reflect indirectly on their personalities, their morals and
their qualities as leaders.

Textual comparison between Bruges 468 and fr. 2650 shows that they closely
agree. There are some exceptions, the most important one of which concerns
an anomaly in the order of the chapters on the battle of Otterburn (August
1388). In Bruges 468 the textual order is as printed in Mirot's edition, but
in fr. 2650, Mirot's base manuscript, the sequence is different. On fol. 307ᵛ,
halfway through § 285, which narrates the leadup to the battle, fr. 2650 skips
ahead to the middle of § 290, which records events in the battle's aftermath.
It then continues with the subsequent eight chapters (§ 291–298), narrating
King Charles VI of France's military expedition against Guelders, which also
took place in August 1388. At the conclusion of this narrative thread (fol. 318ᵛ),
fr. 2650 switches back to the Scottish affairs, repeating part of § 285, preceded
by an introductory sentence which switches the narrative focus. Fr. 2650 then

---

13   Ainsworth (1990); Varvaro (2011).
14   Varvaro (2011: 103–171).
15   Harf-Lancner (2006).

includes the normal narration of the battle of Otterburn (§ 285–291), conclud-ing with § 290–291, which are already found earlier on in the manuscript. Mirot comments on this anomaly and explains it as a scribal error. He suggests that the scribe accidentally skipped a number of leaves after § 285 and only real-ized his mistake after he had copied § 298. According to Mirot the scribe must then have decided to go back in the narrative to include nearly the complete sequence on Otterburn, patching up his error as best as he could.[16]

The fact that Mirot's reconstructed text order matches the text of the Bruges manuscript is indeed a strong indication that in the authorial 'second' redac-tion the order of the chapters was the same as in the first redaction and that the sequence found in fr. 2650 is effectively incorrect. The text skipped between § 285 and § 290 takes up almost exactly 10 leaves in fr. 2650 (fol. 319^v–329^v), which could correspond to an entire quire in the exemplar from which fr. 2650 was copied. An unbound exemplar, from which quires could accidentally be inverted, might indeed offer one possible solution to this textual conundrum.

However, the idea that the text order found in fr. 2650 is simply the result of a copying error is not entirely convincing. There are no signs in the manuscript itself, such as deletions, additions or cross-references, that the scribe was trying to patch up the text, comparable to what can be found in other manuscripts in which copying errors affect the text order, such as KBR, II 88, where an acci-dentally repeated chapter (Book II, § 94) was completely deleted with 'vacat' signs (fol. 15^r). The error and patching up of the text in fr. 2650 could of course have happened in an earlier stage of the transmission, but it is still worth con-sidering an alternative interpretation.

As we will see below there are solid textual arguments to consider the text of fr. 2650 a snapshot of a further authorial rewriting of the text of the 'second' redaction found in the Bruges manuscript. It may therefore also have been the case that Froissart, in this process, was experimenting with a different text order of the narratives on Scotland, France and Guelders. Central elements in Froissart's literary technique are the development of long narrative chains and the use of entrelacement to change the narrative focus between them, in order to evoke simultaneity of different developments and to draw out paral-lels between them.[17] Both the French king's campaign against Guelders and the battle of Otterburn took place in August 1388, so dividing the Otterburn narrat-ive into two and inserting the Guelders narrative in the middle might have been a way of underlining the chronology. Alternatively, the aim may have been to

---

16   Froissart, *Chroniques [Livre III]*. Ed. Mirot and Mirot, vol. 15, 128.
17   Calin (1993).

invite the reader to reflect on the very different approaches to these military operations by the French and English commanders.

While looking for indications that fr. 2650 and Bruges 468 reflect different authorial versions or states of the 'second' redaction, I collated two long samples from both manuscripts, equivalent to §172 and §284–291. These represent 35 chapters in the manuscript and contain just over 20,000 words. Most of these chapters are nearly identical in both authorial versions of Book III (§172, 284–287 and 291) but the sample also includes §288–290, which appear in a substantially refashioned form in the 'second' redaction manuscripts. The fact that the Bruges manuscript and fr. 2650, apart from orthographic variants, nearly always agree on the readings is a strong indication that their scribes (or the scribes of their exemplars) did not set out to regularly interfere in the text, unlike the active scribal rewriting that can be seen in some other witnesses of Book III, such as fr. 6475.

In the selected sample I was able to identify eleven variant places where fr. 2650 has a substantive variant reading that is different from Bruges 468, and where Bruges 468 agrees with the earlier 'first' redaction. Three or four of these could be scribal in origin and be the result either of a scribal error or of a scribe's attempt to correct a perceived deficiency; the others cannot really be explained in this way and are therefore likely to be authorial. Three variants in §172 concern rephrasings: 'ilz se vouloient mettre ensemble' ('they wanted to come together') in fr. 2650, where Bruges 468 and the other manuscripts have 'ilz se meteroient ensemble et' ('they would come together and'); 'puisque vous vouléz qu'ilz soient pris' ('because you want them to be taken') in fr. 2650, where Bruges 468 and the 'first'-redaction manuscripts have 'puisque vous lez voléz prendre' ('because you want to take them'); and 'je sui tout conseilliéz et aussi sommes nous tous et bien aviséz' ('I am fully advised—and so are we all—and of the opinion') in fr. 2650, where Bruges 468 and the other manuscripts have 'nous sommez tout consilliet et tout aviset' ('we are all advised and all of the opinion').[18] One further variant occurs in the part of the text of §290 that is repeated in fr. 2650 but only appears the second time the passage is copied: 'ce bondissement de leurs cornéz' ('this noise made by their horns') where previously, and in all other manuscripts, the reading is simply 'ce bondissement' ('this noise').[19]

Even clearer than the rephrasings are the variants where a complete phrase in one manuscript has no counterpart in the other. Two such variants corres-

---

18   Froissart, *Chroniques* [*Livre III*]. Ed. Mirot and Mirot, vol. 13, 259, l. 4; 263, l. 22–23; 265, 4–6.
19   Froissart, *Chroniques* [*Livre III*]. Ed. Mirot and Mirot, vol. 15, 169, l. 30.

pond to complete phrases that appear neither in the 'first' version nor in Bruges 468, and that are only found in fr. 2650: 'Ensement s'en alerent a l'aventure ce deux chevaulchiees' ('and in this manner both military units went their way in search of battle', § 285); 'mais l'une l'eut pieurre que l'autre' ('but it was worse for one [side] than for the other', § 290).[20] Finally, one variant concerns a phrase that is present in Bruges 468 and in the 'first' redaction but that is absent from fr. 2650: 'mes non furent car mesires Henris ne le trouva point en son consel' ('but they weren't [attacked] because Sir Henry did not think it wise').[21]

Further collation of the Bruges text will probably bring up more examples of such variant readings that are unique to fr. 2650 and absent from Bruges 468. If at least some of these variants may be identified as authorial, then that means that fr. 2650 preserves an authorially revised state of the 'second' redaction. The variants discussed above suggest how the author kept perfecting his text, slightly rephrasing, and adding or deleting words and phrases. The collation of fr. 2650 and Bruges 468 and the comparative study of their variants will therefore lead to important additions in our understanding of the authorial rewriting of Froissart's *Chroniques*.

Bibliography

Primary Sources—Manuscripts
Besançon
Bibliothèque d'étude et de conservation
MS 865

Bruges
Grootseminarie Ten Duinen, Archief
MS 468

Brussels
KBR
MS II 88

---

20   Froissart, *Chroniques* [*Livre III*]. Ed. Mirot and Mirot, vol. 15, 128, l. 12–14; 171, l. 24.
21   Bruges 468, fol. 278ᵛ. This phrase appears in Froissart, *Chroniques* [*Livre III*]. Ed. Mirot and Mirot, vol. 15, 133, between l. 4 and l. 5.

Chicago
Newberry Library
MS f.37

Città del Vaticano
Biblioteca Apostolica Vaticana
Reg. Lat. 869

Kortrijk
Rijksarchief
Handschriften Stadsbibliotheek Kortrijk Cod. 329

Leiden
University Library
VGGF 9, II

London
British Library
Arundel MS 67, vol. III

Paris
Bibliothèque de l'Arsenal
MS 5189
Bibliothèque nationale de France
MS fr. 2650
MS fr. 2653
MS fr. 6475
MS fr. 6477–6479

Primary Sources—Editions

Ainsworth, Peter and Godfried Croenen (2013). *The Online Froissart.* version 1.5. Sheffield: HRIOnline. http://www.dhi.ac.uk/onlinefroissart. Accessed 14 February 2022.

Froissart, Jean, *Chroniques.* 25 vols. Ed. baron [J.M.B.C.] Kervyn de Lettenhove. Brussels, 1870–1877.

Froissart, Jean, *Chroniques* [*Livre I*]. 9 vols. Ed. Siméon Luce. Paris: Société de l'histoire de France, 1869–1888.

Froissart, Jean, *Chroniques* [*Livre II*]. 3 vols. Ed. Gaston Raynaud. Paris: Société de l'histoire de France, 1894–1899.

Froissart, Jean, *Chroniques* [*Livre III*]. 4 vols. Ed. Léon Mirot and Albert Mirot. Paris: Société de l'histoire de France, 1931–1975.

Froissart, Jean, *Chroniques. Livre III*. Ed. Peter F. Ainsworth and Godfried Croenen. Geneva: Droz, 2007.

Secondary Sources

Ainsworth, Peter F. (1990). *Jean Froissart and the Fabric of History: Truth, Myth, and Fiction in the Chroniques*. Oxford: Clarendon Press.

Ainsworth, Peter F. and Godfried Croenen, eds. (2007). See Froissart, *Chroniques. Livre III*. Ed. Ainsworth and Croenen.

Calin, William (1993). 'Narrative Technique in Fourteenth-Century France: Froissart and his *Chroniques*.' In Pickens (1993). 227–236.

Croenen, Godfried (2006). 'Froissart et ses mécènes: quelques problèmes biographiques.' In Zink and Bombarde (2006). 9–32.

Croenen, Godfried (2007). 'Les manuscrits du Troisième Livre: inventaire et description.' In Ainsworth, and Croenen (2007). 27–32.

Croenen, Godfried (2009). 'La tradition manuscrite du Troisième Livre des *Chroniques* de Froissart.' In Fasseur (2009). 15–59.

Croenen, Godfried (2010a). 'A 'Refound' Manuscript of Froissart Revisited: Newberry MS F.37.' *French Studies Bulletin*. 31: 56–60.

Croenen, Godfried (2010b). 'Stemmata, Philology and Textual History: A Response to Alberto Varvaro.' *Medioevo Romanzo*. 34: 398–402.

Croenen, Godfried (2018). 'La guerre en Normandie au XIVe siècle et le problème de l'évolution textuelle des *Chroniques* de Jean Froissart.' In Curry and Gazeau (2018). 111–147.

Curry, Anne and Véronique Gazeau, eds. (2018). *La Guerre en Normandie (X^e–XVe siècle)*. Actes du colloque international de Cerisy, 30 septembre–3 octobre 2015. Caen: Presses universitaires de Caen.

Denaux, Adelbert and Eric Vanden Berghe, eds. (1984). *De Duinenabdij (1627–1796) en het Grootseminarie (1833–1983) te Brugge. Bewoners / Gebouwen / Kunstpatrimonium*. Tielt: Lannoo.

Diller, George T. (1984). *Attitudes chevaleresques et réalités politiques chez Froissart. Microlectures du premier livre des Chroniques*. Geneva: Droz, 1984.

Fasseur, Valérie, ed. (2009). *Froissart à la cour de Béarn: L'écrivain, les arts et le pouvoir*. Turnhout: Brepols.

Guenée, Bernard (2008). *Du Guesclin et Froissart: la fabrication de la renommée*. Paris: Tallandier.

Harf-Lancner, Laurence (2006). 'Froissart, les Anglais et leurs rois.' In Zink and Bombarde (2006). 53–66.

Kervyn de Lettenhove, baron [J.M.B.C.] (1870). 'Recherches sur l'ordre et la date des diverses rédactions des Chroniques.' In Kervyn de Lettenhove (1870–1877), vol. 1/2–3, 1–540.

Kervyn de Lettenhove, baron [J.M.B.C.], ed. (1870–1877). See Froissart, *Chroniques*. Ed. Kervyn de Lettenhove.

Luce (1869–1888). See Froissart, *Chroniques*. Ed. Luce.

Mirot, Léon and Albert Mirot, eds. (1931–1975). See Froissart, *Chroniques* [*Livre III*]. Ed. Mirot and Mirot.

Pickens, Rupert T., ed. (1993). *Studies in Honor of Hans-Erich Keller: Medieval French and Occitan Literature and Romance Linguistics*. Kalamazoo: Medieval Institute Publications.

Raynaud, Gaston, ed. (1894–1899). See Froissart, *Chroniques* [*Livre II*]. Ed. Raynaud.

Schwarze, Michael (2003). *Generische Wahrheit—höfischer Polylog im Werk Jean Froissarts*. Stuttgart: Franz Steiner, 2003.

Soukupová, Věra (2021). *La construction de la réalité historiques chez Jean Froissart: L'historien et sa matière*. Paris: Champion.

Vander Plaetse, Roeland (1984). 'Index van de handschriften van het Grootseminarie van Brugge.' In Denaux and Vanden Berghe (1984). 125–135.

Varvaro, Alberto (2011). *La Tragédie de l'histoire. La dernière œuvre de Jean Froissart*. Paris: Classiques Garnier.

Wuyts, Eva and David Coppoolse (2018). 'Medieval Manuscripts in Flemish Collections: 1000 Jaar handschriften in kaart gebracht.' *Queeste* 25: 115–118.

Zink, Michel (1998). *Froissart et le temps*. Paris: Presses universitaires de France.

Zink, Michel and Odile Bombarde, eds. (2006). *Froissart dans sa forge*. Colloque réuni à Paris, du 4 au 6 novembre 2004. Paris: Académie des Inscriptions et Belles-Lettres.

5

Historian as Hagiographer? Benoît de Sainte-Maure's Saintly Duke of Normandy

Peter Damian-Grint

Abstract

This article examines Benoît de Sainte-Maure's depiction of the dukes of Normandy—in particular Richard the Fearless, the third duke—in his *Estoire des ducs de Normandie*. Benoît's description of the duke, his characterization of him as 'saintisme', and the events he chooses to narrate, raise the question of cross-genre borrowing: is our author writing Richard's life as hagiography? This question is explored with reference to Benoît's translation strategies and to the conventions of Old French and Latin hagiography in his time, as seen specifically in the *vita* of another prince-saint, Edward the Confessor, which has been proposed as a model for Richard's *vita*. The hagiographical elements in Benoît's depiction of Richard are shown to derive closely from his main sources, Robert of Torigni's redaction of the *Gesta Normannorum ducum* and Dudo of Saint-Quentin's *De moribus et actis primorum Normanniæ ducum*, while the pattern of his borrowings from Dudo shows that Benoît downplays rather than emphasises the hagiographical dimension of his text.

1   Benoît's Depiction the Norman Dukes

We know that the Jersey poet Wace began his literary career with a series of hagiographies before making his name as a historian: a *Vie de sainte Marguerite*, *Conception Nostre Dame* and *Vie de saint Nicolas* composed by him all survive. Françoise Le Saux, classifying him as a hagiographer for the early part of his career, points out that his religious writings were something quite unremarkable in the literary context.[1] There is, then, nothing inherently improbable in the proposal that Wace's contemporary and literary rival, Benoît de Sainte-Maure, might have done something similar, but no one to my knowledge has ever proposed that he did; nor has any work of hagiography ever been attrib-

---

1   See Le Saux (2005: 11–12). The section is entitled: 'Wace: Hagiographer'.

uted to him. It is with his resolutely secular *roman antique*, the *Roman de Troie*, that he first comes to public notice.

Despite this, at first glance it is Benoît rather than Wace who appears to draw on hagiography for his descriptions of the lives of the early Norman dukes in his *Estoire des ducs de Normandie*. Thus Rollo, the founder of the dynasty, is presented as guided by God—even before his conversion from paganism—through dreams, which are interpreted by aged and saintly Christians (*Estoire*, 3151–3216, 3523–3800); he calms a storm with his prayer (4203–4360); after his holy death his soul is taken to heaven (10,518–522). All these are elements for which we can find parallels in contemporary hagiography.

Other hagiographical elements can be seen in the *vita* of Rollo's son and successor, William Longsword. The burning desire to become a monk that he expresses (*Estoire*, 13,401–544) can be seen as closely paralleled in the *vita* of the ninth-century count Gerald of Aurillac and, perhaps even more closely, that of the eleventh-century king of the Franks, Robert the Pious.[2] William's murder, which occurs shortly afterwards, is presented explicitly as a 'glorius martire' (*Estoire*, 14,810), and Benoît's description of the event can be seen as closely echoing the well-known account of the martyrdom of a more contemporary 'glorious martyr', St Thomas Becket:

> ... tote la teste out fendue
> e jus la cervelle espandue;
> traites unt les espees nues [...]
> Li dux, li haut, li pretios,
> Li saintismes, li glorios
> que eisi fu martirié.
>
>   *Estoire*, 14,599–601, 14,627–629

(He split his head completely open and scattered the brain; they have drawn naked swords ... The duke, the high, the precious, the most holy and the glorious, who was thus martyred.)[3]

The mention of William's 'haire' (hairshirt: *Estoire*, 14,710) shortly afterwards could be taken as a discreet attempt to underline the parallel—for it was the discovery that Thomas was wearing a hairshirt that assured the monks of Can-

---

2 Odo of Cluny's *Vita sancti Geraldi Auriliacensis* and Helgaud of Fleury's *Epitoma vitæ Regis Rotberti Pii*.

3 See also *Estoire*, 14,627–629 ('martir fu saint e glorius', 14,767). All translations are mine.

terbury that he was a saint—although Benoît's account does not show any literary dependence on contemporary Old French lives of St Thomas.[4]

Even a figure as unlikely as William's grandson and eventual successor Robert the Magnificent (or the Devil) attracts hagiographical tropes, above all in the context of his pilgrimage to Jerusalem, where he visits the Holy Places "nus piez, la haire aprés sa char" ('barefoot, a hairshirt next the skin'; *Estoire*, 33,953); his death, poisoned during the return journey, is not presented explicitly as a martyrdom but is a saintly end:

> Sa fin fu sainte e gloriose;
> por c'est s'arme beneürose
> en celestre Jerusalem.
>
> *Estoire*, 33,979–981

(His end was holy and glorious; this is why his blessed soul is in the heavenly Jerusalem.)

This use of hagiographical figures seems to support an idea that has become something of a cliché: Benoît—according to some scholars—presents the Norman dukes as duke-saints, following the model of Edward the Confessor, king-saint of England (d. 1066), in order to counteract the miracle-working kings of the Capetian line and to appropriate the same sacred power for the Angevin kings.[5]

Sources would not have been hard to come by. The Anglo-Norman *Vie d'Édouard le Confesseur* was composed by a nun of Barking 1163×70, shortly before Benoît began his history; it is doubtful that he would have seen it, but he would almost certainly have known Ælred's popular *Vita sancti Edwardi regis et confessoris*, of which the Barking *Vie* is a close translation.[6]

On one level, the *Vita sancti Edwardi* is not a typical hagiography; Ælred chooses not to dispense with the secular dimension of Edward's life (as he could have done), but draws largely on previous secular biographies of the king, presenting him in secular terms as a layman and a secular ruler within

---

4 There are two: Guernes de Pont-Saint-Maxence's *Vie de saint Thomas Becket* (1174) and the *Vie seint Thomas le glorius martir de Canterbire* (c. 1185) by Benoît, a monk of St Albans.

5 See Gouttebroze (1991: 307–311); Aurell (2003: 11); Laurent (2010). Waugh (2006) points also to the figure of St Edmund the Martyr as a model prince-saint, although the *vitæ* focus on his martyrdom and posthumous miracles. For the 'construction' of Edward's sanctity see Bozoky (2014: 159–171).

6 18 manuscripts survive, and Ælred's work spawned various other *vitæ* of Edward: Pezzini (2008: 333–372).

a nexus of political and dynastic relations.[7] He begins with Edward's lineage, birth and early life, together with a sketch of the English and wider European political context. Richard, duke of Normandy appears here, naturally enough, as the father of Edward's mother Emma: he is described in entirely conventional terms as 'inclytus', and even the description of Richard and his son Robert as 'laudabilis eorum vita et mors nihilominus pretiosa' ('their praiseworthy lives and no less valuable deaths': *Vita sancti Edwardi regis*, §1), while ambiguous, does not go beyond the rhetoric of *laudatio* of famous figures.

But the hagiographical topoi make their presence felt: Ælred introduces the topos of the saint as chosen by God even before birth; we see examples of Edward's goodness, piety and chastity (his virginal marriage to Edith is adduced as a particular case of this virtue); other well-known tropes include his pilgrimages to Rome and his close relations with the pope, and the miracles he works during his lifetime (in which the recovery of sight features prominently). The last quarter of the *Vita* is made up of the traditional collection of postmortem miracle accounts.

2   Benoît's 'Saintisme' Richard

If this is the case, we would expect a hagiographical mode to be most apparent in the life of William's son, Richard the Fearless, who is the focus of Benoît's attention. For of the ten dukes Benoît mentions in his *estoire*, it is Richard who gets the lion's share: around 15,000 verses are devoted to his *vita*, about a third of the entire *Estoire* and almost as much as the space devoted to the two next most important dukes, Rollo and William the Conqueror, combined.

There are a number of significant moments in Benoît's life of Richard that can be proposed as following a hagiographical model. Perhaps the most important of all is his evangelization of the pagan Danes, whom he has asked to help him fight against the king of France (*Estoire*, 25,820–26,580). The duke is portrayed as catechizing them with a long and theologically dense discourse, full of vivid details—beginning with his arresting description of the pains of hell (whence, he tells them, they are headed if they do not believe, *Estoire*, 28,556–562), and mapping out the creation, the Fall, and the Redemption of the human race, and after describing the Last Judgment finishes by urging them to be baptized.

---

7   For the intersection of biography and hagiography in medieval accounts of Edward the Confessor, see Drukker (2006).

No less striking is the more anecdotal episode that appears among a series of adventures ascribed to Richard. The story features an angel and a devil who argue over the soul of a monk who has been drowned while on his way to visit a woman, and in the end agree to put the matter to arbitration: not only is it entirely in the manner of the legends of the saints, but the anecdote appears to be adapted directly from a legend of the Blessed Virgin Mary: here, it is not the Virgin who saves the monk from the clutches of the devil but the duke (*Estoire*, 27,593–28,128).[8]

Also important is the long character description of the duke much earlier in Benoît's *vita* of Richard, which contains a number of hagiographical elements:

> Plain ert de fe e charitos
> e moct par esteit curios
> des sainz commandemenz tenir
> que Dex voct a homme establir
> e fianços de la merite
> que li haut sainz en unt escripte,
> Bien saveit des choses mundaines
> aquerre les celestaines. [...]
> Ne nasquié plus large aumonier;
> ja ne cessast d'estudier
> en buennes ovres n'en jenz faiz.
> > *Estoire*, 23,075–082, 117–119

(He was full of faith and charitable, and very diligent to keep the holy commandments that God wished to establish for men, and trusting in the reward of which the high saints wrote. He knew well how to acquire heavenly things by means of the earthly ... No more generous almsgiver was born; he never ceased to be diligent in good works and noble deeds.)

And Benoît goes on:

> D'atenances portoct grant fés,
> de douce aïe esteit as suens
> e moct en essauçoct les buens.

---

8 The origin of the legend is unclear, but it features in the Latin collections of Marian *miracula* by Anselm of Bury, Dominic of Evesham and William of Malmesbury, as well as in Adgar's Anglo-Norman *Gracial*, all from the 12th century and possible sources for Benoît. Laurent (2014) argues that Benoît, in contrast to Wace, presents this tale as proof of Richard's sanctity.

> Douz, pis, misericordios
> ert vers les povres besoignos;
> joie esteit e garde a chanoines
> e norrissere de sanz moines;
> moct visitoct, ç'aveir en us
> les hermites e les reclus.
>
>   *Estoire*, 23,127–134

(He undertook a great deal of abstinence; he was a kindly help to his own and greatly exalted the good. He was kind, pious and merciful towards the needy poor; he was the joy and protection of canons and the nurse of holy monks; he often visited—it was his custom—hermits and recluses.)[9]

All these signs of holiness are reinforced by Benoît's remarks that Richard is recognized by the people of Normandy as 'saint' or even 'saintisme' (*Estoire*, 28,129–134, 26,939–940).

3   The Model of Edward the Confessor

But how does Benoît's hagiography match up to that of Ælred, his putative model? In spite of the topoi noted above, they are entirely different in atmosphere. Naturally, the political and dynastic elements are very much present; but the signs of sanctity such as the listeners of the time would have expected are conspicuous by their absence. There is no suggestion of a holiness consecrated from a young age, let alone before birth, as we see in Edward's case; nor—even more importantly—is there any hint of thaumaturgic power, before or after his death. As regards a holy life, when Benoît describes Richard as 'moct […] curios / des sainz commandemenz tenir / que Dex voct a homme establir' ('very diligent to follow the holy commandments which God willed to establish for man': *Estoire*, 23,076–079), he is speaking in very general terms; he makes no attempt to suggest that the duke is of irreproachable character.

In the specific case of the virtue of chastity so characteristic of Edward, while Benoît roundly affirms that Richard did practise the virtue, he avoids making his statement absolute. Richard does not surrender to lust or to the pleasures of the flesh *in the way so many others do*; instead he is virtuous and continent

---

9   The full passages is *Estoire*, 23,065–182. Benoît gives three other, shorter, character descriptions: *Estoire*, 14,905–947 (as a child); 19,547–618 (after his return to Normandy); 27,161–196 (introduction to his adventures).

(*Estoire*, 14,929–934); he *often* avoids the pleasures of the flesh (*Estoire*, 23,139–140). Certainly his practice of chastity does not prevent Richard from living with a concubine *more Danica* for some time before he is persuaded by his men to marry her (*Estoire*, 27,012–081); nor does it prevent his taking an unspecified number of unmarried girls to his bed, so that his illegitimate children (whom Benoît does not scruple to list, *Estoire*, 27,147–150) outnumber those born in wedlock.[10]

For the rest, Richard's piety shows itself in the forms traditional to the lay nobility: he rebuilds churches and gives rich gifts to them, he respects the rights of the Holy Church, he gives alms to the poor. When Benoît says that Richard 'knew well how to acquire heavenly things by means of the earthly', this is merely a periphrasis for the duke's generosity towards the poor and religious.

Even the tale of the drowned monk, although it comes directly from the hagiographical tradition, is nevertheless placed in a context that departs radically from hagiography. The tale follows two others which have a preternatural rather than a supernatural content,[11] and Benoît's introduction to them underlines not the duke's holiness but his fearlessness.[12]

> Unc n'out poor, soudes n'esfrei
> ne dotemenz aucun en sei,
> ne onques ne fu, ce dit l'escriz,
> torbez d'error sis esperiz;
> toz jors fu seürs, ce lison,
> sanz dotose tentation.
> De nuiz aloct senz rien doter
> tot autresi cum par jor cler.
> S'ert cil don tote genz saveient
> cui plus fantosmes aveneient,
> plus merveilles, plus deiablies [...]
> Maint' orrible chose sauvage
> veeit sanz muer son corage.
>
> *Estoire*, 27,177–187, 27,191–192

---

10   Richard is not the only duke to take a concubine 'a la danesche manere' (*Estoire*, 11,042): Rollo, William Longsword and Robert the Magnificent do the same (*Estoire*, 6323–327; 11,039–044, 11,911–916; 33,449–708).

11   The other adventures are Richard's encounter with a vampire (*Estoire*, 27197–466), and in an enchanted garden (27467–592). For Cazauran (1991: 22–29), the three adventures show a triple distinction between 'miracle', 'diablerie', et 'merveille'.

12   Cazauran (1991: 27) notes that the key motif in Benoît's tale is not holiness but fear.

(He was never afraid, startled or dismayed, nor had any fear in himself, nor was his mind ever troubled; he was always confident, as we read, without being tempted to fear. He went about without any fear in the night, just as if he were in broad daylight. So, as everyone knew, he was the one who met with the most ghosts, the most wonders, the most devilries ... He saw many wild, fearsome things without losing his courage.)

And this introduction is preceded by a more general portrait of the duke's character in which Benoît describes him primarily in secular and chivalric terms— fame and prowess, generosity and courtesy, summed up in the lapidary 'he greatly upheld chivalry':

> Moct fu li dus Richart preisiez
> e moct fu al secle essaucez;
> moct fu en terre granz sis nons [...]
> Moct ama clers e chevalers,
> moct les essauça volentiers,
> moct ama joie e largece,
> moct oct valor, moct oct proece,
> moct ama sen e corteisie
> e moct maintint chevalerie.
>
> *Estoire*, 27,161–162, 171–176

(Duke Richard was greatly esteemed and greatly praised in this world; he had great renown in his land ... He greatly loved clerics and knights, and he took great pleasure in raising them up; he greatly loved joy and liberality; great was his valour, great was his prowess; he greatly loved wisdom and courtesy, and greatly upheld chivalry.)

Certainly for every reference to Richard as saintly, there are many more that underline his nobility, as a man 'dus e frans e de bon aire' ('gentle and noble and high-born': *Estoire*, 14,919). For the most part, these are qualities explicitly stated by Benoît as being proper to a 'good prince' (see *Estoire*, 43,473–478), and are repeated in the descriptions of the other dukes of Normandy.[13]

---

13   For Rollo see *Estoire*, 2413; William Longsword, 10,169–274, 10,549–594; Richard II, 28,727–
      852; Richard III, 32,079–104; Robert the Magnificent, 32,226–248; William the Conqueror,
      34,888–913; Robert Courteheuse, 42,100, 42,128–130; William Rufus, 42,111–116; Henry I,
      42,073–089.

4   Strategies of Translation

What, then, is Benoît doing? Is his *vita* of Duke Richard biography or hagiography? Arguably, one of the keys to understanding Benoît's intentions can be found in Elisabeth van Houts's remarks in her edition of his main source, the *Gesta Normannorum ducum*, where she presents the vernacular versions as organic to the *Gesta* as a 'living text'; she characterises Wace's version as 'an adaptation rather than a translation', but sees Benoît's as an accurate vernacular version: 'Benoît used Robert of Torigni's redaction and translated it faithfully. Although he occasionally used other sources, mainly Wace's *Roman de Rou*, for minor interpolations, his *Chronique* follows Robert's eight books very closely indeed.'[14] So it is little surprise to find that none of the attributes of sanctity given to Richard in Benoît's *Estoire* are Benoît's doing; they are all to be found in his Latin source. There is, in fact, no evidence of an editorial decision to present Richard as a saint.

But that is not all. Although Benoît's translation is faithful, it is not slavish; it is also an organic development of the 'living text' of the *Gesta* in a way that Wace's adaptation is not. For one of the notable features of Benoît's text is the way in which he continues what we might call Robert of Torigni's work of *ressourcement*. Robert goes back to the original historical source for the dukes of Normandy, Dudo of Saint-Quentin's *De moribus et actis primorum Normanniæ ducum*, and reverses editorial decisions made at an earlier redactional stage of the *Gesta*. William of Jumièges frequently compresses and cuts Dudo's baroque prose and verse; Robert, particularly in his narrative of the life of Rollo, restores many of William's excisions and abbreviations with the original material from *De moribus et actis*. Benoît continues this same process throughout the rest of his *Estoire*, in such a sustained manner that it is hard to avoid the conclusion that it is a programmatic choice.

This programme of restoring material from Dudo is very evident in Benoît's life of Richard. This can be seen from the very beginning of Richard's reign, where the account of King Louis's decision to take Richard as a hostage to the royal court in France, though closely based on Robert of Torigni's redaction, is enlivened by a series of passages of direct speech derived from Dudo which William of Jumièges had simply cut: the Normans express their anger at having allowed Louis to get hold of Richard (*Estoire*, 15,090–121); the king is warned of the danger he is in (15,151–174); he backs down before the enraged mob and hands Richard back to them (15,231–268), but then in a long conversation per-

---

14   Van Houts (1991: xciii–iv); see also Van Houts (1984: 119–120).

suades Bernard the Dane to allow him to take Richard to court (15,307–438). None of these passages appear in Robert of Torigni's redaction, but they add greatly to the effectiveness of Benoît's account as literature.

Benoît's translation strategy includes not only this restoration of much material from Dudo, but also frequent, and often lengthy, expansions on his own account; this, as Françoise Laurent points out, is a deliberate translation strategy of *amplificatio*, understood as an appropriate response to the challenge of creating a vernacular equivalent of a Latin original.[15] What Benoît does not do, either in his *ressourcement* or in his *amplificatio*, is to add any hagiographical topoi to those already incorporated by Dudo into his account of Richard's life. Dudo is operating a fusion of different narrative modes in his text, *historia* with hagiography and epic; Benoît does not remove the mode of hagiography from his *Estoire* altogether, but reduces its prominence in favour of other elements.[16]

A key example of Benoît's minimising strategy is precisely Richard's 'supernatural' adventures. Their place in Benoît's narrative corresponds, in Dudo, to a long passage demonstrating how Richard was a perfect example of the Beatitudes: of the poor in spirit, those who mourn, the meek, those who hunger and thirst for righteousness, the pure in heart, the peacemakers, and those who are persecuted for righteousness' sake, and those who are reviled and persecuted on Christ's account (Mt 5:3–6, 8–11).[17] This passage, a kind of final summary of Richard's life mapped onto the Scriptural notes of sanctity, is an important element in Dudo's hagiographical schema; Benoît's decision not to include it in his own account marks not simply his independence from Dudo's agenda, but an intention to subvert Dudo's supposed duke-saint, replacing him with a very different figure.

To be sure, the hagiographical topoi in Benoît's depiction of Richard (and the other dukes of Normandy) are not an illusion; but neither are they of Benoît's making. His *Estoire* is a close translation of his Latin originals, and his depiction of the dukes is dependent on what Dudo and Robert of Torigni have to say about them—particularly Dudo, as he is the primary source for the early history of Normandy. To renounce *ex toto* Dudo's portrayal of Richard is not to

---

15   See Laurent (2012).

16   For Dudo's combining of literary modes, and Benoît's reticences, see Mathey-Maille (2007), particularly part 2, 'Représentations littéraires du passé. Formes et significations'. On Richard as a saint in Dudo's historiographical project, see Jordan (1991) and Davy (2016).

17   The only Beatitude missing is 'Blessed are the merciful' (Mt 5:7), an understandable omission given Richard's sometimes ruthless administration of justice.

speak of Richard at all. But this does not mean that Benoît intends to make a saint of Richard. Like Dudo, Benoît is writing providential history;[18] and in that history Richard is an exemplary figure; but he is exemplary because he fulfils perfectly the role allotted to him by his biographer.[19] And what is that role? For Jean Dufournet,

> Richard Ier ... apparaît comme un père nourricier qui apporte la richesse et la prospérité, comme un père spirituel qui promeut le christianisme, comme un père protecteur des plus faibles; à quoi s'ajoute, essentielle, la largesse.[20]

These different forms of paternity are all noble Christian roles: but they belong to the prince, not the saint. Benoît's Richard is wise, pious, merciful and generous; he is courageous and noble; but he shows neither the desire for contemplative life exhibited by his father, nor the life of heroic virtue seen in his grandson, and Benoît portrays him not as a saint, but as a Christian prince. There are more ways than one to give *exempla*.

Bibliography

Primary Sources

Ælred of Rievaulx, *Opera omnia VII: Vita sancti Ædwardi regis et confessoris*. Ed. Francesco Marzella. CCCM 3A. Turnhout: Brepols, 2017.

Benoît de Sainte-Maure. *Chronique des ducs de Normandie par Benoit*. 4 vols. Ed. Carin Fahlin. I–II: Bibliotheca Ekmaniana Universitatis Regiae Upsaliensis 56 and 60; III: Östen Södergård, *Glossaire*. Bibliotheca Ekmaniana Universitatis Regiae Upsaliensis 64; IV: Sven Sandqvist, *Notes*. Acta Universitatis Lundensis, Sectio I, 29. Uppsala: Almqvist & Wiksell, 1951–1979.

Dudo of Saint-Quentin. *De moribus et actis primorum Normanniæ ducum*. Ed. Jules Lair. Mémoires de la Société des Antiquaires de Normandie 23. Caen: F. Le Blanc-Hardel, 1865.

---

18   See Laurent (2010), Laurent et al. (2014: 9–22).
19   See Damian-Grint (2006: 48); Blacker (1994: 133–134).
20   'Richard I ... appears as a nurturing father who brings wealth and prosperity, as a spiritual father who promotes Christianity, as a father who protects the weak; to which is added the essential liberality': Dufournet (2010: 717).

William of Jumièges, Orderic Vitalis and Robert of Torigni. *The Gesta Normannorum ducum*. 2 vols. Ed. and trans. Elisabeth M.C. van Houts. Oxford: Clarendon Press, 1992–2000.

Secondary Sources

Aurell, Martin (2003). *L'Empire des Plantagenêt, 1154–1224*. Paris: Perrin.

Aurell, Martin and Noël-Yves Tonnerre, eds. (2006). *Plantagenêts et Capétiens: confrontations et héritages*. Histoires de famille: La Parenté au moyen âge 4. Turnhout: Brepols.

Blacker, Jean (1994). *The Faces of Time: Portrayal of the Past in Old French and Latin Historical Narrative of the Anglo-Norman Regnum*. Austin: University of Texas Press.

Bozoky, Édina (2014). 'La construction de la sainteté d'Édouard le Confesseur et les rois d'Angleterre'. In Laurent et al. (2014). 159–171.

Cazauran, Nicole (1991). 'Richard sans Peur: un personnage en quête d'auteur'. *Travaux de Littérature* 4: 21–44.

Connochie-Bourgne, Chantal and Sebastien Douchet, eds. (2012). *Effets de style au Moyen Âge*. Senefiance 58. Aix-en-Provence: Presses Universitaires de Provence.

Damian-Grint, Peter (2006). 'Propaganda and *Essample* in Benoît de Sainte-Maure's *Chronique des ducs de Normandie*'. *The Medieval Chronicle* 4: 39–52.

Davy, Gilduin (2016). 'Le père, le fils et le saint: les trois piliers de la *Respublica Normannorum*'. In Giraudeau et al. (2016). 15–31.

Drukker, Tamar S. (2006). 'Historicising Sainthood: The Case of Edward the Confessor in Vernacular Narratives'. *The Medieval Chronicle* 4: 53–79.

Dufournet, Jean (2010). 'Benoît de Sainte-Maure et l'historiographie anglo-normande'. *Le Moyen Age* 116: 713–718.

Giraudeau, Géraldine, Cécile Guérin-Bargues and Nicolas Haupais, eds. (2016). *Le Fait religieux dans la construction de l'État*. Perspectives 1. Paris: A. Pedone.

Gosman, Martin and Jaap van Os, eds. (1984). *Non nova sed nove: Mélanges de civilisation médiévale dédiés à Willem Noomen*. Groningen: Bouma's Boekhuis.

Gouttebroze, Jean-Guy (1991). 'Pourquoi congédier un historiographe? Henry II Plantagenêt et Wace (1155–1174)'. *Romania* 112: 289–311.

Isaïa, Marie-Céline and Thomas Granier, eds. (2014). *Normes et hagiographie dans l'Occident latin (Ve–XVIe siècles)*. Hagiologia 9. Turnhout: Brepols.

Jordan, Victoria B. (1991). 'The Role of Kingship in Tenth-Century Normandy: Hagiography of Dudo of Saint-Quentin'. *Haskins Society Journal* 3: 122–135.

Laurent, Françoise (2010). *Pour Dieu et pour le roi: rhétorique et idéologie dans l'Histoire des ducs de Normandie de Benoît de Sainte-Maure*. Essais sur le Moyen Âge 47. Paris: Honoré Champion.

Laurent, Françoise (2012). '"Mises en roman" et faits de style: le *Roman de Rou* de

Wace et l'*Estoire des ducs de Normandie* de Benoît de Sainte-Maure'. In Connochie-Bourgne and Douchet (2012). 115–124.

Laurent, Françoise (2014). '"Saint" Richard de Normandie et le sacristain noyé dans le *Roman de Rou* de Wace et l'*Histoire des ducs de Normandie* de Benoit de Sainte-Maure'. In Isaïa and Granier (2014). 345–358.

Laurent, Françoise, Laurence Mathey-Maille and Michelle Szkilnik, eds. (2014). *Des Saints et des rois: l'hagiographie au service de l'histoire*. Colloques, congrès et conférences sur le Moyen Âge 16. Paris: Champion.

Le Saux, Françoise H.M. (2005). *A Companion to Wace*. Cambridge: D.S. Brewer.

Mathey-Maille, Laurence (2007). *Écritures du passé: histoires des ducs de Normandie*. Essais sur le Moyen Âge 35. Paris: Honoré Champion.

Pezzini, Domenico (2008). *The Translation of Religious Texts in the Middle Ages: Tracts and Rules, Hymns and Saints' Lives*. Bern: Peter Lang.

Van Houts, Elisabeth M.C. (1962). 'Introduction: I'. See *Gesta Normannorum Ducum*.

Van Houts, Elisabeth M.C. (1984). 'The adaptation of the *Gesta Normannorum Ducum* by Wace and Benoît'. In Gosman and Van Os (1984). 115–125.

Waugh, Scott (2006). 'Histoire, hagiographie et le souverain idéal à la cour des Plantagenêt'. In Aurell and Tonnerre (2006). 429–446.

6

The Changing Versions of Froissart's Description of the Battle of Sluys, 1340

Kelly DeVries

Abstract

It is usually thought that Jean Froissart, for the pre-1350 history in his *Chroniques*, relied heavily on Jean le Bel's *Chroniques*. But on rare occasions he did not. This article notes the distinct differences between Le Bel's and Froissart's accounts of the naval battle of Sluys, fought in the Flemish port of 1340, where the English fleet, led by Edward III, ferrying troops across the English Channel encountered a French blockade at Sluys in Flanders. The ensuing naval battle would initiate Edward's first major campaign of the Hundred Years War. While Le Bel's report on the battle is short and lacks details, Froissart's account puts the chronicler directly into the narration—he decries naval warfare because there is nowhere to run if one is defeated—and is filled with many more details. More important for historians of chronicles and their authors is that Froissart rewrote his narrative three times, adding and refocusing on the account's 'point-of-view' which may reflect on who patronized him during his writing of different versions of the *Chroniques*.

Certainly a case can be made that Jean Froissart was the consummate medieval chronicler.[1] Not only did this master of historical narrative compose one of the most intricate and detailed chronicles of the Middle Ages, covering the years 1325 to 1400, he also rewrote and revised it adding new historical information which he had learned or remembered. It is, however, the consummate nature of Froissart's chronicle that is most confusing to modern historians. Few differentiate at all between the various versions of Froissart's *Chroniques*, choosing

---

1 I had not yet received my PhD when, speaking on the battle of Sluys at the Fordham University Medieval Conference: *War and Peace in Medieval Society*, on February 28, 1987, the great fourteenth-century historian, Dr John Henneman, suggested the topic of this article. Unfortunately, he passed on not long after this and was unable to hear me present an earlier version of this at The Third Medieval Chronicle Conference, in Utrecht, the Netherlands, on July 15, 2002. Thanks also to Michael Livingston for his helpful suggestions.

instead to use either the most accessible edition or the bad but often reprinted early nineteenth-century translation by Thomas Johnes.[2]

Modern historians have also dismissed Froissart's use of Jean le Bel as his source for the history of events in the first part of his *Chroniques*, often not investigating whether there is a difference between the two Low Countries' chroniclers' accounts. There is no question that Froissart used Jean le Bel's *Chronique* for his own *Chroniques*. Modern scholars do not diminish Froissart's credibility by pointing this out. As Peter Ainsworth writes:

> To lend greater credibility to his own recital of events from 1307 to 1350, Froissart transcribed virtually word-for-word entire sections from Le Bel's *Chronique*, a practice which we might stigmatise (a little unjustly) as plagiarism, but which even in the later Middle Ages was still a way of signalling respect for an earlier authority.[3]

This means, however, that when Froissart does not transcribe sections of Le Bel virtually word-for-word for this period, he probably has a reason. And if he also then changes his accounts between various versions of his *Chroniques*, it is important that these be investigated to discern why this most 'consummate chronicler' differed from Le Bel and why he changed while writing and rewriting his accounts of the first half of the fourteenth century. Froissart's narrative on the battle of Sluys, fought in 1340, is markedly different from Le Bel's and differs also in three of his *Chroniques*' versions.

While not determining why Froissart chose to vary his account from that of Jean le Bel, the short length of the Liégeois chronicler's narrative of the battle must be noted. It is not at all the length of his accounts of the ensuing siege of Tournai in 1340, the 1346 battle of Crécy, or the 1346–1347 siege of Calais. Le Bel does introduce the battle as 'so large that no one had ever spoken of such a large naval battle' and that it 'lasted from the hour of prime to vespers.'[4] He also indicates that the French naval leader, Hugues Quiéret, thought about leaving,

---

2 *Chronicles of England, France, Spain and the Adjoining Countries*, 4 vols., originally published in 1806 but reprinted throughout the nineteenth and twentieth centuries.

3 Ainsworth (2013). Much the same sentiment is found in Ainsworth (1990). The best edition of Le Bel remains Le Bel, *Chronique*, ed. Viard and Déprez.

4 Le Bel, *Chronique*, 1:178–179: 'Celle bataille fu si grande que ou n'avoit oncques ouy parler de si grosse sur mer, et dura dès l'eure de prime jusques à vespres.' Translation is mine. Since I wrote and presented the original of this article, Nigel Bryant has translated Jean le Bel's work as *The True Chronicles* (this passage there, 86). I prefer my own translation of these passages.

but believed he could not—there is no indication of the French chaining their ships together. Mention is made of the captured English *Christofle*,[5] a *grosse nave* which could destroy many smaller vessels; with it the English stood little chance. But for Edward III: 'the king had taken charge of this battle despite his lack of naval experience, but King Edward held himself so bravely, and he did so many feats of valor [during the battle] that he rallied and gave courage to all the others.' Others, Henry of Grosmont, the Earl of Derby and Sir Walter Mauny are also identified as having 'carried themselves well.' What actions defined this, or any mention of any tactics is absent. Instead, God is mentioned on the English side no fewer than three times and he is given credit for the deaths of many 'French, Normans, Gascons, Bretons, and Genoese ... few escaped.' More than 30,000 were killed 'so it was said,' with several washing up along the shore of Cadzand or Sluys. Among these were Hugues Quiéret and several of his kin. English casualties were also high, but Le Bel notes, the *Christofle* was recaptured.[6]

For Jean le Bel, the battle of Sluys was simple: God was involved in determining victory for the English, Edward and some of the knights fought well, and a huge number of French and English combatants died. For Froissart, the battle of Sluys was less simple. Although he usually makes few changes to Le Bel's account, in this passage he abandons his mentor's material altogether. Perhaps he felt that Le Bel's narrative was too short and lacked detail, or perhaps he had more eyewitness sources of the battle to draw from. Whatever the reason, Froissart wrote a distinctly different, much longer, account of the battle of Sluys. And then he changed it, adding more and altering the focus, until there were three different versions.

Rather than throwing out a meaningless hyperbolic *trope* that claims Sluys was the largest naval battle that anyone had ever described, Froissart places himself into the narrative. He begins his account of Sluys by pointing out that he does not like to describe the events of this, his first naval battle. For him it has no violent equal, certainly not in comparison with the land battles which he has already described or would later describe. Indeed, after giving the location of the battle, how many French ships the English faced, describing them as 'such a great number of vessels that their masts looked exactly like a forest,'[7] Froissart pauses to explain why he feels that naval battles are worse than land battles:

---

5   This large English warship had been captured by the French during their attack of Southampton in 1338.

6   Le Bel, *Chronique*, I:178–179.

7   Froissart, *Chroniques*, ed. Kervyn de Lettenhove, III:194: 'Li roys d'Engleterre et li sien qui s'en

This battle which I describe for you was very foul and very horrible; battles and attacks on the sea are longer and larger than those on land, because one is unable to flee or to retreat.[8]

Despite this hesitation, Froissart still describes the battle of Sluys in more detail than any other author. He notes the numbers of French men and ships, as well as the number of English soldiers who were present at Sluys. He declines to mention, however, the number of English ships present, saying only in the final version of his *Chroniques* (*from* MS. *Rome Reg. lat. 869*) that the French ships outnumbered the English in a four-to-one ratio.[9] Moreover, as he anticipated above, neither the French nor the English fled from their positions. The French wished to defend Sluys 'bien et hardiment,' and the English relished the opportunity finally to meet the French in battle, a detail found in all of Froissart's versions.[10] Before the battle Edward spoke to his men. This is the version given in his first version:

I have for a long time desired to fight these soldiers, if it pleases God and St George. Because indeed they have made me so upset that I want to take revenge, if I can.[11]

---

venoient tout singlant, regardèrent et veirent deviers l'Escluse si grant quantitet de vaissaux que des mas che sambloit droitment ung bois.' See also 199, 203–204.

8   Jean Froissart, *Chroniques*, ed. Kervyn de Lettenhove, III:196: 'Ceste bataille dont je vous parolle, fu moult felenesse et moult orible; car batailles et assaux sur mer sont plus durs et plus fort que sus terre, car on ne puet fuir, ne reculer: si se convient deffendre et vendre et montrer se proèce.' Although I use Kervyn de Lettenhove's edition of the *Chroniques*, it is the *Histoire de France* edition, this volume edited by Simeon Luce, from whom I take the order of Froissart's versions—Kervyn de Lettenhove has this as Froissart's second version. Luce's order, for this account, agrees with Peter Ainsworth and Godfried Croenen's ordering of Froissart's versions on the *On-line Froissart*, https://www.dhi.ac.uk/onlinefroissart/; Ainsworth (2013).

9   Froissart, *Chroniques*, ed. Kervyn de Lettenhove, III:202. See also Froissart, *Chroniques*, ed. Diller, 405–406.

10   Froissart (ed. Kervyn de Lettenhove), III:194.

11   The first version of Froissart's work (ed. Kervyn de Lettenhove, III:199–200) records Edward's speech as:

Dont respondi li rois engles: 'J'ai de lonch temps désiré que les peuisse combatre; si les combaterons, s'il plaist à Dieu et à saint Jorge; car voirement m'ont-il fait tant contriares que j'en voeil prendre le vengance, se j'i puis avenir.'

The English king's speech in Froissart's second redaction (Luce's order) is entirely different (ed. Kervyn de Lettenhove, III:194):

Lors dist li roys: 'Il les nous fault combattre, et se nous les poons desconfire, nostre guerre en avant en sera plus belle; car voirement sont-il moult resongniet de nos amis

Froissart varies this somewhat in his second version:

> If we must fight them, and if we can defeat them, our war ahead will be
> better; for indeed there are many of our allies who are worried and have
> been since they put out to sea. And there are many against us. So, we will
> fight if it pleases God and Saint George.[12]

The final version contains no oration from Edward III.

Edward ordered his ships in lines alternating a ship full of men-at-arms with
two ships of archers.[13] Also present in the English ranks, Froissart reports, was
a ship filled with noblewomen set to join their queen at Ghent—Philippa of
Hainaut had stayed in the city to give birth to John of Ghent (Gaunt). They
were protected by a unit of archers instructed by Edward to 'guard their honour.'[14] The English king then took advantage of the wind, and he turned to face
the French with the sun behind him. All Froissart's versions describe the man-
oeuvre, with this taken from the second:

> When the king of England and his marshal had ordered their lines of
> battle well and wisely they made to submit and draw their sails against
> the wind. And they came to the right to take advantage of the sun which
> in coming there was in the face [of the French].[15]

The French prepared to meet the English, believing themselves to be the more
experienced and superior fighters.[16] They attacked first with the *Christofle*. English longbowmen and Norman/Genoese crossbowmen 'very savagely and very

---

　　　　 et ont ete depuis qu'il se missent sur mer, et nous ont fet pluisseurs contraires. Si les
　　　　 combaterons s'il plest à Dieu et à saint Jorge.'
12　 Froissart, *Chroniques*, ed. Kervyn de Lettenhove, III:194: 'Il les nous fault combattre, et se
　　　　 nous les poons desconfire, nostre guerre en avant en sera plus belle; car voirement sont-
　　　　 il moult resongniet de nos amis et ont ete depuis qu'il se missent sur mer, et nous ont fet
　　　　 pluisseurs contraires. Si les combaterons s'il plest à Dieu et à saint Jorge.'
13　 Froissart, *Chroniques*, ed. Kervyn de Lettenhove, III:194, 200, 204.
14　 Froissart, *Chroniques*, ed. Kervyn de Lettenhove, III:195: 'Et ces dames fist li roys garder
　　　　 bien et songneusement de CCC armures de fer et de Ve archers. Et puis pria li roys à tous
　　　　 que il volsissent pensser dou bien faire et garder sen onneur, et chascun li eult en convent.'
　　　　 See also III:200.
15　 Froissart, *Chroniques*, ed. Kervyn de Lettenhove, III:195: 'Quant li roys d'Engleterre et li
　　　　 marescal eurent ordonnet bellement et sagement leurs batailles, il fisent tendre et traire
　　　　 les voilles contremont, et vinrent sus destre pour avoir l'avantaige du soleil qui en venant
　　　　 leur estoit ou visiage.'
16　 Froissart, *Chroniques*, ed. Kervyn de Lettenhove, III:195–196.

harshly' traded 'very strong and very vigorous' archery fire, but ultimately the English archers proved to be superior to their French counterparts and the *Christofle* was recaptured, returning it to English sailors.[17] But this setback did not stifle the fighting spirit of the French, who fought on for the entire day. In the Rome manuscript Froissart comments on the fighting capabilities of each side:

> And this was a very large and a very perilous battle because the Normans and the Genoese had all been tested in and were accustomed to the sea, and they withstood fatigue well because in all their lives they had done nothing else except pursue armed adventures on the sea. Also it was said that the English were good men of the sea for they were made and nourished in it, and they too could withstand the fatigue.[18]

To this point the different versions of Froissart's *Chroniques* all contain similar versions of the narrative, with the second and third comprising the most detailed accounts of the battle. It is, however, in his conclusions of why the English won and the French lost at Sluys that he shows the widest variations. In each of Froissart's versions of the battle he suggests a different reason for Edward's victory over the French navy.

The first concludes that the superior tactics and valour of the English soldiers, specifically Edward III, determined victory. Edward's strategic use of the sun and wind against the French is highlighted, and added to this is a description of the effective fighting capabilities of English archers and men-at-arms:

> And the archers and the crossbowmen commenced to draw their bows one against the other diversely and rapidly, and the men-at-arms ap-

---

17   Froissart, *Chroniques*, ed. Kervyn de Lettenhove, III:196, 201, 204–205. Some historians, the latest being Parker (1988: 84), believe that the *Christofle* was outfitted with early gunpowder weapons. Froissart, however, indicates nothing about this matter in his text. Parker relied on a quote from Carlo M. Cipolla, *Guns, Sails and Empires: Technological Innovation and the Early Phases of European Expansion, 1400–1700* (New York: Pantheon Books, 1965) without checking if it was accurate. A later *Mariners' Mirror* than that cited by Cipolla corrected the reading of guns on the *Christofel* in 1340 rather than, properly, 1410. For an assessment of the evidence that gunpowder weaponry was used at Sluys see Hall and DeVries (1990).

18   Froissart, *Chroniques*, ed. Diller, 406: 'Et la fu la bataille tres grande et tres-perilleuse; car chil Normant et chil Genevois, estoient tout esqumeur et costumier de la mer, et trop bien en pooient la painne, car en tout lor vivant il n'avoient fait aultre cose que poursiervi[r] les aventures d'armes sur la mer. Aussi, au voir dire, Englois sont bonnes gens de mer, car il en sont fait et nourri, et trop bien en pueent la painne.'

proached and fought hand-to-hand harshly and hardily ... But the English
proved so good and so brave ... that they obtained the place of battle and
the French ships, and the Normans and all those who had fought against
them were dead and defeated, slain and drowned. No one was able to
escape and all were put to death.[19]

Froissart repeats this perception at the end of his second version. It was,
however, not the only factor in the defeat of the French. He adds more to the
end of this account, absent from his first version, which makes clear that the
arrival of Flemish reinforcements at the end of the battle ultimately marked
the defeat of the French:

> And the battle lasted from the first hour to the evening, and finally a great
> number of Flemings arrived because early in the morning the *bailleux* of
> Sluys had sent signals to Bruges and to the nearby villages. So all the vil-
> lagers came and arrived at Sluys on foot, on horse, or along the Roe river,
> coming to aid the English. And there assembled at Sluys a great number of
> Flemings, and they entered into boats and barges and large Spanish ves-
> sels, and they came to the battle all fresh and invigorated, and they gave
> great comfort to the English.[20]

Froissart's third version of the *Chroniques* presents an altogether different perception of why the English defeated the French at Sluys. Removing almost
entirely any mention of English tactical superiority and referring to the Flemish
involvement—including a previously unmentioned tally of 8,000 Flemings on
shore—only as a subsidiary cause of the defeat, Froissart turns to an analysis
of the poor French naval position as the cause of their defeat. Edward simply

19   Froissart, *Chroniques*, ed. Kervyn de Lettenhove, III:201–202: 'Là se commença bataille
      dure et forte de tous costés, et arcier et arbalestrier commencièrent à traire l'un contre
      l'autre diversement et roidement, et gens d'armes à approcier et à combattre main à main
      asprement et hardiment Y Mais il s'esprouvèrent si bien et si vassaument Y qu'il obtiner-
      ent le place et l'yaue, et furent li Normant et tout cil qui là estoient encontre yaus, mort et
      desconfi, péri et noyet, ne onques piés n'en escapa que tout ne fuissent mis à bort.'
20   Froissart, *Chroniques*, ed. Kervyn de Lettenhove, III:196–197: 'Et dura le bataille del heure
      de prisme jusques a revelée, et adont vinrent grant gent de Flandres, car très le matin li
      bailleux de l'Escluse l'avoit fet segnefyer à Bruges et ès villes voisinnes. Si estoient les villes
      touttes esmutes et acouru à piet et à cheval et par le Roe, cheminans qui mieux pour aidier
      les Englés, et s'asamblerent à l'Escluse grant quantité de Flammens et entèrent en nefs et
      en barges et en grans vaissiaux espangnols, et s'en vinrent jusques à le bataille tout fresk
      et tout nouvel, et grandement reconfortèrent les Engles.'

took advantage of this poor positioning, the French ships at rest and chained together, to gain victory:

> Finally the English obtained the sea and the place of battle; and those who were present—Normans, Picards, Genoese, and those from Provençe— all were killed, and very few were saved because they were unable to flee from the defeat. What was the cause of this? I will tell you. The English in coming there had enclosed the French between themselves and Sluys. They [the French] were unable to recoil, as did their enemy, nor to go forward, nor to break the English navy which had blocked all passage to the sea. They and any who wished to save themselves by coming to Sluys were killed at once because the Flemings, who had a great hatred for those who in each and every season had harassed and harried the passage to Sluys and had robbed and pillaged on the sea, took care to kill without pity anyone whom they came upon on land or on the sea.[21]

There seems little doubt that Jean Froissart was unsatisfied by the length and lack of details Jean le Bel records for the battle of Sluys. Clearly, Froissart had more and better information than did his Low Countries' predecessor, whether from eyewitnesses or other written sources closer to the battle cannot be determined.[22]

---

21   Froissart, *Chroniques*, ed. Diller, 408: 'Finablement li Englois obtinrent la mer et la place. Et furent chil esqumeur normant, piqart, genevois, bidau et prouvenciel desconfi; et trop petit s'en sauverent, car a la desconfiture, il ne porent. Cause pourquoi, je le vous dirai. Les Englois en venant les avoient enclos entre euls et l'Escluse. Se ne pooient requler, fors sus lors ennemis, ne aler avant ne rompre la navie d'Engleterre qui avoient pourpris tout la passage de la mer. Chil et auqun, qui se quidierent sauver pour venir a l'Escluse, furent mort d'avantage. Car li Flamenc, qui avoient grant haine a euls, pour tant que toute la saison il avoient cuvriiet et heriiet le passage a l'Escluse et robé et pilliet sus la mer, et n'avoient en cure a qui, les tuoient otant bien sus la terre que en la mer, et n'en avoient nulle pité.'

22   Other written sources that might have been available to Froissart include: letters written by Edward III (those to John de Statford, archbishop of Canterbury, and the citizens of London still exist), chronicles written by Robert of Avesbury, Geoffrey le Baker, Adam Murimuth, Jean de Venette, Richard Lescot, the *Grandes chroniques de France*, the *Chronique Normande*, the first version of the *Chronique de Flandre*, and the poem on the battle by Laurence Minot. Jan de Klerk's *Brabantse yeesten* and *Van den derden Eduwaert* and Giovanni Villani's *Istorie Fiorentine*, would also have been written but, if these were available to him, it is unknown whether he could have read them in their vernacular Brabantese and Italian. None of these sources show enough similarity with Froissart's accounts of the battle to be directly connected to them.

Other conclusions are more speculative. There appears to be a natural progression in the conclusions Froissart makes in each of versions as to what caused victory and defeat at the battle of Sluys. However, what can be drawn from this is difficult to know. It is fairly clear that Siméon Luce won the scholarly argument he had with Baron Kervyn de Lettenhove over the order of Froissart's versions; this order has been confirmed and enlarged by Peter Ainsworth and Godfried Croenen based on more substantial evidence than an account of a single 1340 battle.[23]

Even more speculative is the possibility of ascertaining under whose patronage each of Froissart's versions were written based on his respective conclusions about the outcome of the battle of Sluys. The first conclusion awards victory to the English because of Edward III's superior naval tactics and the valour of the English soldiers. This was likely written when Froissart was in the service of Robert of Namur, a man who would have desired to hear of the English role in the 1340 victory.

The second version, which emphasizes the role of the Flemings at Sluys, might have been written by Froissart while under the patronage of Wenceslas, the duke of Luxembourg and Brabant, for an audience who undoubtedly were interested in the role played at the battle by their fellow southern Low Countries' countrymen. This seems especially likely since at the time of its composition, sometime between 1376 and 1383 according to both Luce and Kervyn de Lettenhove, many Brabantese would have been supportive of the Flemings in their current (1379–1382) rebellion against the French king.[24]

Finally, while it is not disputed that Froissart composed his third version while under the patronage of Guy of Châtillon, duke of Blois, his conclusions as to what caused the victory and defeat at Sluys confirm his service to someone more inclined to a French point of view. Here Froissart's audience was not concerned with the reasons for English victory, rather in the causes of the French defeat. Consequently, in this version Froissart addresses that concern. He tells the reader about the follies of French naval tactics while failing to mention the superior English tactics and valour and, at the same time, downplaying the aid brought by the Flemish reinforcements.

---

23   Ainsworth (2013).

24   It must be noted, however, that Jean Froissart himself does not appear to support the
      Flemings in this revolt. Still, while his commentary on the rebellion is quite long and con-
      tinually praises the French at the expense of the Flemings, it is found only in the third
      version of the *Chroniques* and thus was written while Froissart was under the patronage
      of the adamantly pro-French Guy of Châtillon. See Froissart, *Chroniques*, ed. Kervyn de
      Lettenhove, X:1–242. For Brabantese support of the Ghent rebellions see Nicholas (1978).

Unfortunately, the uncertainty about when Froissart's three versions were written, and under whose patronage, prevents us from drawing such a definitive conclusion from his varying accounts of the battle of Sluys. At most, we can say that the chronicler from Valenciennes purposely changed the Liégeoise chronicler's account of the battle of Sluys, and again, and again.

Bibliography

Primary Sources—Editions

Froissart, Jean. *Chroniques: Dernière rédaction du premier livre. Edition du manuscrit de Rome Reg. lat. 869*, ed. George Diller. Geneva: Libraire Droz, S.A., 1972.

Froissart, Jean. *Chroniques*. In: *Oeuvres de Froissart*. Ed. Henri Marie Bruno Joseph, Baron Kervyn de Lettenhove. 26 vols. Brussels: V. Devaux, 1867–1877.

Froissart, Jean. *Chroniques*. 14 vols. Ed. Siméon Luce et al. Société de l'Histoire de France Paris: Libraire Renouard, 1869–1967.

Le Bel, Jean. *Chronique*. Ed. Jules Viard and Eugène Déprez, 2 vols., Société de l'Histoire de France. Paris: Libraire Renouard, 1904–1905.

Le Bel, Jean. *The True Chronicles of Jean le Bel, 1290–1360*. Trans. Nigel Bryant. Woodbridge: Boydell Press, 2011.

Secondary Sources

Ainsworth, Peter (1990). *Jean Froissart and the Fabric of History: Truth, Myth, and Fiction in the* Chroniques. Oxford: Clarendon Press.

Ainsworth, Peter (2013). 'Jean Froissart: Chronicler, Poet and Writer.' In: *The Online Froissart*. Ed. Peter Ainsworth and Godfried Croenen. v. 1.5. Sheffield: HRIOnline.

Hall, Bert, and Kelly DeVries (1990). 'Review Article: The Military Revolution Reconsidered.' *Technology and Culture* 31: 500–507.

Nicholas, David (1978). 'The Scheldt Trade and the "Ghent War" of 1379–1385.' *Bulletin de la commission royale d'histoire de Belgique* 144: 189–359.

Parker, Geoffrey (1988). *The Military Revolution*. Cambridge: Cambridge University Press.

7

On Friendship as Motivation and Object of the Historiographic Works of Pedro Afonso de Barcelos

Isabel Barros Dias

Abstract

In the Prologue of his *Book of Lineages*, Pedro Afonso, Count of Barcelos considers that his work will stimulate friendship since this feeling is more easily cultivated among people connected by family ties. Although his mindset is traditional by the standards of other Iberian approaches to the concept, his points of view have idiosyncratic traits that should be discussed. His personal concern for the issue is probably rooted in his life experience, both documented and traceable in his historiographic production. This article considers these various levels and argues that this author's approach to the idea of friendship brings together pragmatism and spirituality, the whole being marked by optimism and consciousness of mission that provide an overall sense to his work.

Medieval ideas on friendship stem from but reshape the way Greco-Roman philosophy conceptualized the idea.[1] Whereas ancient thinkers such as Aristotle or Cicero considered the bond of friendship as involving ethical and moral values joining together the virtuous ones in true friendship, and stressed its cohesive and civic force, medieval authors either distrust mundane friendship as a possible source of sin (Augustine, *Confessions*) or reframe it in terms of the supremacy of the love of God and of humanity (Aelred of Rievaulx, *De spiritali amicitia*). Besides, there is a dispersion of meanings, depending on contexts, and the linguistic interchange between love and friendship (or aporia given the frequent use of the pair 'love and friendship'). On the one hand, the clerical and monastic view of friendship seems to object to individual ties, to value the

---

1 For some examples of studies on this subject (combining areas such as philosophy, history of ideas, and history of emotions) see Stern-Gillet and Gurtler (2014); McDonie (2020); Liuzzo Scorpo (2020). This study is part of the project 'Castilla y Portugal en la Baja Edad Media: contactos sociales, culturales y espirituales entre dos monarquías rivales (s. XIII–XV)'—ref. PID2020–114722GB-100 Agencia Estatal de Investigación (AEI), Ministerio de Ciencia e Innovación, del Gobierno de España. All translations in the article are mine.

© KONINKLIJKE BRILL NV, LEIDEN, 2023 | DOI:10.1163/9789004547124_008

spiritual love of the brotherhood, of the believers, of all humankind (even the wicked) and, above all, of God (*vd.* concepts like *caritas* and *compassio*). On the other hand, emotional erotic love emerges in poetry and courtly literature. In between, secular chivalric friendship bonds an elite of warriors sharing the same military values.

Given this frame, the fact that the *Book of Lineages* of Count Pedro de Barcelos begins with an apologia for friendship, stressing its importance as a stimulus for the composition of the work, constitutes a signal of the importance of the topic for this author, and an encouragement to investigate what this concept means to him.[2] In fact, prologues are a fundamental part of any book since they constitute a declaration of the authors' intents. It is here that the main lines and final objectives are defined, and ideological principles and programs are outlined. In this specific case, the idea of friendship as a reason for writing the book seems original and meaningful. So, we will discuss the various aspects of this initial reasoning, also considering the author's personal life experience and his historiographic works.

1 The Social, Legal, and Philosophical Foundations of Friendship

The Prologue of Pedro Afonso de Barcelos' *Book of Lineages* includes a passage on the social, legal and philosophical perception of friendship that derives from the compilation of legislation known as the *Siete Partidas*.[3] Here we can find a title on friendship that includes a definition of the concept, its characteristics and benefits, a classification of its varieties, how to behave and to keep it, and how it can be dissolved.[4] This book was first compiled in the *scriptorium* of King Alfonso X, but it continued to be reworked until it was enacted under his great-

---

2 This Preface has already been commented by Mocelim (2005/6), later incorporated in her master's dissertation (2007: 86–99), and by Ferreira (2012).

3 Ferreira (2012) identified the *Siete Partidas* (*Partida* IV.27) as the source of this passage, determining that the classical echoes of Aristotle (theory of friendship in *Nicomachean Ethics*) and Cicero (*De amicitia*) in D. Pedro's text are second-hand (pp. 97–102). *Partida* IV, in turn, was based in a Latin version of Averroes' commentary on Aristoteles' *Ethics*, made by Herman, associated with the Toledo School of translators. This version was also used by Brunetto Latini in *Li Livres dou Tresor* (Ferreira, 2012: 99; Heusch, 1993: 10–11). The *Siete Partidas* are currently the object of an ongoing project at the Universidad de Valladolid (*7PartidasDigital*—https://7partidas.hypotheses.org).

4 *Partidas* IV.27. The contents of the *Siete Partidas'* IV.27 have been commented by Heusch, 1993 and Liuzzo Scorpo 2020: 68–80.

grandson, Alfonso XI, nephew,[5] and friend of Pedro de Barcelos.[6] This personal connection, probably developed during the Count's exile in Castile (mid-1317–beginning of 1322), explains his acquaintance with and his use of this source. The Count turns to it extensively in this piece of the Prologue, albeit selectively, summarizing and inserting occasional changes.[7] He recalls the rules of the customary laws of Spain that advocated friendship among the nobles, and the principles that regulated its breakdown (mentioned in *Partida* IV, title 27, at the end of law IV as a kind of friendship specific of Spain, related to feudal practices). He considers Aristotle's idea of a perfect society governed by friendship, that would have no need of laws nor rulers (reframing *Partida* IV.27.I). He proceeds by considering the benefits of friendship for all men, both rich and poor, at any age, summarizing law II of *Partida* IV.27. Finally, he focuses on law V and briefly enumerates the duties of those who want to keep friendship: one should not defame friends, nor believe in rumours that denigrate them; secrets must be kept, and works done should not be criticized.

The fourth *Partida* focuses on civil laws, some of which nowadays may seem awkward, but at the time were pragmatic business matters, subject to legislation. Title 27 considers friendship at the end of several issues related to family matters (rules and impediments to marriages, dowries, affinity family, legitimate and illegitimate children, servant and free men, the relationship between vassals and lords …), which signals a difference regarding the ancient concept of friendship, which ignored family ties. This textual context probably contributed to the use of the topic in D. Pedro's prologue: just as the book of laws determined the juridical rules that should regulate society and the families, the *Book of Lineages* would provide in-depth information on who these families were.

---

5   Alfonso XI of Castile was the son of Fernando IV of Leon-Castile and of Constance of Portugal, daughter of King Denis and Queen Isabel. Since Pedro Afonso was natural son of King Denis, he was half-brother to Constance.

6   'Et estando el Rey en este ayuntamiento, veno y Don Pedro Conde de Barcelos, que es en Portugal: et poque este Conde amaba muy verdaderamiente el servicio del Rey, et facia por ello lo que podia, el Rey fizole mucha honra' (*Onceno*: 460).

7   Namely the one highlighted by Ferreira (2012) who explores the rephrasing of 'non habrien meester justicia nin alcalles que los judgasen' (*Partida* IV.27.I) to 'nom haveriam mester reis nem justiças' (*Linhagens*: 55) suggesting a reconfiguration of concepts in the context of the coeval social tensions experienced between the monarchy and the insurgent nobility (pp. 109–116) underlining that Pedro Afonso depreciates 'institutional friendship' over 'true friendship', based on blood ties, and deriving from God, source of all love, while questioning the authority of sovereigns (pp. 116–121).

2   Friendship, and the Recording of Lineages and History

Pedro de Barcelos' *Book of Lineages* reflects one of the most pressing issues of the medieval period in Europe, the concern with origins. The importance of lineages, and of their tracing back to the beginning of the world, as well as their role in legitimizing dominant families, have been established and studied.[8] The introduction of the question of friendship in this type of literature can be viewed as an occurrence that emanates from a very specific context, where a learned nobleman is writing about the ancestors of the members of his social circle, and of himself. At the same time, he conveys his perspective of the coeval social relations, and of what he considers should be the ideal relationships within his own milieu. So, after the presentation of the concept, the Count proceeds to assert the connection between lineage and friendship, according to 'nature' (a broad and significant term also used in the *Partidas*[9]), thus justifying the writing of the book, which would function as a companion enhancing friendship among the nobles by disclosing forgotten family ties.

> E por que nem ũa amizade nom pode ser tam pura segundo natura come daqueles que descendem de ũu sangue, porque estes movem-se mais de ligeiro aas cousas per que a amizade se mantem, houve de declarar este livro per titolos e per alegações que cada ũu fidalgo de ligeiro esto podesse saber, e esta amizade fosse descuberta e nom se perdesse antre aqueles que a deviam haver. (*Linhagens*: 56)

> (And because no friendship can be so pure according to nature as that of those who descend from the same blood, because they are more easily inclined towards the things by which friendship is maintained, I have organized this book by titles and attestations, so that every nobleman could easily know it, and that this friendship would be discovered and not lost among those who should have it.)

The Count of Barcelos then registers seven reasons that have led him to write his work. He summarises the question of friendship as a cohesive force based

---

8   On this subject there is an extensive bibliography, identifying and studying similar cases all over Europe: e.g., the classical works by Bloch (1989) and Melville (1987), and for the Portuguese context Krus (2011).

9   According to *Partida* IV. 27. IV, 'Amistad de natura' applies not only to families but also to animals and to people's relationship with their land and lord. On this concept and its juridical and political implications, see Heusch 1993: 20–25, 45–46; Bautista (2007).

on family ties. This solidarity is considered fundamental for peace and social collaboration against common enemies.[10] Two main ideas stand out from the passage. On the one hand, there is a very broad concept of lineage pointing to the idea of Christianity as a family, as opposed to the infidels that must be fought. Up to a certain point, this idea converges with the notion of global friendship, although restricting it to Christians, which points to the *topos* of the division of the world according to the three lineages that issued from Noah, common information in historiography, also an argument used in the frame of crusade movements, both in the East and in the West. Accordingly, we have here an approach to the idea of the brotherhood of arms. On the other hand, even if in the frame of a basic identity of blood among the elites, the author defends the preeminence of personal value as a determining factor for friendship, which, at first sight, seems to bring him closer to the Aristotelian notion of friendship among the virtuous. Nevertheless, this opposition is between the brave and the weak, which brings us back to the military dimension. The final part of the passage introduces the topic of the intersection of friendship with social stratification and the norms of interpersonal relationships, a typology identical to the one in the advice that a contemporary high-ranking Castilian noble, don Juan Manuel, gives to his son in the *Libro infinido*, dated 1336–1337 (Ayerbe-Chaux 1969). Various parallels can be drawn between Pedro Afonso and Juan Manuel, namely, that they were both literary and historiographic authors often considered as spokesmen of the nobility, having been involved in rebellions, and both lived through troubled times. However, don Juan Manuel's reasoning on friendships differs from D. Pedro Afonso insofar as the former has a more cautious attitude, absent from the latter. Even if to a lesser degree, dissensions and insecurities have also marked Pedro Afonso's life (Lopes 1997; Oliveira 2011) since he lived through aristocratic rebellions and disputes oppos-

---

10   'A terceira, por seerem de ũu coraçom, de haverem de seguir os seus emmigos que som em estroimento da fe de Jesu Christo, ca, pois eles veem de ũu linhagem, e sejam no quarto ou no quinto grao ou dali acima, nom devem poer deferença antre si, e mais que os que som chegados come primos e terceiros, ca mais nobre cousa é e mais santa amar o homem a seu parente alongado per dívido, se bõo é, que amar ao mais chegado, se faleçudo é. E os homẽes que nom som de boo conhecer nom fazem conta do linhagem que hajam, senam d'irmãos e primos cõirmãos e segundos e terceiros. E dos quartos acima nom fazem conta. Estes taes erram a Deus e a si, ca o que tem parente no quinto ou sexto grao ou dali acima, se é de gram poder deve-o servir porque vem de seu sangue. E se é seu igual, deve-o d'ajudar. E se é mais pequeno que si deve de lhe fazer bem, e todos devem seer de ũu coraçom.' (*Linhagens*: 56–57). Liuzzo Scorpo (2020: 199) considers that the preeminence of blood ties in friendship is a common argument in Iberian authors although addressed differently.

ing his half-brothers. In the first 'Manifesto' (Declaration) that King Denis produced against his legitimate only son, Prince Afonso, he expresses his sorrow that his heir managed to recruit his half-brother Pedro Afonso to his ranks, accusing him of having acted for self-serving motives, not genuine friendship.[11]

King Denis' political agenda was marked by an effort towards centralization that gave rise to rebellions of the more powerful aristocrats, which were often articulated with family dissensions (Pizarro, 2005). He faced a civil war against his brother Afonso, and later confrontations that opposed his successor, the future King Afonso IV of Portugal, to his half-brother Afonso Sanches, considered the favourite son of King Denis. Also, Count Pedro Afonso opposed his other half-brother João Afonso and became closer to Prince Afonso, having subsequently seen his territories confiscated and himself exiled, as recalled in King Denis's 'Declaration'.[12]

During his exile, Pedro Afonso attended the court of Maria de Molina, becoming friends with her grandson, and his nephew, Alfonso XI. This period was also particularly difficult for Castile, marked by a pronounced weakness of the monarchy. King Sancho IV (1258–1295) did not live long and his son, Fernando IV (1285–1312) was crowned at the age of 9, the regency being assumed by the mother-queen, Maria de Molina (from 1295 to 1301). Questions about the legitimacy of these rulers further had weakened their power as opposed to the aristocracy.[13] In addition, Fernando IV proved to be a weak

---

11   Lopes (1967). The 'Manifesto de D. Dinis, rei de Portugal, contra seu filho o infante D. Afonso, publicado em Santarém, a 1 de julho de 1320' is transcribed in pp. 5–25. Here we can read: 'Pera se provar craramente como el [Prince Afonso] desama mortalmente todolos que amam El Rey e seguem a sa voontade e o seu serviço, [...] E que seja verdade provasse pelo do Conde Pedro Affonso como dito he, a que el teve senpre maa voontade e peyor que a Affonso Sanches enquanto quiz seguir o serviço e a voontade dEl Rey, e des que o non quiz e o y meterom os seus creedeiros e seus atanjedores do Iffante, logo o amou afaçanhadamente e fiou del' (p. 20).

12   'des enton fyou o Jffante do Conde e o amou e o teve por seu quitemente. E assy o mostrou na assuada que ouve o Conde con Joham Affonso seu yrmãao en que o Conde quisera fazer torto assy come sabudo, en que o Jffante se mostrou por parte do Conde enton envyando os seus vassalos pera el e denodadamente de feito e de dito seendo contra Joham Affonso a que avya feito o mal. E depoys desto indosse o Conde pera Castela e tolhendolhy El Rey a terra por torto que quisera fazer en seu irmão Joham Affonso envyou o Jffante rogar muy aficadamente e muyto ameude a Reya Dona Maria por el que lhy fezesse bem e mostrando amor e fyança ao Conde e aos seus e catava por el.' (Lopes (ed.) 1967: 14–15).

13   Namely the fact that Sancho IV took over the kingdom after the death of his older brother Alfonso, disregarding the fact that he had left children (underaged, but supported by part of the nobility), and the tradition of his father Alfonso X's curse. There were also doubts on the legitimacy of Sancho's marriage to Maria de Molina, which reflected on their son. For an overview, see Arias Guillén (2012).

king, lacking his mother's political ability. Given the early death of Fernando IV, Maria de Molina was once again regent (from 1312 to 1321) during the minority of her grandson Alfonso XI (1311–1350). This last king sought to restore the power of the monarchy, which involved a conflicted relationship with the strong and rebellious nobility.

In 1322 Pedro Afonso is documented to be back in Portugal, assuming a conciliatory posture regarding his family's current dissensions. He shows up on the side of Queen Isabel, collaborating in the promotion of peace between King Denis and Prince Afonso. In the process, the Count was rehabilitated, and his assets were returned to him.[14] Nevertheless, after the death of King Denis, when Afonso IV reached the throne, Count Pedro Afonso retired from the court to his domains, where he subsequently developed his historiographic work. Given the ups and downs of his adventurous life, it becomes easier to perceive the importance that friendship had to him, probably not so much as an abstract concept but as the genuine feeling of an ideal to be fulfilled in life, which enables us to understand its conception as a stimulus to write about the past, recognized as a means of raising awareness and establishing links that could lead to important developments.

3 Friendship as a Stimulus for Writing and to Please God

As we approach the end of this article, we will consider the starting point of the Prologue, that frames the issues already discussed:

> Em nome de Deus que é fonte e padre d'amor, e porque este amor nom sofre nem ũa cousa de mal, porem em servi-lo de coraçom é carreira real, e nem ũu melhor serviço nom pode o homem fazer que ama-lo de todo seu sem, e seu proximo como si mesmo, [...] porem eu, conde dom Pedro, filho do mui nobre rei dom Denis, houve de catar por gram gram trabalho, por muitas terras, escripturas que falavam dos linhagées.
>
> E veendo as escripturas com grande estudo e em como falavam d'outros grandes feitos compuge este livro por gaanhar o seu amor e por meter amor e amizade antre os nobres fidalgos da Espanha. (*Linhagens*: 55)

---

14   Lopes (1970) mentions a request for help that the rebellious Prince Afonso sent in December 1321 to his half-brother Pedro Afonso (p. 68), the latter's involvement in Queen Isabel's pacifying intervention before King Denis, in March 1322 (p. 75), and the subsequent pardon of the rebels (p. 80).

(In the name of God, who is the source and father of love, and because this love does not suffer from any negative element, therefore serving Him with all your heart is the real way, and no better service can a man do than to love Him with all his intelligence, and his neighbour as himself, [...] so I, Count D. Pedro, son of the very noble King Denis, have painstakingly sought throughout many lands, documents that spoke of lineages.

And reading the Scriptures with great study, and as they spoke of other great deeds, I composed this book to win His love and to establish love and friendship among the noble aristocrats of Spain.)

The Count underlines the topic of the book as a guiding companion for nobles to identify their lineages and to consequently develop friendships, thus pleasing God. Therefore, the action of writing the book is, in the long run, a contribution to the fulfilment of God's will on earth. Although these references to God are usual, their use in this Prologue seems to go beyond the *topos*, since they are personalized. This preoccupation may have emerged from Pedro Afonso's closeness to his stepmother, Queen Isabel, later Saint Isabel of Portugal. This relationship may have begun during his upbringing, and subsequently consolidated in adult life, namely during their articulated pacifying actions, as mentioned.

Books of Lineages have been considered as the nobles' reply to royal centralizing policies, since they value ancestry and the positive role of the aristocracy. In a way, they can be viewed as the counterpart to royal chronicles, which are organized according to the succession of kings and concentrate on their deeds. Pedro Afonso is a peculiar author since he is responsible for both a chronicle and a book of lineages. His social situation is also 'in-between'. He is the oldest son of King Denis of Portugal, but illegitimate, therefore hardly eligible for succession, and during his life, at different moments, as presented above, he was both a highly influential aristocrat and a banished nobleman. Therefore, it is our conviction that the life experience of the Count has had a noteworthy influence on his works, namely for what concerns the issue of friendship. Beyond the fact of his biased consideration of the people with whom he had a deeper friendship,[15] if we look at the Count's historiographical works from the point of view of the wish to promote friendship, this is bound to make us reconsider the opposition chronicles / books of lineages and sovereignty / aristocracy. Rather we are led to think of these binomials in a complementary way, each deserving

---

15   See the laudatory passages on Alfonso XI (*Af.X–XI*) and King Denis (*Cr.1344*). On the latter see Dias (2021).

to be valued, and capable of living in harmony. Chronicles and books of lineages present the good and wrong deeds of kings and nobles with a pedagogical inclination (Dias 2003; Mocelim 2005/6; 2007), up to a point, comparable to *specula*, although not normative. In compliance with the Ciceronian maxim, *historia magistra vitae*, models of behaviour are conveyed, not only for warrior and conquering actions but also for moral and affectionate conduct.

One of the characteristics of Pedro Afonso's *Book of Lineages* that has often been commented on is his encompassing vision of the Peninsular aristocratic families. This trait accords with the idea of a united Christendom opposing the enemies of the faith as a means to overcome internal dissensions. It fully agrees with the ideological mainstream of both the *Book of Lineages* and the *Crónica de 1344* where the moments of the union of the Christian kings against Muslim forces are particularly praised. This point of view, being in consonance with religious guidelines also explains the Count's enthusiasm on the battle of Salado or Tarifa (1340) (Ferreira 2010: 91–93) which was the fullest example of the union between nobles and sovereigns and among Christian kings against a Muslim alliance in his lifetime, even if, ironically, Pedro Afonso was not able to participate.[16] This perspective reshapes the previous idea of an Iberian empire, present in Alfonsine historiography since the solidarity advocated by the Count implies the existence of the different peninsular kingdoms.

Pedro Afonso's text on friendship is thus a synthetic but rich reflection. He differs both from the *Siete Partidas* and D. Juan Manuel's views, although he is familiar with them. *Partida* IV considers the juridical status of friendship seeking to apprehend the concept and to frame it socially and politically (Heusch, 1993). Don Juan Manuel's approach is not only political but also suspicious and pragmatic (Ayerbe-Chaux 1969). The Count of Barcelos, having lived in analogous cultural and social environments and having enjoyed a social position and a life experience in some ways similar to those of don Juan Manuel, seems not to have been so negatively affected as his counterpart. His view is also pragmatic and marked by the aristocratic ideas of solidarity, but he involves this interaction in the more spiritual idea of God's service. His approach is both Christian and chivalric and, above all, optimistic since, on the one hand, he seems to believe in the didactic power of example as a stimulus to promote appropriate behaviour and, on the other, his writings display a religious colouring that provides global meaning to his works, as a mission to be fulfilled. In this sense, historiographic writing can be considered an activity that pleases God since

---

16   For health reasons, as explained in ms. U, §135; ms. Q2, §151; ms. S, §177 (*Af.X–XI*).

knowledge of the past is believed to be a means to overcome dissensions and to promote social peace and harmony in the present.

Bibliography

Primary Sources

[*Af.x–xi.*:] *De Afonso x a Afonso xi. Edição e estudo do texto castelhano dos reinados finais da 2ª redacção da Crónica de 1344.* Dir. Maria do Rosário Ferreira. Paris: e-Spania Books, 2015—https://books.openedition.org/esb/698

[*Cr.1344:*] *Crónica Geral de Espanha de 1344.* Ed. L.F. Lindley Cintra. Lisboa: Imprensa Nacional-Casa da Moeda, 1990 (4th vol.).

[*Linhagens:*] Pedro Afonso de Barcelos. *Livro de Linhagens.* Ed. José Mattoso. Lisboa: Academia das Ciências (PMH), 1980 (vol. II/1).

[*Onceno:*] *Cronica de D. Alfonso el Onceno de este nombre ...* Ed Francisco Cerdà y Rico. Madrid: Imprenta D. Antonio de Sancha, 1787 (vol. I).

[*Partidas:*] Alfonso el Sabio, *Las Siete Partidas.* Ed. Real Academia de la Historia. Madrid: Imprenta Real (t.II–Partida segunda–tercera), 1807.

PartidasDigital (edición crítica de las Siete Partidas: Las ediciones históricas). Dir. José Manuel Fradejas Rueda. Universidad Valladolid—https://7partidas.hypotheses.org

Secondary Sources

Arias Guillén, Fernando (2012). 'El linaje maldito de Alfonso x. Conflictos en torno a la legitimidad regia en Castilla (c. 1275–1390)' *Vínculos de Historia* 1: 147–163.

Ayerbe-Chaux, Reinaldo (1969). 'El concepto de la amistad en la obra del infante don Juan Manuel.' *Thesaurus* XXIV/1: 37–49

Bautista, Francisco (2007). '"Como a señor natural": interpretaciones políticas del *Cantar de mio Cid.*' *Olivar* v.8/n°10: 173–184.

Bloch, R. Howard (1989). *Étymologie et généalogie.* Paris: Seuil.

Dias, Isabel Barros (2003). *Metamorfoses de Babel: a historiografia Ibérica (sécs. XIII–XIV), construções e estratégias textuais.* Lisboa: Fundação Calouste Gulbenkian.

Dias, Isabel Barros (2021). 'Pedro Afonso de Barcelos observador e viajante em Castela e Aragão: perspetivas cruzadas.' In C. Olivera Serrano, Ed. *Entre el altar y la corte.* Sevilla: Athenaica ediciones: 165–207.

Ferreira, Maria do Rosário (2010). 'D. Pedro de Barcelos e a representação do passado ibérico'. In *O Contexto Hispânico da Historiografia Portuguesa nos séculos XIII e XIV.* Coimbra: Imprensa da Universidade de Coimbra: 81–106.

Ferreira, Maria do Rosário (2012). '"Amor e amizade antre os nobres fidalgos da Espanha". Apontamentos sobre o prólogo do *Livro de Linhagens* do Conde D. Pedro.' *Cahiers d'études hispaniques médiévales* 35: 93–122.

Heusch, Carlos (1993). 'Les fondements juridiques de l'amitié à travers les *Partidas* d'Alphonse x et le droit medieval' *Cahiers d'études hispaniques médiévales* 18–19: 5–48.

Krus, Luís (2011). *A construção do passado medieval. Textos Inéditos e Publicados.* Lisboa: IEM.

Liuzzo Scorpo, Antonella (2020). *Friendship in Medieval Iberia. Historical, Legal and Literary Perspectives.* London and New York: Routledge.

Lopes, F. Félix (1967). 'O primeiro manifesto de el-Rei D. Dinis contra o Infante D. Afonso seu filho e herdeiro.' *Itinerarium* 55: 17–45 (offprint: 1–31).

Lopes, F. Félix (1970). 'Santa Isabel na contenda entre D. Dinis e o filho (1321–1322)' *Lusitania Sacra* 8: 57–80.

Lopes, F. Félix (1997). 'Alguns documentos respeitantes a D. Pedro conde de Barcelos.' *Colectânea de Estudos de História e Literatura.* Lisboa: Academia Portuguesa da História, vol. III: 223–238.

McDonie, R. Jacob (2020). *Friendship and Rhetoric in the Middle Ages.* New York and London: Routledge.

Melville, M. Gert (1987). 'Vorfahren und Vorgänger. Spätmittelalterliche Genealogien als dynastische Legitimation zur Herrschaft'. In Peter-Johannes Schuler (Hg.). *Die Familie als sozialer und historischer Verband.* Sigmaringen: Thorbecke Verlag. 203–309.

Mocelim, Adriana (2005/6). 'Análise do Prólogo do *Livro de Linhagens*, escrito pelo Conde Pedro de Barcelos em 1340.' *Revista Pós-História* 13–14: 95–105.

Mocelim, Adriana (2007). '"Por meter amor e amizade entre os nobres fidalgos da Espanha": O *Livro de Linhagens* do Conde Pedro Afonso no contexto tardo-medieval português'. Master dissertation in History—Universidade Federal Paraná.

Oliveira, António Resende de (2011). 'O genealogista e as suas linhagens: D. Pedro, Conde de Barcelos.' *e-Spania* 11—https://journals.openedition.org/e-spania/20374

Pizarro, José Augusto de Sotto Mayor (2005). *D. Dinis.* Rio de Mouro: Círculo de Leitores.

Stern-Gillet, Suzanne and Gary M. Gurtler, sj. eds. (2014). *Ancient and Medieval Concepts of Friendship.* Albany: State University of New York Press.

8

Perlocutionary and Illocutionary Chronicling: How an Ostensibly Constative Activity Affects the World around It

Graeme Dunphy

Abstract

J.L. Austin's speech act theory distinguishes between constative and performative utterances, dividing the latter into the subcategories perlocution and illocution, an approach that has since been applied far beyond its original locus in linguistics. Taking examples from fifteenth-century Scottish chronicles, this paper explores how introducing a three-fold distinction between constative, perlocutionary and illocutionary chronicling might more clearly reveal the chronicler reporting, persuading and acting on the political stage.

Chronicles are narrative texts, and as such they tell the stories of the past, they transmit data, they explain connections: chroniclers, it might seem, are in the business of facts.[1] Forty years ago, this would still have been a *communis opinio* in the circles of most of those who drew on these texts as the sources for their scholarship. Leaving aside the fraught question of what we mean by factuality, it would certainly appear that the foregrounding of fact-like material is characteristic of historical writing. However the developments in chronicle studies in recent decades have focussed our attention on the degree to which chronicles are shaped by their perspective and motivated by a purpose, and some are downright partisan, spiritedly agenda-driven polemical compositions. Chroniclers not only tell: they also act. This is now well understood. But as far as I am aware, the opposition between these two spurs to the chronicler's intent—the desire to relate the affairs of the world and the desire to influence them—has not been adequately explored theoretically. How do we conceptualize the relationship between content and agenda? We need a vocabulary to describe these phenomena.

---

1 The first version of this paper was given at the Oxford and Cambridge International Chronicles Symposium, 5th July 2012.

In a recent paper I used the terms "constative" and "performative", drawn from speech act theory, to describe this opposition, in the belief that the usage was self-explanatory.[2] I was challenged by a peer-reviewer for introducing unnecessary neologisms. Well, they are not neologisms, but apparently their application to chronicle studies needs to be explained. Furthermore, since the term performativity is also seen in chronicle studies used in a different, more anthropological and dramaturgical way to refer to the ritual and theatricality of the public reading of the text, a clarification is all the more urgent. What I want to suggest here is that the terminology of performativity as opposed to constativity in the sense of speech act theory, and the insights from the linguistic debates which gave rise to it, can help us to clarify our ideas about the relationship between what the chroniclers say and what they do.

The foundations of speech act theory were laid in 1955 by J.L. Austin,[3] who in a series of lectures called *Doing Things with Words* responded to the new situation created by Wittgenstein's *Philosophical Investigations* (with their focus on what words do rather than what they mean[4]) by working out a theory of performative utterances. This was refined by John Searle,[5] given a deconstructionist dynamic by Jacques Derrida,[6] applied to political theory by Judith Butler,[7] and most recently worked into a theory of historical method by Quentin Skinner.[8] But although Skinner applies it to the historian's reading of utterances by thinkers of the past, he never applies it to what we might call historical writing. The leap to medieval chronicles is yet to be made.

---

2 Dunphy (2012).

3 J.L. Austin (1962), based on lectures held at Harvard in 1955. Austin died in 1960, and his notes were published posthumously.

4 Wittgenstein (1953). Wittgenstein's exploration of meanings inherent in words attempts to show that, while a lexicographer can define words to carry a specific significatory content, the "meaning" of an utterance has more to do with functional context. Even his provisional list of "Language games" in § 23 already puts the focus onto things which are achieved with language: commanding, reporting, obeying, speculating, forming and testing a hypothesis, guessing riddles, asking, thanking, cursing greeting, praying. Even with a relatively fact-based language game like reporting an event, Wittgenstein seems more interested in the activity of reporting. This lends a particular urgency to Austin's question of the relationship between the factual content of an utterance and the effects which the act of uttering produces in the world. The influence of Wittgenstein on Austin would bear further study, but it is probably limited to the raising of some of the questions; Austin did not draw directly on Wittgenstein for his solutions.

5 Searle (1969).

6 Derrida (1977).

7 Butler (1997).

8 Skinner (2002).

Austin's theory begins with a distinction between constative and performative utterances—both terms he coined himself. The term *constative* derives from Latin *constat* 'it is certain'; French *constater* and German *konstatieren* are more everyday words than the English legalese *to constate*, but all mean 'to affirm'. A constative utterance is a statement which conveys information: "In the beginning, God created the heavens and the earth." This is what—before Wittgenstein—would traditionally have been seen as the fundamental purpose of language, to (con)state, assert, communicate what is perceived as being factual. A performative utterance, on the other hand, is a form of words which achieves something through the speaking of them. Austin's favourite example is "I declare you husband and wife", a sentence which, if spoken under the correct circumstances, creates the legal status to which it alludes. A particularly powerful example in a medieval worldview, would be *Hoc est corpus meum*, in which the bread becomes the Body of Christ through the declaration that it is so. These words perform a drama around which the whole of salvation history revolves. Other examples which would have been very real to the medieval mind would be the divine *fiat* with the attendant theology of the Word, but also magic formulae like "abracadabra". But Austin of course is looking for familiar contemporary examples, and suggests such utterances as "I name this ship the *Queen Elizabeth*" or "I give and bequeath my watch to my brother". Such linguistic acts, in which saying a thing makes it so, are termed by Austin "primary performatives". And if they include a self-referential verb of speech which specifically tags the performative element, for example "I declare", "I name", "I give and bequeath", he terms them "explicit performatives".

One of the interesting distinctions Austin makes between constative and performative utterances is that a constative, since it deals with facts, is either true or false, but a performative, because it is not about truth in that sense, must be judged by other categories. If a performative actually produces the desired effect in the world, Austin calls it "felicitous", but if it fails, if for example one writes "I bequeath my watch ..." but on some technicality the will turns out not after all to be valid and the watch remains unbequeathed, then the performative is "infelicitous"—Austin also refers to such an utterance as a "misfire".[9]

This initial definition of a performative is relatively tight, focussing on ceremonial or ritual performances, but as his argument develops, Austin widens the scope greatly, suggesting other senses in which language performs. For

---

9   To be precise, he distinguishes between two kinds of infelicities: "misfires" are attempts at performatives which are botched, whereas "abuses" are insincere utterances where the pretence at a performative is hollow. See Austin (1962: 16–17). However, the "abuse" category is of little further interest to him and will not help us here.

example, a command is performative, assuming the addressee obeys it, for the words have caused something to happen in the world: the professor says "Jump!" and her assistant jumps. This is different from the primary perform-ative, because the speech act does not itself create a new situation, it merely motivates a subsequent action; but it is obviously similar. Interestingly, the same can be said of statements. If I say "Dinner's ready", that is, on the face of it, a constative, but it is performative if it causes hungry children to rush to the table.

Broadening this still further, Austin notices that on a most basic level, to speak is already performing an action, even if no further consequences follow.[10] If the professor says "Jump!" and the assistant declines to jump, the command has been infelicitous, the jumping has failed to materialize, but at least the act of commanding has been performed. In the same way, even the most obvious constative must be performed. If I say "Some cars have wheels", that uninspir-ing insight is hardly likely to change much in the world, but at least it creates a world in which the sentence has been spoken. On this level, of course, every utterance is performative. However, one could as easily say the opposite, that on some level, almost all speech is constative: the words *Hoc est corpus meum* may modify the accidents of the bread and the wine, but at the same time they describe what they are doing. This might suggest that Austin's original distinc-tion has fallen by the wayside, but in fact, as he has developed a hierarchy of performativity from the most demanding primary performatives to the rather weak statement-performance, we might think of speech acts being tendentially more performative or more constative.

Austin next tries to categorize different types of performatives. He distin-guishes two broad groups, for which he coins the terms "illocutionary act" and "perlocutionary act".[11] These he then subdivides into a whole system of types, with which we need not concern ourselves at present;[12] but the illocution-perlocution distinction is very useful. An illocutionary act is one where the speaking itself creates the reality; *in locutione*, "in speaking" I do. This obvi-ously applies to the primary performatives, where the words have legal or magical force, but it also includes autosuggestive statements, like declaring "I

---

10   Austin (1962: 91).

11   In fact Austin appears to distinguish locutionary, illocutionary and perlocutionary aspects of speech in a three-fold classification, but Searle (1969: 23) rejects the locutionary as a comparable category, and we may also leave it out of our classification. By locutionary act, Austin means the physical production of speech.

12   Searle finds Austin's division of illocutionary acts into five categories "ad hoc". It does not appear to be the strongest part of Austin's account, and has not been widely discussed. See Searle (1969: 69, footnote).

am so happy", and in so doing creating within oneself a feeling of happiness.[13] Against this, a perlocutionary act is one which triggers a subsequent action: *per locutione*, "by speaking" I do. Commands have perlocutionary force if they are obeyed, but any speech act which inspires others to act, or discourages them from acting where they otherwise might have, is perlocutionary.[14] And of course the same utterance can be both: if I order a beer, that is illocutionary in the sense that it creates a legal situation where the beer has been ordered (and I am liable to pay for it), and it is perlocutionary if the beer is actually brought.[15]

This then is the terminology on which I wish to draw. Applied to chronicles, it opens possibilities for approaching the question of how a historical text creates in the world the realities which it describes. My starting point was the observation that chronicles are ostensibly constative works, but that this constative façade disguises the extent to which they are in fact performative. Applying the terminology to whole works takes us one major step away from the original speech act theory, though Austin's insistence on the "total speech-act situation" gives us licence.[16] Even in the chronicle context, of course, the designation of individual utterances by Austin's categories may be useful, and Alastair Matthews recently used this to good effect a discussion of the *Kaiserchronik*:

> The characters are not merely pieces in the enactment of a foregone conclusion but experience or create it themselves from one moment to the next; this is especially the case of performative utterances such as Constantine's *nu bevilh ich dir, hêrre | baide lîp unt sêle* ('I now commend both body and soul to you my Lord') on the day after his baptism.[17]

This remains close to Austin's original train of thought and focusses helpfully on what the protagonists in the historical narrative are doing with language. My experiment is to see if we can do the same with what the chroniclers themselves do.

Applying the theory to narrative blocks does of course raise some questions which must remain caveats throughout my discussion. There is the problem that the messages of a whole passage may be harder to identify than that of

---

13 Searle lists examples of illocutionary acts as "stating, questioning, commenting, performing" (1969: 24).

14 Searle lists as perlocutionary acts "persuading, convincing ..." (1969: 25).

15 Austin (1962: 149).

16 Austin (1962: 52).

17 Matthews (2012: 45).

an individual sentence, especially when a complicated textual history might lead to a layering of disparate agendas. One might also object that users—be it lawyers citing historical precedents or later writers drawing on earlier ones— are more likely to cite a chapter and verse than a whole work, so that reception, and hence performative force, often works on a sentence-to-sentence basis. But against that, we know that a literary work is more than the sum of its sentences. In particular, a chronicle locates individual claims about the past within a larger construct of history, and both the individual claims and the larger construct can inspire people. To call chronicles constative is to say that their material is intended to inform. Obviously, on one level, this is true for every chronicle, since we define the genre in terms of its narrative. To call them performative means that in addition to telling, they also act. Far from being purely constative, making statements about what happened, a chronicle generates new "truths" that form paradigms for political and social interaction, and thus it contributes to the next phase of the historical process. In medieval thinking, "truth" was always bound up with morality, so that constating was even more obviously linked to messages about behavioural consequences than in modern assumptions. This may be most obvious when the chronicler has a clear agenda, but any text which has a reader can wield an influence.

A recently published anthology of short Scottish prose chronicles might be an appropriate source of interesting examples, as it has a connection to the dedicatee of the current volume.[18] All of these works focus to some extent on Scottish-English relations. *La Vraie Cronicque d'Escoce* was apparently written in 1464 as briefing notes for French diplomats preparing for negotiations with the English. In places it takes a tendentially pro-Scottish stance, presumably because supporting Scottish claims could undermine English positions, but its general ambivalence reflects Louis XI's willingness to sacrifice the Auld Alliance if such a course suited France's interests. By contrast, the *Ynglis Chronicle* (post-1485) is a bitterly partisan diatribe focussing on those parts of English history that affect Scottish interests and openly declaring its purpose to repudiate English claims. Meanwhile the *Nomina Omnium Regum Scotorum* (late fifteenth century), the *Short Chronicle of 1482* and the *Scottis Originale* (c. 1470–1539) focus on Scottish history, with a clear though less aggressive pro-Scottish agenda. Obviously many passages are packed with information as we might expect from a constative narrative. For example, the *Nomina* gives the exact date of the Battle of Bannockburn, the unusual detail that the opposing kings

---

18   Embree, Kennedy & Daly (2012) appeared in the Boydell series *Medieval Chronicles*; Erik Kooper served on its editorial board.

had agreed in advance on the location of the battlefield, and somewhat inflated figures for the strengths of the two armies (Dalhousie MS 581 ff.), all of which appears to be factual reporting. However when a historian takes sides against those who may feel differently about the events, she or he becomes a player in the reception of history on an altogether more performative level. The author of the *Nomina* cannot resist a satisfied smile at the victory: *libet ad memoriam reducere* ('it is pleasant to recall'). The *Short Chronicle of 1482* speaks of Bannockburn *quhar our ald enemys gat a gret fall* (95), which the *Ynglis Chronicle* proclaims *loving to God* (232). This cheerleading is relatively trivial, but clearly transcends informing to encourage sentiment in a conflict that remained volatile at the time of writing. A more consequential performativity arises when the chroniclers build foundations for legal arguments, as in the many passages on claims and counterclaims to fealty and land rights. The *Nomina* records that in the tenth century, Edmund of England ceded Cumbria to the Scottish throne *in perpetuum* (Dalhousie 283 ff.). In return, the Scots would perform homage for the land. Although the concept of homage often implied acknowledging a feudal superior, in cases like this it involved a far more limited obligation: Scotland would support England against the Danes. Nevertheless, the sentence about homage was dropped from the vernacular translations (Advocates and Asloan MSS) lest it be misunderstood. In such passages we see chroniclers as activists in a continuing conflict.

Perhaps the most fruitful part of Austin's theory for the discussion of chronicle performativity is the distinction between illocutionary and perlocutionary force. Most studies since Austin have focused on illocution, but perlocution seems almost more interesting to me, since it focusses on persuasion—which chroniclers seek to do. A text has perlocutionary force when it influences the thinking or actions of readers or listeners. In chronicles this could include recommending actions, setting examples for others to follow, or establishing legal precedents. One of the most striking repeated motifs in the short Scottish chronicles is the demonization of the English royal line, a perlocutionary tactic to steer the affections of the reader. The *Scottis Originale* claims that, at the outset of the British line, Arthur was made king by the devilry of Merlin when the rightful heir would have been a Scot (Dalhousie 129 ff.). Meanwhile the *Ynglis Chronicle* recalls a detail from the Albion myth, where Queen Albine and her sisters conceived children by demons, and concludes that the entire English nation *ar lynely discendit of þe devil* (16 ff.). Bringing the outrage closer in time, both texts know the story that Geoffrey of Anjou was an incubus, meaning that Henry II "the Tyrant", who, we are reminded, slew St Thomas of Canterbury, was the Devil's grandson (*bot the secund fra the Devill*), of whom St Bernard prophesied *A Diablo existi, et ad Diabolum ibis* ("You came from the Devil and to the

Devil you will go"). Consequently, the entire royal line from *is cummyn doune rycht lyne fra the Devill* (*Scottis Originale*, Dalhousie 213 ff., cf. *Ynglis Chronicle* 133 ff.). Both gleefully cite Higden (*thair awin cronycle of Ingland*) as a witness against his own people. Less scandalously, but equally strategic in its perlocutionary intent, the *Nomina* records how ancient Albion had been inhabited by four peoples, Scots, Picts, Britons and Saxons, the first three of whom fostered the Christian faith, unlike the *gens Saxonum pagana qui nunc Angli dicuntur* ("the heathen Saxon race who are now called English", Dalhousie 233). Such perlocutionary efforts to induce in the reader a general distaste for one of the parties become even more effective if supplemented with partisanship on a specific dispute. The *Vraie Cronique*, following Bower, elucidates the claim of the Kings of Scotland to the English throne on the basis of their descent from Saint Margaret, who was heir to the House of Wessex, concluding approvingly: *le royame et la couronne d'Angleterre compettent et appartiennent et doivent competter et appartenir au roy d'Escose* ("the kingdom and crown of England rightfully belong and should belong to the King of Scotland," 176 ff.). The passage goes on to adduce other reasons for a specific Scottish claim on Cumbria and Northumbria, noting dismissively that the English try to deny this (*veulent dire les Anglois, 205*). We see a perlocutionary force in that the language invites the reader to sympathize with the Scottish claim. It is not always clear whom this propaganda seeks to convince: the *Ynglis Chronicle* addresses the English in the second person: we have read *ʒour fals and fenʒeit writ that ʒe call a cronikle*, and *ʒe sall be answerit* (2 ff.). This has the tone of a prosecution and aims to arm the Scottish reader, not to coax an English one to reconsider. Other chronicles are reminiscent of a weary teacher leading an untalented instructee to understanding, but all in their own way seek control of the narrative. Since there are issues of current national and international policy at stake, the perlocutionary intent to enable and persuade is potentially of great importance.

But what of illocutionary force, the phenomenon that an utterance itself creates a result, not by motivating others, but by the very act of uttering? The most obvious illocutionary move in chronicling is to cite a legal document, for example incorporating a claim of rights into a monastic history. The *Vraie Chronique* reproduces one such document in full, the 1189 *Quitclaim of Canterbury*, by which Richard Lionheart simultaneously proclaimed and enacted a transfer of sovereignty to William the Lion: *Sciatis nos consanguineo nostro Willermo Dei gratia regi Scottorum reddidisse castra sua* ("Know that we have restored to our kinsman William, by the grace of God King of Scots, his castles ..." 267 ff.). The edict itself, formulated in the first-person, is an explicit performative, and is illocutionary in the fullest sense; its inclusion in a pro-Scottish text to make an English voice speak against the English claim is likewise illocutionary. In other ways some of the perlocutionary acts already mentioned resonate an illocutionary dynamic. Judith Butler speaks, in a very different context, of the political power of performativity, and how an utterance can change its own context.[19] For example, Austin insists that an insult is an illocution: "in saying" that you are descended from the Devil I create a situation in which your honour is impugned. There are chronicles that offend, chronicles that praise, chronicles that in claiming something make it so. Since power and legitimacy rest on consensus—a king is king because people believe him to be—the act of declaring a king the rightful heir itself empowers him. Prayer, if one believes in its efficacy, is illocutionary: the *Scottis Originale* references the reigning Scottish Monarch, *quhilk God keep and preserve* (Dalhousie 109). Expressing friendship in words can reinforce that friendship, and especially at a time when the French were lukewarm about the Auld Alliance one can see an illocutionary intent in the attempt of the *Nomina* to trace *the band betuix Scotland and France quhilk lastit as ʒitt, thank be till Almychtty God* (Advocates 175) back to the eighth century, when the University of Paris was ostensibly founded by two itinerant Scotsmen. Perhaps the ultimate illocutionary force of a chronicle lies in the fact that the great constructs within which people's thinking moves are enacted in their words of institution. In formulating the shape of my people's history, I define their identity. Here, *origo gentis* narrations of the sort found in most national chronicles immediately spring to mind, but also, for example, the lines of poetry cited in the *Nomina* on the inspiring first use of the Lion Rampant (Dalhousie, 43).

If chronicles are performative, how do we evaluate them? Historians in search of the facts understandably look at historical writing and ask, "Is it accurate?" But if the passage is more performative than constative, the better question would be, "Did it work?"—Austin's concept of felicity. The devilish ancestry of the English king is presumably not true in its constative dynamic, but it may nevertheless be felicitous as a performative if it enabled a Scottish commander to rally his troops. Obviously, it is only possible to assess this if we know the author's intention. Speech act theorists have discussed at length whether the felicity of a performative utterance depends on the speaker intending the act, or whether an unintended effect would count as performativity. While it is certainly true that the real significance of a work may sometimes be more than its author knew, and indeed there has been a post-modernist trend to question whether an author's intentions are important at all, it must be clear that if a chronicler had an agenda, any impact of the text which ran counter to

---

19   Butler (1997).

this agenda would be a failure of performativity. Since the *Vraie Cronique* was intended to inform diplomats in negotiations between England and France, felicity in the first instance would arise if the French delegation derived an actual advantage from the text, and a misfire if gaps in the information had left the diplomats exposed and unprepared, or if misinformation had wrongfooted them. In fact, the negotiations never took place, and as so often, we are left guessing what the effect might have been. When the vernacular translators of the *Nomina* suppressed all mention of homage in the ceding of Cumbria, they apparently feared that a narrative undergirding Scottish claims might inadvertently have the reverse effect. When it comes to propagandistic vilification of the enemy, felicity may be simply that if you throw enough mud, some will stick. Unfortunately, while we can easily see the writers' concern with the impact of their words, it is usually very difficult to assess that impact in reality, as we seldom have evidence of direct reader responses in individual cases. But occasionally we can observe major political players deploying the advantage the historians render. The transfer of material from the Scottish chronicle tradition into the *Declaration of Arbroath* is a felicity to the extent that the material made available by the chroniclers was believed and weaponized in political debate outwith the genre. To the extent that the *Declaration* motivated Pope John to exhort the English side to make peace, it was more felicitous still. That it continued to galvanize Scottish national feeling down through the centuries, and is echoed in the discourse of the independence movement to the present day, shows how the waves can ripple further than their originators could have imagined. When the *Declaration of Arbroath* cites chronicles as a source of precedence, these documents have found their locus in the political debate, and we have a measurement of felicity.

Agenda-driven aspects of chronicles have been highlighted frequently in recent research: chronicles establishing precedents, enlisting support for parties in disputes and spreading the information and misinformation that shapes worldviews. The application of theoretical categories to this may allow more subtle readings. We have seen how Austin distinguishes constative and performative utterances, dividing the latter into the subcategories perlocution and illocution. The term "performance" might be confusing as it is used in literary studies in other ways, but a three-fold distinction between constative, perlocutionary and illocutionary chronicling can help us study the chronicler who reports, persuades and acts on the political stage. As the historian refines a construction of history, she or he enters into a dialogue with readers, whose thinking and thus whose subsequent actions are forever changed as the new constructs are internalized. A chronicler may pretend to constate the past, but is in fact performing in the world.

Bibliography

Austin, J.L. [John Langshaw] (1962), *How to do things with Words*. Oxford: Clarendon Press.

Butler, Judith (1997), *Excitable Speech. A Politics of the Performative*. New York and London: Routledge.

Derrida, Jacques (1977), "Signature Event Context" in: *Limited inc*. Baltimore: Johns Hopkins University Press.

Dunphy, Graeme (2012). 'Perspicax ingenium mihi collatum est: Strategies of Authority in Chronicles Written by Women' in: *Authority and Gender in Medieval and Renaissance Chronicles*, ed. Juliana Dresvina and Nicholas Sparks. Cambridge: Cambridge Scholars Publishing. 166–201.

Embry, Dan, Edward Donald Kennedy and Kathleen Daly with Susan Edgington (2012), *Short Scottish Prose Chronicles*. Woodbridge: The Boydell Press.

Matthews, Alastair (2012), *The Kaiserchronik: A Medieval Narrative*. Oxford: Oxford University Press.

Searle, John (1969), *Speech Acts. An Essay in the Philosophy of Language*. Cambridge: Cambridge University Press.

Skinner, Quentin (2002), *Visions of Politics*. Cambridge: Cambridge University Press.

Wittgenstein, Ludwig (1953), *Philosophical Investigations*. Trans. G.E.M. Anscombe. Oxford: Blackwell.

9

The Southern Principalities of Rus' in the First Novgorodian Chronicle

Márta Font

Abstract

With the disintegration of the Kievan Rus', local centres of chronicle-writing emerged. Since the Novgorodian Chronicles mainly recorded local events, the occasional inclusion of events in the southern region of Rus' is significant, and it is instructive to note what was selected. The present study examines such passages in the First Novgorodian Chronicle, comparing them with reports from the Kievan and Galician-Volhynian chronicles in the southwestern part of Rus'. We conclude that the information transfer between Novgorod and the southern part of Rus' was tied to individuals whose activities had been significant both for Novgorod and for other areas of Rus'.

1   The Regions of the Kievan Rus'

The disintegration of the Kievan Rus' cannot be denoted by a single year: the importance of Kiev declined gradually as a result of several factors. The Cuman tribes emerging in the steppes played a role in this, not only as a threat to the southern centres, but also as a potential force, that is, an aid to achieving independence from Kiev.[1] From the economic point of view, this reduced the role of Kiev but enhanced the position of the Principality of Galicia located by the Dniester. The events of the eleventh and twelfth centuries testify that the princes of Chernigov used the military assistance of the Cumans numerous times, and the chroniclers denounced them for their connection with the "pagans", although this is undoubtedly a one-sided position.[2]

In the twelfth century, this supplementing of the local elite was a phenomenon known throughout Rus', manifested in the intensity of the operation of the *veche*. One of the most prominent illustrations relates to Novgorod. In

---

1 Font (2005: 267–276); Kovács (2014: 48–64).
2 Noonan (1987: 384–443); Zaytsev (2009: 45–59).

1136, Vsevolod Mstislavich, the prince sent from Kiev, was removed.[3] The *veche* played a significant role in the competition between the princely branches in terms of the acquisition of Kiev. The "summoning" of the prince was often affected by the demands of the neighbouring area and family kinship. In Novgorod, mainly the North Eastern Rus' (Vladimir–Suzdal), in Galicia–Volhynia the western neighbours. In some cases, the Rurik kinship also appeared in Novgorod from afar (e.g., from Chernigov).[4]

In addition to the withdrawing forces, there were also factors pointing in the direction of unity.[5]

The unity of the regions is demonstrated by the customary law, ecclesiastical structure and cult of Saints.[6] The continuous application of customary norms, early laws and ecclesiastical provisions is revealed in the numerous manuscripts. Among the narrative sources, chronicle-writing (*letopisanie*) plays a prominent role, showing both similar features and, in parallel, regional differences throughout Rus'. At the beginning of the twelfth century, *The Tale of Bygone Years* (*Povest' vremennykh let* = PVL) was created as an imprint of the entire contemporary Rus'. PVL was known in all three regional centres of chronicle-writing (Novgorod, Galicia–Volhynia and Vladimir–Suzdal), and several versions of the codex were maintained.[7] In the twelfth century, chronicle writing in the southern region was still based in Kiev. The *Kievan Chronicle* (KC) originated in the same Saint Michael Monastery in Vydubychi where the PVL had originated in the late twelfth century.

In the northern region, the peculiarities of the local dialect appeared in the texts originated in Novgorod. The text of the Vladimir–Suzdalian *svods*[8] harmonizes with that of Kiev in some places. The *Galician–Volhynian Chronicle* (GVC), compiled in the late thirteenth century, represents a new departure in the Galician–Volynian historiographical tradition, marking the beginnings of the *gesta* as a genre.[9]

---

3   ChronikNov I. (1971: 24); Froyanov (1992: 186–207).
4   Font (2021: 169–173).
5   Dimnik (2016: 379–383); Litvina and Uspenskiy (2006: 265–266).
6   Fennell (1995: 54); Lenhoff (1989).
7   Nikitin (2006: 5–16); Font (2016: 809–825).
8   The oldest codex of the chronicle of Vladimir–Suzdal is the Laurentian Codex (edition: PSRL I.), from which the antecedents of the late twelfth and early thirteenth centuries were reconstructed. These are the so-called *svods* (supposed chronicle-redactions). See: EMC II:1158–1159 (Guimon, Timofei V.); Font (2016: 831–833).
9   MPH KHW xlvii–lii; Font (2021: 63–75); Presumably, chronicling did not begin in Galicia–Volhynia in the thirteenth century. Evidence of this is the chronicle of the Polish Długosz,

The regionalization of chronicle-writing did not mean that information would not progress from one centre to another. One way to proceed was to "migrate" or copy manuscripts and the other was by word-of-mouth. The former can be presented by comparing the manuscripts (*spiski*), and the latter was authenticated by a more detailed discussion of each event. In the following, by analyzing the Chronicle of Novgorod, we will show what generated the interest of the people of Novgorod in the events of the southern region.

The Novgorodian chronicles are represented in five different texts.[10] The present study aims to address only the earliest one, the *First Novgorodian Chronicle* (*Novgorodskaia Pervaia Letopis* = NPL). The text of the NPL is known in two versions (*izvod*) and from several codices. The oldest one is the *Synodal manuscript* (*Synodalny spisok*), compiled from earlier texts in the Saint George Monastery in Novgorod between 1337 and 1345.[11] This is the only manuscript of this version of the text. The other version is the *Commissionny spisok*, which is known from several later codices: the Commissionny and the Akademichesky in the fifteenth century, the Troicky in the sixteenth century. The *Commissionny spisok* includes authentic texts of twelfth and thirteenth century. These two versions are published side by side,[12] as it is a widely recognized opinion that the two oldest manuscripts can be traced back to a common antecedent (*protograph*).

The *Synodal manuscript* consists of 169 folios and was written in several different calligraphies. The manuscript begins with the details of the PVL, but the beginning of the text, the part regarding events before 1016, is missing. The part written as a continuation of the PVL was dedicated to local events since the twelfth century, and it was essentially documentary in nature. Unlike other groups of chronicles, it lacks theological reasoning and literary borrowing.[13] The first compilation of early records may have originated in the second half of the thirteenth century, presumably before 1273, as no events between 1273 and 1298 are recorded.[14] Additional coverage of the years 1300–1330 were recorded around the middle of the fourteenth century. Short additions were added

---

which has preserved episodes from the history of this region that are unknown in Eastern Slavic sources. See: Font (2021: 50–53).

10   Likhachev (1947: 440–451).

11   The manuscript is preserved in the Gosudarstvenny Istorichesky Muzei in Moscow: ГИМ *Синод.собр.Under № 786*. See: Bobrov (2011: 270).

12   NPL (1950); PSRL III.; Nikitin (2011); The German edition differs from this, which only reports the Synodal version: ChronikNov I. (1971); English transl. ChronicleNov I. (1914); The English edition reflects Shakhmatov's position, which is now outdated.

13   ChronikNov I. (1971: 28).

14   Yanin (1981: 164–166).

to the chronicle to the years 1337, 1345 and 1352. Consequently, the merging of the thirteenth- and early fourteenth-century parts could not have taken place before 1352. Yury Bobrov has shown that the *Commissionny spisok* was compiled in the 1440s in the Khutynsky Monastery near Novgorod.[15] This chronicle is preserved in a codex containing a collection of diverse texts.[16] There are several differences between the Synodalny and the Commissionny manuscripts, which should be seen as later insertions.[17]

	Synodalny	Commissionny
Before 1016		PVL text prior to 1016
6726 (1218/1219)	Fratricides in Riazan'	
6748 (1240/1241)		Battle of Alexandr Nevsky along the Neva
6750 (1242/1243)		Battle of Aleksandr Nevsky on Lake Chud
6753 (1245/1246)		narration of the death of Mikhail Chernigov in the court of the Mongol Khan
6759 (1251/1252)– 6771 (1263/1264)		Comments on Alexandr Nevsky
6781–6806 (1273/1274– 1298/1299)		lasting, annual text

There is a section that is considered a later insertion in both versions, but this may have been included in the text of the common *protograph*.[18] It is revealing that all three additions are related to events outside of Novgorod, although they undoubtedly had an impact on the fate of the area afterwards.

---

15   Bobrov (2001: 73).
16   The manuscript is preserved by the Saint Petersburg Section of the Institute of History of the Russian Academy of Sciences: *СПб. собр. Археографической комиссии № 240*. Folio 28–264 of the manuscript contains the text of the chronicle. The section preceding the 28th folio consists of a list of princes, and the text of the chronicle is followed by legal texts (*Russkaia Pravda* and *Zakon Sudny Ljudem*). See: Bobrov (2001: 67–70, 272); Nikitin (2011: 27–28).
17   Nikitin (2011: 14–15).
18   Nikitin (2011: 14).

6711 (1203/1204)	Constantinople is occupied by the Crusaders
6732 (1224/1225)	Testimony on the battle at river Kalka
6746 (1238/1239)	Batu's campaign against Riazan' and Vladimir–Suzdal

The structure of the *Synodalny spisok* can be divided into two distinguishable units: the first part is between 1016–1272 and the second is between 1299–1352. From 1016 to 1117/1118 it goes along with the text of the PVL. The records beginning in 1118 can be interpreted specifically as Novgorodian. In the southern part of Rus', Chernigov and Kiev were independent political factors until the Mongol conquest. Galicia–Volhynia held out a little longer, until the end of the thirteenth century, from which time the Polish influence was strengthened until the principality became part of the Kingdom of Poland in 1340. Further investigation is based on NPL news reports 1118–1272.

Information on the southern region can be obtained by comparing the *Ipatiev Codex* (IP) which consists of three parts: the PVL, the KC and the GVC. The IP was discontinued by the end of the thirteenth century, so it is evident that for the purpose of comparison the twelfth/thirteenth-century passages were chosen. The twelfth-century part of the IP (KC) in Kiev was compiled in 1198/1199 by Moisei, abbot of the Vydubychi Monastery near Kiev. In this section we find information from Kiev, Galician–Volhynia and Chernigov at the same time. Historiography dates back to the eleventh century in Kiev and presumably in the early twelfth century in Galicia. The historiography of Chernigov, the third major centre in the southern region, is unknown. The Chernigov area came under Mongol rule after 1239, and even if there were early records, they certainly disappeared by the fourteenth century. From the history of Chernigov, we know as much as the KC and the GVC have preserved.

The following is a summary of the data of the *Synodalny spisok* from 1118 to 1272 that reported events in the southern part of Rus'. As a comparison, the data of KC 1118–1198 / 1199 and GVC 1200–1292 are also included in our table.[19]

---

19   See: Tables no. 1. and no. 2.

2   NPL on Southern Rus' in the Twelfth Century: Struggles for Kiev

Vladimir Monomakh was succeeded on the throne of Kiev (1125–1132) by his eldest son, Mstislav, who had previously spent longer periods of time in Novgorod (1088–1093, 1095–1117). He in turn was succeeded by his son, Vsevolod (1117–1136).[20] Mstislav's second son, Iziaslav Mstislavich, became Grand Prince of Kiev (1146–1154). Mstislav's third son, Rostislav Mstislavich, was promoted to Grand Prince between 1159–1167. Iziaslav's son, Mstislav Iziaslavich, named after his grandfather, was only able to acquire Kiev for a short period of time (1167–1169 / 1170). Volhynia was the base of Mstislav's son, Roman Mstislavich, who no longer sought to acquire Kiev, but instead extended his rule to the neighbouring Galicia: thus, the Principality of Galicia–Volhynia was established in 1199. The Novgorod connection reappeared here: the NPL recorded that Roman's father sent him to Novgorod, but he had to leave soon.

The other descendent of Vladimir Monomakh to receive special attention in the NPL was his youngest child, Yury Dolgoruky. In 1150, Yury fought for Kiev with his nephew, Iziaslav, but was unable to keep it. Nevertheless, he ended his life as the Grand Prince of Kiev, which he occupied after the death of Iziaslav (1154–1157). Yury resided in Vladimir–Suzdal (1132–1154), permanently living in the neighbourhood of Novgorod. He laid the foundation for the ambitions of the Vladimir–Suzdal princes towards Novgorod.

The separation of Novgorod from Rus' is dated to 1136. In reality, the independence of Novgorod developed more slowly. Novgorod still paid taxes after 1136, but it was not clear who this income would belong to, the Grand Prince of Kiev, or was Novgorod already owned by the neighbouring Vladimir–Suzdal. In the conflict between Iziaslav Mstislavich and Yury Dolgoruky, this debate created another controversy.[21] Another evidence that Novgorod still functioned as a part of Rus' even after 1136: in 1145, when the Grand Prince of Kiev of Chernigov origin, Vsevolod Olgovich (1139–1146) was gathering his army as he marched against Galicia, some of the members of his troops were of Novgorod origin. Galicia was mentioned by the Novgorod chronicler only because of the participation of the Novgorod army. The army of Novgorod supported Iziaslav's campaign against Rostov in 1148.[22] A similar case occurred in 1180/1181, when Novgorodians fought against Vsevolod of Vladimir–Suzdal on the side of

---

20   Rapov (1977: 139–140, 144–145).
21   PSRL II, col. 388.
22   ChronikNov I. (1971: 28).

Sviatoslav Vsevolodovich (1176–1194) from the Chernigov clan of the Grand Prince of Kiev. The case is understandable: Sviatoslav's son, Vladimir, was the prince of Novgorod.[23]

Vsevolod Olgovich, as Grand Prince of Kiev, was a remarkable person according to the author of the NPL. After Vsevolod, his brother, Igor Olgovich, wanted to be Grand Prince of Kiev, but in the battles for the position of Grand Prince, Igor was killed. All this was known to the chronicler of Novgorod, but the princes of Kiev from the Chernigov clan in the second half of the twelfth century were no longer in the reports of the NPL. The long reigning Sviatoslav Vsevolodovich (1176–1194) became a point of interest only because he wanted his son to rule Novgorod, which was ultimately unsuccessful.

3   NPL on Southern Rus' in the Thirteenth Century: Personalities Associated with Novgorod

In the thirteenth century text of the NPL, the "southern" news can be grouped around two people. One of these is Mstislav Mstislavich Udaloy / Udatny (the Daring / the Bold), the grandson of the twelfth century Grand Prince of Kiev, Rostislav Mstislavich, and a descendant of the Monomakh clan from Mstislav.[24] The other is Mikhail Vsevolodovich of Chernigov, who fought for Novgorod, but attracted the attention of its people primarily because of his martyrdom and ecclesiastical respect in the Mongol court.[25]

Mstislav Mstislavich's father was Mstislav Rostislavich "Khrabry" (the Brave),[26] Prince of Novgorod (1179–1180). At the birth of Mstislav Mstislavich, his father was no longer alive. According to Rus' naming traditions the name of a living father was never given to a newborn child.[27] Mstislav Mstislavich manoeuvred between Novgorod and southern Rus'. He first accepted the summons of the Novgorodians,[28] but later gave up his position in Novgorod and tried to hold on to the south of Rus'. This is indicated by his marriage to the daughter of the Cuman Kotian. He received help from a group of Cumans led by Kotian.

---

23   ChronikNov I. (1971: 36–37).
24   LexMA VI:1306–1310 (Poppe, Andrzej); Dimnik (2008: 67–113).
25   Dimnik (1981).
26   Rapov (1977: 163); Dąbrowski (2015: 461–464).
27   Litvina and Uspensky (2010: 165); Dąbrowski (2015: 533); Gyóni (2018: 196).
28   On the reign of Novgorod see Gyóni (2018: 197–203); Mstislav defended Novgorod against Vladimir–Suzdal's vigorous attempt to expand; and he was the first to establish a contractual relationship with the Novgorod community. See: Gyóni (2018: 197–201).

He captured the castle of Halych and seized the territory of Galicia.[29] In early 1223, he embraced the request of his father-in-law, Kotian, who asked for help in the fight of the Cumans against the Mongols. His arguments were accepted and supported by both the princes of Kiev and Chernigov. Deploying the full force of the princes of southern Rus', they embarked on a battle that ended in defeat along the river Kalka. Thanks to Mstislav the Bold, the NPL deals in great detail with the events of the Battle at river Kalka, which provide new information even compared to the meticulous GVC.[30]

Mikhail Vsevolodovich, became the prince of Chernigov (1223–1246)[31] shortly after the battle along the Kalka river, at which his predecessor had lost his life.[32] In the twelfth century the Principality of Chernigov, stretched along the rivers Seim and Desna, was defenceless towards the steppe.[33] It is no coincidence that members of the local clan were already turning to the west in the early thirteenth century, trying to hold on to one of the principalities. An example of this is the attempt by the Igorevich family in the first decade of the thirteenth century to hold on to Galicia.[34] Mikhail, the new prince of 1223, tried to get a role in Novgorod from Chernigov. In the conflict between Novgorod and Vladimir–Suzdal, Mikhail's person represented a compromise: in 1225/26 he became the prince of Novgorod. His reign did not last long. Mikhail was in Novgorod again in 1228 but did not leave Chernigov permanently; his young son, Rostislav, represented him in Novgorod. Afterwards, neither Mikhail nor his son showed interest in Novgorod; they tried to seize *volost'* in Galicia in the South-Western part of Rus' and occupy Kiev. For both, they battled with Daniel Romanovich, and their struggle was ended by the Mongol campaigns. Mikhail tried to negotiate with the Mongols, but the visit to Sarai cost him his life. Daniel's and Mikhail's struggle was briefly reported by the Novgorod chronicler. Mikhail's Mongolian "adventure" was only recorded by the *Commissionny spisok* of the NPL.[35] This passage is undoubtedly a later insertion and cannot be explained by Mikhail's earlier presence in Novgorod, only by his martyrdom.

29   Font (2021: 185–190).
30   Font (2018: 136–141).
31   Rapov (1977: 123–124).
32   PSRL II, cols. 744–745; ChronikNov I. (1971: 63).
33   Zaytsev (2009); Kovács (2014: 126–133).
34   PSRL II, cols. 719–720; Font (2021: 169–170).
35   Nikitin (2011: 240–243).

Conclusion

The NPL's news coverage of the southern regions of Rus' highlights Novgorod's declining interest in what is happening in the southern regions. The secession from the centre of Kiev was the result of a process that took place in the twelfth century. After the expulsion of the prince sent there in 1136, tax payment continued, and occasionally Novgorodians appeared as part of the Rus' army. After 1169, Novgorod was more interested in Vladimir–Suzdal than Rus' in the south, as this was seen as the greater threat. During the decades of the reign of Mstislav Vladimirovich's the Great (Veliky), his descendants were in the focus until the end of the twelfth century. From the 1170s onwards, only those who played a role in the life of Novgorod itself received much attention. From the last third of the twelfth century, neither Kiev nor members of the reigning Chernigov clan were important to Novgorod. In the thirteenth century, the importance of Galicia only mattered if it concerned the efforts of Mstislav Mstislavich regarding Novgorod. Interestingly, neither Galicia's nor Volhynia's the battles with the Lithuanians are covered. Presumably, they were confronted with different Lithuanian clans. The unification of the Lithuanian tribes did not take place until the fourteenth century, by which time Galicia had ceased to be an independent political force in the region.

Translated by Alexandra Hatter

Appendix

TABLE 9.1   Events Recorded in the NPL about the Southern Regions—Twelfth century

Years	Events	NPL text editions		Kievan Chronicle (KC) PSRL II. cols. 285–715.
		ChronikNov (1971) (Synodalny)	Nikitin (2011) Synodalny and Commiss.	
6653 (1145/46)	All of Russia marched against Galicia [...] Help arrived to the Kievans even from Novgorod (1146)	27.	76.	cols. 314–316. (6652=1144) cols. 319–320. (6654=1146)
6654 (1146/47)	After the death of Vsevolod Olgovich (1146) Iziaslav Mstislavich became the Grand Prince of Kiev (1146) Igor Olgovich was killed (1146)	28.	77.	col. 321. (1146) col. 327. (1146) cols. 326–327. (mention: col. 355)

TABLE 9.1   Events Recorded in the NPL about the Southern Regions—Twelfth century (*cont.*)

| Years | Events | NPL text editions | | Kievan Chronicle (KC) PSRL II. cols. 285–715. |
		ChronikNov (1971) (Synodalny)	Nikitin (2011) Synodalny and Commiss.	
6656 (1148/49)	Iziaslav marched against Rostov, and the Novgorodians also took part in the campaign (1148)	28.	77–78.	cols. 368–369. (1148)
6657 (1149/50)	The bishop of Novgorod, Niphont, was imprisoned in Kiev Yury Dolgoruky marched on Kiev and released the bishop	28.	78.	col. 383. Occupation of Kiev: Aug 23, 1149
6659 (1151/52)	Iziaslav Mstislavich defeats Yury Dolgoruky (July 17, 1151)	28.	79.	cols. 433–441. (1151, but without an exact date)
6662 (1154/55)	April 17, 1154 Rostislav Mstislavich was staying in Novgorod On November 14, 1154, Iziaslav Mstislavich died	29.	79–80.	Rostislav is only mentioned regarding his short rule of Kiev (cols. 470–471.) After the death of Iziaslav (col. 469.)
6663 (1155/56)	On Holy Week, Yury Dolgoruky marched on Kiev	29.	80.	cols. 477–478. (1155, but without an exact date)
6666 (1158/59)	Mstislav Iziaslavich banished Iziaslav Davidovich from Kiev	30.	82.	cols. 489–490.
6667 (1159/60)	Rostislav Mstislavich began to rule in Kiev	30.	82.	col. 504.
6669 (1161/62)	Rostislav Mstislavich agrees with Andrei Yurievich of Vladimir that the grandson of the latter will become the Prince of Novgorod	31.	83.	col. 511.
6674 (1166/67)	Rostislav Mstislavich died on the road from Novgorod to Kiev	32.	84.	Rostislav in Novgorod cols. 528–530.; Death (1169) cols. 531–532.
6675 (1167/68)	Mstislav Iziaslavich became the Grand Duke of Kiev	32.	84.	cols. 535. (1169)
6676 (1168/69)	April 14, 1168 Roman Mstislavich arrived in Novgorod and from there he went to Volhynia	33.	86.	This news is not included here.

TABLE 9.1   Events Recorded in the NPL about the Southern Regions—Twelfth century (*cont.*)

| Years | Events | NPL text editions | | Kievan Chronicle (KC) PSRL II. cols. 285–715. |
		ChronikNov (1971) (Synodalny)	Nikitin (2011) Synodalny and Commiss.	
6688/6689 (1180/1182)	Son of Sviatoslav Vsevolodovich, Vladimir invited to Novgorod, next year he was expelled	36–37.	92–93.	Only about connection between Sviatoslav and Vsevolod Yurievich

TABLE 9.2   Events Recorded in the NPL about the Southern Regions—Thirteenth century

| Years | Events | NPL text editions | | Galician-Volhynian Chronicle (GVC) PSRL II. cols. 715–938. |
		ChronikNov (1971) Synodalny	Nikitin (2011) Synodalny and Commiss.	
6711 (1203/04)	The Cumans led a campaign against Kiev (January 1, 1204) [followed by a counterattack by the Russian princes: Rurik Rostislavich, Roman Mstislavich and Mstislav Mstislavich]	45.	108. [only in Commiss.]	This news is not included here.
6718 (1210/11)	Mstislav Mstislavich arrived in Novgorod (1210)	52.	112.	This news is not included here.
6723 (1215/16)	Mstislav Mstislavich left for Kiev of his own will (1215) and then returned	53.	116.	This news is not included here.
6725 (1217/18)	Mstislav Mstislavich went to Kiev, leaving his wife and son in Novgorod	57.	121.	col. 736.
6727 (1219/20)	Mstislav Mstislavich marched into Halych and captured the Hungarian prince and his wife	59.	126.	cols. 737–738. (1219)
6732 (1224/25)	Battle along Kalka, in which the army of the Russian princes and the Cumans were defeated by the Mongols (May 31, 1223)	61–63.	130–133.	cols. 740–745.
6737 (1229/30)	Mikhail of Chernigov became the Prince of Novgorod, leaving his son Rostislav there in his place	68–70.	140–141.	This news is not included here.
6739 (1231/32)	The Novgorodians fought against Chernigov	71.	146.	This news is not included here.

TABLE 9.2   Events Recorded in the NPL about the Southern Regions—Thirteenth century (*cont.*)

| Years | Events | NPL text editions | | Galician-Volhynian Chronicle (GVC) PSRL II. cols. 715–938. |
		ChronikNov (1971) Synodalny	Nikitin (2011) Synodalny and Commiss.	
6743 (1235/36)	Daniil Romanovich of Halych and Mikhail Vsevolodovich of Chernigov fought for Halych and Kiev	73–74.	150.	col. 772. (6742 = 1234/35) cols. 774–775. (1235/36)
6753 (1245/46)	Mikhail of Chernigov died a martyr's death in the court of the Mongol Khan	This news is not included here.	only in Commissionny 240–243.	col. 795.

Bibliography

Primary Sources—Editions

ChronicleNov I. (1914). = *The Chronicle of Novgorod 1016–1471.* (1914) transl. Robert Michell. London: Offices of the Society.

ChronikNov I. (1971). = *Die erste Novgoroder Chronik nach ihrer ältesten Redaktion. Synodalhandschrift 1016–1333/1352.* Edition des altrussischen textes und Faksimile der Handschrift im Nachdruck. hrsg. von Dietze, Joachim. München: Sagner.

MPH KHW (2017). = *Kronika Halicko-Wołyńska (Kronika Romanowiczów).* wyd. wstęp i propisami Dąbrowski, Dariusz and Jusupović, Adrian. przy współpracy Jurjewa, Irina and Majorow, Aleksandr and Vilkul, Tatiana. Kraków and Warszawa: PAU and Institut Historii PAN. (Monumenta Poloniae Historica. Nova Series. XVI)

Nikitin, Andrei (2006). = Никитин, Андрей Л. (2006). *Текстология русских летописей XI- начала XIV вв.* вып. 1: *Киево-Печерское летописание до 1112 г.* Москва: Минувшее

Nikitin, Andrei (2011). = Никитин, Андрей Л. (2011). *Текстология русских летописей XI- начала XIV вв.* вып. 4: *Новгородское летописание XII—первой половины XIV в.* Москва: Минувшее

NPL (1950) = *Новгородская Первая летопись старшего и младшего изводов.* ред. Насонов, Арсений Н. Москва и Ленинград: Академия наук СССР.

PSRL I. = *Лаврентьевская летопись.* Полное собрание русских летописей. т. I. изд. Клосс, Борис М. Москва: Языки славянской культуры, 2001. (2nd)

PSRL II. = *Ипатьевская летопись.* Полное собрание русских летописей. т. II. изд. Клосс, Борис М. Москва: Языки славянской культуры, 2001. (2nd)

PSRL III. = *Новгородская Первая летопись старшего и младшего изводов.* Полное собрание русских летописей. т. III. изд. Клосс, Борис М. Москва: Языки славянской культуры, 2000. (2nd)

Secondary Sources

Bobrov, Alexandr (2001). = Бобров, Александр Г. (2001). *Новгородские летописи XV века.* Санкт-Петербург: Дмитрий Буланин.

Dąbrowski, Dariusz (2015). = Домбровский, Дариуш (2015). *Генеалогия Мстиславичей: Первые поколения (до начала XIV в.).* Санкт-Петербург: Дмитрий Буланин.

Dimnik, Martin (1981). *Mikhail, Prince of Chernigov and Grand Prince of Kiev 1224–1246.* Toronto: Pontifical Institute of Mediaeval Studies.

Dimnik, Martin (2016). *Power Politics in Kievan Rus': Vladimir Monomakh and His Dynasty (1054–1246).* Toronto: Pontifical Institute of Mediaeval Studies.

EMC = *Encyclopedia of Medieval Chronicle* (2010). Ed. Dunphy, Graeme. I–II. Leiden–Boston: Brill.

Fennell, John (1995). *A History of Russian Church to 1448.* London and New York: Longman.

Font, Márta (2005). 'Old-Russian Principalities and their Nomadic Neighbours: Stereotypes of Chronicles and Diplomatic Practice of the Princes.' *Acta Orientalia Academiae Scientiarum Hungaricae* 48 (3): 267–276.

Font, Márta (2016). 'Die Chronistik der Ostslawen.' *Handbuch Chroniken des Mittelalters.* hrsg. von Wolf, Gerhard and Ott, Norbert H. Berlin and Boston: De Gruyter. 805–835.

Font, Márta (2018). 'A Kalka menti csata (1223).' Font, Márta (2018). *Dinasztikus érdekek nyomában: Árpádok, Piastok, Rurikok az európai politikában.* Pécs: Kronosz. 121–143.

Font, Márta (2021). *The Kings of the House of Árpád and the Rurikid Princes.* Budapest: Research Centre for the Humanities.

Froyanov, Igor Ya. (1992) = Фроянов, Игорь Я. (1992). *Мятежный Новгород.* Санкт-Петербург: Изд. С-Петербургского Университета.

Gyóni, Gábor (2018). *A középkori Novgorod politikatörténete.* Budapest: Russica Pannonicana. (Ruszisztikai Könyvek XLVI)

Kovács, Szilvia (2014). *A kunok története a mongol hódításig.* Budapest: Balassi. (Magyar Őstörténeti Könyvtár 29)

Lenhoff, Gail (1989). *The Martyred Princes Boris and Gleb: A Socio-Cultural Study of Cult and Text.* Columbus: Slavica.

LexMA = *Lexicon des Mittelalters* (2003). Bände I–IX. Red. Avella-Widhalm, Gloria et al. München: DTV Verlag.

Likhachev, Dmitry S. (1947) = Лихачев, Дмитрий С. (1947). *Русские летописи и их культурно-историческое значение.* Москва и Ленинград: Академия наук СССР.

Litvina, Anna F. and Uspensky, Fedor B. (2006). = Литвина, Анна Ф. Успенский, Федор

Б. (2006). *Выбор имени у русских князей в X–XVI вв.: Династическая история сквозь призму антропонимики*. Москва: Языки славянской культуры.

Litvina, Anna F. and Uspensky, Fedor B. (2010). = Литвина, Анна Ф. Успенский, Федор Б. (2010). *Траектории традиции*. Москва: Языки славянской культуры.

Noonan, Thomas S. (1987). 'The Monetary History of Rus' in Soviet Historiography.' *Harvard Ukrainian Studies* 9 (3–4): 384–443.

Rapov, Oleg (1977). = Рапов, Олег М. (1977). *Княжеские владения на Руси в X—первой половине XIII вв.* Москва: Московский университет.

Yanin, Vladimir (1981). = Янин, Владимир Л. (1981). 'К вопросу о роли Синодального списка Новгородской I летописи в русском летописании XV в.' *Летописи и хроники 1980 г.: В.Н.Татищев и изучение русского летописания.* ред. Рыбаков, Б.А. и другие. Москва: Наука. 153–181.

Zaytsev, Alexei (2009) = Зайцев, Алексей К. (2009). *Черниговское княжество X–XIII вв.* Москва: Квадрига.

10

English Translation of John Strecche's Chronicle for the Reign of Henry IV

Chris Given-Wilson

Abstract

Book Five of the 'History of the Kings of England' by John Strecche was written in the early 1420s, probably at Kenilworth Priory in Warwickshire, and covers the reigns of Henry IV of England (1399–1413) and his son and successor, Henry V (1413–1422). The portion of the text covering Henry V's reign is well known and much used, having been edited in full more than a century ago and recently also published in translation, but the portion on Henry IV's reign has never been printed either in its original Latin or in translation. The main aim of this article is to provide a translation of the text, because, as I hope to demonstrate with both the text itself and my introduction, Strecche's account of Henry IV's rule contains much of interest to scholars of early fifteenth-century England and he presents a fascinating portrait of the king's character and final illness.

Book Five of John Strecche's *Historia regum Anglie* (*HRA*), the unique manuscript of which is in Additional MS 35,295 in the British Library, London, and was first described in detail by Kingsford in 1913, falls into two unequal parts: the reign of Henry IV (fols 262^r–265^r) and the reign of Henry V (fols 265^r–279^v). The Henry V section was edited and printed in its entirety by Frank Taylor in 1932, has been used extensively by historians of his reign since then, and has recently been translated by Geoffrey Hilton.[1] However, the former part, although occasionally used by historians of Henry IV's reign, has never been published. The principal purpose of this article is to remedy that deficiency. Ideally, a previously unpublished medieval text should be presented in its original language (in this case, Latin), preferably with accompanying translation, but the constraint of a strict word-limit has precluded that, so it seemed on balance more useful to provide a translation, although for some significant or potentially ambiguous passages, the original Latin is given in brackets.

---

1 Kingsford (1913: 39–43); Taylor (1932: 137–187); Hilton (2014).

Little is known of Strecche. He was an Augustinian canon of St Mary's priory at Kenilworth (Warwickshire) and was made prior of its dependent cell at Brooke (Rutland) in 1407. He resigned this post in 1425, but whether he returned to Kenilworth, when he died, or indeed when he was born, is unknown. Apart from his chronicle, he wrote or copied a number of works on poetry, on the Augustinian order and on ancient history and fables. He was certainly keen that his authorship of the HRA should not be forgotten, for he revealed it via acrostics, monograms (IS) and a colophon on fol. 246ᵛ declaring that 'the name of the compiler of this work is contained in the capital letters of the chapters of the said three books immediately preceding'—i.e. the first three books of HRA. The acrostics referred to read *Iohannes Strecche Canonicus*.[2]

Following a brief prologue and a poem on the Fall of Troy, Additional MS 35,295 contains three main items: firstly (fols 6ʳ–136ᵛ), a copy of the *Historia Destructionis Troiae* ('History of the Destruction of Troy') by the thirteenth-century Sicilian poet Guido delle Colonne; secondly (fols 137ʳ–232ᵛ), the history of the British kingdom, beginning with Brutus and ultimately derived from Geoffrey of Monmouth; thirdly (fols 233ʳ–279ᵛ), the five books of the HRA, which take the story from the arrival of the Saxons through the Saxon, Danish, Norman and subsequent kings, ending in 1422. The manuscript was compiled—by Strecche himself, apparently—early in the reign of Henry VI.

It was also at this time, in the early or mid 1420s, that Strecche wrote the HRA, apparently at the request of Thomas Kidderminster, prior of Kenilworth (1403–1439).[3] Largely based on the *Polychronicon* of Ranulf Higden, it has no value as an independent source for English history until the end of the fourteenth century, although it is of undoubted value for the history of Kenilworth priory, notices of which are frequently inserted in the narrative.[4] From 1399 onwards, however, Strecche was writing of events he had witnessed, on which he had opinions and for which he depended on no other known source. Not surprisingly, historians have focussed very largely on what he wrote about Henry V, whom he admired without reservation and about whose reign he preserved important and original details. Yet this is also the case, albeit to a lesser degree, for what he said about Henry IV.

That Strecche admired Henry IV is something he makes clear from the start: in particular, he admired the king's military triumphs, his crusading fervour

---

2 Taylor (1932: 137 n. 10); Gransden (1982: 405–408); Kingsford printed the colophon (1913: 40 n. 1).

3 Hilton (2014: 63).

4 Book Four of the HRA covers the kings of England from 1066 to 1399. For Strecche and Kenilworth, see Hilton (2003: 23–36).

and his musical and scholarly interests.[5] Strecche's subsequent statement that Henry's people were 'so moved by the sight of him' that images of his face were set up at numerous locations around the kingdom is a fascinating and, for a medieval monarch, unique claim, more suggestive of the personality cult of a modern dictator, although it is neither corroborated nor verifiable. However, he also pointed out that by failing to keep the promises he made at the beginning of his reign, Henry subsequently 'lost the love of many ordinary people'.

Following these introductory remarks about the king, Strecche's narrative of the reign concentrates largely on the familiar, memorable events, as one might expect from someone writing a decade or more after the king's death: the Epiphany Rising of January 1400; the battle of Shrewsbury in 1403 and the subsequent fate of the Percy family; the 1404 parliament at Coventry; the rising of Archbishop Scrope and the earl of Nottingham in the summer of 1405; the simultaneous and subsequent (1408) rebellions of the earl of Northumberland and Thomas Lord Bardolf; the creation of the king's son Thomas as duke of Clarence; the revolt of Wales under Owain Glyndwr, and Owain's fate; and Henry IV's creeping and ultimately debilitating illness. The chronicle ends with the last parliament of the reign (February 1413), a graphic description of the king's body at the time of his death, and his dying advice to his son.

Strecche makes no attempt to provide a consecutive register of the events of Henry IV's reign, merely a few highlights (and lowlights). Parliaments and foreign affairs are almost completely ignored. The value of his account lies rather in the occasional details and motivational perceptions which he includes, such as the fact that 'some people say' that the Welsh rebelled because of the killing of Richard II 'who greatly pleased the Welsh', or that Henry failed to keep his promises because he was 'led astray by the advice of greedy men'. Also interesting are his comment that during the 1404 parliament 'many people secretly plotted many things against the king' and that this led to the 1405 risings; his unambiguous account of Prince John's duplicitous entrapment of Scrope and Nottingham; his description of the citizens of York emerging 'almost naked in linen cloths' to beg the king's pardon and throw the blame on the archbishop, and of Scrope's beheading 'beneath a certain windmill';[6] and his claim that Henry gave the citizens of Berwick enough wood to rebuild their town. Apart from his character portrait of Henry IV, already discussed, two of Strec-

---

5   Strecche's description of Henry as 'brilliant at music' (see below) is supported by an Italian chronicler who met him or heard about him when he visited Treviso on return from the Holy Land in April 1393 and described him as 'learned in many things, especially mathematics and music': Muratori (1731: 792–793). My thanks to Professor Michael Bennett for this reference.
6   Both of these claims are corroborated by other sources: Given-Wilson (2016: 269 and Plate 10).

che's most interesting passages are his account of the king's blessing of his son Thomas when he created him duke of Clarence, which, like Isaac's blessing of Jacob, favoured the second son over the first-born, although Strecche makes the point by allusion rather than directly; and his description of the king's death, his 46-year-old body dreadfully wasted by disease but his mind still focussed on the prospect of revisiting the Holy Land and the future of his dynasty.[7]

Like many chroniclers, Strecche also liked to mention events in his native county,[8] and his chronicle, apparently compiled as a teaching aid for the Kenilworth canons, was barely known outside Warwickshire. The only other chronicler known to have used it was John Rous (*d.* 1491), chaplain of Guy's Cliff (Warwick). Following this it remained almost entirely unknown until purchased by the British Museum in the late nineteenth century as part of the Ashburnham House Library manuscript collection and, shortly afterwards, the publication of Kingsford's assessment of the text.

Appendix

London, *British Library*, Additional MS 35,295, fols 262ʳ–265ʳ. (Headings and marginals in red ink in the manuscript are given in italics.)

Here begins the fifth book of this work, concerning King Henry IV, the son of John   fol. 262ʳ
of Gaunt, duke of Lancaster, who following his banishment (deportacione), *his father having died, returning to England and reclaiming* (vendicans) *his inheritance, was raised up to be king of England after King Richard.*

Chapter One: The noble prince Henry duke of Lancaster, once he had returned from exile to England, was, with the greatest enthusiasm of the inhabitants of the realm (*a regnicolis amore ferventissimo*) on account of his reputation for probity and his remarkable military accomplishments, anointed and crowned as king of England on 13 October, the feast of St Edward, king and confessor, by Thomas Arundel archbishop of Canterbury at Westminster, as already noted in the last chapter of the previous book.[9] This King Henry was elegantly built, of great strength, a vigorous knight, brave in arms, wise and circumspect

---

7   Cf. Adam Usk's similarly gruesome account of Henry's disease-ridden body: Given-Wilson (1997: 242).

8   His first account of the Epiphany Rising at the end of Book Four (fols 261ʳ–261ᵛ) says as much about the fate of the Warwickshire knight William Bagot as all the conspirators combined.

9   Strecche briefly mentioned Henry's coronation at the end of Book Four.

in his youthful behaviour (*actu tirocinii*), always fortunate in battle, successful in his deeds and gloriously victorious everywhere, brilliant at music and marvellously learned, especially in ethics (*in musica micans et mirabilis litterature et maxime in morali*). And all the people of the realm were so moved (*affectuosus*) by the sight of him that in many towns his face, a sweet sight to his friends, a fearsome one to his enemies, was painted and fashioned in prominent places so that people could always gaze at him and observe his countenance and features (*pingeretur et formeretur in locis spectabilibus ut sic quod ad eum sepius posset populus intueri et eius formam faciei vultumque videre*). When he was an earl, he undertook warlike feats in far off lands such as Lithuania, where as a youth he earned praise in his first campaign against unbelievers by terrifying and comprehensively triumphing against the Turks, for love of the cross of Our Saviour (*ob amorem crucifixi nostri salvatoris*). A leader of many, never defeated, he had few equals.

Soon after his coronation, this King Henry recalled Thomas earl of Warwick, who had been banished to the Isle of Man, to his home and restored and reinstated him to his former status. He also recalled to his lands the son of Richard earl of Arundel, as well as bringing the son of his uncle Thomas of Woodstock, former duke of Gloucester, from exile in Ireland, but on his arrival at Beaumaris he was struck down by disease (*morbo captus*), died and was buried. This king also promised in his early days to abolish many things which had previously been burdensome to his people and oppressive to those who dwelt in the realm, but, led astray by the advice of greedy men (*cupidorum consilio ductus*), he later failed to fulfil his promises, whereby he lost the love of many ordinary people (*unde magnam partem amoris perdidit popularis*).

Chapter Two: In the first year of his reign, as noted above, certain evil men (*malivoli*) rose up against this king, such as the earl of Kent, the earl of Salisbury, and John Holand, duke of Exeter. For what happened to them, and how, see above, the last chapter of the fourth book.[10] Others also rebelled against the king after the feast of the Epiphany in the same year, some from the south and some from the north, such as Lord Bernard Brocas from the south and Lord Ralph de Lumley from the north, but all of these men and their accomplices were executed at Oxford, some being beheaded in Oxford castle, others hanged until dead on gallows set up on a fine hill close to Oxford (*in bello monte iuxta Oxon'*).

---

10   The conclusion to Richard II's reign (fols 261^r–261^v) includes a preliminary account of the Epiphany Rising.

When he was earl of Derby, this King Henry IV, at the bidding (*iniuncto*) of his father John | duke of Lancaster, married the noble Mary, daughter of the earl of Hereford, by whom he fathered four illustrious (*inclitos*) sons, namely, Henry the first-born, later prince of the Welsh, Lord Thomas duke of Clarence, Lord John duke of Bedford, and Lord Humphrey duke of Gloucester; also two daughters, namely Blanche and Philippa, one of whom married the emperor and the other married the king of the Danes. However, their mother Mary died in childbirth at Peterborough, and she was respectfully (*honeste*) buried in the Newark (*Novo Opere*) at Leicester.

fol. 262ᵛ

[*The remainder of fol. 262ᵛ and most of fol. 263ʳ recount the history of Kenilworth Priory under prior Thomas Merston (1384–1400) and prior Walter Brayle (July 1400–January 1403). Brayle resigned in 1403 and was succeeded by Thomas Kidderminster, formerly prior of Brooke (Rutland), a dependent cell of Kenilworth.*][11]

Chapter Four [sic]: *How King Henry IV married Queen Joan.*
    In the third year of his reign, about the feast of the Purification of the Blessed Mary [2 February], King Henry IV married Joan, the widow of the duke of Brittany (*Britannie Minoris*) and daughter of the king of Navarre, who soon after this was crowned queen in London and was endowed (*dotata*) with ten thousand [marks] of annual rent in England.[12]

fol. 263ʳ

    The Battle of Shrewsbury: Also, in the fourth year of his reign, King Henry fought a lethal battle (*bellum habuit letale*) with Henry Percy, son of the earl of Northumberland, on the River Severn close to Shrewsbury. This Henry rose up against King Henry with a great army of northerners (*borialum*) as well as men from the county of Chester and joined battle, in which battle eleven thousand Englishmen on both sides (*ex utraque parte*) died. On one side, that of the king |, died the noble earl of Stafford; on the other side, Henry Percy met his fate, along with his uncle Thomas Percy, then earl of Worcester, who was beheaded. Also in this battle Henry prince of Wales, first-born son and successor (*primogenitus serie regens*) of King Henry IV, when he was standing in the very thick of the battle (*maximum pondus belli*), was gravely wounded in the face by an arrow, and after the battle he came with his wounds (*cum suis lesis*) to Kenilworth castle, where he was cured by the skill of a physician (*per artem medicine*). Also in this battle the earl of Douglas from Scotland was taken prisoner; he was the captive of Henry Percy, having been captured in the previous

fol. 263ᵛ

---

11   Kidderminster remained prior of Kenilworth until 1439.
12   Henry married Joan of Navarre on 7 February 1403 (his fourth regnal year).

year by the aforesaid Henry Percy at Homildon Hill (*ad montem de Humbel-don*), at the same time as five hundred Scots were captured or killed or fled or surrendered from the time of this battle or date (*bello sive dato*).

King Henry sent accusingly (*concr[im]inie*) for Henry, earl of Northumber-land, the father of Henry Percy, and imprisoned him for some time in a certain tower at Baginton near Coventry. And then King Henry granted and assigned the keeping of the lands of the said earl, along with part of the north of England (*cum parte boriali Anglie*), to his son Lord John. However, within six months King Henry released the said earl from custody on his faith (*sub sua fide*) and allowed him to go free.

The Coventry Parliament: Soon after this, around the feast of St Denis [9 October] in the year of the Incarnation of the Lord 1405 and the sixth year of his reign,[13] King Henry held a parliament at Coventry, in which parliament many people secretly plotted many things against the king (*multi multa contra regem secretius conspiraverunt*), as a result of which in that same year, around the feast of Pentecost, Richard archbishop of York and the earl of Nottingham with other well-armed knights rose up in rebellion against the king and took the field near York. But Lord John the king's son, the governor of the northern parts (*borialum gubernator*), arrived quickly with his army and confronted the said arch-bishop and earl and cunningly spoke such words of peace and advice to them (*cum eisdem sub tali cautela et consilio tractavit in verbis pacificis*) that he per-suaded them to draw apart from the body of their army, and he detained their messengers with him. Then the aforesaid Lord John sent a messenger to the body of the army assuring them that everything had been peacefully resolved between them and that everyone should return in peace to his home. Hear-ing this, the army soon dispersed and went into the city of York. But when this news came to the ears of King Henry, he quickened his step and approached York with a great army. The citizens of that city, almost naked in linen cloths (*quasi nudi in lineis*), came out of the city to meet the king, prostrating them-selves before the king and miserably beseeching his grace and mercy, throwing all the blame wholly on the archbishop (*omnino culpam in archiepiscopum pen-itus retorquendo*). And once they had been received into the king's grace and restored to their possessions, the king forthwith ordered the aforesaid earl and archbishop to be adjudged to death as traitors. Then, when they had been judi-cially (*sententialiter*) condemned to death and led outside the walls of the city, they were both beheaded beneath a certain windmill (*sub quodam molendino*

---

13   The Coventry Parliament met from 6 October–14 November 1404.

ventrico) on 8 June in the year of the Incarnation of the Lord 1406 and the eighth year of King Henry IV.[14]

After this King Henry hastened without delay to Berwick, where the earl of Northumberland and Lord Richard[15] Bardolf, a baron, and many other knights were rebelling, but when they heard that the king was coming the said earl and baron fled with all their men to Scotland, taking with them the son of Henry | fol. 264ʳ Percy. And when the earl had left the town of Berwick, the Scots set fire to it, so when the king arrived he gave the citizens of the town enough wood from his forest there to rebuild it. And the king besieged and seized all the castles, lordships and fortifications belonging to the aforesaid earl and his son Henry Percy, such as Alnwick, Jedworth and Warkworth, as well as their other lands and possessions, and granted them to his son John and made him governor of all the northern parts. And all the rebels he found in these towns and castles, such as Baron Greystoke and many others, he promptly either pardoned or put to the sword (*gladio trucidavit*). And then the king returned to York.

Chapter Seven [sic]: *The earl of Northumberland.* In the ninth year of the reign of King Henry IV, the year of the Incarnation of the Lord 1408, the afore-mentioned earl of Northumberland, accompanied by [Thomas] Bardolf, came well-armed from Scotland into England, believing the country to be on his side so that it would rise up with him against the king (*putans patriam sibi favore sic cum eo contra regem insurgere*). But when the sheriff of York heard of his arrival, he raised up the people of the country by virtue of his office (*vigore offi-cii sui*) and confronted the said earl and his rebels with a powerful force near Tadcaster, and he overcame the said earl in battle and promptly decapitated him, and he sent the earl's head to King Henry, who was then staying at Stony Stratford, hurrying northwards. He also captured [Thomas] Bardolf, who was mortally wounded in this battle and soon drew his last breath (*spirum exha-lavit*). The aforesaid sheriff also killed many of these rebels, put some to flight, and imprisoned others to await the king's mercy.

In the tenth year of his reign and the year of the Incarnation of the Lord 1409,[16] this King Henry IV also made his son Thomas duke of Clarence, to whom he gave his paternal blessing and, by the same measure, confirmed all his pos-sessions to him and placed his other lords beneath him (*eidem modulo suo omnia bona sua stabilivit et eius dominos ceteros subiecit*), weeping and kissing and declaring, "Just as Isaac the patriarch in his old age blessed his son Jacob by paternal right (*effectu paternali*), so now I bless you, and I pronounce you the

---

14   *Recte* 1405, Henry's seventh year.
15   *Recte* Thomas.
16   *Recte* July 1412, Henry's thirteenth year.

favoured one (*faustum*), and fortunate in war". And concerning this most noble Thomas, prince and most fortunate in war, and concerning his death, more is said below in the Life of Henry V which follows this, in the chapter which begins thus: 'All these (*Hiis omnibus*)'.[17]

Chapter Eight: Concerning the Welsh rebel Owain Glyndwr: It should be noted here that throughout the time (*omnibus diebus*) of King Henry IV a certain Welsh esquire (*armiger Wallicus*), Owain Glyndwr, rose up and rebelled against the king in North Wales with all the Welsh people, and he captured and razed the king's coastal castles (*castella maritima*) in Wales. And some people say that the reason for this (*et hec causa fuit, ut quidam dicunt*) was because of the death of Richard former king of England, who greatly pleased the Welsh (*qui Wallicis multum placuit*). So King Henry undertook numerous military campaigns against this Owain, who repeatedly fled from place to place so that, by hiding in the mountains, nowhere did he fall into the hands of the king, who daily (*de die in die*) captured and killed numerous Welshmen at that time, includ-

fol. 264ᵛ ing the son of Owain | whom he imprisoned in the Tower of London, where he died. Rhys ap Tudor and Rhys Dhu, along with many others who supported him, were also captured, drawn and hanged by the king at various times. However, Owain, a wary warrior, always kept house in the open (*cautus belliger, sub divo semper larem fovit*) with his Welshmen, hiding in the mountains so that he never appeared publicly to the king's men, and although constantly harried, nowhere could he be captured. In the eleventh and twelfth years of his reign, this King Henry IV became so debilitated by bodily infirmity (*in tantum madit corporis infirmitatem*) that he could scarcely undertake further military operations, so his body was committed to the care of doctors (*medicorum cura fuerat comissus*).

How Prince Henry pursued Owain Glyndwr: However, the noble Henry, prince of the Welsh, the first-born son of King Henry IV, pursued the aforesaid Owain in those parts, both in the mountains and in the forests, so that there was nowhere in all Wales that he could find a place to rest (*quod in tota Wallia quiescendi locum non invenit*). And thus the aforesaid prince seized and killed and captured numerous Welshmen every day. But in about the last year of the reign of King Henry IV, the said Owain, without violence (*sine conflictu*), eventually ended his life and died and was buried, whereupon, following this, all the Welsh during the time of King Henry V maintained a firm peace (*pacem firmam*) and

---

17   Chapter 26 of Book Five, which relates Clarence's death in 1421, begins 'Hiis omnibus': Taylor (1932: 184).

willingly submitted themselves to the rule of the king and his crown in all things (*et regis regimini et eius corone se libenter in omnibus subdiderunt*).

The Death of Henry IV: King Henry, having suffered grievously for a long time with disease, as mentioned above, eventually, in the fourteenth and final year of his reign and the year of the Incarnation of the Lord 1413, held a great parliament at Westminster in which the king appeared publicly before all the people, saying, "If God wills it and my life permits, I am the person who shall restore the Holy Cross into the hands of Christians, and to arrange for this to be accomplished I need assistance. Will you provide it (*apponere velitis*)?" And having said this he secured in parliament for his proposed expedition one tenth from the clergy and one fifteenth from the people, and then he retired. Soon after this, however, while this parliament was continuing, when he was lying in a certain chamber within the abbey of Westminster which has long been called Jerusalem (*infra abbathiam Westmonasterii in camera quadam iacens que ab antiquo Ierusalem vocabatur*), understanding and sensing the inevitability of approaching death, he sent for his first-born son and heir Henry prince of Wales, and he showed him his body, by then dreadfully shrunken and wasted by disease, with flesh eaten away and skin quivering, so that his intestines and all the other interior parts of his body were openly visible, except that his limbs had been carefully bandaged and wrapped in linen cloths (*corpus suum ex nimia tunc infirmitate decoctum et tabefactum, consumptis carnibus et cute micanto, quod eius viscera et omnia alia interiora sui corporis visum fuerant patefacta, nisi quod in pannis lineis fota fuerant eius membra ligata et involuta*). And the king said to his son: "See, son, your father's body, which once was tall and strong and feared by many and most noble, but now, son, behold, is like the food given to worms, for I am approaching death. Fear God, my son, and observe his commandments; embellish and honour his church; cherish your brothers; pay my debts; rule the people; judge justly; conduct yourself in all things according to God. For this kingdom, in which we have striven greatly, I leave to you, together with all my earthly goods, with the grace and benevolence of Our Saviour and with my everlasting blessing. For I hope to see God in the land of the living, and I await my death here under my God's most gentle mercy (*nam ego spero Deum videre in viventium terra, et hic ego mortem prestolor sub Dei mei mitissima misericordia*)".

Having said which and made his farewells to all, on the thirteenth kalends of April, the feast of St Cuthbert, he yielded up his life into the hands of the Saviour (*spem suum in manus reddidit Salvatoris*).[18] He ruled for thirteen years

---

18   Henry died at Westminster on 20 March 1413.

and five months and two weeks and three days; and he was honourably (*honorifice*) buried in Canterbury cathedral. May God take his soul. Amen.

Bibliography

Primary Sources—Manuscripts
London
British Library
Additional MS 35,295

Secondary Sources

Given-Wilson, Chris (1997). *The Chronicle of Adam Usk 1377–1421*. Oxford: Oxford Medieval Texts.

Given-Wilson, Chris (2016). *Henry IV*. New Haven and London: Yale English Monarchs.

Gransden, Antonia (1982). *Historical Writing in England 2: c. 1307 to the Early Sixteenth Century*. London: Routledge

Hilton, Geoffrey (2003). 'The Chronicle of John Strecche and its place in medieval historical records of England and Kenilworth Priory', *Bulletin of the John Rylands Library* 85: 23–36.

Hilton, Geoffrey (2014). *The Deeds of King Henry V told by John Strecche*: Kenilworth.

Kingsford, C.L. (1913). *English Historical Literature in the Fifteenth Century*: Oxford: Clarendon Press.

Muratori, L.A. (1731). 'Chronicon Tarvisinum', in *Rerum Italicarum Scriptores* XIX. Milan.

Taylor, Frank (1932). 'The Chronicle of John Strecche for the Reign of Henry V (1414–1422)', *Bulletin of the John Rylands Library* 16: 137–187.

11

Lost Polish Chronicle(s) in the Hungarian-Polish Chronicle

Ryszard Grzesik

Abstract

The *Hungarian-Polish Chronicle* is a narrative composed at the turn of the 1230s, probably in Slavonia at the court of Coloman, former king of Halich, and of his wife Salomea, the daughter of Leszek the White, duke of Cracow. It was based on three written sources: a *Hungarian Chronicle* (the lost *Gesta Ungarorum*), a *Vita sancti Stephani* (the *Life of Saint Stephen*, the shorter version of the *Legenda Hartviciana*), and a lost *Polish Chronicle* (the *Chronica Polonorum*). This paper argues that the latter was more specifically dedicated to the Polish-Hungarian relationships and written for Salomea, who was married to Coloman. In this work, we find traces of another narrative which describes the deeds of Bolesław II the Generous and which was written before 1076, the year of his coronation. The information presented in this lost eleventh-century narrative (the marriage of Adelaide with a Hungarian prince, the Polish legation for a crown, the description of the Polish-Hungarian border and the Polish involvement in the civil war in Hungary) was changed and falsified at the beginning of the thirteenth century in order to diminish the role of Bolesław, the murderer of St Stanislaus. These elements enriched the Polish historical tradition after the only manuscript of the *Hungarian-Polish Chronicle* was transported by Salomea to Poland.

In September 1988, I discussed the next stage of my studies with my tutor, Prof. Brygida Kürbis and she advised me to research the *Hungarian-Polish Chronicle*.[1] At that time, I knew nothing about this text, so I started to read the *Chronicle* as well as the studies devoted to it, and thus began a lifetime journey. I was very surprised when I read the *Chronicle* for the first time.

It was a vivid narration about the travelling Hungarians, who plundered several European countries from Lithuania to Scotia and from Dacia to Apulia.

---

1 In the 1950s and '60s, there was a plan for an edition of the Chronicle in Poland. According to Professor Piotr Węcowski, the manuscript was partially ready without commentaries. I do not know its fate. Węcowski (2021: 30–31).

Their leader Aquila was directed to Croatia by an angel when he planned to conquer Rome. The Hungarians avenged Casimir, prince of the Slavs and of the Croatians, and decided to settle in the territory of Slavonia, which they named Hungary. They created their own state there and married local women. Afterwards, Aquila gave lands to his barons, established the rule of succession to the throne, and died. Further, the narration concentrated on Yesse (Géza), the great grandson of Aquila, who was married to the princess Adelaide of Cracow, the sister of prince Mieszko. Adelaide converted her husband to Christianity and both spouses had visions: Yesse on the visit of the bishop of Prague, St Adalbert, and pregnant Adelaide on her son Stephen, who became the new hero of the Chronicle. In the following chapters, we read about the Hungarian-Polish rivalry for the crown after Pope Leo gave the crown, which was made for prince Mieszko, to the Hungarian envoy Astricus. This vivid scene with dialogues contains a negative description of the Poles as people who like forests more than vineyards, and were amateurs of drinking and hunting, which is rather surprising if we remember the way of life of medieval European elites. The chronicler then relates Stephen's coronation as well as the peaceful meeting of Stephen and Mieszko at the supposed Hungarian-Polish border, near Esztergom on the Danube. The next chapters deal with the holy life and death of St Stephen, an event underlined by the mention of the lamentations of his subjects.

The subsequent narration of the following years of Hungarian history can confuse any historian who knows the eleventh-century history of the country. We read that the dead king had three sons who escaped to Poland and sought refuge at the court of prince Bolesław, then eighteen years old, in order to flee their German mother-in-law and her brother Henry, who established a tyrannical rule in Hungary. After sixteen years, the three orphans asked Bolesław for help: the Polish ruler in turn asked his mother Dąbrówka for permission and then organized an expedition against Henry. The German prince was killed, as was the tutor of the Hungarian princes, the palatine Aba. Bolesław crowned Levente as king in Székesfehérvár, and elevated Levente's brothers Peter and Béla to the dignity of princes. Once the coronation was performed, the Polish ruler went hunting in his borough of Salis. Following the death of Levente, Bolesław crowned Peter and led a war expedition in Carinthia, Austria and Germany. After Peter's death, it was the turn of Béla to be crowned by his Polish ally. Finally the youngest of Béla's sons, Ladislas, married the daughter of Mstislav, the prince of Halich, and so became king of Hungary, being crowned with the consent of his brother Salomon.[2]

---

2   Chron., *passim*. The only one vernacular (Polish) translation of the Chronicle until the begin-

At the end of the nineteenth century, a new, shorter redaction of the *Chronicle* was published.[3] The biography of St Stephen was the main focus of this variant of the text. It presented an abbreviated version of Hungarian 'prehistory' with Attila as leader, mentioned the avenged king of Croatia as Trezimir (= Krešimir), and described the canonization and miracles of St Stephen instead of the political history of Hungary before St Ladislas.

At the time, I also studied the publications about the *Chronicle* and the various references to the work; most of them were written in the nineteenth century, when detailed philological studies were popular. Researchers had concentrated on the sources used by the chronicler and on the form of the archetype. Some scholars, inspired by legal history and studies of charters, sought to identify interpolations, which "polluted" the "clear" text of the *Chronicle*; some fragments, considered by one group of scholars to be interpolations, were appreciated as originals by others. These different studies enabled me to elaborate my own vision of the *Chronicle*, which I presented in my Ph.D. thesis. I concentrated on the philological comparison of the textual variants, but I also tried to analyse the ideological side of the narrative. I focussed on the Hungarian sources, which were for me a great discovery as well as a source of fascination. I compared the *Chronicle* with the text of the *Legenda Hartviciana*—the youngest and the longest *Life of St Stephen*, written before 1116 by bishop Hartvic. It was one of the three main written sources of the *Chronicle* as well as the basis for its narration about St Stephen. I compared several variants of the *Legenda* using the critical apparatus in Emma Bartoniek's edition: however, I could not confirm her observation that the text of the *Chronicle* was based on the variant preserved in two fifteenth-century manuscripts from Vienna and Munich. In my opinion, the basis was close to the archetype of the *Legenda Hartviciana*, albeit with several surprising omissions.[4] At the time of this research, I did not know an article by László N. Szelestei about a new manuscript of *Legenda Hartviciana* from the second half of the fourteenth century which contains an abbreviated text of the *Legenda*. The omissions are identical with the ones that can be observed in the *Hungarian-Polish Chronicle*, and the hypothesis of the author that this variant of the *Legenda* transmitted a text similar to the *Chronicle* confirms my observations.[5] I also noticed that the *Chronicle* belongs to the

ning of the 21st century: Kownacki (1823)—its language was already archaic at the time of its edition. About the *Chronicle* cf. Grzesik (2010a: 348–349).

3 Kętrzyński (1897: 365–373).
4 Grzesik (1999: 26–51); Legenda 374; Grzesik (2010c: 755–756). English translation: Hartvic (175–198).
5 Szelestei (1991: 1–19).

group of sources derived from the lost archetype of Hungarian chronicle writ-ing, the so-called *Gesta Ungarorum*.[6] I studied the Croatian tradition as well, concluding that the early version of the king Zvonimir tradition was used.[7] Now I think that the traces of the older Great-Moravian tradition were preserved in the Zvonimir story.[8] I determined the time of writing of the *Chronicle* at the turn of the thirties of the thirteenth century, because the story of Ladislas' marriage reflects the real marriage of prince Andrew, the son of king Andrew II, with a daughter of the ruler of Halich, Mstislav, before 1227. I also thought that the *Chronicle* was written in the Slavonian court of Coloman, the former king of Halich, and his wife, Salomea, the daughter of Leszek the White, prince of Cra-cow. It was probably Salomea who carried the *Chronicle* to Poland when she returned to her homeland after her husband's death in 1241.[9]

The relationship of the *Chronicle* with Polish medieval historiography is complicated. Some episodes were unknown earlier and appear in Polish sources only from the end of the thirteenth century. Our *Chronicle* was undoubtedly the source of the references to Adelaide in several Polish annals, as well as the basis of the description of the Polish-Hungarian rivalry for the crown in the Silesian chronicles and of the critical view of Poland in the St Stanislaus hagiography.[10]

Although I did not investigate the question of the possible use of a Polish written source by the chronicler at that time, the answer seems to be positive. The incipit of the *Chronicle* in the Zamoyski manuscript already suggests it: 'The Hungarian chronicle begins connected and mixed with the Polish chron-icle and with the Life of St Stephen'.[11] I tried to explain the presence of some Polish elements by knowledge of Polish oral tradition by the chronicler, but this hypothesis was rightfully critiqued by Wojciech Drelicharz. He took the view that there had to have been a Polish narrative source, standing maybe close to the lost Polish state annals, the so-called *Annales Regni Poloniae deperditi*.[12] I came to the same conclusion in a study published in volume 9 of *The Medieval Chronicle*. There, I attempted to show that a *Chronica Polonorum* was written about 1214 in Cracow for Salomea, who was married to Coloman. The story of Adelaide, the narration of the meeting of rulers on the common border and

---

6   Grzesik (2010b: 701–702).

7   Grzesik (1999: 51–91).

8   Homza (2009: 56); Homza and Rácová (2010: 104).

9   Grzesik (1999: 208–212).

10   Grzesik (1999: 93–129).

11   Chron., 9: 'Incipit Cronica Vngarorum iuncta et mixta cum cronicis polonorum et uita sancti Stephani.'

12   Drelicharz (2012: 101, 105 n. 30).

the deeds of Prince Bolesław could be derived from it. I saw the basis for the chronicle mainly in the Polish oral tradition about Bolesław II the Generous,[13] but how do we explain some anachronisms, such as the existence of *dambor-ouca* near Sieciech in the circle of Prince Bolesław? We must keep in mind that Sieciech was a palatine of Władysław Herman, the younger brother of Bolesław the Generous, who ruled Poland in the last two decades of the eleventh century, after the escape and death of Bolesław. Dąbrówka or Dobrawa was the Bohemian wife of the first historical ruler of Poland, Mieszko I, and the mother of Bolesław I the Brave. She died in 977, a hundred years before Sieciech's period of activity.[14] The mention of Dąbrówka could have been a conscious forgery of the *Chronica Polonorum*, whose author may have known that the real mother of Bolesław II the Generous was Dobroniega, not Dobrawa, but may have wanted to erase the person of the ruler and to suggest that it was another Bolesław, Bolesław I the Brave, who was the real hero of the Polish-Hungarian relationship.

Poland, and especially Cracow, for about 150 years lived in the shadows of a political tragedy which divided the political elites into two parties, namely the conflict between King Bolesław II the Generous and the bishop of Cracow, St Stanislaus. The result was the death of the bishop, a revolt of the subjects against the king, and the rule of Władysław Herman, his younger brother.[15] Gallus Anonymus, who worked at the court of Herman's son, Bolesław III the Wry-Mouthed, wrote about the conflict in a very laconic and careful manner. The bishop was presented as a traitor, but the king was also condemned by the chronicler.[16] During the twelfth century, the black legend of King Bolesław II was created.[17] The martyrdom and early canonization of the archbishop of Canterbury, Thomas Becket, was noticed in Cracow and gave a new impulse to the intensification of trials to proclaim Stanislaus a saint, which took place

---

13   Grzesik (2014: 189–203).

14   Chron., 63–64; Jasiński (1992: 61–64); Kurtyka (1996: 495–509).

15   Wojciechowski (2004: 173–231). This book was published in 1904 and determined the discussion on the conflict in Polish historiography of the twentieth century. Cf. Labuda (2000).

16   Gallus I 27, 96–98: 'Qualiter autem rex Bolezlauus de Polonia sit eiectus longum existit enarrare, sed hoc dicere licet, quia non debuit christus in christum peccatum quodlibet corporaliter vindicare. Illud enim sibi nocuit, cum peccato peccatum adhibuit, cum pro traditione pontificem truncationi membrorum adhibuit. Neque enim traditorem episcopum excusamus, neque regem vindicantem sic se turpiter commendamus, sed hoc in medio deseramus et ut in Vngaria receptus fuerit disseramus.' Cf. von Guttner-Sporzyński (2010: 659–660).

17   Banaszkiewicz (1981: 353–390); Banaszkiewicz (2012: 27–100).

only in 1253.[18] The chronicler and later bishop of Cracow, Vincent Kadłubek, belonged to the circles interested in these trials: the milieu involved in this canonization process was composed of two generations of Cracow elites who were connected to the prince's court and to the bishopric and also supported the Gregorian reforms of the Church in Poland as well as the alliance with Hungary. It seems likely that a member or perhaps some members of these Cracow elites composed the *Chronica Polonorum* for Salomea. This *Chronicle* described the Polish-Hungarian relationship expressing the Poles' pride in being the dominant partner in the history of Polish-Hungarian relationships.[19]

However, an oral tradition could not be the basis of this *Chronicle* since its account of the second half of the eleventh century, which is presented from the Polish point of view, is too detailed. We can thus propose the hypothesis that another text might have served as a source for the *Chronica*. It could have been a narrative belonging to the *Gesta* genre, and it was probably focussed on the deeds of Bolesław II the Generous; therefore, I propose to call it *Gesta Boleslai Largi*. It could have contained the story of a princess named Adelaide married to a Hungarian ruler, whereas the genealogical additions (the princess came from Cracow, she was married to Yesse [Géza], and she gave birth to St Stephen instead of St Ladislas) could have been the result of the alterations made by the author(s) of the *Chronica Polonorum*, i.e., the member(s) of the Cracow elite. The description of the Polish-Hungarian border, which is very close to the present day Post-Trianon border line of Hungary and Slovakia, seems to reflect the border of the Nitra Duchy, which was ruled by the cadet branch of the Árpáds, i.e., the line supported by Bolesław II the Generous.[20] The information of the great role played by Sieciech in the Polish prince's court seems to be important, as it suggests that he was already a powerful aristocrat in the time of Bolesław.[21] Notably, Bolesław is presented as a prince, which could show that the hypothetical *Gesta* were written before 1076, when he was crowned.

The story of the Polish-Hungarian rivalry for a crown also seems interesting in the light of the hypothesis postulating a lost *Gesta Boleslai Largi* from the 1060s or the first half of the 1070s. Its roots are Hungarian and lie in the *Legenda Hartviciana*, where the main focus was placed on the Hungarian legation. We read that St Stephen sent his envoy Astricus, also called Anastasius,

---

18   Annales Capituli Cracoviensis: 'MCLXX Thomas archiepiscopus martirizatus est.' *Najdawniejsze roczniki*, 62; Labuda (2000: *passim*); Derwich 2010 (58–59).

19   Grzesik (2016: 74–75); Grzesik (2018, 161).

20   Grzesik (2019: 99–108).

21   Kurtyka (1996: 495–509). He doubted that Sieciech could play so important role so early. Sieciech was the most powerful person in Poland in the time of Władysław Herman.

to Rome for a crown. At the same time, the Polish prince Mieszko sent a legation for a crown. The pope prepared a crown for Mieszko, but the angel ordered
him in a vision to give the diadem to the Hungarians.[22] The *Hungarian-Polish
Chronicle* continued this story in a vivid and dramatic way. We read about the
arrival of the Polish legation, about the explanation of the papal decision and
the strong words of accusation against the Poles followed by the proclamation
of the eternal Polish-Hungarian peace by Pope Leo.[23] Lambert, the Polish leg-
ate, is the principal hero of this part of the *Hungarian-Polish Chronicle*, and
he could have been a historical person as well as Pope Leo. The pope's name
seems to be an anachronism if we consider that the related events took place
around the year 1000, when Sylvester II was sitting on the apostolic throne,
and the Polish annals already corrected the pope's name to Sylvester. Some
researchers thought that meant was Leo VIII, who was pope at the time of
the Christianization of Poland; others stated that the name was derived from
the Attila legends.[24] However, nobody seems to have considered pope Leo IX,
who ruled in the years 1049–1054. We know Lambert from the *Annales Capituli
Cracoviensis*: he was called by the Polish name Suła and was bishop of Cracow
from 1061 until his death in 1071; St Stanislaus was his successor. Suła-Lambert
was probably one of the authors of the annalistic entries in the lost annals of
the Polish court known as *Annales Regni Poloniae deperditi*, which were preserved in the *Annals of the Cracow Chapter*; it is worth pointing out that those
annals also mention his priestly ordination in 1037.[25] It is very likely that he
was really the envoy of a Polish ruler—Casimir the Restorer (died 1058) rather
than Bolesław II the Generous—to the Holy See, sent to request that a crown
should be given anew to Poland after the deep crisis of the state in the 1030s.
The legation could have taken place in the early 1050s, before the pope's death
(1054). The episcopal dignity of Lambert could be a late remuneration for this
legation, analogous to the case of Bishop Hartvic (Arduin) of Győr, who represented Coloman the Learned in his efforts to obtain the hand of the daughter
of a Sicilian Norman ruler.[26] The description of Lambert's legation could have
been a part of the hypothetical *Gesta Boleslai Largi*.

---

22   Legenda, 412–414.
23   Chron., 30–37.
24   Grzesik (1999: 154–155).
25   Annales Capituli Cracoviensis: 'MXXXVII ordinatus est Sula presbiter,' *Najdawniejsze
      roczniki*, 47; 'M°LXI Zula in episcopum Cracouiensem ordinatur et tunc cognominatus est
      Lambertus,' *Najdawniejsze roczniki*, 49; 'MLXXI Sula cognominatus Lambertus episcopus
      Cracouiensis obiit,' *Najdawniejsze roczniki*, 50; 'MLXXII Stanyzlaus succedit;' ib. 74.
26   Pauler (1883: 803–804).

In Hungary, the tradition of two legations for a crown in the beginning of the eleventh century originated independently. Hartvic's aim was—according to Hungarian medievalists—to emphasize the Gregorian point of view on the coronation, i.e., that the pope was the only one entitled to grant consent to the coronation.[27] I see here an attempt to explain why Hungary was a kingdom, whereas the powerful Poland was not. There was no Polish-Hungarian rivalry in the year 1000, but the narration created by Hartvic was known relatively early in Poland. I think that the information of Vincent Kadłubek about the patron saints of Poland and Hungary, Adalbert and Stephen, demonstrates that the *Legenda Hartviciana* was known to him.[28] The story of the alleged Polish-Hungarian rivalry for the crown could have been interpolated with the description of Lambert's legation by the author(s) of the *Chronica Polonorum*. The criticism of the Poles' way of life could also be an invention of the *Chronica Polonorum*, which condemned the behaviour of Bolesław II the Generous. Furthermore, Hartvic's story could have inspired the author(s) of the *Chronica Polonorum* to move in time the story of Adelaide and to falsify the chronological background of prince Bolesław's activity.

My study of the *Chronica Polonorum*, one of the three written sources of the *Hungarian-Polish Chronicle*, has led me to propose that this lost *Chronicle* was written c. 1214 for Salomea and described the Polish-Hungarian relationships. However, it also used the hypothetical lost *Gesta Boleslai Largi*, which presented the military deeds of Bolesław II the Generous in Hungary, and might also have mentioned the marriage of Adelaide to the Hungarian ruler and the legation for a crown by Lambert, later bishop of Cracow. If this conjecture is correct, it would mean that the hypothetical *Gesta* would probably have been written at the beginning of the second half of the eleventh century, which means that this lost work would be the oldest Polish chronicle, as it would have been created about half a century earlier than Gallus Anonymus' *Gesta*. It was probably destroyed after its rewriting as the *Chronica Polonorum*, when the information was changed in order to erase its main hero, Bolesław II the Generous. The cen-

---

27   Bagi (2011: 175–186); Bagi (2017: 340–342).
28   Kadłubek IV 18,1, 165–166: 'Regis quoque Pannoniorum federa, idem qui eadem dissoluisse arguebatur, palatii princeps Nicolaus cum sepe memorato Cracouiensium presule Fulcone ad perfectum redintegrant, iuxta sanctorum instituta: regis uidelicet beati Stephani et sanctissimi Polonorum patroni Adalberti: communiter debere coli utriusque regni amicitias, communiter alterius utrius hostilitates insectari, communes fore prosperitatum successus et indifferentes necessitatum succursus.'

sorship of those times created new, falsified historiographical episodes, which enriched both the medieval and the modern Polish historiography until the present day.[29]

Acknowledgements

I am very grateful to Dr Adrien Quéret-Podesta for his language correction.

Bibliography

Primary Sources

[Chron.:] *Chronica Hungaro-Polonica. Pars 1: (Textus cum varietate lectionum)*. Ed. Béla Karácsonyi. Szeged 1969. Acta Universitatis Szegedensis de Attila József nominatae, Acta Historica 26.

[Gallus:] *Gesta principium Polonorum. The Deeds of the Princes of the Poles*, ed. Paul W. Knoll and Frank Schaer with a preface by Thomas N. Bisson. Budapest—New York: CEU Press: 2003.

Hartvic, *Life of King Stephen of Hungary*. Transl. Nora Berend. In: *Medieval Hagiography. An Anthology*. Ed. Thomas Head. New York & London: Garland Publishing, Inc., 2000. 175–198.

[Kadłubek:] *Mistrza Wincentego zwanego Kadłubkiem Kronika polska. Magistri Vincenti dicti Kadłubek Chronica Polonorum*. Ed. Marian Plezia. *Monumenta Poloniae historica, series nova* 11. Cracow: Nakładem Polskiej Akademii Umiejętności, Wydawnictwo i Drukarnia "Secesja", 1994.

Kownacki, Hipolit, ed. (1823). *Kronika Węgierska na początku wieku XII. Kronika Czeska na początku wieku XI. W łacińskim języku pisane: z tłomaczeniem na polski język. Tudzież Ziemopismo Bedy wieku VIII. List popa Jana wieku XIII. Z rękopismow rożnych Bibliotek*. Warsaw.

[Legenda:] *Sancti Stephani regis maior et minor, atque Legenda ab Hartvico episcopo conscripta*. Ed. Emma Bartoniek. In: Scriptores rerum Hungaricarum, ed. Emericus Szentpétery, vol. 2, Budapestini 1938: 363–440.

Najdawniejsze roczniki krakowskie i kalendarz. Ed. Zofia Kozłowska-Budkowa. *Monumenta Poloniae historica, series nova* 5. Warsaw: Państwowe Wydawnictwo Naukowe, 1978.

---

29   Grzesik (2022: 31–56)—with a lexicon explaining main heroes of the Polish-Hungarian history of the eleventh-thirteenth century.

Secondary Sources

EMC—*The Encyclopedia of the Medieval Chronicle*. Ed. Graeme Dunphy. 1–2. Leiden— Boston: Brill, 2010.

Bagi, Daniel (2011). 'Papieskie przysłanie korony dla św. Stefana w Legendzie św. Stefana pióra biskupa Hartwika.' In: *Gnieźnieńskie koronacje królewskie i ich środkowoeuropejskie konteksty*. Ed. Józef Dobosz, Marzena Matla and Leszek Wetesko. Gniezno: Urząd Miejski w Gnieźnie, Instytut Kultury Europejskiej UAM w Gnieźnie, Instytut Historii UAM, 175–186.

Bagi, Dániel (2017). *Divisio Regni. Országmegosztás, trónviszály és dinasztikus történetírás az Árpádok, Piastok és Přemyslidák birodalmában a 11. és a korai 12. században*. Pécs: Kronosz Kiadó.

Banaszkiewicz, Jacek (1981). 'Czarna i biała legenda Bolesława Śmiałego.' *Kwartalnik Historyczny* 88, 353–390.

Banaszkiewicz, Jacek (2012). 'Czarna i biała legenda Bolesława Śmiałego.' In: Banaszkiewicz, Jacek. *Takie sobie średniowieczne bajeczki*. Cracow: AVALON.

Derwich, Marek. 'Annales capituli Cracoviensis'. *EMC* 1, 58–59.

Drelicharz, Wojciech (2012). *Idea zjednoczenia królestwa w średniowiecznym dziejopisarstwie polskim*. Cracow: Towarzystwo Naukowe Societas Vistulana.

Grzesik, Ryszard (1999). *Kronika węgiersko-polska. Z dziejów polsko-węgierskich kontaktów kulturalnych w średniowieczu*. Poznań: Wydawnictwo Poznańskiego Towarzystwa Przyjaciół Nauk.

Grzesik, Ryszard (2010a). 'Chronicon Hungarico-Polonicum (Hungarian-Polish Chronicle).' *EMC* 1, 348–349.

Grzesik, Ryszard. 'Gesta Ungarorum deperdita.' *EMC* 1, 701–702.

Grzesik, Ryszard (2010c). 'Hartwich of Győr.' *EMC* 1, 755–756.

Grzesik, Ryszard (2014). 'Some New Remarks on the Hungarian-Polish Chronicle.' *The Medieval Chronicle* 9, 189–203.

Grzesik, Ryszard (2016). 'Jedna lub dwie zaginione kroniki polskie z wczesnego średniowiecza.' In: *Stilo et animo. Prace historyczne ofiarowane Profesorowi Tomaszowi Jasińskiemu w 65. rocznicę urodzin*. Ed. Maciej Dorna, Marzena Matla, Miłosz Sosnowski, Ewa Syska, Wojciech Baran-Kozłowski. Poznań: Instytut Historii UAM, 67–76.

Grzesik, Ryszard (2018). 'Chronica Polonorum as One of the Basic Sources of the Hungarian-Polish Chronicle.' In: *Hadi és más nevezetes történetek. Tanulmányok Veszprémy László tiszteletére*. Ed. Katalin Mária Kincses. Budapest: HM Hadtörténeti Intézet és Múzeum, 157–162.

Grzesik, Ryszard (2019). 'Granica polsko-węgierska w Kronice węgiersko-polskiej'. In: *Silesia—Polonia—Europa. Studia historyczne dedykowane Profesorowi Idziemu Panicowi*. Ed. Jerzy Sperka. Katowice—Bielsko Biała: Wydawnictwo Cum Laude; PTH, Oddział w Cieszynie, 99–108.

Grzesik, Ryszard (2022). 'Kronika węgiersko-polska—fałszerstwo doskonałe?'. In: *Surasti tiesą. Pabalginiai istorijos mokslai falsifikatų tyrime. Mokslinių straipsnių rinkinys.* Ed. Rūta Čapaitė. Vilnius: Lietuvos istorijos institutas, 31–56.

Homza, Martin (2009). *Uhorsko-poľská kronika. Nedocenený prameň k dejinám strednej Európy.* Bratislava: Libri Historiae, Post Scriptum.

Homza, Martin and Rácová, Naďa (2010). *K vývinu slovenskej myšlienky do polovice 18. storočia. Kapitoly k základom slovenskej historiografie. Učebné texty.* Bratislava: Vydavateľstvo Stimul.

Jasiński, Kazimierz (1992). *Rodowód pierwszych Piastów.* Warszawa—Wrocław: Oficyna Wydawnicza Volumen. Reprint with the same pagination: Poznań: Wydawnictwo Poznańskiego Towarzystwa Przyjaciół Nauk, 2004.

Kętrzyński, Wojciech (1897). 'O Kronice Węgiersko-Polskiej (Vita sancti Stephani, regis Ungariae, Ungarico-Polona).' *Rozprawy Akademii Umiejętności w Krakowie. Wydział Historyczno-Filozoficzny* 34, 355–392.

Kurtyka, Janusz (1996). 'Sieciech.' In: *Polski słownik biograficzny* 36, 495–509.

Labuda, Gerard (2000). *Święty Stanisław biskup krakowski, patron Polski. Śladami zabójstwa—męczeństwa—kanonizacji.* Poznań: Instytut Historii UAM.

Pauler, Gyula (1883). 'Ki volt Hartvic püspök?' *Századok* 17, 803–804.

Szelestei, N. László (1991). 'A seitzi legendárium Szent István-legendája.' *Magyar Könyvszemle* 107, 1–2: 1–19.

von Guttner Sporzyński, Darius. 'Gallus Anonymus.' *EMC* 1, 659–660.

Węcowski, Piotr (2021). 'Dzieje naukowej współpracy Aleksandra Gieysztora i Brygidy Kürbis w świetle ich korespondencji.' In: *Źródłoznawstwo historyczne Brygidy Kürbis. Teoria—praktyka—konteksty.* Ed. Edward Skibiński and Paweł Stróżyk. Poznań: Wydawnictwo Nauka i Innowacje sp. z o.o., 11–59.

Wojciechowski, Tadeusz (2004). *Szkice historyczne jedynastego* [sic] *wieku.* 5th edn. Poznań: Wydawnictwo Poznańskie. 1st edn.: Cracow: Nakładem Akademii Umiejętności, 1904.

12

À l'ombre des fleurs de lys : l'Abrégé du Ménestrel d'Alphonse de Poitiers

Isabelle Guyot-Bachy

Résumé

Known as the *Abrégé du ménestrel d'Alphonse de Poitiers* in the 19th century, the *Geste des nobles rois de France*, written between 1249 and 1271, is one of the first dynastic histories written in French, even before the *Roman des rois* de Primat. Yet no specific study has been devoted to it. The study below examines the manuscript tradition (13 witnesses) and highlights three recensions. None of them was initiated by the monks of Saint-Denis nor commissioned by the king, but they have close links with the princes of the fleurs de lys. The first two works were dedicated to Alphonse de Poitiers, Louis IX's younger brother. Their author should be sought in the shared circle of the two princes, and undoubtedly benefited from the support of some Cistercian monasteries in Burgundy for the transmission of Latin sources. The third recension was composed between 1286 and 1297. It proposes important reworkings and was commissioned by a Capetian prince of Philip the Fair's generation, maybe Robert II, Count of Artois.

Mentionné dans les travaux érudits qui, depuis le dix-neuvième siècle[1] scrutent la genèse des *Grandes chroniques de France*, très partiellement publié, *l'Abrégé du ménestrel d'Alphonse de Poitiers* n'a jamais fait l'objet d'étude spécifique. C'est à tenter de combler cette lacune que voudrait s'employer cette courte synthèse sur l'une des premières histoires dynastiques en langue vernaculaire.

---

1   Paris (1836 : xviii) ; Wailly (1847) ; Béthune (1903) ; en dernier lieu Guenée (2016 : 51-54, 93). Mes remerciements les plus vifs vont à Marie-Laure Savoye et Anne-Françoise Leurquin (IRHT), à Florian Mittenhuber (Burgerbibliotek Bern), à Maxime Ferroli (Département des Patrimoines écrits-Médiathèque du Grand Dole) pour l'aide précieuse apportée dans la préparation de cette étude, ainsi qu'à Gaël Chenard, pour ses remarques stimulantes, et à Xavier Hélary pour m'avoir donné l'occasion de démarrer cette recherche voici dix ans dans le cadre d'un séminaire du projet CAPETIENS.

La base Jonas de l'IRHT recense aujourd'hui treize témoins, tous produits entre la seconde moitié du treizième siècle et le milieu du quatorzième siècle[2]. Ce moment de production, bref mais dense, fut prolongé par une circulation des témoins jusqu'à la fin du Moyen Âge et même au-delà. Quelques témoins attestent même d'une présence dans les milieux curiaux : BnF, fr. 4961, réalisé dans le Nord de la France au début du quatorzième siècle, porte l'ex-libris de Charles d'Orléans[3] ; Genève fr. 081, réalisé en Italie du Nord, appartenait en 1407 à la famille Gonzague de Mantoue[4].

1 La première recension et l'*Historia ou Gesta Francorum usque ad annum 1214*

L'examen des différentes composantes de l'œuvre permet de classer ces treize témoins en trois recensions. La première est représentée par cinq témoins (Genève, Bibliothèque de Genève, fr. 081 ; London, British Library, Cotton Vespasianus A.VI (1) ; Paris, BnF, fr. 13565 ; Vatican, Biblioteca apostolica Vaticana, Reg. lat. 0789 et Reg. lat. 0839). La dédicace à Alphonse 'comte de Poitiers et de Toulouse' permet d'en situer la composition entre 1249 et 1271, plus vraisemblablement à partir de 1250, année du retour du frère de Louis IX de Terre sainte. Cette dédicace est suivie d'un prologue ouvrant une histoire dynastique organisée en trois livres, correspondant aux trois lignées mérovingienne, carolingienne et capétienne. Chacun des livres est découpé en chapitres dont les titres sont rassemblés dans une table placée entre le prologue et l'incipit 'Après la mort de Josue el tens que li yuis estoient en granz tribulacions et desoulz divers yuges et desoulz divers seingnorez, lors ravi Alixandres Paris Eleynne'. Dans sept des treize témoins, le texte est précédé ou suivi d'un arbre généalogique de chacune des lignées[5]. Le récit a pour explicit : 'une grant partie d'Aquitaine desserva li rois Philippes del roiaume d'Engleterre et l'ajouta au royaumes de France', terme confirmé dans les manuscrits du Vatican et le fr. 5700 par la formule : 'Explicit la geste des [nobles] rois de France'. Tel était donc le titre initial de l'œuvre rebaptisée au dix-neuvième siècle *Abrégé du ménestrel d'Alphonse de Poitiers*.

---

2 https://jonas.irht.cnrs.fr/consulter/oeuvre/detail_oeuvre.php?oeuvre=2435 [consulté le 28/02/2022].

3 Ouy (2007 : 80) ; Laffitte (2018 : 24).

4 https://www.rialfri.eu/rialfriWP/manoscritti/geneve-bibliotheque-publique-et-universitaire-ms-fr-81.

5 Dans Genève, fr. 081, le feuillet portant l'arbre des Capétiens est manquant.

Cette première recension eut pour matrice – plus que pour source princi-pale dont elle ne serait que la traduction – un texte latin, désigné sous le titre d'*Historia* ou *Gesta Francorum usque ad annum 1214*, première synthèse de l'his-toire du royaume depuis les origines. Sorte de 'défense et illustration des hauts faits de la royauté', centrée sur les affaires séculières (*secularibus negotiis*), sur le roi et sur le peuple des Francs, elle a été conçue avant 1216 (elle tient Jean sans Terre pour vivant)[6], vraisemblablement dans le contexte de la trêve de Thouars (1206).

Outre un prologue, qui répond parfaitement aux règles du genre et dans lequel l'auteur expose un projet mûri et ambitieux, cette œuvre latine a aussi fourni à l'*Abrégé* son plan en trois livres, introduit chacun par une table des cha-pitres[7]. Son récit, compilation revendiquée de sources nombreuses et annon-cées dans le prologue, offrait toutes les garanties d'autorité pour une adaptation en langue vernaculaire. Quelques années auparavant, l'Anonyme de Béthune et l'Anonyme de Chantilly ne s'y étaient pas trompés et s'en étaient largement servi (Labory 1990, 315 et 318).

Natalis de Wailly avait identifié cette œuvre latine dans un manuscrit de la bibliothèque de Saint-Victor (BnF, lat. 14663, fols 194-249). L'humaniste Simon Plumetot l'avait fait copier au sein d'un recueil de textes historiographiques[8]. Mais trois autres exemplaires, plus anciens, attestent qu'elle a circulé, en parti-culier en Angleterre et en Irlande, peut-être dans le monde cistercien[9].

Parmi ses sources, l'auteur de l'*Historia* revendiquait un livret (*libellus*) *qui de Gestis Francorum loquitur, qui apud S. Germanum de Pratis iuxta Parisius reperitur*. La formule désigne la compilation d'Aimoin de Fleury, réalisée vers 1103 à Saint-Germain-des-Prés, sur laquelle ont été greffées ensuite les vies de Louis VI et Louis VII (Paris, BnF, lat. 12711). Auguste Molinier en avait déduit que cette *Historia* avait été composés à Saint-Germain-des-Prés, une hypothèse, recevable, qu'aucun indice textuel cependant n'étaye.

---

6 *Ex historia regum Francorum*, RHGF 9: 43 'Johannes frater ejus qui modo regnat.'
7 Le livre III comporte vingt-deux chapitres, répartition que l'on retrouve dans la première recension.
8 Une copie en a été réalisée au XVIIe siècle (BnF, lat. 17008, fols 1-49).
9 Dôle, BM 13-MS-M-3 (anc. 348-349), XIVe siècle ; London, College of Arms, 1, XIVe siècle ; Trinity College Dublin, 493, XIIIe siècle. Dans ces trois manuscrits, l'*Historia* [ou *Gesta*] *regum Fran-corum* est associée à l'*Historia Britonum* de Geoffroi de Monmouth, cf. Crick (1991: n° 3637) et Dumville (1977: 25).

2   La seconde recension et la traduction du *Chronicon* de Robert
     d'Auxerre

Six autres manuscrits (Bern, Burgerbibliothek, Cod. 590 et Cod. 607 (1); Chantilly, Bibliothèque du Château (Musée Condé), 0871; Oxford, Bodleian Library,
Douce 297; Paris, BnF, fr. 4961 et fr. 5700) portent une version qui prolonge
le récit jusqu'à la libération de Ferrand, comte de Flandre à l'épiphanie 1227
(explicit: 'fu delivrez entor la thiphanie par raençon de grant avoir'). Cette
continuation, organisée en cinq chapitres, dont les titres viennent compléter
la table initiale (XXIII-XXVII)[10], est étrangère aux notes qui complètent l'*Historia* jusqu'en 1214. Dès 1897, Léopold Delisle faisait le rapprochement entre la
dernière partie de cette recension de l'*Abrégé* et une traduction du *Chronicon*
de Robert d'Auxerre, resserrée sur l'histoire du royaume de France, présente
aux fols 1ʳ-106ᵛ du manuscrit Condé 871[11]. Examinant cette traduction du *Chronicon*, Delisle démontrait qu'elle tenait à la version allant jusqu'en 1211 avec les
additions portées par Robert, la continuation réalisée à l'abbaye cistercienne
d'Écharlis dans les années 1220, et une série de notes allant de 1100 à 1227, que
l'on désigne d'ordinaire sous le titre d'*Abrégé de la Mazarine* (Paris, Mazarine
1715, fols 150-164)[12]. S'appuyant sur un autre témoin de la même recension de
l'*Abrégé* (Berne, Burgerbibliotek 590), portant lui aussi la traduction du *Chronicon*, mais incorporant, outre des fragments des textes complémentaires que
Robert avait ajoutés en tête de son œuvre, des listes de rois de France et des
empereurs continuées dans cet exemplaire jusqu'à Saint Louis et Frédéric II,
Delisle concluait que cette traduction de l'œuvre latine de Robert d'Auxerre
avait été réalisée vers le milieu du treizième siècle.

Associée à l'*Abrégé* dans deux exemplaires du corpus, la traduction du *Chronicon* de Robert d'Auxerre a visiblement joué un rôle dans la mise en œuvre de
la seconde recension et l'on peut supposer que les trois entreprises (première
recension, traduction du *Chronicon* et seconde recension) ont été menées à peu
de temps d'écart et sans doute dans des environnements reliés.

L'adresse 'A son très cher seigneur, le très bon crestien, la très vaillante
personne, conte de Poitiers et de Tholouse' désigne sans hésitation le dédicataire de l'œuvre. Un dédicataire qui figure dans l'arbre généalogique capétien
de deux des plus anciens témoins, avec ses frères Robert [d'Artois] et Charles

---

10   'Li XXVII parole du couronnement Loeys le roy qui ore est' [Louis IX].
11   Delisle (1897).
12   Rech (1994): l'*Abrégé de la Mazarine* résultait d'une compilation d'éléments dans le
      manuscrit original du *Chronicon*, enrichie ensuite à partir de la version d'Écharlis. Rech
      l'attribue à Jean de Mailly peu après 1227.

[d'Anjou], tous trois entourant le nom de leur père Louis VIII, à qui a succédé Louis, l'aîné de la fratrie[13]. Alphonse est ainsi intégré à l'histoire dynastique dont l'*Abrégé* rend compte.

Dans huit des treize exemplaires, cette histoire est introduite par une miniature dont le roi sacré occupe le centre. Ce personnage sur la tête duquel descend une colombe (Condé 871, fol. 109^r) ne saurait être confondu avec le dédicataire[14]. Mais ce dernier est sans doute présent dans l'image : peut-être à droite, en pleine discussion (fr. 5700 fol. 6) ? Portant les mêmes vêtements que le roi, à genou devant lui et lui présentant le livre, tandis qu'un autre présente une épée (Bern Burgerbibliotek Cod. 607 (1), fol. 4^r) ? À genoux encore, mais cette fois en costume militaire, sans livre mais offrant ses mains dans le geste de l'hommage (Condé 871, fol. 109^r) ? Ce personnage, dans lequel Delisle voyait le ménestrel-auteur, ne peut être qu'Alphonse de Poitiers. Compte tenu des divergences qui ont tenu les deux frères éloignés l'un de l'autre pendant de nombreuses années, il faudrait donc situer la réalisation de l'*Abrégé* après 1266/7, au moment où la préparation de la dernière croisade les rapproche[15].

Et le ménestrel ? C'est Paulin Paris qui le premier désigna ainsi l'auteur de l'*Abrégé*, en se focalisant sur l'un des termes par lesquels celui-ci se désignait dans la dédicace. Mais par ses sources savantes comme par sa manière de traiter l'histoire, ce 'ménestrel' ne ressemble guère à son contemporain dénommé le 'ménestrel de Reims'. Ce dernier est assurément un poète de cour, qui entend distraire un public nobiliaire par ses récits historico-facétieux. L'auteur de l'*Abrégé* est bien plus sérieux et sans doute n'est-il pas ménestrel. Pour appréhender le statut de l'auteur, il convient en fait de rapprocher ce terme de 'menestrel' des deux autres qui l'encadrent dans la formule de présentation ('cil qui est ses serjans, ses menestereus et ses obeïssans'), et de les envisager sous leur sens premier, venu du latin (*serviens* et *ministerialis*). Redondants, les trois termes désignent en fait un 'serviteur' ou un 'officier' du prince. Clerc ou laïc ? Ni la lecture du texte, ni même l'usage de la langue vernaculaire ne permet de trancher. Il y a fort à parier en tout cas qu'il appartient au cercle des familiers d'Alphonse de Poitiers, un cercle qui recoupait souvent celui du roi Louis IX. Pourrait-il être Pierre de Villebéon dont le copiste du fr. 5700 a voulu inscrire la mémoire dans le médaillon de ce roi[16] ? Chambellan de celui-ci, Pierre fut

---

13   Bern Burgerbibliotek Cod. 590, fol. 127 ; BnF fr. 13565, fol. 203.

14   *Contra* Delisle (1897 : 528).

15   Chenard (2017 : 185-187).

16   BnF, fr. 5700, fol. 4vo : 'Cest Loeis devant diz fu rois XLV anz et fu morz en Cartage et fu enterrez au moustier Saint Denis en France en l'an de grace mil deus cenz soisante et onze le venredi devant Penthecoste et fu enterrez a ses piez mesire Pierres li chanberlans.'

aussi l'un des exécuteurs testamentaires du comte de Poitiers. Ou Philippe de Gometz, trésorier de Saint-Hilaire, 'premier parmi les serviteurs du comte'[17]? Plausibles, ces hypothèses ne sont pas vérifiables.

En arrière-plan de l'identité du commanditaire-dédicataire, une autre question se profile : la proximité avec l'*Historia regum Francorum*, dont la source principale est le *Chronicon* de Robert d'Auxerre, comme avec la traduction de cette chronique universelle, suggère la réalisation d'un *scriptorium* monastique. Il ne peut s'agir de celui de Saint-Denis (Mandach : 150-151). Parce que l'*Abrégé* est très largement une traduction de cette *Historia* que l'on supposait produite à Saint-Germain-des-Prés, parce qu'il a conservé l'allusion au *libellus* qui y avait été composé, d'aucuns l'ont rattaché à l'atelier sangermanien, dont l'activité au treizième siècle, il faut le reconnaître, est bien mal documentée[18]. Il est vrai qu'entre 1246 et 1255, l'abbaye est dirigée par Thomas de Mauléon, originaire des terres saintongeaises d'Alphonse de Poitiers. Le frère de Louis IX paraît cependant avoir fait bien peu cas des moines de Saint-Germain-des-Prés pour lesquels il ne prévit aucun legs testamentaire.

La forte influence du *Chronicon* de Robert d'Auxerre, les emprunts à la compilation d'Aimoin de Fleury, interpolée vers 1175 par un moine bourguignon, et ceux faits à une 'Chronique de la Charité-sur-Loire', confèrent à l'*Historia* une coloration nettement bourguignonne. Elle n'est pas démentie à la génération suivante par l'*Abrégé du ménestrel*. Non seulement il reçoit et traduit deux versions du *Chronicon* mais il leur adjoint encore les notes auxerroises et nivernaises de l'*Abrégé de la Mazarine*.

Si l'on retient l'hypothèse selon laquelle l'*Historia* aurait été produite à Saint-Germain-des-Prés, l'influence bourguignonne peut s'expliquer par la succession de trois abbés originaires de Vézelay entre 1155 et 1224[19]. Ce premier canal fut peut-être bien doublé d'un autre. C'est en effet par l'entremise des cisterciens que sont parvenues à Paris les différentes versions du *Chronicon*, justement depuis leurs monastères bourguignons de Pontigny et d'Écharlis. Bien implantée entre Paris et Auxerre, ayant des contacts documentés avec l'abbaye prémontrée de Saint-Marien – berceau du *Chronicon* – il y avait aussi la communauté cistercienne de Barbeau, fondée par Louis VII[20].

Discrète, la place des cisterciens est marquée en deux endroits significatifs de l'*Historia*, tous deux maintenus dans l'*Abrégé* : la naissance de Cîteaux mentionnée à la 42e année du règne de Philippe Ier ; la sépulture de Louis VII à

---

17   Chenard (2017 : 311).
18   Hourlier (1957 : 91) ; Armogathe et Denoël In Recht and Zink (2015).
19   Hourlier (1957 : 90).
20   Colpart (1995 : 49, 78, 86).

Barbeau, accompagnée de la citation *in extenso* d'une épitaphe que nul autre chroniqueur ne rapporte[21]. L'existence d'un lien entre ces abbayes cisterciennes et Saint-Germain-des-Prés reste à démontrer. La faveur d'Alphonse de Poitiers pour les fils de saint Bernard est en revanche avérée. N'a-t-il pas accepté en 1253 le patronage du tout récent collège parisien des Bernardins[22]?

3   Troisième recension : variantes, remaniements et changement d'orientation

Deux derniers manuscrits (Paris, BnF, fr. 2815 et naq fr. 10043)[23] présentent un texte continué jusqu'en 1286, dans lequel Charles-Victor Langlois reconnaissait l'une des chroniques mieux informées qui soit pour le règne de Philippe III[24]. Cette continuation a été découpée en deux chapitres intégrés à la liste originelle[25]. Dans cette recension, la partie originale a subi trois modifications importantes : l'adresse à Alphonse de Poitiers et les arbres généalogiques ont été supprimés ; l'interpolation du Ps.Turpin diverge radicalement de ce que l'on peut trouver dans les autres manuscrits[26] ; à partir de 1060 (avènement de Philippe Ier), on lit désormais un texte très proche de celui du *Roman des rois*, prolongé par la vie de Louis VIII, traduite des *Gesta Ludovici VIII*[27]. Enfin, dans le fr. 2815, au cycle iconographique initial, qui suivait la structure en trois livres pour les trois lignées, vient se superposer une nouvelle trame qui place une miniature au début de chacun des règnes (le règne de Philippe Auguste étant, lui, doté de quatre miniatures).

Il ressort de l'examen de la continuation que le récit du règne de Louis IX ne présente aucune similitude avec les œuvres du *scriptorium* de Saint-Denis. Au contraire, celui du règne de Philippe III suit assez régulièrement les *Gesta Philippi tercii* de Guillaume de Nangis, dont le texte latin est recopié dans le recueil des chroniques latines de Saint-Denis (BnF, lat. 5925) vers 1286-1287 et dont une traduction française est réalisée vers 1298. Mais c'est bien la version latine que la continuation compile. La matière en est drastiquement sélectionnée et le chroniqueur signale ses abrègements par une formule stylistique 'Que vous iroie-je

---

21   RHGF 12 : 221.
22   Chenard (2017 : 66-67).
23   Ce témoin porte les modifications du texte original mais sans la continuation.
24   Langlois (1887 : IV).
25   BnF, fr. 2815, fol. 5^v.
26   Mandach (1970) reprenant Short (1969).
27   Sans toutefois qu'ait été conservé le premier chapitre établissant l'ascendance carolingienne du roi.

disant?/que vous iroie-je contant?' qui imprime un rythme propre à faciliter la lecture, tout en établissant un contact fictif entre l'auteur et son public. Une pratique, étrangère au *scriptorium* sandionysien.

Nous avons affaire à un récit dont l'information et la construction – bien plus proche du genre historique qu'annalistique – sont largement originales. La rédaction a dû intervenir entre 1286 et 1297 : évoquant en 1269 la prédication de la croisade par Simon de Brie, le chroniqueur précise 'et puis fu il esleus à estre apostoille et le fu', ce qui suppose le décès du prélat[28] ; tout en qualifiant Louis IX de *saint roi Louis*, la canonisation n'est pas mentionnée et, au moment où il écrit, le chroniqueur ignore le mariage des deux filles de Philippe III et le fils de Robert d'Artois, Philippe, est encore en vie[29].

La connaissance du latin dont il fait preuve lorsqu'il traduit les *Gesta Philippi*, la réintroduction de la longue discussion théologique du ch. XVII du Ps-Turpin (omise dans la version standard), un zèle exacerbé pour la croisade et la référence constante à la volonté de Dieu plaident en faveur du statut de clerc de l'auteur. C'est d'ailleurs sous les traits d'un clerc qu'il est représenté dans la lettre initiale au fol. 1 du fr. 2815[30]. Ce clerc n'est cependant pas insensible aux plaisirs chevaleresques : il n'a pas oublié les tournois autorisés par le roi à Compiègne et à Senlis à l'occasion de la visite du prince de Salerne, un détail que les chroniqueurs sandionysiens se sont bien gardés de mentionner.

Il est en tout cas parisien[31]. De longue date visiblement puisqu'il se souvient qu'en 1256-1257, le prix du setier de blé avait atteint 20 sous parisis[32]. Il est attentif aux entrées royales, celle de Louis IX au retour de sa première croisade, celle de Philippe après le sacre de Reims[33].

Cette troisième recension, nous l'avons dit, efface les liens que l'*Abrégé* entretenait avec Alphonse de Poitiers, dont la mort n'est même pas signalée. La rubrique qui ouvre la continuation invite le lecteur à regarder à présent en direction d'un autre frère du prince, Charles d'Anjou[34]. Celui-ci entre dans le récit le 25 août 1270, débarquant devant le camp de Carthage où Louis IX vient

---

28   Martin IV mourut en 1285.

29   RHGF 21:102 et 94. Marguerite fut mariée à Édouard Ier d'Angleterre en 1299 et Blanche fut promise à Rodolphe de Habsbourg lors de l'entrevue de Vaucouleurs la même année. Philippe d'Artois mourut en 1298.

30   Sur les compétences de l'auteur en latin, Hélary (2021:358-361).

31   Holder-Egger (1882) : introduction 603.

32   RHGF 21 : 84.

33   RHGF 21 : 83, 91. Dans le premier cas, les chroniqueurs de Saint-Denis relatait plutôt la visite à l'abbaye et dans le second cas, les déplacements en Vermandois et à Arras.

34   RHGF 21 : 81 : 'Ci commencent lestoire du Saint roys Loys et de Charles son frere Roy de Sezile'.

de rendre l'âme. Il prend aussitôt la direction des opérations et très vite impose le retour en France à son jeune neveu, Philippe. Le chroniqueur profite de l'étape sicilienne, où Charles accueille somptueusement le nouveau roi, pour retracer en une longue parenthèse l'origine de la dévolution du royaume de Sicile à Charles et sa conquête, au cours de laquelle Dieu n'a cessé de lui montrer sa faveur[35]. Charles d'Anjou reste un personnage-clef du récit du règne de Philippe III, tout spécialement après l'exécution de Pierre de La Broce[36]. Sa mort à Naples le 07 janvier 1285 est inscrite dans une dimension téléologique : comme autant de présages, le chroniqueur lui associe une série de catastrophes naturelles[37] ; elle ouvre surtout – comme une conséquence immédiate – l'épisode final du règne de Philippe III, la croisade d'Aragon.

La datation de la continuation, postérieure à la mort de Charles d'Anjou, interdit de voir en celui-ci son commanditaire. Mais ce dernier doit appartenir au premier cercle de l'entourage royal, à ces parents dont le roi pouvait bien se repentir de ne pas avoir écouté les avertissements au sujet de Pierre de La Broce, en qui, lui reproche le chroniqueur, il avait 'grigneur fiance que [en ses] frères[38]. Des frères de Philippe III encore en vie après 1285, seul reste Robert de Clermont. Ses accès de démence depuis 1279 semble le disqualifier. Mais n'oublions pas qu'au cours de ces mêmes années 1280-1290 Philippe de Beaumanoir lui dédia le *Livre des Coustumes et usages du Beauvaisis* et Gilles de Rome son *Liber Hexameron*[39]. Sans l'ignorer, la continuation ne lui prête toutefois guère attention. Il faut donc élargir le cercle familial aux cousins, Charles II d'Anjou et Robert II d'Artois. Le premier, installé à Naples en 1289 après des années de captivité peut être écarté. Reste alors Robert, dont le soutien à la branche angevine dans les campagnes militaires comme au Conseil sont bien connus, comme l'est aussi l'appui offert à sa cousine germaine, la reine Marie de Brabant, en butte aux attaques de Pierre de La Broce[40]. La prouesse de Robert devant Pampelune en 1276 est vantée par le chroniqueur qui n'ignore rien des deux mariages ni de la descendance du comte[41]. Quant à Marie de Brabant, elle fait à deux reprises l'objet d'un éloge appuyé, qui souligne à l'envie son amour et sa loyauté à l'égard du roi. Avançons avec prudence et sans certitude que le pro-

---

35	RHGF 21 : 86-90.
36	RHGF 21 : 96-102.
37	RHGF 21 : 98. Ces mentions apparaissent dans les chroniques contemporaines, mais en ordre dispersé.
38	RHGF 21 : 95.
39	Carolus-Barré (1989 : 58, 60).
40	Hélary (2012).
41	RHGF 21 : 93-94.

fil de Robert d'Artois, de retour en France à la fin de l'année 1291, correspondrait assez bien à celui du commanditaire de la troisième recension.

Comme les entreprises de l'Anonyme de Béthune et de l'Anonyme de Chantilly qui le précèdent de peu, l'*Abrégé du ménestrel d'Alphonse de Poitiers* répond à l'ambition de donner en prose vernaculaire une histoire dynastique depuis les origines, en faisant fond sur l'autorité des chroniques latines (Labory 2004:16). Ces premières expériences, dont relèvent la première et la seconde recension de l'*Abrégé*, ne doivent rien à Saint-Denis. Le rôle de Saint-Germain-des-Prés reste à préciser, celui des cisterciens, assurant depuis la Bourgogne la diffusion du *Chronicon* de Robert d'Auxerre, semble se dessiner en arrière-plan.

Dans le dernier tiers du treizième siècle, l'*Abrégé* jouissait en tout cas d'une réelle autorité : son prologue servit de modèle à Primat et il n'est pas impossible que l'enlumineur de l'exemplaire du *Roman des rois* offert à Philippe III (Paris, Bibl. Sainte-Geneviève, 782) se soit inspiré de sa miniature d'ouverture[42]; vers 1318 le libraire Thomas de Maubeuge s'y référait encore pour organiser la version des *Grandes Chroniques* commandée par Pierre Honoré de Neufchâtel[43]. Il n'est donc pas étonnant que l'on revint vers cette œuvre dans les toutes premières années du règne de Philippe le Bel pour la continuer. Mais l'histoire dynastique conçue à Saint-Denis et désormais disponible en langue vernaculaire s'invite alors dans le jeu : à travers les remaniements, elle marque de son empreinte la troisième recension, qui conserve néanmoins son indépendance à l'égard du *scriptorium* sandionysien. Au gré de ses trois recensions, l'*Abrégé* manifeste finalement l'ambition d'une histoire dynastique qui, sans être une priorité du pouvoir royal, semble clairement assumée par l'entourage des princes des fleurs de lys.

Bibliographie

Sources

[*Abrégé du ménestrel d'Alphonse de Poitiers*] *Chronique anonyme finissant en M.CC. LXXXVI*. Ed. Joseph-Daniel Guigniaut et Natalis de Wailly. RHGF 21. Paris, Imprimerie impériale, 1855: 80-102.

[*Historia regum Francorum usque ad annum 1214*] *Ex historia regum Francorum*, RHGF 9 (1874): 41-45; 10 (1874): 277; 11 (1876): 319.

---

42   Mandach (1970: 151-152).
43   Hedeman (1991: 37).

[*Historia regum Francorum usque ad annum 1214*] *Ex libro III Historiae regum Francorum.* RHGF 12 (1877): 217-221; 17 (1878): 417-428.

Ex historia Francorum usque ad annum 1214. Ed. Auguste Molinier. MGH SS XXVI. Hanovre, 1882: 394-396.

[*Abrégé du ménestrel d'Alphonse de Poitiers*] *Extraits d'un abrégé de l'Histoire de France.* RHGF 10 (1874): 278-280; 11 (1876): 386; 12 (1877): 222-227; 17 (1878): 429-432.

[*Abrégé du ménestrel d'Alphonse de Poitiers*] *Ex historiae regum Franciae continuatione Parisiensi,* éd. O. Holder-Egger, MGH SS XXVI, Hanovre, 1882: 603-610.

Les Grandes chroniques de France selon qu'elles sont conservées en l'église de Saint-Denis en France. Ed Paulin Paris et Édouard Mennechet, t. I, Paris: Techener Libraire, 1836.

Études

Carolus-Barré, Louis (1989). 'Robert de France, sixième fils de saint Louis, comte de Clermont-en-Beauvaisis et sire de Bourbonnais (1256-1318)'. In *Autour du donjon de Clermont, témoin de l'histoire (Colloque de Clermont, 1987)*. Beauvais, Groupe d'étude des monuments et œuvres d'art de l'Oise et du Beauvaisis: 42-64.

Chenard, Gaël (2017). *L'administration d'Alphonse de Poitiers (1241-1271)*. Paris: Classiques Garnier.

Colpart, Luc (1995). 'L'Abbaye de Barbeau au Moyen Âge'. *Paris et Ile-de-France – Mémoires*, 46: 11-90.

Crick, Julia Catherine (1991). *The Historia Regum Britannie. Dissemination and reception in the later Middle Ages*, IV, Cambridge: D.S. Brewer.

Delisle, Léopold (1897). 'Notice sur un abrégé de la Chronique universelle de Robert de Saint-Marien d'Auxerre d'après un manuscrit du Musée Condé.' *Bibliothèque de l'École des Chartes* 58: 525-553.

Dumville, David N. (1977). 'Celtic-Latin texts in northern England, c. 1150-c. 1250'. *Celtica*, 12: 19-49.

Guenée, Bernard (2016). *Comment on écrit l'histoire au XIIIᵉ siècle. Primat et le Roman des roys.* Paris: CNRS Éditions.

Hélary, Xavier (2012). 'Robert d'Artois et les angevins (1274-1302), d'après le chartrier des comtes d'Artois.' In Provost (2012).

Provost, Alain (2012). *Les comtes d'Artois et leurs archives. Histoire, mémoire et pouvoir au Moyen Âge.* Arras: Artois Presses Université.

Hélary, Xavier (2021). *L'ascension et la chute de Pierre de La Broce, chambellan du roi (†1278). Étude sur le pouvoir royal au temps de Saint Louis et de Philippe III (v. 1250-v. 1280).* Paris: Honoré Champion.

Hedeman, Anne D. (1991). *The Royal Image. Illustrations of the 'Grandes chroniques de France', 1274-1422.* Berkeley-Los Angeles-Oxford: University of California Press.

Hourlier, Jacques (1957). 'La vie monastique à Saint-Germain-des-Prés.' *Revue d'histoire de l'Église de France, tome 43, n°140.* Mémorial du XIVᵉ centenaire de l'abbaye de

Saint-Germain-des-Prés. Recueil de travaux sur le monastère et la congrégation de Saint-Maur: 81-100.

Labory, Gillette (1990). 'Essai d'une histoire nationale au XIIIe siècle: la chronique de l'anonyme de Chantilly-Vatican.' *Bibliothèque de l'École des chartes*, 148/2: 301-354.

Labory, Gillette (2004). 'Les débuts de la chronique en français (12e et 13e siècles)'. *The Medieval Chronicle* III. Proceedings of the 3rd International Conference on the Medieval Chronicle. Doorn/Utrecht 12-17 July 2002. Amsterdam: Rodopi: 1-26.

Langlois, Charles-Victor (1887). *Le Règne de Philippe III le Hardi; [Suivi du] catalogue des mandements de Philippe III*. Paris: Hachette.

Lehoux, Françoise (1951). *Le bourg Saint-Germain-des-Prés: depuis ses origines jusqu'à la fin de la Guerre de Cent ans*. Paris.

Mandach André de (1970). 'Chronique dite Saintongeaise, texte franco-occitan inédit "Lee". À la découverte d'une chronique gasconne du XIIIe siècle et de sa poitevinisation.' *Beihefte zur Zeitschrift für romanische Philologie* 120. Tübingen: Niemeyer.

Paris, Paulin, ed. (1836). 'Introduction'. See *Les Grandes chroniques de France selon qu'elles sont conservées en l'église de Saint-Denis en France*. t. I, Paris: Techener Libraire.

Rech, Régis (1994). *Lecture et lecteurs de Géraud de Frachet*, DEA, EPHE, IVe section, 1994, dact.

Recht, Roland and Zink, Michel, eds. (2015). *Saint-Germain-des-Prés. Mille ans d'une abbaye à Paris*. Actes du colloque international des 3-4 décembre 2014 publiés avec le concours du Fonds de dotation pour le rayonnement de l'Église Saint-Germain-des-Prés. Paris: Académie des Inscriptions et Belles-Lettres.

Short, Ian Robert (1969). 'The Pseudo-Turpin Chronicle: Some Unnoticed Versions and their Sources'. *Medium Aevum* 38: 1-22.

Wailly, Natalys de (1847). *Examen de quelques questions relatives à l'origine des chroniques de Saint-Denis*, Mémoires de l'Institut Royal de France. Académie des Inscriptions et Belles Lettres, 17: 1: 379-407.

Laffitte, Marie-Pierre (2018). 'À propos de la librairie de la chambre du roi: manuscrits de la bibliothèque personnelle de François Ier hérités des comtes d'Angoulême (1445-1496)'. *Bulletin du bibliophile*: 11-52.

Ouy, Gilbert (2007) *La Librairie des frères captifs. Les manuscrits de Charles d'Orléans et Jean d'Angoulême*. Texte, Codex et Contexte, 4, Turnhout, Brepols.

13

Three Chronicles by London Clergymen and the Yorkist Version of the First War of the Roses

Michael Hicks

Abstract

A score of chronicles document English politics from 1440–1462, the preamble to and onset of the Wars of the Roses. Although all the chronicles were anonymous and none were original, there are clues to the text of the date of composition and the domicile, age, qualification, and livelihood of the authors. The fullest three chronicles discussed here, the chronicles known as *Benet's Chronicle*, the *English Chronicle*, and *Gregory's Chronicle*, were written years later by highly educated clerics resident in London. Such data enables assessment of their testimony. Two credible authors are suggested. All shared a metropolitan outlook that assimilated Yorkist propaganda and that evolved via criticism of governance eventually to Yorkist dynasticism.

Fifteenth-century English people accessed their history principally by the multiple-volume Latin *Polychronicon* that survives in over a hundred copies, through the Middle English Prose *Brut* of which 203 copies of the Common Version survive, and the London chronicles, of which 44 remain of literally hundreds that once existed.[1] The *Brut* was structured by regnal years and the London chronicles by mayoral years. Eleven 'Peculiar Versions' of the *Brut* and miscellaneous London chronicles treat the preamble to the Wars of the Roses from 1449 and the First Phase itself of 1459–1461. The chronicles known as *Benet's Chronicle*, *Gregory's Chronicle*, and the *English Chronicle*, the three best, are the subject of this paper.[2] This paper shows that all three chroniclers were secular clerks who apparently drew on other London chronicles. Modern historians have not realized that as least six of the chronicles supposedly of London cit-

---

1   Taylor (1966: 51); Matheson (1998: 67–77); McLaren (2002: 98). Erik Kooper researched the *Brut* for earlier centuries. This chapter benefits from feedback on three papers delivered at conferences on the Medieval Chronicle in Belfast in 2008 and in Pecs in 2016, organized by Erik Kooper, and the Fifteenth-Century at Aberystwyth in 2008.
2   *Benet's Chronicle*, 151–232.

izens were actually the work of clergymen. Whilst some Londoners updated their annals each year, others (including these three) did not. Prompted to continue by memorable local events, notably Jack Cade's rebellion of 1450 and the Yorkist victory of 1461, they backfilled the gaps since the last completed annal by borrowing from one another. Historians cannot establish who copied who or the sources of particular items or indeed perhaps whole continuations that once existed.

Only the *Second Anonymous Crowland Continuation* of 1459–1486 surveyed the Wars of the Roses as a whole.[3] Crowland is respected and often followed by modern historians, who quarry the rest for their own narratives and unconsciously imbibe their Yorkist bias. Yet these lesser chronicles deserve more regular scrutiny. Although undoubtedly contemporary, how contemporary are they, how reliable and well-informed, and how independent of one another? Teasing out what sort of man a chronicler was, where he was well-informed and authoritative or where not, his prejudices and biases, assists today's historians when weighing his work against other narratives. Were chronicles written at once or after the event? How influenced were they by the propaganda of the victors? The titles by which chronicles are now known rarely denote the authors, but rather the owners of the manuscript (Benet, Rawlinson), the copyists (Benet, Warkworth, Worcester), and even the modern editors (Giles, Davies). Whilst much can be deduced from an original manuscript, these chronicles are not originals, but survive instead in commonplace books. They are fair copies distanced from the original compilation, perhaps through multiple recensions, though fortunately copyists slavishly repeated what they found, relevant or redundant. The *Warkworth* chronicler famously incorporated his instructions into his transcript. Copies were liable to interpolation, compilation, abbreviation, marginalia, and silent changes of authorship. Robert *Bale's Chronicle*, Rawlinson B355, Gough London 10, the *English Chronicle*, and *Warkworth's Chronicle* have all been found to be incomplete. Two modern editors rashly assumed that the two surviving texts each of the *English Chronicle* and *Warkworth Chronicle* were once identical.[4]

Yet evidence is embedded in the surviving texts about the date and provenance of particular annals or sequences of annals and of authorship, sometimes transferred from earlier sources. The chronicles of Bale, Giles, Rawlinson, and

---

3   He was a secular clerk employed in a royal writing office, Hicks (2005: 172–190).

4   Baskerville (1913: 123–127); *Six Town Chronicles*, 76; Kleineke (2014: 744–750). Whilst Marx did locate the start to the *English Chronicle*, his version terminated in 1450 short of the Davies MS in 1461, *The English Chronicle 1377–1461*, 70 n. 1. The Hunter MS of *Warkworth's Chronicle* lacks the beginning, *Death & Dissent*, 72.

pseudo-Worcester share such features. Annals that look forward to later events must therefore have been written later. A Latin text or the Roman calendar normally betray a cleric, occasionally a notary like Bale or a secretary like Worcester. Dating by dominical letters reveals a clergyman who delivered the liturgy. Laymen normally wrote in English. Latin is a more precise language that often reveals the location and actions of the authors. A Latin verb test can indicate the location of the chronicler from time to time. This test when applied in the Crowland Continuation was revealing.[5] The verb test also works for the Rawlinson manuscript.[6] It cannot work for the *English Chronicle* or other English texts or chronicles that incorporate material from several sources. Some of these deductions apply to the Benet, Gregory and English chronicles.

1   *Benet's Chronicle*[7]

All these clues are relevant to *Benet's Chronicle*: the best and the most splendidly edited. It continues the Latin *Brut* (Matheson Peculiar Version D_1) from 1440–1462 and was copied in 1462–1468 into the commonplace book of John Benet, vicar of Harlingdon (Bucks.), who was not the original chronicler. *Benet's Chronicle* was written up regularly, close to events or after a short lapse in time.

In this instance the Latin verb test works well. The verbs *venir* and *revenir*, to come to the author, occur frequently, and similarly *irer, abire, exire, transire*, to go from the author. Other more neutral verbs are also used, such as rode (*equitavit*), entered (*intravit*), and proceed (*profectus*). Not surprisingly, international travel involves people *coming* to England or *going* abroad. Thus Cardinal Beaufort entered (*intravit*) England in 1428, the king returned (*revenit*) from his French coronation in 1431, many indulgences of Pope Eugenius *entered* England around Christmas 1439, Talbot *came* from Normandy in 1442, the defeated Edmund Duke of Somerset returned (*revenit*) without profit and ambassadors empty handed in 1443, Queen Margaret's entourage came (*venit*) to England in 1444, French ambassadors came (*venerunt*) and York returned (*revenit*) from his lieutenancy in France in 1445, Edmund Duke of Somerset took up the baton in France in 1448, Somerset from France and York from Ireland *returned* to England in 1450, Yorkist earls entered (*intraverunt*) England and York came (*venit*) from Ireland to England (1460), James II of Scotland

---

5   Hicks (2005: 176–178, 188–189).
6   *Six Town Chronicles, passim.* The verb test does not apparently work for the chronicles in English.
7   The section is based on *Benet's Chronicle*.

attacked the North (*venit*) in 1456 and the French attacked (*intraverunt*) Sandwich in 1457.[8] The king, cardinal and others crossed to France (*transfretavit,
transivit, transierunt*) on many occasions.[9] *Venire, revenire* or similar verbs are
used many times over for people coming to London or Westminster and variants of go (*ire*), rode (*equitavit*), or were sent (*misit*) for those leaving them
for overseas or the provinces. John Duke of Bedford came (*venit*) with his new
wife Jacquetta of Luxemberg to parliament in 1433 and the sorceress Eleanor
Cobham moved prisons (*exiens*) from London to Chester.[10] Never does anyone come somewhere else from London, indicating that it was there that the
chronicler resided, the earliest instance being in 1445. The verb test works particularly well in 1450, when Jack Cade's rebels came from Kent to Blackheath
and Clerkenwell (*venerunt*), left (*exivit*), came again to Blackheath and London and Cornhill in the City (*venerunt*), and again went away (*abierunt*), whilst
the king came twice (*venit*) and summoned Lord Say secretly to come to him.
York *came* to London, all the dukes, earls and barons *came* to London.[11] People
went to Coventry, Leicester, and other provincial locations. People *came* from
abroad to England and *came* from other places in England to London from
1445—occasionally from other regions to localities, e.g., Yorkists to St Albans
near London and the Lancastrians to the south in 1461. They *went, rode, shipped*
elsewhere. The king held his great councils and parliaments and festivals at
Westminster, to which people *came*. When such events were held at Leicester
or Coventry, people *went* there. But people *came* to a great council at Sheen
and *came* in 1453 to parliament at Reading, which suggests the chronicler was
there, and to Ludford in 1459, *came* to Guines in 1460 and *came* to the battle of
Northampton, which suggests the chronicler *went* into exile with the Yorkists.
For chronicles originating outside London, the verb test may not work so well.

    Benet's Chronicle is extremely informative about events at great councils,
parliaments and convocations and what happened within them, to the point
where it is difficult to believe that the chronicler was elsewhere. It does seem
likely that he was at the great council at Sheen in 1449 to which came 'all the
dukes, earls, barons, knights and esquires of England'.[12] An ecclesiastic, he was
not a bishop, abbot nor prior, with a right to a personal summons, but maybe
he was in the entourage of such people. When the Reading parliament of 1453
was prorogued and then re-prorogued by Cardinal Kemp, archbishop of Canter-

---

8   *Benet's Chronicle*, 181, 183, 186, 189, 190, 191, 194, 202, 217, 218, 225, 227.

9   Ibid. 182, 184, 185, 186, 187, 189, 190, 198.

10   Ibid. 184, 189.

11   Ibid. 191, 198–202.

12   Ibid. 196.

bury and Lord Chancellor, the chronicler reports that he came (*venit*) to do it:[13] an indication surely that he too was there, perhaps in company with another bishop?

To categorize an anonymous chronicler is easier than firmly identifying him. Benet himself was from the diocese of Lincoln—the most extensive diocese spanning eight counties!—and regarded himself as a northerner. Never at Oxford University, Benet was probably not therefore the eyewitness identified in a marginal note to a riot of 1441 by southerners against the northerners of White Hall, Oxford, whose principal was William Witham. Witham may be our chronicler, whose career he closely paralleled. Principal of Broadgates Hall in 1436 and then White Hall, he was a civil lawyer, graduating doctor in 1444 and practising in the admiralty court from 1441. He was senior enough to know the university's response to Duke Humphrey's gift of books and was keeper of the key to the University chest as late as 1449. The southerners acted 'almost without cause', indicating the chronicler knew reasons he did not divulge. Principal then (*tunc*),[14] Witham had departed at the time of writing, moving on to London. His legal expertise was esteemed by both archbishops, the bishops of Lincoln, London, and Bath and Wells, and by the crown. He may have accompanied them to convocation and to the parliament. He had important connections to the diocese and successive bishops of Lincoln, where he served three livings from 1438, six prebends successively from 1447 and two archdeaconries from 1454. He had other prebends at Southwell Minster and at Hastings. Witham was instituted to and resigned from a bewildering number of churches, was dispensed to hold two incompatible benefices, and then, in 1453, three. Bishop Gilbert of London ordained him priest in 1444, collated to the rectory of Laindon (Essex) and to a prebend at St Paul's, and named him his executor in 1448. In 1446 Witham was presented by the chapter of St Paul's to the first of three City rectories. From 1448 he was dean of court of arches in St Mary Bow, the premier court of the province of Canterbury, and from 1450 he was chancellor of Lincoln, exercisable from the episcopal house at the Old Temple.[15]

Up to 1444–1445 the chronicle is retrospective and derivative.[16] Possibly the whole early part was written up in 1450 under the stimulus of great events, the impeachment of the duke of Suffolk and rebellion of Jack Cade. Thereafter

---

13   Ibid. 210–211.
14   Ibid. 164.
15   Emden (1957–1959: iii.2065–2066).
16   *Benet's Chronicle*, 161; Matheson (1998: 156). Neither Benet's immediate source nor the original *Brut* apparently survive and it is not therefore known whether the years 1435–1445 were written in annually or retrospectively.

each crisis was shaped by Yorkist propaganda and apparently composed separately. The whole sequence from 1456 may date after the Yorkist triumph of
1460. For this era the text is somewhat abbreviated, with many annals consisting of a whole series of events loosely linked by 'et' (and). Numerous references
to dates '*circa*' or '*circiter*' (about) particular feasts indicate memories recalled
rather than those set down instantaneously and indicate that the same author
was responsible for datings before and after 1440. Only brief comments on the
effectiveness of campaigns etc seem original to annals before 1445.

A few references in the text to later events indicate that compilation was a
little in retrospect. An annal for 1441 about Eleanor Cobham's imprisonment at
Chester dates in or after 1442, Witham became doctor of civil law not by 1441
but in 1444, and the creation of the duke of Warwick in 1444 actually happened
in 1445.[17] The author was critical of the war effort in the early 1440s, declaring fruitless the campaigns of John Earl of Shrewsbury in 1442 ('*et nihil pro-
fuit*') or of John Duke of Somerset in 1443 ('*cum nihil prefecit*') (*which profited
nothing*).[18] From 1447 descriptive adjectives applied to leading figures betray
political stances. Humphrey Duke of Gloucester had been mentioned several
times before his arrest in 1447, when he is described as '*verissimus*' (truest) and
'*strenuissimus*' (most strenuous) and died 'to much sorrow' (*in multa tristicia*);
on the latter page Master John Stopingdon died most noble (*nobilissimus*).[19]
William de la Pole, earl of Suffolk occurs several times, on campaign, embassy,
escorting the new queen, and in 1448 created duke,[20] but only from 1449 is he
described as '*iniquus*' (iniquitous). His malign counsel is blamed for Richard
Duke of York's exile to Ireland which had raised no such connotations when
it happened. This is a sharp change in tone. Suffolk's malignity had not been
noticed before. Altogether Suffolk is called '*iniquus*' ten times in 1449–1450.[21]
Such language might indicate the change in authorship that Harriss postu-
lates. More probably, however, it indicates the retrospective influence of the
crisis of 1450 and perhaps York's open letters circulated then. The death of Lord
Delawarr dated to 1446 actually happened in 1450.[22] It is likely therefore that the
whole sequence from 1445 was written in the light of the crisis of 1449–1450. By
then the chronicler was hostile to Suffolk, regarding the charges against him
as proven, and sympathetic to the cause of reform, Jack Cade, very daring and

---

17   *Benet's Chronicle*, 187, 189, 190; Emden (1957–1959: iii.2065).
18   *Benet's Chronicle*, 189, 190, 194. 'Et sic nihil profecit' (1460), ibid. 225.
19   Ibid. 192, 193.
20   Ibid. 179, 182, 190, 194.
21   Ibid. 195–198.
22   Ibid. 191 and n.

discreet (*valde audax et discretus*), and York. Surprisingly for someone trained in law, he accepts the popular attribution of treachery to those acting against the public interest as the populace saw it, even though this very definitely was not the legal definition of treason.[23] It was in 1449–1450 that Suffolk's offences and from 1450 that Good Duke Humphrey's unjust demise can be shown to have become popular currency. This re-interpretation of the past was shaped by knowledge of Suffolk's trial and fall in 1449–1450. The strict ordering by annal perceived up to 1450 is briefly lost as events up to York's submission at St Paul's after the Dartford episode on March 1452 are recounted without a break: the new annal for 1452 starts after Easter.[24] Perhaps the crisis of 1450 stimulated the chronicler to write up or revisit the previous years and to continue the sequence down to 1452. Although the adjectives might be later additions to an existing text by the copyist, they fit the existing interpretation.

The chronicler presents York's justification of his rebellion in 1452, 'against the traitors of the king and kingdom of England and for the good of England and not against the king',[25] praises effusively York's First Protectorate of 1453–1455, and the Yorkist justification of the First Battle of St Albans between the 'good' York and the 'bad' Somerset, which derives from the Yorkist *Stow Relation*.[26] *Benet's Chronicle* (and indeed the other Yorkist chroniclers) indicate the success of the reformers in the propaganda war within London. This is perhaps all the more surprising given the chronicler's contacts with the court and government. He shares the successive Yorkist critiques in turn on Edmund Beaufort, duke of Somerset (d. 1455), Queen Margaret of Anjou, and eventually Henry VI himself, who were not presented in this hostile way in earlier annals. Beaufort occurs repeatedly fighting, promoted, and defeated without further comment up to 1452, when he becomes ignominious (*ignominiose*). In 1453 he was accused of treachery and became iniquitous (*iniquus*). His evil government 'almost destroyed the realm of England'.[27] Similarly Queen Margaret is treated with respect in the 1440s and early 1450s but suddenly leaps into political prominence and condemnation in 1456.[28] *Benet's Chronicle* records John Halton's slander that the Queen's son was not fathered by the king, dated to 23 February 1456. King's Bench records indicate that this actually occurred two years afterwards: the passage was therefore written in 1458 or probably rather

---

23   See Hicks (2002: 134–140 at 136–137).
24   *Benet's Chronicle*, 207.
25   Ibid. 206: 'contra traditores Regis et regni Anglie et pro bono Anglie et non contra regem'.
26   Ibid. 206–207, 212, 213.
27   Ibid. 187–188, 192, 194, 202–206 (at 203), 210–211, 213.
28   Ibid. 190–191, 207.

later, perhaps in 1459.[29] Only in 1461 is Henry VI said to have 'ruled tyrannically like his father and grandfather' before him ('Quia tirannice regnavit sicut Avus et pater suus'). Hitherto the chronicle had accepted the Lancastrian dynasty without question and was sympathetic and apparently intimate too. It records the king's hunting at Rockingham all summer 1434. It records his moods (*iratus*) and decisions. In 1449 it labelled him most illustrious (*illustrissimi*) in 1441, the most noble and most Christian (*nobilissimo et Christianissimo*), and in 1454 the chronicler recorded his recovery of sanity to the grace of God.[30] The chronicle becomes much fuller in 1459–1461, taking an overtly Yorkist line, and the annal for 1461 indeed spills over into 1462 when it abruptly ceases.

2   The English Chronicle[31]

The continuation of the *Brut* known of the *English Chronicle of 1377–1461* survives as two manuscripts out of at least four that once existed: at the National Library of Wales (NLW) at Aberystwyth (A), dated by watermarks and palaeography to c. 1475, and Bodleian MS. Lyell 34 (L), apparently completed in 1461.[32] The NLW manuscript has linguistic features particular to Shropshire/Denbighshire and the Bodleian to Surrey/Kent, whereas the original was written in London. The NLW manuscript broke off in 1450. The heading for Henry VI's reign was interpolated: it spans the 28 years from 1422 to 1450. Actually the authorship changed in 1440. The *English Chronicle* is most useful for 1458–1461, when a distinct prologue or watershed justified York's rebellion and the usurpation of the Yorkists and the narrative is supported by Yorkist propaganda that is otherwise unrecorded. The editor's judgement that the whole period 1440–1461 was a self-conscious pro-Yorkist unity, with 'a Yorkist bias and a Yorkist narrative', is questionable. The annals from 1440–1458 are intermittent and retrospective: the narrative lapsed and resumed in 1440, in 1449–1450, and in 1455. The whole sequence from 1440 may date to 1452 or after, when Eleanor Cobham, duchess of Gloucester died.[33] The chronicler strongly approved of the trials of

---

29   Ibid. 190–191, 216–217. Harriss states the bastardy story to be current in 1459, citing in support the *English Chronicle* which was written in 1461.
30   Ibid. 184, 189, 195, 204, 212.
31   The source of this section is *The English Chronicle 1377–1461*. Originally there were four MSS.
32   *The English Chronicle 1377–1461*. Unless otherwise stated, this authoritative edition is relied upon. Marx gives primacy to the NLW version and repeatedly ignores Davies, which therefore is not superseded, see *An English Chronicle*.
33   Griffiths (1981: 252).

two Lollards, the duchess, and her necromancer, but added little of the ensuing decade. His annals for the treaty of Troyes (1444) and the death of the duke of Warwick date to 1449 or later. So, perhaps, may the death of Humphrey Duke of Gloucester in 1447. There is a full account of Jack Cade's Rebellion of 1450, a sketchy one of the impeachment of Suffolk (1449–1450), nothing at all about York's two returns from Ireland and his attempted coup in 1450–1451, only the briefest mention of his capitulation at Dartford in 1452, and Yorkist version of the First Battle of St Albans in 1455. The Reading parliament of 1453, Henry VI's madness, and York's first and second protectorates are altogether overlooked. The author down to 1457 (and probably 1461) lived in London and relied on hearsay for the events beyond. He used the Roman kalends and twice remarked when religious festivals coincided,[34] information from the Sarum ordinal or pye that ensured that priests celebrated the office of the appropriate day. He was therefore a secular clerk, most probably rector of a City parish, with expertise in theology and the Bible. Credulous about portents, he disapproved of heresy, sorcery, the errors of Bishop Reynold Pecock, and violence to William Aiscough 'their father and bishop'. Probably he attended the convocation at St Paul's in 1460. Whilst critical of the 'simple commons' and parvenus, he was in touch with the common voice, and repeated popular rumours and hearsay. His continuation from 1440 to 1461 was not 'carefully constructed Yorkist propaganda or, more accurately, mythmaking', nor an 'official [Yorkist] version of events'.[35] Although critical of the regime, he was no fan of York nor foe to the king until 1458–1461, of which his account was composed as a unit before the battle of Towton ended the First War.

3   Gregory's Chronicle[36]

The third example is Gregory's Chronicle, which from 1440 splits from Cotton Vitellius AXVI, a London chronicle. The final section in a commonplace book, it is difficult to distinguish between the original, the continuation and any borrowings. Possibly the well-known annal that appeared to identify as author the skinner and mayor William Gregory was such a borrowing. All modern commentators recognize a single author, not Gregory, for the years 1451–1469. This chronicle is another major source for Cade's Rebellion in 1450 and for

---

34   The English Chronicle 1377–1461, 64, 66, 71.
35   The English Chronicle 1377–1461, cii.
36   Gregory's Chronicle; Contemporary English Chronicles, which regrettably omits the annals for 1448–1450.

the First Phase of the Wars of the Roses, 1459–1461. Internal cross-references indicate that the annals for the 1440s were composed in 1450, 1450 in 1461, the early 1460s in 1465, and 1465–1469 at the time. Scarcely anything relates to the 1440s—Henry VI's 28th regnal year is omitted—and this sequence may be retrospective, as the entry for 1448–1450 certainly is. A reference to Richard Duke of York in 1447 must date from 1460 or even later. Cade's uprising, fall of Suffolk, and York's failed coup preceded an account of the 1450s that omitted the 32nd regnal year, York's Dartford Rebellion (1452), the birth of Prince Edward (1453), Henry VI's madness (1453–1454), and both of York's protectorates (1454–1456). There is scarcely any narrative at all. The compiler absorbed the propagandist critiques against Suffolk and his allies, Cade's complaints, and the perverse Yorkist justification of the First Battle of St Albans. 'The more parte of thys londe hadde pytte that they were attaynte and proclaimed trayters by the parlement [that] was holde of Couyntre' (1459). Only in 1460 did the chronicler back the Yorkist dynasty. If focused on London, familiar with its church, streets, gates, chronicles, and indeed 'the lord bishop', the chronicler was not obviously a London alderman—whether Gregory, Forster or Jocelin who have been suggested—or indeed a layman.

The author need not reside in London continuously: how could he place the loveday of St Paul's at Coventry? The case is less compelling for another secular priest, but nevertheless this chronicler was prone to pious utterances and to controversial views. Seven times he quoted Latin proverbs or sayings, citing *Genesis* 27:28, *Gesta Romanorum, Counsel of Conscience*, the homilies of St Gregory, and a couplet from a Latin schoolbook that befitted a schoolmaster. Only a churchman needing to perform the right services would date by the dominical letter D![37] A credible candidate is the theologian William Ive, master of Winchester College in 1445–1453 and a likely source for several Hampshire anecdotes. From 1465 he was master of Whittington College at St Michael Paternoster Royal in London until in 1470 he moved to Salisbury as cathedral chancellor.[38]

---

37   *Contemporary English Chronicles*, 74, 197.
38   Thomson (2013: 94–97); Walker (2004: 445–446).

4   Conclusion

Almost all the chronicles of the Wars of the Roses share a metropolitan outlook. Some chroniclers were cockneys by birth, residence, and citizenship, but
others immigrated to City livings and offices of church and state. The verb test
tracks their location. Such clerics were part of the 'social milieu' and attitudes
of London, which changed over time. In touch with both the London elite and
London mob, they were immersed in London's grievances, issues and pride,
into hostility to foreigners, to Fleet Street lawyers, and to any (like Henry VI)
who pursued what were regarded as anti-London policies. To be governed from
London was self-evidently right—not from Coventry, York, or by wild northerners of Queen Margaret. Londoners experienced the mid-century depres-
sion and blamed it, unfairly, on the government. They approved the treaty of
Tours of 1444, Henry VI's wedding, and Suffolk's conduct until the loss of Normandy, when with hindsight Duke Humphrey became 'good' and poisoned
and York was exiled to Ireland. Initially the chroniclers. like Londoners generally, accepted the complaints of Cade's Kentishmen, but then disapproved
when they lynched and pillaged. Whilst they accepted the Yorkists' interpretation of First St Albans in 1455 and deplored their condemnation in 1459, the
chroniclers also welcomed Henry VI's peace-making (the loveday of St Paul's)
and remained loyal subjects until York's overt bid for the crown in 1460s. They
internalized critiques of governance, now witnessed principally in *John Vale's
Book*,[39] and demonstrate by omission how ineffective any official broadcasts
were on shaping metropolitan and Kentish opinion. No provincial chronicles
enshrine what may have been the majority response. The Yorkist accession consolidated Yorkist narratives that were retrospectively revised by these chroniclers and those of Caxton, Vale and Warkworth and have become the established narrative ever since. It is difficult to break free.[40] Understanding which
was contemporary, even by just a few years, distinguishes eyewitness testimony
from retrospective memories and what became official propaganda.

---

39   *John Vale's Book*, 178–212.
40   Hicks (2010), part 2, tried to do this.

Bibliography

Primary Sources—Editions

[*Benet's Chronicle*]: 'John Benet's Chronicle for the year 1400–1462'. Ed. Gerald L. Harriss and Mary A. Harriss, *Camden Miscellany* xxiv. CS. 1972.

Chronicles of London, ed. Charles L. Kingsford, Oxford University Press 1905.

Contemporary English Chronicles of the Wars of the Roses, ed by Dan Embree and Teresa Tavormina. Woodbridge: Boydell. 2019.

Death and Dissent. The Dethe of the Kyng of Scottis and Warkworth's Chronicle. Ed. Lister M. Matheson. Woodbridge; Boydell. 1999.

An English Chronicle of the reign of Richard II, Henry IV, Henry V and Henry VI. Ed. John Sylvester Davies. CS 64. 1856.

The English Chronicle 1377–1461: A New edition. Ed. William Marx. Woodbridge: Boydell. 2003.

[*Gregory's Chronicle*]: *Historical Collections of a Citizen of London in the Fifteenth Century*. Ed. James Gairdner. CS new series xvii (1876).

[*John Vale's Book*]: *Politics of Fifteenth Century England; John Vale's Book*. Ed. Margaret l. Kekewich, Colin Richmond, Anne Sutton, Livia Visser-Fuch, and John l. Watts. Stroud: Alan Sutton. 1995.

Six Town Chronicles. Ed. Ralph Flenley. Oxford: Oxford University Press. 1911.

Secondary Sources

Baskerville, G. (1913) 'A London Chronicle of 1460', *English Historical Review* 28, 123–127.

Emden, Alfred B. (1957–1959) *A Biographical Register of the University of Oxford to AD 1500*. 3 vols. Oxford University Press: Oxford.

Given-Wilson, Chris (2003), 'Chronicles of the Mortimer Family, c. 1250–1450', *Family and Dynasty in Late Medieval England*, ed. Richard Eales and Sean Tyas, Paul Watkin, Donington: Paul Watkins. 67–86

Griffiths, Ralph A. (1981), *King and Country*, Hambledon: London.

Hicks, Michael A. (2002) *English Political Culture in the Fifteenth Century*. Routledge: London.

Hicks, Michael A. (2005). 'Crowland's World: A Westminster View of the Yorkist Age', *History* 90: 172–190.

Hicks, Michael A. (2010) *Wars of the Roses*. London: Yale University Press.

Kleineke, Hannes (2014). 'Robert Bale's Chronicle and the Second Battle of St Albans', *Historical Research* 87: 744–750.

Matheson, Lister M. (1998). *The Prose Brut: The Development of a Middle English Chronicle*. Medieval and Renaissance Text Studies 180. Tempe.

McLaren, Mary-Rose (2002). *The London Chronicles of the Fifteenth Century: a Revolution in English Writing*. Woodbridge: Boydell.

Rajsic, Jaclyn, Kooper, Erik, and Heche, Dominique (2016), *The Prose Brut and other Medieval Chronicles*, Woodbridge: York University Press.

Taylor, John (2004). 'Higden, Ranulf (d. 1364), Benedictine monk and chronicler', ODNB 27, 49–50.

Taylor, John (1966). *The 'Universal Chronicle' of Ranulf Higden*. Oxford: Oxford University Press.

Thomson, John A.F. (2013). 'Continuation of' Gregory's Chronicle—a possible author?', *Piety and Politics in Britain, 14th–15th Centuries*. Ed. Graeme Small. Farnham: Ashgate. 94–97.

Walker, Simon (2004) 'Ive [Ivy], William (d. 1486), theologian', ODNB xxix: Oxford. 445–446.

14

Creative Copyists

Numerical Problems in a Manuscript of the Crónica de Don Álvaro de Luna *from the Bibliotheca Phillippica (MS 8415) and Their Implications for Future Editions*

David Hook

Abstract

A hitherto unstudied manuscript of the *Historia de Don Álvaro de Luna*, the Condestable of King Juan II of Castile, formerly in the collection of Richard Heber and then that of Sir Thomas Phillipps (MS 8415), contains some blank spaces where the copyist has not provided an expected numerical indicator of distance, duration, number, or quantity. Examination of the equivalent readings in some other textual witnesses reveals differing solutions to what was evidently a problem in an early witness to the text from which all these must descend. The implications of this situation for any future edition are briefly considered.

There have been long-standing debates over the authorship, development, and genre classification of the *Crónica* or *Historia de Don Álvaro de Luna*, to which a range of labels from 'crónica particular' to biography has been attached over the decades. Its internal self-description as 'la historia' suggests that the aim of some sections of this multi-phase text is less to give a chronological account of events than to present an interpretation of them. The complex organization and development of the text have been examined by Montero Garrido and González Delgado, and are conveniently summarized by Beltrán, while Montiel has perceptively analysed its diverse uses.[1] Whilst the presentation of its titular protagonist has overtones of that of a chivalresque hero, the moral dimension of its subject has, it has been pointed out, notable Christological overtones; and a recent observation by Ellis that the work is 'nearly hagiographic' will command some assent, at least in relation to particular sections of it.[2]

---

1   Montero Garrido (1995), Beltrán (2001), Montiel (1997), González Delgado (2012).
2   Ellis (2020: 246).

This paper offers a brief description of a previously unstudied manuscript, first recorded in the library of Richard Heber from which it came into that of Sir Thomas Phillipps as his MS 8415; and discusses some textual implications of certain readings in it. These, it suggests, could indicate that some readings transmitted in other witnesses are in fact later, non-authorial constructions created to resolve blank spaces or illegible phrases or numerals in an early exemplar. These problems underline the need for a new critical edition of the work that takes into account all the known witnesses to its textual transmission. As noted by Beltrán, to the nine MSS listed by Carriazo others should be added;[3] indeed, the number has risen to the nineteen witnesses (including MS 8415) known to the Philobiblon database at the University of California, Berkeley (consulted July 2021).

The Heber/Phillipps manuscript is currently MS C-4 in my library. Its recorded provenance begins with its ownership by a religious foundation in Madrid, from whose library the number '36' inked at the head of the spine presumably dates; an ownership inscription at the head of the first folio has at some point been hidden by a paper strip, subsequently removed, leaving the original inscription at best partially legible thanks to the residue of the glue. Optimistically rendered as 'the Discalced Franciscan convent of Madrid' in the 1976 Sotheby's auction catalogue cited below, with a computer-enhanced image of the inscription this may be read as 'Libreria g. delos Ps d..mos De la co de Madrid', which may be conjecturally resolved as 'Libreria general de los Padres dominicos (?) de la corte (?) de Madrid'. Of an eroded and faded single-line full-width inscription at the head of the limp vellum wrapper of the volume, presumably a title, I am unable to decipher even sufficient individual letters to hazard a reconstructive transcription. Since the volume was later owned by Richard Heber (1774–1833), it may be reasonably presumed that it probably left Madrid in the wake of the disruptions of the Napoleonic period or the temporary restoration of the Constitution of Cádiz (1820) and the subsequent French invasion (1823), rather than later. The subsequent provenance of the manuscript since the 1830s is clear and continuous; it appeared as lot 1004 in the sale of Heber's MSS (*Bibliotheca Heberiana*, XI) in London in 1836; and was acquired there by the London bookdealer Payne for Sir Thomas Phillipps (1792–1872). These two phases are attested by the relevant printed catalogues, but also by the two spine-labels bearing these numbers, in manuscript for the Heber sale, and printed from the Bibliotheca Phillippica.[4] From the dispersal sales of the

---

3   Carriazo (1940: XVI–XXI); Beltrán (2001: 74–75).
4   Hook (2017: II, plate X). On Heber, see Hunt (2001) and Munby (1977).

Bibliotheca Phillippica (New Series, VI, 1970) it was bought by Señor Joan Gili of the Dolphin Book Company of Oxford, from whom I purchased it in 1991.

From the course of this piece of book history, we have four catalogue entries for this MS, which variously assign it to the XVIth, XVIIth, and XVIIIth century. These are as follows:

1. *Bibliotheca Heberiana* XI:

    1004 Luna. Comienca la Historia de los claros fechos e animosos, del muy virtuoso y muy esforcado caballero Don Alvaro de Luna. Cod. del Siglo XVII. In double columns. [fol.]

2. Entry by Phillipps in his *Catalogus*:

    8415   1004 D. Alvaro de Luna Historia di Mastre de St. Iago.
    117 leaves. f. ch. s. xvi.

3. Entry in Catalogue 'F', now MS Phillipps-Robinson b.213 in the Bodleian Library, a handwritten list of Spanish MSS drawn up in 1924 by Phillipps' grandson Thomas Fitzroy Fenwick, who leaves an ellipsis for text that he was presumably unable to decipher.[5]

    8415

    Historia de los claros fechos e animosos ..... del muy virtuoso y muy esfor-cado Caballero Don Alvaro de Luna, &c. In the original vellum cover. 234 pp. Folio. XVII cent.

4. BPNS VI (16 June 1970) auction catalogue, lot 1281:

    1281 Historia de Don Alvaro de Luna maistre de santiago, 116 ll., double column, contemporary vellum, from the library of the Discalced Francis-can convent of Madrid, Phillipps MS. 8415, from the Heber collection (sale 10 February 1836, lot 1004). folio [18th century]. * Printed by Sancha in 1783–1784.

These descriptions illustrate the pitfalls awaiting studies based on historic cata-logue entries. Here, the transcription of the title varies from entry to entry, but none of the versions cited is a fully accurate rendering. Ignoring minor mis-readings, none gives, in the absence of any titlepage in the manuscript, the full heading of the first page of text after the prologue (which is separately headed 'Prologo deesta historia de don aluaro De luna maestre De *santiago*'). This is as follows, written in full-width lines across the page above the two-column arrangement of the text proper (contractions and abbreviations, marked and unmarked, are here expanded in italics; all translations are mine):

---

5 For Fenwick's catalogue, see Hook (2017: I, 194–199, 248–261; II: 328).

Comienca la historia de los claros fechos e animosos dichos notables fazañas deel muy virtuoso y muy esforçado cavallero Don Aluaro de luna Maestre de la orden de la Cavalleria de el vien aventurado Appostol santiago del espada; Condestable de castilla: e conde de santisvan, y señor del infaztazgo [sic, for 'infantazgo']

([Here] begins the history of the distinguished feats, spirited words, [and] notable deeds of the most virtuous and most valiant knight Don Álvaro de Luna, Master of the Military Order of the blessed Apostle St James the warrior, Constable of Castile, Count of Santistéban, and Lord of the Infantazgo.)

The work is thus presented here as an 'historia', not a 'crónica' as in the printed editions of Milan (1546), Flores (1784) and Carriazo (1940), and this is maintained in its colophon: 'fenesce la estoria del inclito don aluaro de luna maestre de santiago de la espada.' (fol. 114ᵛ of pencil sequence, 113ᵛ of ink).

The different dates assigned to the manuscript underline the difficulty of dating this class of script; my personal view is that Ph8415 is at the earliest a seventeenth-century copy.[6] It will also have been noticed that the number of leaves cited varies from 117 (Phillipps) to 116 (Sotheby). The explanation is not loss of a leaf during the intervening years, but lies partly in the peculiarities of an early ink foliation in Arabic numerals. This has lost a final digit in the right-hand corner of the head margin of some leaves following fol. 100 thanks to cropping by the binder; the last complete number in the sequence is 114, followed by two leaves of text and a final blank (but also numbered) folio, which before cropping would have been '115–116' and '117' respectively. In giving the total number of leaves, Phillipps has followed the logic of the ink foliation, and Sotheby's that of the last leaf containing text. The final blank, however, is conjoint with fol. 113 of the ink foliation, and is thus an integral part of the structure of the final quire; this point is further discussed below. The early ink foliation, moreover, is inaccurate in the volume as a whole, with disruption to its sequence following fol. 44 (= 44, 46, 57, 58, 49, 50 ...); a blank folio (H6) after fol. 62 is left unfoliated (the continuity of the text is unaffected by its presence); then further disruption is caused by a repetition after fol. 63 (= 64, 64, 65, 66 ...). My own pencil foliation correctly records fols 1–118 (including the integral blank leaf between ink fols 62–63) as the 'text leaves', with 119 as the

---

6 Its watermark (for which I can offer no precisely-dated parallel) is a device of an outline Latin cross within a near-cordiform circle, below which are the Roman capitals MB. The general arrangement can be paralleled from the second half of the sixteenth century.

final, blank but structurally integral, leaf. The explanation of the odd number is that fol. 112 of the ink foliation (113 of my pencil sequence) is a singleton, now glued to the final leaf of the penultimate quire 'O'. Since such a situation could indicate some textual disruption in the history of this copy, a detailed examination of the quire structure is necessary. There is clear evidence that fol. 112 (ink)/113 (pencil) is not a later inserted singleton, but was originally an integral part of the final quire. This is because what is currently the pastedown of the rear cover (now fully detached from the final folio of the text quires) was originally folio 118 of the ink foliation (which would be fol. 120 of my sequence): it still bears, in the same position at top right, the uncropped first two digits of that ink numbering, in identical ink to, and of the same size as, the numerals on the preceding leaves. This makes the final quire 'P' a regular 8-leaf quire like all the others in the manuscript, its outer bifolium being the pair represented by the now separated fols 112 and [118] of the ink numbering, and its central bifolium by fols 115–116. In that original state, quire P ended with two blank leaves. Its current state does not therefore indicate any textual problems at this point during production of the copy, nor any later textual splicing to remedy a deficiency. Although the quire signatures are occasionally inconsistent in terms of capitalization and the number of leaves per quire on which they are inscribed, they follow a clear alphabetical sequence (omitting J) throughout the manuscript (AbcDefGHIKLMNOP$_8$). Folios 14–16 have some textual discontinuity arising in copying rather than binding; the correct textual sequence is indicated in early marginal *signes de renvoi*.

This MS escaped the attention of Usoz in his survey of some of Heber's Spanish acquisitions.[7] Having entered the Bibliotheca Phillippica, it unsurprisingly also eluded the modern editor of the chronicle, Carriazo; there was historically little awareness in Spain of the Hispanic material in Sir Thomas' library, mainly because of the inaccessibility there of his *Catalogus*. Although noted by Beltrán in his important study, Ph8415 has not been consulted by any modern scholars who have dealt with this chronicle.[8]

A variety of evidence suggests that Ph8415 was not copied from the printed tradition; for example, its numbering of the chapters does not follow the single overall sequence of 128 chapters or *títulos* plus an epilogue found in the printed editions, but reflects a state in which the text was subdivided into four separate sequences of chapter numbers (specifically, 1–73, 1–8, 1–7, 1–29): a complication unlikely to have been introduced by a copyist working from a printed exemplar with unitary numbering. This detail recalls a much less fragmented,

---

7 Usoz (1842).
8 Beltrán (2001: 74).

but still non-unitary, sequence found in an early witness, MS 10141 of the Biblioteca Nacional, Madrid, described by Montero Garrido.[9] Ph8415 also leaves blank spaces at various points in the text where the printed tradition has an uninterrupted and continuous text with content that is more or less meaningful and coherent. It seems likely that in such cases the printed editions were coping with a problematic reading from earlier in the transmission, for which they concocted a workable solution (even if occasionally one that raises new problems), whilst the copyist of Ph8415, facing the same difficulty in his exemplar, left it unresolved by leaving a blank, probably for future attention which in some cases never materialized. This MS is thus an excellent illustration both of the potential importance of relatively late manuscripts, and of how the study of a previously unexamined witness can affect our understanding of textual quirks in, and textual relationships among, long-known witnesses. There follow selected examples of these problems; chapter or *título* numbers are those common to the printed editions of 1546 (Milan) and 1784 (Flores). Additionally, Carriazo's edition (1940) is included as representing Biblioteca Nacional, Madrid, MSS 10141 (A, his base text) and 2127 (B, used by him to 'correct' A in 'necessary', but alas unspecified, circumstances).[10]

1. The distance from Calatayud to Cetina:
   (a) Ph8415, tit. xxiii, fol. 25ra (ink and pencil foliations)
       entre los otros lugares entro por fuerça vn buen lugar \IV/ ...... a leguas de Calatayud que dizian çetina[11]
   (b) Milan, tit. XXIII, fol. 19va:
       Entre los otros lugares entro por fuerça vn buen lugar a çerca de Calatayud que dezian çetiba
   (c) Flores, tit. XXIII, p. 79:
       Entre los otros logares entró por fuerza un buen logar á dos leguas de Calatayud que descian Cetiba
   (d) Carriazo, cap. XXIII, p. 91:
       Entre los otros logares, entró por fuerça un buen logar a dos leguas de Calatayud, que dezían Cetina

A blank space in Ph8415 with a numeral seemingly added in it later, a vague phrase in Milan, and a different distance in Flores and Carriazo from that in Ph8415 alert us to a problem resolved in different ways by these witnesses,

9   Montero Garrido (1995: 96).
10 Carriazo (1940: XXI); see comments by Beltrán (2001: 75).
11 In passages quoted, oblique strokes designate later textual insertions. 'Among the other places, he stormed a goodly settlement \4/ ... leagues from Calatayud, which was called Çetina.'

probably caused by an illegible numerical or verbal expression of the distance between Calatayud and Cetina, which in modern terms is roughly thirty kilometres.

2. The number of casualties from an 'industrial accident':

   (a) Ph8415, cap. iiij, fol. 70va ink/71va pencil:

   cayeron los maestros todos enel Rio que no quedo sino solo vno de buen numero que eran y alli fenescieron sus dias.[12]

   (b) Milan, tit. XCV, fol. 59vb:

   cayero*n* los mismos Maestros todos enel Rio: que non quedo dellos sino vno solo: assi que fenesçieron alli sus dias.

   (c) Flores, cap. XCV, p. 248:

   cayeron los mismos maestros todos en el rio, que non quedó dellos si non solo uno de fasta en número de mas de treinta: assi que fenescieron alli sus dias.

   (d) Carriazo, cap. XCV, p. 282:

   cayeron los mismos maestros todos en el río, que non quedó dello si non sólo uno de fasta en número de más de ..., ansí que fenesçieron allí sus días.

The garrison's engineers or carpenters fall into a river on the collapse of a wooden structure undergoing modification; all except one drown. It will be observed that the term 'número' is used in three witnesses (with a close verbal resemblance here between Carriazo and Flores), but that a specific number is cited only in Flores. Ph8415 generalises with 'buen numero', and Milan 1546 omits the reference to the total number completely. This suggests that the problem predates MSS A and B, Milan, and whatever ancestor Ph8415 copied, which was obviously not the printed tradition. As will be seen, similar problems affect other readings which could involve specific numbers, with either omission or textual manipulation being used to cover the gap or dodge the difficulty.

3. The date of attendance at Mass with King Juan II:

   (a) Ph8415: tit. lv, fol. 47va pencil/'58'va ink:

   Otro dia sabado .... dias del mes de junio [*written over* julio] siendo manana oyeron el Rey y maestre missa Armados.[13]

   (b) Milan, tit. LXIII, fol. 39va:

   Otro dia sabado andados algunos dias del mes de Junio bien de da mañana oyeron el Rey & el Maestre missa armados

---

12   'All the master carpenters fell into the river, so that only one of them remained of all their sizeable number, and there they ended their days.'

13   'Next day, Saturday the .... day of the month of June, in the morning the King and the Master attended Mass in full armour.'

(c)   Flores, tit. LXIII, p. 164:

Otro dia sabado andados algunos dias del mes de Junio, bien de mañana oyeron el Rey é el Maestre Misa armados

(d)   Carriazo, cap. LXIII, p. 187:

Otro día, sábado, ... días del mes de junio, bien de mañana, oyeron el Rey e el Maestre misa armados

Leaving aside the problem of 'siendo' versus 'bien de', the wording of Ph8415 and that of Carriazo invites completion of the blank by insertion of a specific number; the printed tradition by contrast agrees on a vague 'algunos' here. Again the problem was obviously in an exemplar earlier than MSS A, B, and Ph8415.

4.   The duration of the royal presence at the siege of Palenzuela:

(a)   Ph8415, cap. iiij, fol. 72rb pencil/71rb ink:

e despues de los fechos ansi concluydos el Rey e su maestre e sus gentes se parten del cerco de palençuela a cauo de aver estado en el por espacio de .... poco mas o menos e se van a portillo villa del mesmo maestre.[14]

(b)   Milan, tit. XCV, fol. 60rb:

y despues de los fechos assi concluydos: el Rey: & su Maestre: y sus gentes: se parten del çerco de Palençuela acabo de hauer estado enel. Algunos se van a Portillo Villa del mismo Maestre.

(c)   Flores, tit. XCV, p. 250:

E despues de los fechos assi concluidos el Rey, é su Maestre é sus gentes se parten del cerco de Palenzuela, al cavo de aver estado en él por espacio de ciertos dias, é se van á Portillo, villa del mismo Maestre.

(d)   Carriazo, cap. XCV, p. 285:

E después de los fechos así concluídos, el Rey e su Maestre e sus gentes se parten del çerco de Palençuela, al cabo de aver estado en él por espaçio de ... días, e se van a Portillo, villa del mismo Maestre.

Similar to previous examples in so far as the logic of Ph8415 and Carriazo invites a specific numerical insertion to fill the blank concerning the duration of the king's visit to the siege camp at Palenzuela. Milan is clearly barely satisfactory and achieves such meaning as it has only through a radical restructuring of the text; Flores again opts for vagueness ('por espacio de ciertos dias') to avoid providing a specific number. Whilst Ph8415 and Flores agree that after

---

14   'And after these matters were thus concluded, the King and the Master and their company departed from the siege of Palenzuela after having been there for more or less ..... and went to Portillo, a town held by the Master himself.'

the king had been at the siege for some time the entire company went on from Palenzuela to Portillo, Milan states that only some ('Algunos') did so. An hypothesis can be advanced that this 'Algunos' may be a repurposed remnant of a longer but semi-legible phrase, namely the chronological statement concerning the length of the king's stay at the siege of Palenzuela such as is invited by the blank in Ph8415; here one could hazard something like 'a cabo de hauer estado en el por espacio de algunos dias; e se van ...'. In this case, we would have at least three steps: an illegible word or blank space in one exemplar, followed by a tidying-up operation involving the insertion of a vague statement such as 'algunos dias' and finally deletion of the entire duration clause except for 'algunos', the semantic antecedent of which now becomes 'gentes'. (Where the rest of the company went, we are not told.) The difficulty, whatever it was, that provoked the differing solutions offered by Ph8415 and Milan was clearly encountered in an exemplar predating 1546.

5. The distance from Portillo to Brazuelas/Brazuelos:
    (a) Ph8415, cap. xiiii, fol. 88ra pencil/87ra ink:
         era vno que se llamaua Alfon gonçales de leon señor de un lugar ques fasta .... leguas de portillo el qual se llamaua braçuelas.[15]
    (b) Milan, tit. CXII, fol. 72rb:
         era vno que se llamaua Alonso Gonçalez de Leon señor de vn lugar que es çerca de Portillo. El qual se llama Braçuelas.
    (c) Flores, tit. CXII, p. 301:
         era uno que se llamaba Alfonso Gonzalez de Leon, señor de un logar que es cerca de Portillo, el qual se llama Brazuelos
    (d) Carriazo, cap. CXII, p. 342:
         era uno que se llamaba Alonso Gonçález de León, señor de un lugar que es fasta ... leguas de Portillo, el qual se llama Brazuelos

The verbal formulation in Ph8415 and Carriazo's sources invites a specific numerical expression of distance in leagues from the settlement of Portillo. The printed tradition is non-specific in merely stating that Brazuelas is 'near' Portillo, again dodging the problem at the price of vagueness.

6. The quantity of coin in the moneybags:
    (a) Ph8415, cap. xxiii, fol. 103vb pencil/102vb ink:
         e dioles a cada vno sendos talegones de aquellos que podria aver en cada vno dellos fasta \seys/ \dos mill doblas/ =doblas=.[16]

---

15 'It was a man called Alfonso Gonçales de León, Lord of a place that is about ..... leagues from Portillo, which is called Braçuelas.'

16 'And he gave to each of them one of those moneybags, in which there could have been in every one up to \six/\two thousand *doblas*/. ~~doblas~~.'

(b)   Milan, tit. CXXII, f. 82vb:

y dioles cada sendos talegones de aquellas doblas: que podia hauer en cada uno de aquellos fasta de moneda mucho numero.

(c)   Flores, tit. CXXII, p. 349:

é dióles cada sendos talegones de aquellas doblas, que podria aver en cada uno de aquellos fasta dos mill.

(d)   Carriazo, cap. CXXII, p. 398:

e dióles cada sendos talegones de aquellas doblas, que podría aver en cada uno de aquellos fasta ... .

In describing Álvaro de Luna's hasty arrangements, when faced with imminent arrest and execution, to dispose of quantities of coin held in his dwelling in Burgos and to reward members of his household, the chronicle narrates how he fills moneybags with *doblas* which he distributes to them. The texts vary on the quantity involved. The blank space originally left in Ph8415 has been filled first by 'dos' which has later been overwritten to read 'seys'; in filling the blank, 'doblas' has been duplicated, and the original 'doblas' which followed the blank space has been marked for deletion by two pairs of oblique lines (here represented by = signs). Carriazo's two manuscript sources seem to leave a blank; Flores agrees with the 'dos' provided in Ph8415; but Milan has clearly not found a number in its exemplar, and in that line of transmission a vague indicator of large quantity ('mucho numero') has been provided to cover this deficiency.

Other cases of blank spaces left in the text of Ph8415 involve aspects such as personal names, placenames and lordships, but the point is already clear from the numerical instances cited here. Any future edition should be based on a full collation of all extant witnesses in order to identify all those readings which may embody non-authorial textual modifications generated in order to resolve a problem of information deficiency caused by omission or illegibility, notably but not solely associated with numerical expression, that obviously arose at a very early point in the manuscript transmission of the text. History may indeed be, as Montero Garrido's title states, a literary creation; but in addition to the creativity of chroniclers, it is necessary (as these problems in MS Ph 8415 remind us) to take into account the creative contributions of copyists to the texts preserved in our extant witnesses.

Bibliography

Primary Sources—Manuscript

La historia de los claros fechos e animosos dichos notables fazañas deel muy virtuoso y muy esforçado cavallero Don Aluaro de luna Maestre de la orden de la Cavalleria de el vien aventurado Appostol santiago del espada; Condestable de castilla: e conde de santisvan, y señor del infaztazgo [sic, for 'infantazgo']. MS Phillipps 8415; currently MS C-4, private library of the author.

Primary Sources—Printed

Carriazo, Juan de Mata, ed. (1940). *Crónica de Don Álvaro de Luna, Condestable de Castilla, Maestre de Santiago.* Colección de Crónicas Españolas, 2. Madrid: Espasa-Calpe. [Representing BNM MSS 10141 (A) and 2127(B).]

Comiença la Coronica de don Aluaro de Luna Condestable de los Reynos de Castilla y de Leon: Maestre y administrador de la orden y caualleria de Santiago. (1546). Milan: printed by Juan Antonio de Castellono.

Flores, Josef Miguel de, ed. (1784). *Cronica de D. Alvaro de Luna, Condestable de los reynos de Castilla y de Leon, Maestre y Administrador de la Orden y Caballeria de Santiago.* 'segunda impresión'. Madrid: printed by Antonio de Sancha.

Secondary Sources

Beltrán, Rafael. (2001). 'Don Juan de Mata Carriazo, editor de crónicas medievales', in Juan Luis Carriazo Rubio, ed., *Juan de Mata Carriazo y Arroquia: perfiles de un centenario, 1899–1999.* Sevilla: Secretariado de Publicaciones, Universidad de Sevilla: 59–109, at 73–79.

Bibliotheca Heberiana, XI. (1836). *Catalogue of the Library of the late Richard Heber, Esq. Part the eleventh. Manuscripts. Which will be sold by Auction, by Mr. Evans, at his House, no. 93, Pall Mall. On Wednesday, February 10th, and Nine following days, Sunday excepted.* London: Evans.

de Ricci, Seymour. (1930). *English Collectors of Books and Manuscripts (1530–1930) and their Marks of Ownership.* New York: The Macmillan Company; and Cambridge: University Press.

Ellis, James. (2020). 'Enemies that should be friends: knightly disloyalty and rebellion at the court of Juan II of Castile', in Kim Bergqvist, Kurt Villads Jensen, and Anthony John Lappin, eds. *War, Diplomacy and Peacemaking in Medieval Iberia.* Newcastle upon Tyne: Cambridge Scholars Publishing: 237–263.

Fenwick, Thomas Fitzroy: see Hook, D.

González Delgado, Ramiro. (2012). 'Tradición clásica y doble autoría en la *Crónica de don Álvaro de Luna*'. *Bulletin hispanique*, 114-2: 839–851.

Hook, David. (2017). *The Hispanic, Portuguese, and Latin American Manuscripts of Sir*

Thomas Phillipps, 2 vols, Publications of the Magdalen Iberian Medieval Studies Seminar, 5. Westbury on Trym: Fontaine Notre Dame/David Hook.

Hunt, Arnold. (1996). '*Bibliotheca Heberiana*', in Robin Myers and Michael Harris, eds., *Antiquaries, Book Collectors and the Circles of Learning*. Winchester: St Paul's Bibliographies, and New Castle, Delaware: Oak Knoll Press: 83–112.

Hunt, Arnold. (2001). 'The sale of Richard Heber's Library', in Robin Myers, Michael Harris, and Giles Mandelbrote, eds., *Under the Hammer: book auctions since the seventeenth century*. New Castle, Delaware: Oak Knoll Press, and London: The British Library: 143–171; includes as Appendix 2 Marc Vaulbert de Chantilly, 'The statistics of the London Heber Sales': 170–171.

Montero Garrido, Cruz. (1995). *La historia, creación literaria. El ejemplo del Cuatrocientos*. Fuentes cronísticas de la historia de España, 8. Madrid: Fundación Ramón Menéndez Pidal, and Universidad Autónoma de Madrid.

Montiel Roig, Gonzalo. (1997). 'Los móviles de la redacción de la *Crónica de Don Álvaro de Luna*'. *Revista de Literatura Medieval*, 9: 173–195.

Munby, A.N.L. (1977). 'Father and Son: The Rev. Reginald Heber's vain attempt to stem the rising tide of his son Richard's bibliomania', reprinted in Munby, *Essays and Papers*, ed. Nicolas Barker. London: The Scolar Press: 225–234.

[Phillipps, Sir Thomas]. (2001). *The Phillipps Manuscripts. Catalogus librorum manuscriptorum in Bibliotheca D. Thomae Phillipps, Bt. Impressum Typis Medio-Montanis 1837–1871. With an introduction by A.N.L. Munby*. London: The Holland Press, 1968; rpt. [London]: Orskey-Johnson.

Philobiblon: https://bancroft.berkeley.edu/philobiblon *or* https://pb.lib.berkeley.edu (*consulted 06 June 2021*).

Sotheby & Co. (1970). *Bibliotheca Phillippica. Catalogue of French, Spanish, Portuguese, Greek, Yugoslav and Slavonic Manuscripts from the Celebrated Collection formed by Sir Thomas Phillipps, Bt. (1792–1872). New Series: Sixth Part* [...] London: Sotheby & Co. [Sale date: 15–16 June 1970.]

'U' [= Usoz y Río, Luis]. (1842). 'Noticia de manuscritos españoles existentes fuera de España', *Revista andaluza*, 4: 735–746.

15

The Printing of the Middle English Prose *Brut* and the Early Stages of Anglo-Dutch Publishing

Sjoerd Levelt

Abstract

The Middle English Prose *Brut* was printed four times between 1480 and 1493: twice by William Caxton in Westminster (1480 and 1482), once by William de Machlinia in London (c. 1486), and finally by Gerard Leeu in Antwerp (1493), in an edition completed shortly after Leeu's death from a stab wound inflicted by his punch cutter. This study of Gerard Leeu's edition in relation to its predecessors sheds new light not only on Leeu's edition, but also on the wider development of printing in English in its earliest decades. It leads us to a more nuanced view of the relations between these three early publishers of works in English, and shows the industry they helped establish to have been more fundamentally Anglo-Dutch in nature than has previously been acknowledged. Finally, the evidence makes it possible to add Gerard Leeu to the list of early publishers of English works in the Dutch Low Countries who not only printed, but personally knew English.

1 The Death of a Publisher

In 1493, a Middle English chronicle of England, a version of the Middle English Prose *Brut*, was printed in Antwerp.[1] Its colophon is a remarkable piece of writing in several respects:

> Here ben endyd the Cronycles of the Reame of Englond with their apperteignaunces. Enprentyd In the Duchye of Braband. in the towne of Andewarpe In the yere of owr lord .M.cccc.xciij. By maistir Gerard de leew. a man of grete wysedom in all maner of kunnyng: whych nowe is come from

---

1 ISTC icoo481000; I thank my colleagues Elisabeth van Houts and Moreed Arbabzadah for our collaboration from which this work stems, Ad Putter for his comments on an earlier version, and the Leverhulme Trust for its generous financial support.

© KONINKLIJKE BRILL NV, LEIDEN, 2023 | DOI:10.1163/9789004547124_016

lyfe vnto the deth / which is grete harme for many a poure man. On whos
sowle god almyghty for hys hygh grace haue mercy

A M E N[2]

The passage is a rare surviving specimen of English written in the medieval
Dutch Low Countries. Coming at the end of an edition of the Middle English
Brut by Gerard Leeu, printer originally from Gouda who had relocated to Antwerp in 1484, it is followed by Leeu's printer's device (Figure 1). It was, however,
obviously printed after Leeu's passing, and the colophon therefore attests not
only to Leeu's ability to publish work in English, but also to the presence of
English-speaking personnel in Leeu's workshop—a presence which will have
made such publications possible. That the colophon was written by a member of Leeu's personnel is clear from the heartfelt, yet perhaps somewhat self-
centered lament that Leeu's death was 'grete harme for many a poure man'.

What the colophon does not disclose is *how* Leeu died, but this we know
from other sources; and again a member of personnel of Leeu's workshop was
involved. A record of account from Jan van Ranst, sheriff (*schout*) of Antwerp,[3]
of 1493, tells:

> Van eenen geheyten Henric Van Symmen, in de Wandelinge, letterstekere,
> dairmen boecken mede print, vuyt Hollant, van dat hy die een arm geselle
> was, om desselfs syns ambachts wille, midts dat hy met meesteren Geerde,
> boecpryntere, salige gedachten, nyet wercken en woude, mair op hem-
> selven om meerder winningen tedoene, van denselven meesteren Geerde
> met quaden woerden, ende oic faictelic veroverlast zynde, denselven
> meesteren Geerde een cleyn steecxken gaf in syn hooft, soe dat hy bynnen
> twee of drie dagen dairna dairaf sterf; midts welcken feyte, hy, den voirs-
> chreven meesteren Geerde, noch liggende in levende lyve, tot Andwerpen
> gevangen werdt, partyelic voir ende na de doot lange vervolght mit rechte,
> ende want de vriende genoech bevonden dat 't feyt onnoselic gebuerde,
> soe hebben zy, denselven tot genaden ende soenen laten comen, midts
> denwelcken ic van Myns genedichs Heeren wegen, gemerct den redenen
> voirschreven, insgelicx denselven hebben laten componeren, ende dairaf
> gecregen tot Myns genedichs Heeren behoef, XL gulden, te X stuvers 't
> stuck, qui valent V liv. grooten.[4]

---

2   Leeu, sig. [z8]v.
3   Rijns (2013).
4   Ruelens (1864: 7).

¶ Here ben endyd the Cronycles of the Reame of Englond with their
apperteignaunces. Enprietyd In the Duchye of Braband, in the towne
of Andewarpe In the yere of owr lord . M.cccc.rciij. By maistir Gerard
de leew. a man of grete wysedom in all maner of künyng: whych nowe
is come from lyfe vnto the deth/which is grete harme for many a poure
man. On whos sowle god almyghty for hys hygh grace haue mercy
A M E N

FIGURE 15.1   Colophon and printer's mark in Gerard Leeu's edition of the Middle English
            Prose *Brut*. The Hague, Koninklijke Bibliotheek, KW 172 A 5, sig. [z8]v.

(About one called Henric van Symmen, of occupation a cutter of letters for the printing of books, from Holland: because he was a poor journeyman, for the sake of his trade, therefore he no longer wanted to work with Master Gerard, book printer, of blessed memory, but by himself, to make greater profits, away from that Master Gerard. With angry words, and also being truly anguished, he gave this same Master Gerard a small cut in his head, so that he died within two or three days thereafter. Because of this event, while the aforementioned Master Gerard was still lying alive, he was arrested in Antwerp, and both before and after his death legally prosecuted. And because the nominated arbiters of both parties concluded that the event happened accidentally, they have let them come to mercy and to reconciliation. For this I on behalf of my merciful lords' ways, having taken into account the aforementioned reasons, likewise have let the same be settled, and to my lords' desire received 40 guilders (at 10 stuyvers a piece), that is 5 pounds groats.)

Henric van Symmen, also known as Hendrik Lettersnyder, who gave Leeu the stab wound from which he died, subsequently indeed established himself as an independent printer, if only briefly.[5]

2   William Caxton and the Low Countries

Another rare, and slightly earlier, example, of Middle English writing from the Dutch Low Countries is William Caxton's *Recuyell of the Historyes of Troye*, published in Ghent or Bruges in 1473/4,[6] and the first book ever to be printed in English. In it, Caxton noted that his work of translating his French source, Raoul Lefèvre's *Recueil des Histoires de Troye*, 'was begonne in Brugis, & contynued in gaunt And finysshid in Coleyn In the tyme of þe troublous world, and of the grete deuysions beyng and reygnyng as well in the royames of englond and fraunce as in all other places vnyuersally thurgh the world that is to wete the yere of our lord a thousand four honderd lxxi.'[7] A further example of English written in the medieval Dutch Low Countries is presented by *The Game and Playe of the Chesse*, published by Caxton in 1474 while still in Flanders, and also

5   Valkema Blouw (2013: 9–12).
6   ISTC il00117000.
7   Oxford, Bodleian Library, S.Seld. d.1, fol. 251ᵛ.

translated by him, from Jacobus de Cessolis' *Liber de moribus hominum et officiis nobilium ac popularium super ludo scachorum*.[8]

William Caxton, born in Kent, was a mercer from London, who from the early 1450s spent most of his time in Flanders, primarily in Bruges, where by 1462 he had become governor of the English nation. Between 1464 and 1467 the English merchants were forced to relocate to Utrecht; Caxton accompanied them in their relocation, but soon returned to Bruges to negotiate for their return. By 1471, Caxton had resigned his governorship, and relocated to Cologne, where he got involved in a new trade: that of the printed book. While in Cologne, he acquired the experience, the collaborators and the press necessary to set up his own publishing business when having returned to Flanders in 1472, developing his early publishing venture in collaboration with local book producers and traders.[9]

Ad Putter has shown Caxton to have been thoroughly bilingual by this time, his English infused with Dutch, even when translating from French rather than from Dutch itself.[10] In 1475/6, after spending the better part of three decades in the Low Countries, Caxton moved from Flanders to England, where he set up England's first press in Westminster. It is quite likely that the first of Caxton's translations which he published after resettling in Westminster was a work he had already written during his time in Flanders.[11] But even when he set to translating new works for publication, he did not entirely cut his ties to Flanders, his homeland for three decades: in 1481 he published his translation, from Dutch, of the beast epic *Reynard the Fox*, Flemish both in origin and in setting,[12] even if the version Caxton set to translate came not from Flanders, but from Holland: namely, from the press of Gerard Leeu in Gouda.[13]

---

8   ISTC ico0413000.

9   Blake (2004a).

10   Levelt and Putter (2021: 257–260); putter (2021).

11   *The historie of Jason*, ISTC iloo112000.

12   ISTC iroo137000.

13   *Historie van Reynaert die vos* (1479), ISTC iroo135800; confirmed to be Caxton's direct source by Blake (1970: xlvii–xlviii).

3   The Middle English Prose *Brut*, William Caxton, and William
         de Machlinia

From Westminster, Caxton set to explore new genres of publishing for the English market, and one genre for which he soon found an eager audience turned
out to be historical writing. In 1480, he published his version of the Middle English Prose *Brut* chronicle—in large part relying on the text as transmitted in the
manuscript tradition, with what is believed to be his own continuation for the
years 1419 to 1461.[14] The publication was a success, and was soon followed by a
second edition, also by Caxton, in 1482.[15]

Lotte Hellinga has noted that Caxton's *Brut*-edition of 1480 marks a development for Caxton toward increased independence from his Low Countries
background: 'its production coincides with considerable renewal and expansion of the materials in his printing house in the form of a new fount of type
and a new, improved press, both pointing to plans to increase his capacity for
production. The new fount of type, known to bibliographers as Type 4: 95B,
was much more economical than the two much larger *de luxe* founts brought
from Flanders that he had used from 1476 in the early years in Westminster.'[16]
The 1482 edition saw modernization of the text of the *Brut*, as Caxton adjus-
ted vocabulary and spellings in 'an effort to remove all remaining traces of a
slightly old-fashioned origin of the text, and also of the irregularities in spacing
that had crept in as a result of copy-fitting.'[17]

The text of Caxton's *Brut* was then repurposed, with the addition of universal historical information and historical information concerning the succession
of popes and the Christian church, for an expanded edition first published in
St Albans, which was printed nine times between 1483 and 1528.[18] This text will
remain outside the scope of this chapter. A further edition of Caxton's own *Brut*,
however, by William de Machlinia, followed in c. 1486.[19] Machlinia, or William
Maclyn, was a printer who from his name appears to have been from Mechelen
in Brabant, who had been active in London since 1482. Unlike Caxton, who had
founded his publishing business in Westminster, Machlinia established himself
in London, first with collaborator John Lettou near All Saints' Church, and then

---

14   ISTC ic00477000. For the printing of the Middle English Prose *Brut*, see Matheson (1998:
      339–348); Matheson (1985); Weijer (2016); for Caxton's exemplar for the years to 1419, Hunt-
      ington Library MS HM 136, see Wakelin (2011); Takagi (2012); Hellinga (2017).
15   ISTC ic00478000.
16   Hellinga (2017: 322).
17   Hellinga (2017: 324).
18   STC 9995–10002.
19   ISTC ic00480000.

independently first at Fleet Bridge and subsequently, from 1486, in Holborn. It is here that he published the *Chronicles of England*.[20] Except for his collaboration with John Lettou on six publications in 1482/3—indeed Machlinia is in all probability to be identified with printer William Ravenswalde who is recorded as living with Lettou in the 1483 poll tax for aliens,[21] and who married Lettou's widow, the Dutchwoman Elizabeth—,[22] and his list of twenty-two named or attributed French, Latin and English publications between 1483 and 1490, there is, unfortunately, nothing more that we know about Machlinia.[23]

4   Gerard Leeu

While the St Albans chronicle was only just starting its long run of editions, the run of the *Brut* soon came to an end: it was reprinted only one more time, in 1493, two years after William Caxton's death, by Gerard Leeu in Antwerp.[24] Gerard Leeu was born in the middle of the fifteenth century from a family with long ties to Gouda. He established himself as printer in Gouda in 1477, where he continued publishing until moving to Antwerp in 1484. Thus, Leeu will in all likelihood have been in Gouda when William Caxton visited the town on a number of occasions in 1475 as part of a diplomatic delegation, as 'factor van den coninc van ingelant' ('representative to the king of England')[25]—it is, however, by no means certain that the two men met at that time.[26] Over the decade and a half of his printing career, Leeu was responsible for at least 228 editions, initially exclusively in Dutch and (to a much smaller extent) French, but once he had acquired the necessary type with Latin ligatures and abbreviations, soon overtaken by Latin editions, which eventually made up almost two thirds of his list.[27] Desiderius Erasmus, who had strong familial and professional ties to Gouda himself, in 1489 recommended Leeu to one of his friends as 'impressoriae artis opifex, vir sane lepidus'[28] ('an artisan of the art of printing, and a good-natured man').

---

20   Blake (2004b).

21   Sutton (2014: 128); Sutton (1994: 136).

22   Christianson (1999: 138–139).

23   Blake (2004b).

24   ISTC ic00481000.

25   Gouda, Streekarchief Hollands Midden, OA 1140, fol. 145, reproduced by Klein (2003: 176).

26   Klein (2003: 175–181).

27   Rijns (2013).

28   Erasmus, *Opus epistolarum* I, 127.

Besides Dutch, Latin and French, from the 1480s Leeu also printed in English: from 1488, for example, is his edition of *Vulgaria Terentii*, a book of Latin sentences with English translations, copied from an edition by William de Machlinia.[29] A Directorium (a guide for praying Divine Office) from 1488 is specifically for English readers,[30] but this edition is far from the only Latin work by Leeu that survives predominantly or even exclusively in English collections,[31] suggesting that with several of his titles throughout the second half of the 1480s he deliberately targeted the English market for books. While Leeu had previously concentrated primarily on Latin texts that could be sold both on the continent and in England, and on Dutch texts that could be sold locally, after the death of Caxton in 1492, Leeu promptly stepped in to fill the gap left by England's first printer in the area of texts in English or exclusively for English readers, too: in very quick succession, Leeu published a Sarum Book of Hours,[32] *Salomon and Marcolphus*,[33] *Parys and Vyenne*,[34] and *The History of Jason*,[35] the last two reprints of earlier Caxton editions (and indeed texts translated by Caxton himself).[36] Concluding this series, Leeu was responsible for the final edition of Caxton's Middle English Prose *Brut*, which appeared from his press posthumously, in 1493; Leeu had died in December 1492.[37]

In fact, there is a real possibility that the strong trade links with England were a significant factor in Leeu's decision to relocate from Gouda to Antwerp, where the English Merchant Adventurers had their headquarters in this period. The question remains whether Leeu's English trade in the 1480s was in competition, or in coordination with Caxton's; it is quite possible that Caxton, knowing his press was not able to satisfy the local appetite for printed books, coordinated his own output with that of Leeu—in other words: that Leeu was working as a franchise holder of Caxton's publishing venture for the English market,[38] which was at the time far less saturated by supply than was the Dutch.[39] And it was

---

29   ISTC itoo111050; Wakelin (2014: 229); Brodie (1972: 323). Hellinga (2018a: 342, n. 7) asserts
       the exemplar to have been a copy from the fifteenth-century Oxford press instead.
30   ISTC idoo265250.
31   E.g., ISTC ia00426600; ij00003540; ig00076150; ig00075850; ie00135300; il00019900;
       ij00273540; ia00197000.
32   ISTC ih00420430; Hellinga (2018a: 342, n. 7).
33   ISTC is00102800.
34   ISTC ip00113600.
35   ISTC il00112100.
36   ISTC ip00113500; il00112000.
37   For the evidence, see Bradbury and Bradbury (2012: 'Introduction').
38   Hellinga (2018a).
39   Pleij (1987).

not only Leeu who would borrow titles from Caxton; the reverse was true, too, as Caxton translated his *History of Reynard the Fox* (Westminster, 1481) from Leeu's prose *Historie van Reynaert die vos* (Gouda 1479, or a slightly earlier edition). That Leeu only commenced printing a significant number of books *in* English just after Caxton's death further supports the hypothesis that there was coordination between the two printers. However, Caxton was not the only English printer with whom Leeu may have been in contact: William de Machlinia, whose edition of *Vulgaria Terentii* Leeu had reprinted in 1488, was another.

5   Gerard Leeu's *Cronycles of the londe of Englond*

The 1493 edition of the Middle English *Brut* followed the previous three editions of Caxton's text closely, but had two notable additions: the aforementioned colophon (Figure 1), and a title page (Figure 2). The first title page to an English book had been printed by William de Machlinia in 1485. In that case, however, the page had no decoration, and simply stated the title: 'A passing gode lityll boke necessarye & behouefull a3enst the pestilence'.[40] The first title page to a book in Dutch had been printed by Leeu himself, in 1477.[41] Title pages—absent in manuscript production—had initially served a double function: to protect the first pages of text during transport, and to inform shop keepers and customers of the content of the book.[42] The first title pages were not illustrated, but decorative elements were soon introduced, initially primarily to facilitate the printing process: the additional elements across the full page made it easier to make the impression. Leeu's decorated title page, however, is not merely decorative, but meaningful—and the woodcut may well have been produced for the purpose: the angels depicted in the illustration hold up the English royal coat of arms, perfectly suited to a chronicle of the kings of England.

A further change from the previous editions is Leeu's chosen layout in two columns; the Caxton and Machlinia editions had been single-column (as had the first edition of the St Albans chronicle, which was later reset in two columns by Wynkyn de Worde—another early English printer of Dutch origin—in 1497).[43]

Collation of Leeu's text with the earlier editions delivers a result that invites us to reconsider the relations between the people involved. The editions by

---

40   ISTC ij00013600.
41   ISTC ic00902000; Klein (2003: 189).
42   Cole (1971: 303–316); Smith (2000).
43   ISTC ic00479000; Hellinga (2018b).

FIGURE 15.2   Title page of Gerard Leeu's edition of the Middle English Prose *Brut*. The
Hague, Koninklijke Bibliotheek, KW 172 A 5, title page.

Caxton and Machlinia textually differed only in detail. Caxton himself had somewhat revised his text for his second edition, and it is clear from variants that Machlinia based his text on Caxton's first edition, of 1480,[44] and followed its text very closely. Leeu intervened in the text much more actively, in effect delivering a revised version—but variants show him to have based his text not on either of Caxton's editions,[45] but on that of William de Machlinia.

Reliance on Machlinia is particularly clear in those places where Machlinia botched his copy—leading Leeu to attempt to restore the text. At the opening of Chapter 1, Leeu rather extraordinarily calls Eneas 'a noble king'. He was called 'a noble knyght' in both Caxton editions, but Machlinia erroneously printed 'kynght', leading Leeu astray.[46] The Verschlimmbesserung that definitively confirms Leeu's reliance on Machlinia occurs in chapter 247, where the text mentions 'the sixthe counte of Nerborne'. Caxton's text had 'the viscounte of Nerbonne'—in the second edition spelled 'vysecounte'. Leeu's reading, however, is explained by that in Machlinia—not only is the e in -oe- there a little defective, enabling Leeu's misreading of the name; the word 'viscount' is separated over two lines, with omission of the -s-: 'the vi / counte of Nerboenne'. In Leeu's edition, the hanging 'vi' of 'vi[s]counte' was interpreted as a number, and written out, creating 'the sixthe counte'.[47] Surveying such variants, it can be concluded with certainty that Leeu's edition is based on that of Machlinia, and that of Machlinia alone.[48]

The two Caxton editions and that of Machlinia are remarkably close to each other. Caxton did rid the text of some archaisms in his second edition, but the changes are limited to substitution of vocabulary and changes of spelling. Machlinia's text is overall, except for occasional introduction of errors, loyal to its copy, Caxton's first edition. Leeu's edition, on the other hand, presents a much revised text. This is clear from the very start of the text, where Caxton's opening '[I]N the noble lande of Sirrie ther was a noble kyng and myhty' is re-written: 'THer was in the noble lande of Surre a noble myghti king'.[49] Notable is that such restructurings of sentences consistently follow the preferred

---

44   Matheson (1998: 342); cf., e.g., Caxton 1480, sig. a2^r, 'sompnynge' / Caxton 1482 sig. a2^r, 'somenyng' / Machlinia sig. [a1]r, 'sōpnynge'; Caxton 1480 sig. a3^r, 'scomfited' / Caxton 1482, sig. a3^r, 'discomfyted' / Machlinia sig. a3^r, 'scōfited'.

45   *Pace* Matheson (1998: 342).

46   Caxton 1480 & 1482, sig. a2^v; Machlinia, sig. [a1]v; Leeu, sig. a3^r.

47   Caxton 1480 & 1482, sig. [u6]v; Machlinia, sig. [bb8]r; Leeu, sig. [×5]r.

48   With thanks to Henrike Lähnemann and Moreed Arbabzadah for supplying me with photographs of copies of the Machlinia edition from Oxford (Bodleian Library, Douce 156) and Cambridge (Pembroke College, LC.I.30) respectively, which allowed me to collate the text of the different editions.

49   Caxton 1480 & 1482, sig. a2^r; Machlinia, sig. [a1]r; Leeu, sig. a1^r.

Dutch sentence structure, replacing word orders acceptable in English: thus, for example, where Caxton wrote that Albina's husband wrote a letter, and 'the letter sent to Dioclisian hir fadre', Leeu has instead that he 'sent the letter to dioclisian hyr fadre'.[50]

Everything points at the presence, in Leeu's printing house, of a compositor with excellent grasp of English, but a predilection for Dutch grammatical custom. Importantly, however, there is a shift over the course of the text: toward the end, such interventions become very rare, pointing at a change of practice in the production process—and such a change may well have been occasioned by a change in the personnel involved in the production process. And such a change of personnel, we know there indeed had been: the production was, after all, completed posthumously, after Leeu's killing, leaving his print workshop to complete the work without him. The marked shift in the text of the Leeu edition of Caxton's *Brut* in relation to its exemplar, William de Machlinia's edition of that text, strongly suggests it was Leeu himself who was responsible for the edits—and thus, that Gerard Leeu knew English.

6   Conclusion

The history of the printing of the Middle English Prose *Brut* is a history of three stages of Dutch involvement in early English printing: from William Caxton, an Englishman who spent most of his career in Flanders before bringing England its first printing house, to William of Machlinia, one of the Low Countries tradesmen who helped expand printing in England, to Gerard Leeu, who, while not migrating to England himself, does appear to have learned English, and brought English printing back home to the Dutch Low Countries. The network of links between these three men should be seen as foundational to the next generation of Anglo-Dutch printers. Its final development, the return of English printing to the Low Countries, was briefly aborted by Leeu's unfortunate death, but was then continued by the next generation of book producers, in the early sixteenth century, with an edition of Richard Arnold's *Chronicle* published in Antwerp in 1503.[51] Publisher Jan van Doesborch put printing in English in the Dutch Low Countries on a firm footing through his prolific output. Doesborch, like Leeu, knew English; in Doesborch's case enough not only to compose the

---

50   Caxton 1480 & 1482, sig. a2^v; Machlinia, sig. [a1]v; Leeu, sig. a1^v.
51   Variously attributed to Adriaen van Berghen and Jan van Doesborgh; if the latter, it would be his earliest engagement with the English language.

pages of his English-language publications himself, but even to translate *into* the language. Doesborch was followed two decades later by early exiled English reformers like William Tyndale and Miles Coverdale, through whose activities and collaborations with local merchants like Jacob van Meteren and printers like Merten de Keyser English literary production became more firmly established in the Dutch Low Countries. We thus see how William Caxton's translations and the colophon to Gerard Leeu's edition of the *Brut*, are heralds of a new development: the start of a tradition not only of publishing, but also writing in English in the Dutch Low Countries.

Sigla

Caxton 1480:   ISTC ic00477000.
Caxton 1482:   ISTC ic00478000.
Leeu: ISTC ic00481000.
Machlinia: ISTC ic00480000.

Bibliography

Blake, N.F. (2004a). 'Caxton, William (1415×24–1492), printer, merchant, and diplomat'. *ODNB* ⟨doi.org/10.1093/ref:odnb/4963⟩.

Blake, N.F. (2004b). 'Maclyn [de Machlinia], William (fl. 1482–1490), printer'. *ODNB*. ⟨doi.org/10.1093/ref:odnb/17536⟩.

Blake, N.F., ed. (1970). *The History of Reynard the Fox, Translated from the Dutch Original by William Caxton*. Oxford: Oxford University Press.

Bradbury, Nancy Mason, and Scott Bradbury (2012). *The Dialogue of Solomon and Marcolf: A Dual-Language Edition from Latin and Middle English Printed Editions*. Kalamazoo, MI: Medieval Institute Publications. ⟨d.lib.rochester.edu/teams/text/bradbury-solomon-and-marcolf-intro⟩.

Brodie, Alexander H. (1972). 'The Vularia Terentii', *The Library*, 5th ser., 27: 320–325.

Christianson, C. (1999). 'The Rise of London's Book-trade'. In: Lotte Hellinga and J.B. Trapp, eds. *The Cambridge History of the Book*, vol. 3. Cambridge: Cambridge University Press. 128–147.

Cole, Garold (1971). 'The Historical Development of the Title Page'. *The Journal of Library History* 6: 303–316.

Erasmus, Desiderius, *Opus epistolarum* I. Ed. P.S. Allen. Oxford, 1906.

Hellinga, Lotte (2017), 'Caxton's *Chronicles of England* and its Printer's Copy', *The Library* 18 (2017), pp. 316–324.

Hellinga, Lotte (2018a). 'Aesopus Moralisatus, Antwerp, 1488 in England'. In her *Incunabula in Transit: People and Trade*. Leiden: Brill. 340–352.

Hellinga, Lotte (2018b), 'Wynkyn de Worde's Native Land'. In her *Incunabula in Transit: People and Trade*. Leiden: Brill. 323–339.

Klein, Jan Willem (2003). 'The Leeu(w) van Gouda: New Facts, New Possibilities'. *Quaerendo* 33: 175–190.

Levelt, Sjoerd, and Ad Putter (2021). *North Sea Crossings: The Literary Heritage of Anglo-Dutch Relations 1066–1688*. Oxford: Bodleian Library Publishing.

Matheson, Lister M. (1985). 'Printer and Scribe: Caxton, the Polychronicon, and the Brut'. *Speculum* 60: 593–614.

Matheson, Lister M. (1998). *The Prose Brut: The Development of a Middle English Chronicle*. Tempe, Arizona: Arizona State University.

Pleij, Herman (1987). 'Dutch Literature and the Printing Press: The First Fifty Years'. *Gutenberg Jahrbuch* 62: 47–58.

Putter, Ad (2021). 'Dutch, French and English in Caxton's *Recuyell of the Historyes of Troye*'. In: A.S.G. Edwards, ed. *Medieval Romance, Arthurian Literature. Essays in Honour of Elizabeth Archibald*. Cambridge: D.S. Brewer. 205–226.

Rijns, Hans, ed. (2013). *Gheraert Leeu, Dye hystorien ende fabulen van Esopus.* ⟨dbnl.org/tekst/leeu002hysto2_01⟩.

Ruelens, Ch. (1864). 'La mort de Gérard Leeu'. *Annales du Bibliophile Belge et Hollandais* 1: 5–7.

Smith, Margaret M. (2000). *The Title-Page: Its Early Development, 1460–1510*. London: British Library.

Sutton, Anne F. (1994). 'Caxton was a Mercer: his Social Milieu and Friends'. In: Nicholas Rogers, ed. *England in the Fifteenth Century: Proceedings of the 1992 Harlaxton Symposium*. Stamford: Paul Watkins, 1994. 118–148.

Sutton, Anne F. (2014). 'Merchants'. In: Vincent J. Gillespie and Susan Powell, eds. *A Companion to the Early Printed Book in Britain: 1476–1558*. Woodbridge: Boydell & Brewer. 127–133.

Takagi, Masako (2012). 'Caxton's Exemplar and a Copy from Caxton's Edition of the *Chronicles of England*: MS HM136 and BL Additional 10099'. *Arthuriana* 22: 120–139.

Valkema Blouw, Paul (2013). *Dutch Typography in the Sixteenth Century: The Collected Works of Paul Valkema Blouw, ed. by Paul Dijstelberge and A.R.A. Croiset van Uchelen*. Leiden: Brill.

Wakelin, Daniel (2011). 'Caxton's Exemplar for *The Chronicles of England*?'. *Journal of the Early Book Society* 14: 75–113.

Wakelin, Daniel (2014). 'Humanism and Printing'. In: Vincent J. Gillespie and Susan Powell, eds. *A Companion to the Early Printed Book in Britain: 1476–1558*. Woodbridge: Boydell & Brewer. 227–247.

Weijer, Neil (2016). 'Re-printing or Remaking? The Early Printed Editions of the *Chronicles of England*'. In: Jaclyn Rajsic, Erik Kooper and Dominique Hoche, eds. *The Prose Brut and Other Late Medieval Chronicles. Books have their Histories. Essays in Honour of Lister M. Matheson*. Cambridge: Cambridge University Press. 125–146.

16

A City of Two Tales: Late Medieval Siena

Alison Williams Lewin

Abstract

Italians living during the Great Schism (1378–1417) experienced turmoil on a regular basis as division in the Church exacerbated rivalries both great and small across the peninsula. While noble rivals, each backed by a pope, fought for dominance in Italy and brought in armies of mercenaries, Italians suffered from their depredations, in addition to the usual hazards of medieval life such as plague, famine, flooding and fire. As a fairly important city, Siena could escape neither normal disasters nor diplomatic and military entanglements. Two contemporary Sienese chroniclers each left detailed accounts of these tumultuous decades, yet the two accounts barely overlap in content. This paper explores possible explanations for the two very different accounts from artisan authors who might well have known one another and who surely lived through the same shared experiences.

The late William Bowsky began one of his early articles by stating, 'Rarely does the medievalist treat a theme of such contemporary interest as that of this paper.'[1] I feel much the same, though my contemporary concern differs from Bowsky's. Ten years ago, I would have been baffled that two people living in the same place and time, possessed of similar political and social status, could present such radically different views of events within and beyond their beloved commune of Siena. In the United States of America,[2] in 2022, however, such division and alternate realities have become the norm. My two medieval Sienese chroniclers were perhaps more fortunate than we because their differences concerned what we might call personal choices rather than overtly hostile perspectives—and though each moved in lively social circles, no malicious algorithms seized and manipulated their words.

Who are the two chroniclers? One is Bindino da Travale. We know little of his life beyond bare essentials: he moved to Siena from Travale, a tiny town on the

---

1 Bowsky (1967: 1).
2 More accurately, divided states of America.

outskirts of Sienese territory at some point in the 1370s and became a citizen. By the time he began composing his work, he lived with his two adult sons, Giovanni and Mariano; all three were included in the list of painters in the *Breve dell'arte*. Giovanni especially served as his amanuensis when he began composing his chronicle, more accurately described as a memoir, which focuses on 1384–1416 (though he briefly notes a few earlier events).[3] I have published an annotated, slightly abridged version of his work, so will refer to that version.

The second chronicle, attributed to Paolo di Tommaso Montauri, was obviously the work of several authors and spans several centuries; I have focused on sections that coincide with the bulk of Bindino's *Cronaca*. If we know little of Bindino's life, we know even less about Montauri and his alleged work. The whole covers two large chunks of time: 1170–1315, and 1381–1432,[4] though the sole extant copy dates from around 1490. Supposedly a certain Antonio di Martino faithfully copied the whole chronicle from a manuscript given to him by the goldsmith Paolo di Tommaso Montauri who, in turn, is believed by some to be its author; a prominent metalworker of this name appears in the city records in the late 1300s.[5]

The two authors are unusual because unlike most Italian chroniclers, they were neither notaries nor merchants,[6] but artisans—though goldsmiths were usually far wealthier than painters. If Montauri really was a goldsmith, Bindino probably knew him or at least the work of his colleagues; several sections of Bindino's account describe dazzling and elaborate works in gold and silver, embellished with dozens of different jewels.[7]

As Duane Osheim has noted, however, 'most of all they were townsmen, and it is in the city that their accounts are situated'.[8] Yet their Sienas could not be more different. The city lies at the centre of both their narratives, but Bindino focuses far more on his city's role in pan-Italian and even pan-European affairs, whereas Montauri keeps his focus close to home, recounting what seem to be

---

3   Lewin (2021: 26–27). It is not clear whether he and his sons were producing a final copy from earlier notes but some brief asides in the text suggest he was referring to earlier notes. If he was, the notes have not survived. A somewhat flawed transcription of the entire work exists both in print and online: Bindino da Travale, *La Cronaca di Bindino da Travale (1315–1416)*, ed. Vittorio Lusini, 2nd ed. (Florence: B. Seeber Succ. Di Loescher, 1903).

4   I have restricted my focus in Montauri to the years that overlap with the bulk of Bindino's account: 1380–1416.

5   Boggi (2021). A transcription of this account, with some repetitions omitted, is in Montauri, *Chronache senesi*. The pandemic has prevented me from consulting the manuscript; I hope to soon.

6   Dale, Lewin and Osheim (2007: x).

7   Bindino, *Cronaca*, ed. Lewin, 164–166 and 243–244.

8   Dale, Lewin and Osheim (2007: x).

an endless series of trials and disasters that afflict the Sienese. Both probably had access to much the same information; Bindino's house was close to a street that was home to several goldsmiths[9] (two of whom he names), and both record ambassadorial arrivals and departures, among other events.

It is their styles that diverge most dramatically, as an examination of several events or spans of time reveals. We might take several approaches to this difference; I find two particularly useful. First, that associated with Hayden White and later with Dominick LaCapra, 'the linguistic turn', which first makes texts contemporaneous with the person reading them, and more importantly, states that 'events are judged real not because they occurred but rather because they are both remembered and then judged important enough to be included in a chronological sequence'.[10] Montauri's account presents far more detailed and specific information about daily events, and thus seems to draw on short-term recall; Bindino's reveals both in its (dis)organization, gaps, and unevenness that a great deal clearly comes from much earlier memories, aided perhaps by now-absent notes. In both cases, however, the authors included those events that appeared most important to them.

Second, this framework presents the open acknowledgement of 'the tension between the historical account that claims authority from reality itself and the narrative process that gives form, coherence, and authority to the text'.[11] Here too a clear distinction arises; whereas Montauri overall generally and convincingly appears to present factual material, such as the price of grain in a given month, Bindino emphasizes the dramatic rise and many triumphs of Ladislaus of Durazzo, even as he ignores the great suffering his chivalric hero inflicts on Siena and the Sienese. Thus if Bindino promotes a strong narrative framework that emphasized a literary genre, Montauri presents a more gritty and immediate record of his own times.

Independent records allow us to assess the accuracy of both accounts. As far as the first point goes, Lusini's transcription contains hundreds of footnotes from official communal records, and many corrections regarding the accuracy of both the contents and the dates Bindino reports. Even more visibly, however, Bindino clearly privileges the narrative process over the authority from reality itself. First, he favours his own memories and impressions over the reality of Siena's precarious position, both internally and externally, for much of the time spanned in his account. Second, even more strikingly, his account reads in large part as a chivalric romance, casting Siena's largest threat, Ladislaus of Naples, as

9   Bindino, *Cronaca*, ed. Lewin, 27.
10   Dale, Lewin and Osheim (2007: xvi).
11   Dale, Lewin and Osheim (2007: xvi, esp. n. 1 & 4).

its unlikely hero.[12] Finally, he constantly asserts his authorship—almost all of the 250+ sections open with, either 'Bindino is writing', or 'Giovanni di Bindino is writing what Bindino presents (*pone*)'—and inserts frequent and charming commentaries about himself, letting the reader know that he is old (60), that his mind is melting like ice, or flies around erratically, and that he used to herd swine, among other titbits.

Here we can turn to another comprehensive framework, one which moreover 'emphasizes the interests, culture, and experiences of the author or compilers of a text ... as a writer who is part of a complex intellectual tradition'.[13] In Bindino's case, so fixed is he on the romantic tale of Ladislaus and his family (including a dramatic account of Ladislaus's murder of his father and his gallantry even as a youth) that he completely omits the dominant figure of the end of the fourteenth century, Giangaleazzo Visconti. This omission, along with many others, makes it easy to see his account as a crafted story rather than as any attempt to present an accurate record of events.[14]

The richness of Bindino's descriptions, the little poems threaded throughout his chronicle and vivid recreations of speeches and encounters led me initially to judge Montauri rather harshly at first. I wrote that his work 'lacks Bindino's quirks and colloquialisms'.[15] He employs much clearer syntax, uses far more standard Italian than dialect, and, in the few places where he does use Latin, seems to have a firmer grip on that language than Bindino. These traits, combined with his generally more annalistic presentation overall, contribute to a sense of greater distance and dryness overall. He might just have had less of a dramatic or poetic flair, been more affected by specific miseries (as a goldsmith, for example, he doubtless paid far more in taxes than a humble painter would), or have had a more fatalistic or lugubrious disposition. Indeed, by reading just his account, the reader marvels that anyone was still alive in Siena by 1416, given the steady litany of plagues, floods, droughts, famines, and mercenary marauders he presents.

On closer examination, however, Montauri also reveals some hints about himself and his subtler agenda, though far less frequently and directly than Bindino. He clearly favours more concrete information and coherent chronology over narrative structure, only infrequently revealing his interests, culture, or experiences. Unlike Bindino, who operates on a literary and some-

---

12   Lewin (2008: 147–160).
13   Dale, Lewin and Osheim (2007: xvii).
14   For a thorough account of Giangaleazzo's involvement with and eventual lordship over Siena, see Favale (1936).
15   Bindino, *Cronaca*, ed. Lewin, 26, n. 2.

what remote plane, Montauri frequently presents the suffering of those many victims of the ambitions of the powerful. For example, when Arezzo in 1381 became the focal point of conflict between two factions,[16] Montauri describes the general destruction, adding compassionately, 'Think of those who were killed, and è those who fled in shirt and skirt; lucky those men and women who were able to save themselves and their children'. He adds that all the women who had remained in the city were raped by the soldiers.[17] He shows similar compassion when recording the many incidents of plagues, famines, floods, droughts and other everyday disasters of medieval life, frequently stating that 'I just cannot write' or 'it is impossible to write' how great the suffering was.[18]

He also makes no attempt to gloss over the great damage inflicted on the Sienese *contado* by the Florentines (who Bindino presents, at least directly, as steadfast allies; he does manage to insert some pretty pointed barbs through the speeches of others). Florentine troops raided Sienese territory and rode up to the city's very gates, taking 600 pair of cattle, more than 15,000 sheep and pigs, along with a great deal of grain, woollen and linen cloths, and beds, so much that the procession resembled a huge line of ants (*formicaio*). The attacks were even more egregious considering the Florentine ambassadors were in the middle of 'showing the sun for the moon' (lying), receiving 15,000 florins from the Sienese; moreover, 'it was even worse so that I cannot write about the Florentine brotherhood towards the Sienese'.[19] Again in 1387, a large coalition of troops led by Florence aroused such fear in Siena 'with so many injuries and such harsh and innumerable threats, so many that they could never be written', that the Sienese appointed a *Balìa* (special emergency commission) to appeal to Giangaleazzo Visconti for help.[20] Montauri surrenders his ability to write about Florentine damages, even as he describes them, again in 1390 and in 1398.[21]

A comparison also emphasizes how surprisingly bloodless Bindino's account is. He tells us of the death in battle of several outstanding captains or soldiers

---

16   The two accounts diverge widely, both in terms of what happened and who the major figures involved were; Bindino, *Cronaca*, ed. Lewin, 44–47 and Montauri, *Chronache*, 690–693.

17   'Pensate chi vi rimase morto e chi fugì in camicia e in gonella; beato colui e colei che scanpare poteva sè e suoi fanciulii'. Montauri, *Chronache*, 691.

18   For example, Montauri, *Chronache*, 692.

19   '[E]d è anco pegio ch'io non escrive de' fratelli Fiorentini co' Sanesi'; Montauri, *Chronache*, 713–714.

20   '[T]ante ingurie e aspre minace e tante minace, che tante non si potrebe mai scrivare'; Montauri, *Chronache*, 721.

21   Montauri, *Chronache*, 738, 753.

of his day or rulers,[22] as befits his chivalric framework, but very little of the frequent murders and subsequent executions that punctuated life. Whereas Bindino focuses extensively on large-scale military manoeuvres and battles, Montauri is far more interested in individual executions, listing no fewer than thirty in the relevant years, in addition to the mass execution in 1391 of twenty-seven rebels who had conspired with the Florentines. Montauri even copied the verses that accompanied each one's 'infamous portrait' displayed on the walls of the Palazzo della Repubblica.[23] In keeping with his outward focus, Bindino passes over this major threat to Siena's government in silence.

While most individual executions occurred in Siena and focused on Sienese inhabitants, several took place elsewhere. Montauri revels a bit in florid detail, certainly more than his compatriot. While both reported the execution of four of the 'Eight Saints' who had headed the Florentine regime from 1378–1382, only Montauri adds the additional detail that 'whoever proclaimed XIIII [sic— should be XXIIII] arts, [the Florentines] killed like rabid dogs ...'.[24] When the Florentines attacked the inhabitants of Tolfa, in Lazio near Rome, Montauri adds a full paragraph describing the suffering inflicted; once again, it would be impossible to recount how many men died in battle, and moreover those imprisoned 'who died of starvation, and had their teeth and eyes gouged out, and ate ears, noses, and hands and other limbs, and such great dark deeds that I cannot write them here ...'.[25]

We can also relate these accounts to the fascinating analysis Graeme Dunphy presents in this volume: Dunphy draws on the speech act theory, especially of J.L. Austin, in distinguishing a constative statement, which informs, from a performative statement, which 'generates new "truths" that form paradigms for political and social interaction and thus contributes to the next phase of the historical process'.[26] Unlike Dunphy's Scottish chronicles, neither Bindino's nor Montauri's chronicle circulated widely, as far as we know; each survives in a single manuscript copy. It is therefore difficult to see their effects on later his-

---

22 For example, he describes, inaccurately, the murders of both King Andrew, spouse of Joanna I of Naples, and the revenge taken on his murderers by Andrew's brother, Louis I of Hungary; Bindino, *Cronaca*, ed. Lewin, 40–41.

23 Montauri, *Chronache*, 743.

24 Bindino, *Cronaca*, ed. Lewin, 53; Montauri, *Chronache*, 691: 'ucidenvansi come cani arabiati ...'.

25 '[e] anco l'uomini morti ..., e anco de' prigioni presi e messi nelle prigioni e morivanvi di fame, e di cavare di denti ed ochi e di mangiare urechie, nasi e mani, e altri menbri, e facevasi magiori scurità ch'io non vi scrivo ...'; Montauri, *Chronache*, 738.

26 Graeme Dunphy's contribution to this volume. I am grateful to Professor Dunphy for sharing this with me pre-publication.

torical writing, but it does seem reasonable to claim that their written accounts reflect to some extent the conversations they surely engaged in with their fellow Sienese.

Specifically, Montauri includes several striking examples of sin followed by immediate punishment,[27] which underscores another of Dunphy's important points: 'In medieval thinking, "truth" was always bound up with morality, so that constating was even more obviously linked to messages about behavioural consequences than in modern assumptions'.[28] In March of 1401,[29] Montauri reported, 'Some young men had set up to play dice near the church of Saint Vincent in Siena late in the evening ...; it was on the day of Easter, and one of these gamers, called Lomo, having lost a great deal, turned towards an Annunciation that was painted on the front of the said church [and claimed] that the Virgin Mary had been the reason for his loss, and not the devil, who had already entered him. And with fury and without any words took a rock and, in a rage, threw it at the said figure of the Virgin Mary.' He then lost the power of speech, lost consciousness, and in the middle of the night died miserably.[30]

Another account of divine vengeance immediately follows. A shoemaker was working on the feast day of Saint Laurence. When a good friend reproached him, he replied, 'Saint Laurence can do what he wants; what I want is to work so that I have something to eat'. Montauri continues, 'As soon as he said these words, his mouth turned around towards the nape of his neck and he lost his voice and one of his arms dried up so that he could not feed himself, eat or drink ....; and he lived like this for some months and then died miserably in great misery and disgrace'. In case anyone had doubts, Montauri adds, 'And thus Saint Laurence punished him for making a mockery of his name day'.[31]

Gambling again provokes a loser to blasphemy. In 1405 [1406 n.s.], One Jacomo detto al Cola was gambling on a feast day, 'and having lost, turned towards God and the Virgin cursing all the saints of heaven with many filthy and ugly words; he suddenly fell dead on the gaming table in front of many citizens; and

---

27   My thanks to Isabel Maria de Barros Dias who pointed out that these dramatic reports of sin and punishment are common in books of miracles, namely Marian ones; she pointed to several examples of many in *The Oxford Cantigas de Santa Maria Database*, https://csm .mml.ox.ac.uk.

28   Graeme Dunphy in the current volume.

29   New style—Italians started the new year on 25 March, the day of the Incarnation.

30   Montauri, *Chronache*, 760.

31   '[E] subito come ebe detto quelle parole, senza indugio si li volse la boca drieto e a la cicotola e perdè la voce e secosoli un bracio per sì fatto modo che non si poteva imbocare e mangiare, nè bere ....; e così vise alquanti mesi e poi morì miseramente con grande stento e vitoperio ...'; Montauri, *Chronache*, 760–761.

thus it was believed that the devil had carried him away, and this was a just miracle of God and the Virgin'.[32] In all three cases, the sinner commits the crime of blasphemy by attacking or ignoring the divine.

One final example of diabolical power presents a far more complicated scenario. Though it begins with a young man gambling in a castle of Arcidosso in the *contado* of Siena, and losing, he, unlike the others, 'commends himself to the devil, saying, "Take me away from such troubles", and suddenly many people appeared. The young man was carried away, and no one knew to where'. A few days later, the wife and sons of the aforementioned gambler '... [they] immediately went to the said ditch and called, "Oh, our father!" He responded, "What do you want, my children?" They answered, "Do you want us to do anything for you, any office or mass for your soul?" He answered no, "that everything that is done for me causes more pain, so do not do anything for me, given that I am damned."' And having said that he disappeared and left, and this was in December 1416.[33]

If Montauri's performative goals were to teach reverence for God and the saints, and instil fear of diabolical retribution, Bindino stays true to form in paying far more attention to the larger picture and sinner: the institutional church. Many of his reports of ambassadorial missions and their speeches as he imagines them address the running sore of the Great Schism. For the most part he reports fairly objectively on the various communications with the Roman and later, Pisan, popes. The only cleric whom he criticizes, indirectly, is Pope John XXIII, by repeating his own version of the charges lodged against the Pisan pope at the Council of Constance.[34]

The real attacks on the institutional Church come from the supposed speeches of Master Jan Hus. The speeches he reports present far lengthier and harsher attacks than any other account of the council; in his initial attack, Bindino has Hus address several constituents of the clergy, highlighting each one's sins and failings. Clearly Hus/Bindino has other charges to lay, but instead he says, 'But to say more briefly, I am not here writing every bit of what I, Bindino, could describe'.[35] This statement does not mean that Hus is finished in

---

32 Montauri, *Chronache*, 762.
33 I have omitted part of the story in the interests of space; Montauri, *Chronache*, 787.
34 Not even his closest friends would pretend Baldassare Cossa, *quondam* pope, had any spiritual inclinations whatsoever. The speeches Bindino puts in the mouths of various legates and ambassadors present the standard accusations against him: he has lived by simony, lived a sinful life, broken his word repeatedly, lacks all virtue and, alone of all clerics, was like a rapacious wolf. Bindino, *Cronaca*, ed. Lewin, 244–247, which omits several of the speeches because they repeat the others.
35 Bindino, *Cronaca*, ed. Lewin, 249.

Bindino's telling as he then turns to the secular priests, and finally the claimants to the Holy See.[36]

Even more dramatic than this lengthy excoriation of the clergy is what Bindino portrays as the sympathy Hus aroused for his position in King Sigismund, presiding over the council. When the assembled clerics began to yell, 'Kill him! Let him be put to death!' Sigismund 'began to be dismayed, because it seemed to the king that the said master in sacred theory had known very well what to say [i.e., his accusations were valid]'. As a result of this confrontation, 'The master was taken in this uproar and had irons put on his legs and was put in prison. His disciples and the king were greatly saddened by this. In its anger the council wanted to burn him. The king ordered that he did not wish it under such circumstances,' and instead remanded him to prison for eight days.[37]

Showing his own hand more clearly, Bindino reports that 'according to what the former Travalese has discovered and attested to ... there was great agitation throughout Constance because he was a great doctor of law. He had learned disciples of great worth .... The king and his barons were in great distress over this; they knew Master Jan Hus had a great mind. The king had great sorrow and suffering from his death but the king, to spare his own person, had the clergy reunite' and that at this meeting, 'that which [M]aster Jan Hus has said will be erased and his book erased. He will ask pardon of you and you must pardon him'.[38]

Hus of course did no such thing, a fact which leaves Bindino 'stunned and crazed because of what he has described.' Instead, Hus dug in more deeply, concluding, 'I will die before I wish to mar my book or remove anything from it. You will see that I will die ..., but you can do nothing to wound my Spirit.'

Again emphasizing the king's sympathy for Hus, Bindino reports that though 'everyone present was stupefied and saddened and melancholy; the king, hearing such a speech, immediately could not restrain his tears ... [and] felt such deep sorrow that he wished [Hus] to survive. But because the clergy would have him die immediately ... he was put in prison ... [A]ccording to what Bindino has found out and thus is having put down and written, how the king tried to spare Jan Hus'. Sigismund had Hus held for another two months to give him one more chance to recant; when Hus refused 'with great melancholy, he [the king] wished him and his spirit well'.[39] Bindino then presents a generally accurate

---

36   The texts of the specific attacks appear in Bindino, *Cronaca*, ed. Lewin, 249–250.

37   Bindino, *Cronaca*, ed. Lewin, 251; presumably Sigismund hoped tempers would cool in the interval.

38   Bindino, *Cronaca*, ed. Lewin, 252.

39   Both the reported speeches and Sigismund's sympathies seem unique to Bindino. See

summary of Hus's main teachings and describes his death and that of a young disciple, who threw himself into the river after his master's death.[40]

By using the two perspectives of the linguistic turn and the relative emphases on constative and performative writing, we can to some degree reconcile the initially jarring discrepancies that occur between the two chronicles.[41] Despite its somewhat murky production history, the specificity and liveliness of Montauri's account inclines me to believe that it was at least initially a record of immediate or recent events, which may have been copied at a later date. By contrast, Bindino's rambling and often chronologically chaotic opus suggests rather that many years after the fact he wished to record major events of his time, but still more, to give free rein to an obviously vivid imagination in a retrospective retelling of the most important and appealing narratives. He chose to play on a large stage, both geographically and stylistically, Montauri on a much smaller one.

In the second framework, that of constative and performative accounting, Montauri is an invaluable resource for his presentation of not only what affected the lives of his fellow Sienese, but also the acknowledgement of both the great suffering many endured as well as a persistent belief in the immediacy of both the saints and the devil to monitor and intervene in those same people's lives if necessary. At the same time, Bindino was preserving and replicating a different worldview, one which valued rhyme, romance, and the dramatic storytelling of the *cantastorie*. As much as Bindino reveals and preserves a fascination with chivalric romance and elevated speech, Montauri brings the reader down to earth in subtly sympathetic and admonitory fashion.

We know that as townsmen, as members of Siena's guilds, possibly as neighbours, both men would have been out on the streets, observing one another's work (as Bindino clearly watched the goldsmiths nearby), and above all, **talking** with one another about far-flung and local events, each would have reified his own mental framework and doubtless played a role in altering, albeit subtly, the worldviews of other Sienese. What might each have hoped to achieve? To the extent that Bindino shared his worldview with his contemporaries, he surely wished to draw their attention to the need for major religious reform,

Spinka (1968), which reports the silencing of Hus on 259. Dr Thomas Fudge reported other sources portray Sigismund as partisan against Hus; email February 2020.

40   Bindino, *Cronaca*, ed. Lewin, 254–257. On 257, Bindino again emphasizes the describes the king's 'great sorrow'.

41   I hesitate to call them 'contemporary', given the uncertain genesis and historical record for the Montauri family and manuscript. Dr Philippa Jackson confirms that in 1493 a Paulo di Tommaso Montauri was listed in *Archivio di Stato, Concistoro*, 2664, at 37, BCS, P.III.23, 45ᵛ.

both institutionally and doctrinally. For his part, Montauri's depressing litany of catastrophe and misfortune, juxtaposed with the occasional swift punishments for blasphemy, suggests that the impiety of the Sienese was to blame for their constant woes and suggests, indirectly, that greater devotion would alleviate their misery.

In different proportions, each chronicle thus functions as both a constative and performative work presenting information but aiming also to instruct. They also reveal the degree to which individual talents and inclinations of individuals shape their accounts. Awareness of these frameworks can help us to see others not as wrong, but rather as having different priorities and different perspectives from our own. 'It is well known, as the great thinker Kant has it: we see things not as they are, but as we are.'[42]

Bibliography

Primary Sources

Archivio di Stato di Siena (*ASS*), *Concistoro*, 2664, at 37, BCS, P.III.23, 45ᵛ

Bindino da Travale, *La Cronaca di Bindino da Travale* (*1315–1416*), ed. Vittorio Lusini, 2nd ed. (Florence: B. Seeber Succ. Di Loescher, 1903).

Bindino da Travale, *Cronaca*: Lewin, Alison Williams, ed. (2021). *Chronicle* (*1315–1416*). Toronto: Centre for Reformation and Renaissance Studies.

Montauri, Paolo di Tommaso. *Chronache senesi*. Ed. A. Lisini & F. Iacometti. *Rerum Italicarum Scriptores* (*RIS*), vol. 15, part 6 (1931–1939), 179–252 and 689–835.

Secondary Sources

Boggi, Flavio (2021). 'Cronaca senese conosciuta sotto il nome di Paolo di Tommaso Montauri'. *EMC*.

Bowsky, William M. (1967) 'The Medieval Commune and Internal Violence: Police Power and Public Safety in Siena, 1287–1355.' *The American Historical Review*, 73: 1–17.

Sharon Dale, Alison Williams Lewin and Duane Osheim (2007). *Chronicling History*. State College PA: Pennsylvania State Press.

Favale, Sarah (1936). "Siena nel quadro della politica viscontea," in *Bullettino senese di storia patria*, 43: 315–382.

Lewin, Alison Williams (2008). 'Chivalry and Romance in the Chronicle of Bindino da Travale and King Ladislao of Naples.' In *The Medieval Chronicle V*, ed. Erik Kooper. Amsterdam & NY: Rodopi. 147–160.

---

42   Scharling (1876: 211).

Lewin, Alison Williams, ed. (2021). *Bindino da Travale. Chronicle (1315–1416)*. Toronto: Centre for Reformation and Renaissance Studies.

Scharling, Henrik (1876). *Nicolai's Marriage: A Picture of Danish Family Life*, vol. II. Translated from Danish. London: Richard Bentley and son.

Spinka, Matthew (1968). *John Hus: A Biography*. Princeton NJ: Princeton University Press.

17

Stumps, Branches and Trees: Patterns of Manuscript Survival versus Patterns of Textual Influence in the Prose *Brut* Tradition

Julia Marvin

Abstract

Since the first scholarly edition of the oldest surviving version of the Anglo-Norman prose *Brut* appeared in 2006, scholars (Erik Kooper notable among them) have increasingly traced the chronicle's presence and influence in late-medieval historiographic works in Anglo-Norman, Middle English and Latin. This essay will focus on one manuscript included in the variants of that edition, Oxford, Bodleian Libraries, MS Wood empt. 8, whose version of the text is clearly not a direct ancestor of the subsequent dominant Anglo-Norman and Middle English versions. At the time, it appeared to be a unique outlier. Now, with the discovery of another full manuscript of this version, and of its role as a source for other texts, the Wood version can be seen to have had an influence and circulation of its own. This case study helps reveal the variety of ways in which *Brut* texts were deployed and reworked in the fourteenth and early fifteenth century, as well as the challenges of evaluating textual traditions on the basis of surviving manuscripts that may or may not be representative.

The vernacular prose *Brut* tradition not only offered late-medieval audiences access to the legendary history of Britain but also became a locus for the writing of contemporary history. With over fifty known surviving manuscripts in several versions, the Anglo-Norman prose *Brut* chronicle (hereafter ANPB) is a major cultural presence in fourteenth- and fifteenth-century English culture. Throughout the twentieth century, just as the dialect of Anglo-Norman French itself was often dismissed as an oddity, the ANPB was mostly regarded (when it was regarded at all) as a mere antecedent to its more obviously significant translation, the Middle English prose *Brut* chronicle (hereafter MEPB), with its huge number of manuscripts, continuations offering the promise of contemporaneity, and influence on early printed histories of England.[1] Since modern

---

1 Brie's edition remains the only full modern publication of a MEPB (*The Brut*, 1906–1908). For

editions of versions of the ANPB have begun to appear, scholars have been able to begin to trace its broader influence on other texts.[2] The ANPB played a substantial role in both the transmission of British history and the development of vernacular historiography, and thus of vernacular authorship itself. In this essay, I will focus on one version of the chronicle that on first examination seemed to be an isolated case: that found in Oxford, Bodleian Libraries, MS Wood empt. 8 (hereafter Wood).

In appearance, Wood seems to be a typical fourteenth-century ANPB manuscript: modest in size, with a seemingly unfinished scheme of decoration or rubrication, written in a tidy documentary anglicana formata script.[3] Its content, however, is atypical. In my 2006 edition of the Oldest Version of the ANPB (by which I meant the oldest known surviving version, concluding in 1272), I said of Wood (or **W**):

> The text of the *Brut* is meticulously given, with few careless errors. In a number of places **W** more closely resembles the sources of the Oldest Version than do the other manuscripts; it also contains an account of the second and third years of the reign of Henry II not found in any other prose *Brut* text that I have seen. It may be that **W** represents the earliest surviving state of the text. However, the text also shows evidence throughout of editing for clarity and concision of style, and in, for instance, supplying proper names when an antecedent is unclear. Because of the signs of minor revision and because of the presence of the beginning of a continuation, **W** cannot be considered a 'pure' text of the Oldest Version, and I have not chosen it as base text, despite its many good qualities.[4]

Definitely not the version of the text that gave rise to subsequent versions of the ANPB and therefore the MEPB, Wood appeared to be an outlier. As it seemed likely to provide some evidence of an earlier state of the chronicle than my base

---

the recent boom and basic resources in *Brut* studies and for unpublished editions, see, e.g., the bibliographies of Marvin (2017) and Rajsic et al. (2016).

2 *The Oldest Anglo-Norman Prose 'Brut' Chronicle* and *Prose 'Brut' to 1332*, an edition of a three-manuscript subgroup of the Short Version that is not ancestral to common later prose *Brut* versions but is of course valuable in its own right.

3 For a fuller description and an image see *Oldest*, 61–67, and Marvin (2017: 194–195 and plate 15).

4 *Oldest*, 62–63.

text, I decided it would be worthwhile to represent its readings in the edition. Since that time, three other texts have been identified as closely related to the Wood version.

1   **Wood and Saint Petersburg, National Library of Russia, MS Fr.Q.v.IV.8**

Saint Petersburg, National Library of Russia (hereafter NLR), MS Fr.Q.v.IV.8 was unknown to early scholars of the *Brut* tradition. Although the library did identify it as a *Brut* chronicle in its typewritten 1989 catalogue of French manuscripts, the manuscript did not receive wider recognition until Gillette Labory noted it on a visit to the library and passed on the information to Ruth Dean for inclusion in her indispensable guide to Anglo-Norman manuscripts.[5] Like Wood, it is a modest if nicely prepared volume, in a mid-fourteenth-century documentary anglicana script, written by one or possibly two scribes, with a completed program of rubrication and initials.[6] It is misbound, with a number of misplaced and missing folios that make identification and analysis that much more challenging. In 2006 I speculated that the NLR manuscript might be 'a Short Version manuscript without prologue'.[7] But examination of the NLR manuscript has shown it to be something quite different. In addition to a core *Brut* text very closely related to the Wood version, it contains two continuations, one for Edward I and one for Edward II.

The NLR manuscript cannot be a direct, exclusive ancestor or descendant of any of the extant Oldest Version manuscripts, including Wood, since it lacks text that they all have and contains text that they all lack.[8] But it is extremely close to Wood, agreeing with it against other Oldest Version manuscripts in

---

5   Dean and Boulton (1999: no. 45), with the old Soviet name for the library and the shelfmark mistakenly given as Fr.F.v.IV.8, an error that I promulgated until my 2017 visit to the library.

6   It came to the Russian imperial library through the 1794 expropriation of the Załuski collection in Warsaw. An inscription on the front pastedown indicates that it belonged to Joseph Butler, bishop of Durham, and it is still in an English binding.

7   *Oldest*, 49 n. 179. The large group of *Brut* manuscripts labeled as the Short Version represent a later stage, extending the narrative into the early 1330s, with the precise endpoint varying among manuscripts; most also contain a verse prologue with the Albina story. For overviews of and bibliography on the different versions of the Anglo-Norman and Middle English prose *Brut* chronicles, see Matheson (1998: 1–49), *Oldest* (2006: 15–57) and Marvin (2017: 6–11).

8   E.g., at *Oldest*, ll. 223, 423 and 427, NLR (fols 6ᵛ, 11ʳ) agrees with other manuscripts against Wood or contains material lacking in Wood but found in other manuscripts, while at *Oldest*, ll. 278 and 1121, Wood agrees with other manuscripts against NLR (fols 7ᵛ, 27ʳ) or contains material lacking in NLR. Space constraints do not permit fuller comparison here.

ways that manifest greater correspondence to the chronicle's known sources and analogues.[9] Their most striking shared attribute is the account of the second and third years of the reign of Henry II mentioned above.[10] Since the information in this passage shows no definitive connection to the text's major known analogue at this point, it is conceivable that it represents an independent supplementation of the text.[11] It seems probable, however, that it was skipped in a manuscript ancestral to the great majority of prose *Brut* manuscripts, and that it too bespeaks the Wood version's closer relation to an ur-text.

Wood and NLR share another important distinctive element beyond their *Brut* text to 1272: their continuation on the reign of Edward I. Only the beginning and end of this continuation survive in the badly worn and damaged last quire of Wood, but NLR contains the whole (and makes it possible to ascertain that the last page of Wood, only partially legible even under ultraviolet light, indeed contains the same text).[12]

The best-known context in which this account of Edward I occurs is the *Petit Bruit* of Rauf de Boun, composed in 1309 according to its opening lines but surviving complete in only one later sixteenth-century manuscript, London, British Library (hereafter BL), MS Harley 902.[13] The *Petit Bruit* covers the entire history of Britain from the arrival of Brut to the death of Edward I in fewer than 20 printed pages, and the reign of Edward I constitutes a little under 20 percent of the whole. This section's content bears a general resemblance to the verse chronicle of Peter Langtoft and is far more staid than the earlier part's idiosyncratic version of British history. Its prose also appears to be somewhat less labored, although I have not yet conducted a full comparative study. Given its length, detail and focus (mostly on Edward's conflicts in Wales, Scotland and the continent), it seems likely to have been an existing account that Rauf used to finish his work with the 'playne procés de tout sa vie', the full account of Edward's whole life, that he promises at the beginning.[14]

---

9 See, e.g., *Oldest*, ll. 1388–1426, 2691–2704, 3963–3975, 4185–4191, and explanatory notes.

10 See *Oldest*, ll. 3471–3479 and explanatory notes, corresponding to NLR, fol. 71ᵛ. See also below on its presence in Cambridge University Library, MS Dd.32.10.

11 For this analogue, the Latin chronicle of the Praemonstratensian house of Barlings, see *Oldest*, 25–39 and 332–346.

12 For the Wood continuation, see *Oldest*, 411–412. The Latin beast prophecies later added on the final page have now been identified as coming from the *Historia regum Britanniae* of Geoffrey of Monmouth; see Marvin (2017: 245).

13 Rauf, *Petit Bruit*.

14 Rauf, *Petit Bruit*, 5.

John Spence has identified this text in two other fourteenth-century histo-rio-genealogical manuscripts that do not contain prose *Brut* chronicles as such: the roll BL Additional 47170 and the codex BL Harley 1348.[15] The roll contains material added from both the earlier and later parts of the *Petit Bruit*, includ-ing one of Rauf's self-references (which appear only in the earlier portion), so its descent from Rauf is unquestionable.[16] The codex, whose common material appears to relate only to Edward I, contains no such references.

Just as with Wood and NLR themselves, the absence and presence of par-ticular passages show that none of these fourteenth-century manuscripts can be direct, exclusive ancestors or descendants of one another, nor ancestors of Harley 902. Thus neither Wood nor NLR can represent the exact version of the 'grant Bruit' from which Rauf tantalizingly says his work is taken, but they do at least demonstrate that books that could be considered 'grant Bruits' con-taining text shared with the *Petit Bruit* did in fact exist.[17] The circulation of the Edward I text independent of the rest of the *Petit Bruit* casts further doubt on Rauf's authorship of this portion and indicates that it must have been com-posed very early in the reign of Edward II to be already available to Rauf in 1309.

It is possible that the Edward I text was originally composed as a prose *Brut* continuation. It is also quite possible that, like the makers of the roll BL Add. 47170, someone found the account of Edward I and added it into an ANPB. Its style and focus differ enough from the main text of the Oldest Version that I think there is very little possibility that it was part of an original text of which the 1272 version could be a truncation. Similarly, its wordiness, clumsy syntax and frequent ambiguity make it unlikely to have been the work of the sharp editor responsible for the Wood version. It is even conceivable that the Edward I text entered into independent circulation by means of extraction from the *Petit Bruit*, whose history up to Henry III may have looked as strange to Rauf's con-temporaries as it does to us.

The NLR manuscript has yet more to offer. In its main text, sometimes at the end of a section, it includes a number of pithy, character-revealing anec-dotes not so far found in any other ANPB manuscripts, analogous to moments in William of Malmesbury or other earlier historians. For instance, it tells the story of the ten-year old Aethelred (the Unready) developing a terror of candles after his mother uses one to beat him, and of William Rufus demanding more

---

15   Spence (2005: 63–66), with a very helpful account of previous scholarship.
16   Spence (2005: 64–65, 76).
17   Rauf, *Petit Bruit*, 5.

STUMPS, BRANCHES AND TREES

expensive hose, with the result that his canny servant satisfies him with even cheaper hose while pocketing the money saved.[18]

NLR's additional continuation on the reign of Edward II is much more fluently written than the account of Edward I, with a detailed account of Edward's final flight and capture, and a notably positive view of the king. It is, as far as I now know, unique to the NLR manuscript.[19] Although it is not possible to tell from the NLR manuscript alone if the brief introduced episodes and the account of Edward II were supplied at the same time by the same person, the shared interest they show in human character and moments of lively dialogue suggest that this is a real possibility.

Running seamlessly from each section to the next, NLR shows no signs of being the original manuscript in which these additional elements appeared: it implies the existence of another manuscript from which it was immediately copied and at least one more ancestral manuscript from which both of these closely related versions sprang. The basic Wood version is therefore not an isolated one-off but was transmitted and further developed in multiple manuscripts. As of course is the case in the Galfridian tradition more broadly, adaptation and expansion of prose *Brut* texts can be seen to occur practically from the beginning of the tradition.

2   Wood and Cambridge University Library, MS Dd.10.32

Whereas the Wood version of the ANPB uses an Edward I text to continue its narrative, the fourteenth-century manuscript Cambridge University Library (hereafter CUL), MS Dd.10.32 uses the Wood version itself to continue a copy of the *Historia regum Britanniae*, as Heather Pagan and Geert De Wilde demonstrate in their edition.[20] This continuation runs from the wicked king Osbright to the death of Henry III, with substantial abridgment and light modification of the Wood version's content and what looks to be an ad hoc five-line account

---

18   NLR, fols 53^r, 67^r, corresponding to William, *Gesta*, 2.164 (I, 268) and 4.313 (I, 556–558). Another passage, in which Richard I banters with a Cistercian monk, corresponds to Roger of Howden, *Chronica*, IV, 76–77.

19   Fols 108^r–118^r. Andy King and I are currently making an edition and translation of both continuations.

20   Dean and Boulton (1999: no. 25); 'The Anglo-Norman *Prose Chronicle of Early British Kings* or the Abbreviated Prose *Brut*', esp. 230–232. The text displays many distinctive similarities to Wood, including the longer account of Henry II noted above ('Abbreviated', ll. 864–871), corresponding to *Oldest*, ll. 3471–3479.

of Edward I filling out the last folio.[21] Both the Latin and Anglo-Norman texts are in anglicana scripts 'rather of charter type', as M.R. James puts it in his notes on the manuscript.[22] But the transition to the Anglo-Norman text is marked by a conspicuous change of ink colour, hand and script, to a far looser anglicana typical of many ANPB manuscripts.[23] It thus appears that the supplementation occurs in and for this manuscript in particular, early enough in its life that both parts of it have coloured initials and red touching of proper names and the like.

This abridged extract not only provides further evidence of the circulation of the Wood version but also demonstrates the probable existence of still another lost or unknown manuscript, for its content shows that, close as it is, it cannot be directly, exclusively descended from either Wood or NLR.[24] The CUL manuscript also makes for a lovely example of the dragon biting its own tail, or of the complexities of the genetics of manuscript transmission, as this text with no content in common with the *Historia regum Britanniae*, but nonetheless descended from it, is grafted directly onto its remote ancestor.

3   Wood and Longleat House MS 55

Longleat House MS 55, known as the Red Book of Bath, which dates from the early fifteenth century, contains nearly forty items in Latin, French and Anglo-Norman, several with Bath connections, and the language of its Middle English items localizable to Somerset.[25] On fols 35ᵛ–53ᵛ appears a Latin prose chronicle running from Brut's arrival in Britain to the death of Richard II, in the middle of which the text breaks into English verse for most of the life of Arthur. In the last

---

21   Cf. *Oldest*, ll. 2334–4218; see 'Abbreviated', 232.

22   James (2021).

23   See 'Abbreviated', 235, for an image of the transition on fol. 63ʳ. See Marvin (2017: 132–133) on the legal community's involvement in *Brut* production.

24   *Pace* Pagan and De Wilde, who cautiously propose that Wood could be the immediate source ('Abbreviated', 230, 232). E.g., at ll. 185–186 and 1019–1020, the CUL text has matter lacking in Wood (see *Oldest*, ll. 2548, 3642–3643 and textual notes), and at ll. 184–185 and 543, it has matter lacking in NLR (fols 49ᵛ, 61ʳ). The CUL manuscript's few sentences on Edward I do not offer content distinctive enough to tell whether there is any relation to the Edward I continuation of Wood and NLR; the direct manuscript source for the CUL text may well not have gone past Henry III, in which case it would represent a stage prior to Wood and NLR.

25   For general description of the manuscript and extensive bibliography, see *Arthur*, 239–246, and Kooper (2016: 75–77).

few lines of the poem, the poet twice tells his audience to 'reed on the Frensch boke' for more: it turns out that he means it.[26]

When Marije Pots and Erik Kooper were preparing a new edition of this Middle English poem, entitled *Arthur*, they determined that it derived from an Anglo-Norman prose *Brut*. With further work, Kooper and I were able to identify the Wood version in particular as its main source.[27] With still further work, Kooper concluded that the surrounding Latin chronicle is also discernibly descended from an ANPB and, drastically abbreviated though its content is, it should be considered part of the Latin prose *Brut* tradition.[28]

I have so far found nothing in the poem that would further narrow the possibilities and prove or disprove Wood or NLR in particular as its immediate source: its obviously distinctive moments are common to both manuscripts. And although in his test passages Kooper shows the Latin chronicle to be closer to the Oldest Version than to the corresponding moments in the *Historia regum Britanniae*, Wace's *Roman de Brut* or Gaimar's *Estoire des Engleis*, these passages do not present differences between the Wood version and the Oldest Version that are telling enough to enable a closer identification of its source.[29]

The question as to whether the maker of the Latin chronicle should also be considered the author of the ME *Arthur* remains fraught, partly because past scholars have identified the language of the poem to be mid-fourteenth century and thus to predate the Latin text.[30] Until and unless a finer discrimination can be made, it remains unclear whether the same writer used the same source at the same time to create the Latin chronicle and the Middle English poem; or the Latin chronicle and poem were written by different people at different times with access to the same source (perhaps part of a local Bath collection of texts); or the use of related source material is sheer coincidence (in that case coincidence suggestive of the wide availability of ANPB texts). In any case, Longleat 55 shows further circulation of the Wood version while also showing the versatility and creativity of writers' use of *Brut* material across languages and literary forms.

---

26   *Arthur*, ll. 634 (quoted), 642.
27   *Arthur*, 244, Kooper and Marvin (2012).
28   Kooper (2016).
29   Kooper (2016: 89–91).
30   See *Arthur*, 239, for an account of thought on the matter.

4   Conclusions

In my Oldest Version edition, I said that the Wood manuscript 'cannot be regarded as a typical *Brut* text or one influential in the transmission of the chronicle'.[31] Now I would say that although its version of the text is not a direct ancestor of the main stream of Anglo-Norman and Middle English *Bruts* and their early printed descendants, it had circulation, influence and descendants of its own.

These manuscripts and their complex relationships also raise a number of broader issues: they provide further evidence for the continuing compos-ition of Anglo-Norman works into the fourteenth century, for the ANPB as fertile ground for more continuations than had been previously realized, for the multilingualism of scribal and authorial culture, and also for the creation of works of historiography by (as far as the evidence suggests) secular indi-viduals not simply receiving and copying, but adapting and supplementing, existing texts.[32] ANPB scribes coming from the legal community would have been comfortable with Anglo-Norman as a language of composition, may have had access to a range of texts (as well as their own independent knowledge and opinion), and may well have felt considerable freedom to remake these vernacular narratives to suit their interests and practical needs. The case of Longleat 55 is a reminder that writers in Middle English did not necessarily prefer sources in English, even when they might have been available. The prose *Brut* tradition can more than ever be seen to have played a real role in creating a vernacular culture not just of reading but of composition.[33] As more editions of Latin and vernacular historiographic works appear, the picture will no doubt become clearer in some ways, and more complicated in many.

These manuscripts also raise the messy and apparently eternal question of how to define and present texts that exist in many forms, especially now that adaptable digital options exist. Had I defined the Oldest Version more strictly and omitted Wood, my edition would have been cleaner—but it also would have provided less information for comparative use. Similarly, the eclectic vari-

---

31   *Oldest*, 67.
32   For studies of scribal innovation in a range of late-medieval historiography in Britain, see Fischer (2012).
33   Scholarship on the complexities of *Brut* production and transmission is advancing rapidly. For an Anglo-Norman case, see Marvin (2017: 136–162). For a spectacular Middle English case, see Bryan (2009), and on Middle English production more broadly, Mooney and Matheson (2003).

ants of nineteenth- and earlier twentieth-century editions are a treasure trove, however maddening they may sometimes be.

Hypothetical manuscripts and versions of texts feature in the history of most medieval works with any staying power. It is important, but in practice difficult, to remember that the manuscripts that survive do not necessarily constitute a representative sample. The record may be especially gappy where the ANPB tradition is concerned: its manuscripts tend to be relatively cheap rather than treasured luxury objects, its texts became less useful as its language become more obsolete, and its content also became obsolete as updated versions began to appear in English, and eventually in print. Many of these manuscripts were probably destroyed when their parchment became most valuable as raw material for other uses.

It is easy to regard as important a manuscript that represents a particularly handsome specimen or a dominant version of a text, or that benefits from being housed in a major repository, or that happened to be used in an early scholarly edition, or that has a named author associated with it: the named author and dating of the *Petit Bruit* have surely gained it attention that it would not have gotten as an anonymous work in one post-medieval copy. Seen through only the lens of what became the mainstream of the prose *Brut* tradition over the fourteenth and fifteenth centuries, a non-ancestral manuscript like Wood can appear to be less significant. But there is more than one kind of textual life and afterlife: the fact that it now can be seen to be part of a branch, and not just a stump, on the family tree may enhance—but does not constitute—its significance.

And finally for now, this case study is only one of many that could be presented to show how generously and significantly Erik Kooper has contributed to the study of medieval historiography in his own scholarship, as a mentor and colleague, and through the journal that he founded alongside the Medieval Chronicle Society.

Bibliography

Primary Sources—Manuscripts
Cambridge
Cambridge University Library
Dd.10.32

London

British Library
   Additional 47170
   Harley 902, 1348

Longleat

Longleat House
   55

Oxford

Bodleian Library
   Wood empt. 8

Saint Petersburg

National Library of Russia
   Fr.Q.v.IV.8

Primary Sources—Editions

'The Anglo-Norman *Prose Chronicle of Early British Kings* or the Abbreviated Prose *Brut*.' Ed. Heather Pagan and Geert De Wilde. *The Medieval Chronicle* 10 (2015): 225–319.

'*Arthur*: A New Critical Edition of the Fifteenth-Century Middle English Verse Chronicle.' Ed. Marije Pots and Erik Kooper. *The Medieval Chronicle* 7 (2011): 239–266.

The Brut; or, the Chronicles of England. Ed. F.W.D. Brie. 2 vols. Early English Text Society, os, 131, 136. London, 1906–1908.

The Oldest Anglo-Norman Prose 'Brut' Chronicle: An Edition and Translation. Ed. and trans. Julia Marvin. Medieval Chronicles, 4. Woodbridge, Suffolk: Boydell, 2006.

Prose 'Brut' to 1332. Ed. Heather Pagan. Manchester: Anglo-Norman Text Society, 2011.

Rauf de Boun. *Le Petit Bruit*. Ed. Diana B. Tyson. Anglo-Norman Text Society, Plain Texts Series, 4. London: Anglo-Norman Text Society, 1987.

Roger of Howden. *Chronica Magistri Rogeri de Houedene*. Ed. W. Stubbs. 4 vols. Rolls Series, 51. London, 1868–1871.

William of Malmesbury. *Gesta regum Anglorum: The History of the English Kings*. Ed. and trans. R.A.B. Mynors, R.M. Thomson, and M. Winterbottom. 2 vols. Oxford: Clarendon, 1998–1999.

Secondary Sources

Bryan, Elizabeth J. (2009). 'Rauner Codex MS 003183: The Beeleigh Abbey *Brut* at Dartmouth College.' *Journal of the Early Book Society* 12: 207–243.

Dean, Ruth J., and Maureen B.M. Boulton. (1999). *Anglo-Norman Literature: A Guide to Texts and Manuscripts*. London: Anglo-Norman Text Society.

Fisher, Matthew (2012). *Scribal Authorship and the Writing of History in Medieval England*. Columbus OH: Ohio State University Press.

James, M.R. (2021). *Unpublished description by M.R. James of Cambridge, University Library, MS Dd.10.32 (Geoffrey of Monmouth, Historia regum Britanniae, with a continuation in French)* [Dataset], accessed 22 February 2022. https://doi.org/10.17863/CAM.67707

Kooper, Erik (2016). 'Longleat House MS 55: An Unacknowledged *Brut* Manuscript?' In Rajsic et al. (2016: 75–93).

Kooper, Erik, and Julia Marvin (2012). 'A Source for the Middle English Poem *Arthur*.' *Arthuriana* 22: 25–45.

Matheson, Lister M. (1998). *The Prose 'Brut': The Development of a Middle English Chronicle*. Tempe, Arizona: Medieval and Renaissance Texts and Studies.

Mooney, Linne R., and Lister M. Matheson (2003). 'The Beryn Scribe and His Texts: Evidence for Multiple-Copy Production of Manuscripts in Fifteenth-Century England.' *The Library* 7th s. 4: 347–370.

Rajsic, Jaclyn, Erik Kooper, and Dominique Hoche, eds. (2016). *The Prose 'Brut' and Other Late Medieval Chronicles: Books Have Their Histories—Essays in Honour of Lister M. Matheson*. York: York Medieval Press.

Spence, John (2005). 'The Identity of Rauf de Boun, Author of the *Petit Bruit*.' *Reading Medieval Studies* 31: 59–76.

18

The Image of Alexander the Great in Persian History, Epic and Romance

Charles Melville and Firuza Abdullaeva

Abstract

The figure of Alexander the Great (Iskandar) features large in the historical and roman-tic literature of East and West. This paper compares the treatment of Alexander in different genres of Persian writings, particularly the way his career is illustrated in manuscript painting. We see, first, an enormous corpus of images depicting scenes from the early eleventh-century epic poem, the *Shahnama* of Firdausi, in manuscripts dating from the early fourteenth century to the early modern period. We then see how a later literary development of Firdausi's work in the romance epic by the twelfth-century poet Nizami treats Iskandar's life as a philosopher and seeker of truth. In striking contrast, only a handful of Persian chronicles purporting to provide a 'histor-ical' account of his reign, which are also illustrated from the fourteenth century, depict only two episodes: Iskandar and the dying Dara (Darius) and Iskandar entering the northern darkness. This visual repertoire remains constant regardless of the text, but it is remarkable that the self-identified historical works contain a far more restrained illustrative programme than those that aim for a more popular audience with a strongly narrative and mystical purpose.

Alexander the Great († 323 BC), one of the most celebrated figures in world his-tory and as much a subject of discussion and analysis in the ancient world as he is today, has generated a massive historiography in classical studies, history and art history that leaves few stones unturned. Although an unequivocally real historical figure, this historical reality has become obscured by the accre-tion of myths and legends and the transformation of Alexander's personality into that of a philosopher king, prophet or saint.[1] This is largely due to the fact

---

1   Abdullaeva (2012, 2017), also Manteghi (2018: 72–78) among many others. Among the latest publications, see the catalogue (Stoneman, 2022) of the current exhibition *Alexander the Great: The Making of a Myth* in the British Library (21 October 2022–19 February 2023).

that such contemporary sources as Cleitarchus and Onesikritos, who accompanied Alexander in his conquests, have either not survived at all, or only as incorporated, either piecemeal or in translation, into the histories of later authors, like Diodorus of Sicily of the third quarter of the first century BC, the Greek history of Arrian (second century AD) and the Latin works of Justinus (c. AD 200) and Curtius Rufus (first century AD): that is, compiled some 300–400 years after Alexander's death. There are two consequences of this: first, a proliferation of fictional or legendary accounts of his life via the work wrongly attributed to Callisthenes, the historian associated with Alexander's court, and composed around the third century AD before being translated from the Greek into Latin by Julius Valerius (†c. AD 340), essentially unrestrained by a secure factual basis. Secondly, scholarship has concentrated on the study of the so-called Alexander Romance literature and its dissemination across East and West, at the expense of more focused historiographical writing.[2]

There are two major versions of this fictional romance, with a common theme—one produced in Egypt and the other in Iran—due to the damage inflicted on the imperial ambitions of their dynasties by Alexander's invasion.[3] In the case of Egypt it was the last native ruler Nectanebo II, in the case of Iran it was king Dara (Darius), the last Kayanid (the dynasty which could be correlated at the end with the Achaemenids). Rather than being conquered by a foreign invader, they were revealed as his relatives, which made him a legitimate heir to their thrones. In the case of Egypt, it was Nectanebo II who travelled to the court of Philip of Macedon and seduced his wife in her husband's absence. In the case of Dara it was his mother, the daughter of Philip, who was sent from Greece to Iran but after the wedding night was returned on the pretext of her bad breath. This made the last Iranian ruler Alexander's half-brother, treacherously killed with Alexander arriving too late to save him but in time to receive his blessing.

There is not much difference in practice between the transmission of the legendary history of Alexander in medieval European historiographical works and those of romance literature, characterized by a progressive mingling of the two genres, together with the additional elements of Christian salvation history (mirrored also in the Islamic context, starting with the Qur'an).[4] In the case of European manuscripts, examples of both historiographical texts and the Alexander Romance are richly illustrated, the latter perhaps more so than the

---

2 Jamzadeh (2012: 2–6), Gaullier-Bougassas (2011: 5–9 and *passim*).
3 Bertels (1948: 9).
4 Sura 18: 82; Nöldeke (1890: 27, 32).

former, though with a wide range of scenes and topics depicted in both, the distinction being perhaps more to do with the context of the illustrations—that is, the genre of work in which they appear, such as universal chronicles—than the nature of the text being illustrated.[5] It is evident, for example, that several works of the thirteenth to the sixteenth century owed much to the stories relayed in the Alexander Romance,[6] and the same may be said of the three French chronicles discussed by Alison Stones, who nevertheless distinguishes her discussion of these 'historical compendia' from the numerous verse and prose copies of the Alexander Romance.[7] Although the distinction between 'history' and 'literature' is only a consideration lurking in the background here, it is helpful as a way to frame the strongly contrasting ways in which Alexander is visualized in Persian historical and literary texts, which provides the subject of our brief contribution.[8]

The first thing to note is that the history of Alexander—Iskandar in the Arab and Iranian tradition—in Persian literature is all derived from the Pseudo-Callisthenes Romance, which was spread also through Armenian, Syriac, Coptic and Ethiopian translations and possibly in Iran via a Middle Persian (Pahlavi) version.[9] The important point remains that the life of Alexander that entered early Islamic literature—in Arabic and later, Persian—was the essentially fictitious construction of the Romance and the source for both ostensibly historical works as well as epics and later romantic and mystical literature. But while these works all narrated the same basic storylines, despite inevitable variations of length and accretions of detail, the level of illustration of the texts diverged considerably. The second point to note is that as far as the historical works are concerned, the reign of Iskandar is included within the framework of a 'universal chronicle'—covering the ancient, pre-Islamic world up to the authors' own times—rather than any discrete work dedicated to the

---

5   See the several papers in Gaullier-Bougassas (2015) and the extensive references cited; Gaullier-Bougassas (2011) does not consider the topic of illustration in the historical repertoire.

6   Koroleva (2015: 389–391; 2019: 7–10).

7   Stones (2019: 12), referring to the rich bibliography on this subject, to which she has made a significant contribution.

8   Offered in friendship and admiration for our dedicatee, inspired in the first author at the Medieval Chronicle conference in Utrecht in 1999. This research is supported by a Leverhulme Trust Emeritus Fellowship, EM-2018–033\5.

9   Bertel's (1948: 10–11). Hämeen-Anttila (2018: 45–51) remains skeptical but Manteghi (2018: 41–45) argues convincingly for a Middle Persian intermediary produced at the Sasanian court, on the basis of an analysis of the contents of the different strands of transmission, rather than linguistic considerations.

conqueror. As far as we are aware, there is no illustrated copy of the prose *Iskandarnama* ('Book of Alexander'), the thirteenth-century Persian text of the Alexander Romance,[10] although there are some examples of the other popular prose romance also associated with Iskandar, namely the *Darabnama* ('Book of Darius'),[11] for one incomplete copy of which, see for example the British Library manuscript Or. 4615.[12]

1   The Persian Epic

Far removed from these popular, and certainly later, prose compositions, the earliest full account of Iskandar in Persian, derived from pseudo-Callisthenes, is the epic masterpiece of Firdausi, the *Shahnama* ('Book of Kings', c. 1010). In the most authoritative printed edition of the text, the poem runs to 459 verses in the reign of Dara (Darius) and 1,908 verses in the chapter on Iskandar.[13] Numerous manuscripts of the text were illustrated copiously from the early fourteenth century, the story of Iskandar among them.[14] The Cambridge Shahnama Project website identifies eight subjects illustrated in the reign of Dara son of Darab, with over 200 paintings, and around sixty subjects in the reign of Iskandar, with well over 600 paintings, making his career the sixth most heavily illustrated in the whole poem.[15] Of these subjects, by far the most popular is the scene of Iskandar attending the dying Dara, with over 140 paintings, followed by his battle against the Fur of Hind (Porus), his visit to Qaydafa (Candace) and his construction of the wall against Gog and Magog, respectively 65, 51 and 45 examples recorded so far. In all cases, the peak of this activity of illustration was in the sixteenth and seventeenth centuries, although interestingly—in view of the historical context of the irruption of the Mongols into southwest Asia in the thirteenth century—one-fifth of recorded paintings

---

10   For which, see Hanaway (1998) and the more recent translation by Venetis (2017), who places its original composition in the eleventh century.

11   Again, Hanaway (1994) for a detailed overview, and briefly Manteghi (2018: 6–7) for its place in Alexander scholarship.

12   See https://blogs.bl.uk/asian-and-african/2014/03/the-tales-of-darab-a-medieval-persian-prose-romance.html [accessed 27 February 2022].

13   Firdausi, *Shahnama*, v, 529–565, vi, 3–129.

14   See, briefly, Rubanovich (2018) and Milstein (2018); and van den Berg (2011, 2020): all focusing on the illustration of themes across different texts, see also below.

15   Regrettably the original Shahnama Project website is now inaccessible to the public and is in the course of being transferred to the Cambridge Digital Library, at: https://cudl.lib .cam.ac.uk/collections/shahnama/1 [accessed 28 February 2022].

of Iskandar's wall against the people of Gog and Magog, were made in the four-teenth century (when the first *Shahnama* manuscripts were illustrated).[16]

This purely statistical overview is sufficient to underline the enormous appetite for images of Iskandar as visualized in the national epic, which indeed only presents an identifiable historical reality at this point in the demise of the Achaemenid Empire. Iskandar's image as a world-conqueror is particu-larly marked in the so-called 'Great Mongol' *Shahnama* of the early fourteenth century, reflecting the contemporary history of the world-conquering Mongol khans in Iran.[17]

2   Religion and Romance

The martial age of the Turko-Mongol invasions and the conquests of Timur that followed gave way to the transformation of Iskandar's legendary persona into a more philosophical role in a narrative of a quest for knowledge and dis-course on earthly rule, within the context of Islamic scriptural traditions. The first softening and sublimation of Iskandar was already undertaken by the poet Nizami of Ganja (†1209), whose *Khamsa* ('Quintet') saw a refashioning and expansion of many of the episodes found in Firdausi's *Shahnama*, and partic-ularly in the Alexander cycle, now versified in the *Iskandarnama*, consisting of two books, the *Sharafnama* ('Book of Nobility') and *Iqbalnama* ('Book of Fortune').[18] This trend was accelerated in later epochs as sufism (Islamic mys-ticism) came increasingly to dominate Persian poetic idiom and religious liter-ature, and works such as the *Falnama* ('Book of Omens') and *Qisas al-anbiya* ('Stories of the Prophets') reflected the changing spirituality of the Safavid era of the sixteenth and seventeenth centuries.[19]

The literary and artistic enrichment of the Alexander stories, including the way in which the iconography of the paintings achieved a life independent of the texts, reached the point whereby the pictures could even influence the texts

---

16   van den Berg (2011: 78–81, 86; 2020: 16–28) for a particular focus on the story of Gog and Magog.

17   Grabar and Blair (1980: 112–135), with all 13 paintings illustrated; Soudavar (1996), in which the scenes of Iskandar are treated thematically; see also Rubanovich (2015: 224–228).

18   The bibliography on Nizami's poetry and thought is perhaps even richer than that con-cerning the *Shahnama*; of the references already cited, concerning Iskandar, see especially Manteghi (2018: 71–157) and the collection of essays in Bürgel and van Ruymbeke (2011).

19   See for example, Milstein (2018) and Milstein et al. (1999), and van den Berg (2020: 28–42).

themselves, such was their fluidity, particularly in the case of the *Shahnama*.[20] For our present purpose, what is of interest is the prolixity and range of the illustrations of Iskandar's *vita*, in both secular and spiritual epics and their chief focus.

A statistical analysis of the Iskandar paintings in manuscripts of Nizami's *Iskandarnama* has identified 127 themes (or scenes) out of a total of 338 across the whole *Khamsa*, of which the most popular is once more the scene of Iskandar and the dying Dara (86 examples), and with Qaidafa (here called Nushaba) attracting 45.[21] Only nine paintings, however, depict the story of the iron ramparts built against Gog and Magog, of which some additional ones have been noted since.[22] This is in stark contrast to the preferred choice of scene in the stories of the prophets, nine out thirteen paintings in the *Qisas al-anbiya* texts treating this episode.[23]

Overall, several scenes are illustrated repeatedly over the whole range of these texts—which include Amir Khusrau Dehlavi's *A'ina-yi Iskandari* ('Alexandrine Mirror') of c. 1300, and 'Abd al-Rahman Jami's mystical poem, *Khirad-nama-yi Iskandari* ('Alexandrian Book of Wisdom') of c. 1485, both written in emulation of Nizami, not discussed here.[24]

Thus, there is a vast body of manuscript illustrations of the story of Iskandar, both in the Persian epic and in mystical romance literature, covering a range of topics and subjects. The same is not the case in the equally voluminous body of historical texts, to which we now turn.

3 Historical Literature

Given this considerable volume of paintings in manuscripts of the story of Iskandar in secular, philosophical and religious poetic literature, it would be reasonable to expect the same in the illustrated copies of Persian chronicles and overtly historiographical works, particularly since, as noted, elements of

---

20 See Abdullaeva (2010), concerning Iskandar's flight into the heavens and Abdullaeva and Melville (2021), regarding his search for the water of life.

21 van den Berg (2011: 87–88), summarising the study by Dodkhudoeva (1985: 306–307). For a collection of paintings of the *Khamsa*, see Suleimanova (1985).

22 van den Berg (2011: 88–91).

23 Milstein et al. (1999: 83), identifying it also as the most often illustrated in the *Falnama* manuscripts studied; van den Berg (2020: 36–42).

24 See again, Rubanovich (2018), Milstein (2018) and van den Berg (2020: 31–33); for illustrations of Amir Khusrau, see Brend (2003: 272–275) and for Jami's *Khiradnama*, less often illustrated, Simpson (1997: 384).

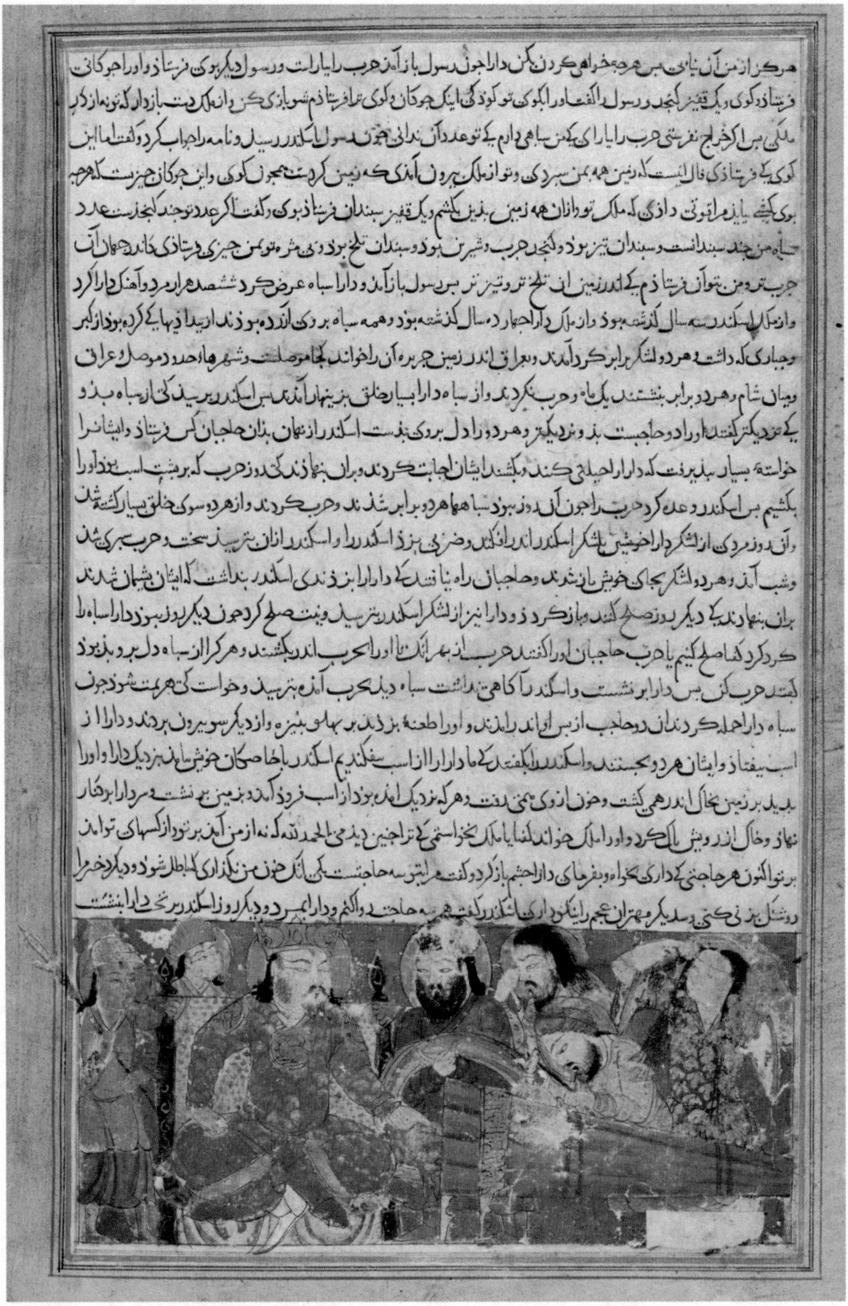

FIGURE 18.1　'Alexander contemplates the Coffin of Darius from his throne'. Freer Gallery of Art, Smithsonian Institution, Washington, D.C.: Purchase—Charles Lang Freer Endowment, F1957.16, fol. 90ᵛ

FIGURE 18.2   'Alexander enters the Northern Lands'. University of Edinburgh, Or. MS 20, fol. 19ʳ

the same narrative are found across these different genres. In fact, however, historical texts, which are mainly related, contain remarkably few illustrations of Iskandar, which must explain why they have received almost no attention.[25]

The first picture identified shows Iskandar on the throne of Iran, contemplating the coffin of Dara (see Fig. 1), in a manuscript of Abu 'Ali Bal'ami's tenth-century *Tarikhnama* ('History'), a substantial reworking and translation of Tabari's History of the Kings and Prophets.[26] Bal'ami's account, which predates Firdausi's *Shahnama*, is relatively brief, referring to the murder of Dara by his chamberlains and their subsequent execution, a minimal notice of his travels to India and China, his failure to find the water of life and his death in Shahrzur. The picture is inserted where the text reads: 'the next day [Alexander] sat on the throne' and after the typically telegraphic report, 'Dara died. Iskandar put him in a coffin'.[27] This is followed by a more extended account of the construction of the *sadd-i Iskandar* (Alexander's dam) against Gog and Magog, in the persona of Dhu'l-qarnain (the 'two horned'), richly laced with Qur'anic quotations.[28] This reflects the fact that this very early Persian prose work builds not only on the Romance but also on Islamic traditions, and that the history of the pre-Islamic prophets is also narrated as part of Iran's ancient history, derived partly from Sasanian mirrors for princes, like the *Khwaday-namag*.[29]

Bal'ami was certainly one of the sources used by Rashid al-Din (†1318), whose *Jami' al-tawarikh* ('Compendium of Histories') contains a history of the Mongol Empire as well as the people with whom the Mongols came into contact.[30] As yet there is no critical edition of the section devoted to the history of Iran and Islam, which also has considerable verbal affinities with the work by Qadi Baidawi, almost contemporary with Rashid al-Din.[31] The original copy of the *Jami' al-tawarikh*, dated AD 1314, in Arabic, is incomplete and shared between two separate collections. It contains only one painting of Iskandar, entering the 'northern darkness'—that is, a precursor to encountering the iron-working people of Gog and Magog, describing a land shrouded in fog, where

25   See briefly Milstein (2018: 52, 57).

26   Freer Gallery of Art, Washington D.C., F1957.16, fol. 90ᵛ. The manuscript is undated but thought to be an early fourteenth-century production, probably from Iraq (Mosul?) in the early Mongol period, commissioned as an aid to converting the Mongols; see Fitzherbert (2006: 404–405).

27   Bal'ami, *Tarikhnama*, 487–488. The picture thus reflects the edited text, but the manuscript omits the sentence 'Iskandar put him in a coffin'.

28   Bal'ami, *Tarikhnama*, 490–495.

29   Hämeen-Anttila (2018: 147–148); Manteghi (2018: 22–28).

30   Kamola (2019: 187–191) for the work and its recensions.

31   Melville (2016), with a critique of the existing edition; see further Ghiasian 2023.

the sun is seldom found (see Fig. 2).[32] The painting is described at length by Min Yong Cho, remarking on the confident approach of Iskandar and the hesitancy of his three followers, but also the disconnect between the description of the landscape and any relevant activity on the part of Iskandar.[33] The scene rounds out the scope of Iskandar's travels, following his visits to China, India and the Maghrib and, therefore, depicts him as a discoverer, perhaps reflecting the wide-ranging encounter of the Mongols with the other peoples of the world.[34] The iconography bears strong resemblance to pictures in manuscripts of the *Shahnama* of Iskandar contemplating the people of Gog and Magog,[35] or entering the land of the Brahmins in the Great Mongol *Shahnama*.[36]

Another, insipid, rendering of the same scene is found in an almost contemporary manuscript of the same work, dated AD 1317, but illustrated in the fifteenth century; the picture is located at the same place in the text.[37] The possibility of the existence of a third image of the same scene in another contemporary manuscript originating in Rashid al-Din's atelier—and therefore presumed to be following the same format—cannot be substantiated, because this section of the text, concerning the pre-Islamic past, is a replacement text copied by its author, Hafiz Abru in 1425.[38]

By contrast, this latter manuscript, H. 1653, does contain a picture of Iskandar with the dying Dara,[39] showing the conqueror cradling the prostrate Darius in his lap (and receiving his deathbed wishes). It is perhaps no surprise, therefore, that a second picture dedicated to this scene is contained in yet another in this group of interrelated manuscripts containing and amplifying the work of Rashid al-Din. This is a widely dispersed copy of Hafiz Abru's own *Majma' al-tawarikh* (c. 1425), this section of which, as noted above, was copied into the *Jami' al-tawarikh* manuscript H. 1653.[40] Both pictures occur in almost the same

32 Edinburgh Or. MS 20, fol. 19ʳ; for the equivalent Persian text, see BL Add. 2768, fols 28ʳ⁻ᵛ. In Bal'ami, *Tarikh*, 489, Iskandar's trip to the 'darkness', following journeys to East and West, is couched in connection with his vain search for the water of life, an episode not narrated by Rashid al-Din.

33 Min Yong Cho (2008: 79–81, 128–131); she does not, however, connect this to the story of Gog and Magog that follows.

34 See also Milstein (2018: 52).

35 E.g. the 'Inju' *Shahnama* of 1341 in the David Collection, Copenhagen, 13/1990.

36 Sackler 1986.105a, reproduced among others by Hillenbrand (2002: 163) and Milstein (2018: 54).

37 Istanbul H. 1654, fol. 26ʳ.

38 See the recent work of Ghiasian (2018: 62–79) concerning H. 1653, and in general for the relationships and illustrations of all three early copies of Rashid al-Din.

39 Istanbul H. 1653, fol. 91ʳ.

40 Ghiasian (2018: 57–62). New York Metropolitan Museum of Art, 52.20.3.

place in the text, close to an unillustrated manuscript of the *Jami' al-tawarikh*.[41] The question remains whether there was once an image of this scene in the original Arabic version of 1314, the surviving copy of which is incomplete.[42] On the face of it, and given the connection of both Rashid al-Din and Hafiz Abru with the work of Bal'ami, one might expect all this group to have included this iconic scene of the transfer of power to a foreign conqueror. Although the Mongols' own conquest of Iran certainly was not effected in such a sympathetic and accommodating manner, the scene might have encouraged this greater sensitivity towards the defeated Iranians.

Iskandar and Dara are depicted in two other unique illustrated manuscripts of different works. The first is the *Tabaqat-i Nasiri*, a general history of Iran arranged by dynasty, composed by Minhaj b. Siraj Juzjani in AD 1260.[43] It is one of only two illustrations in the manuscript, giving it a certain emphasis; it was produced in Shiraz in 1411, perhaps by the Timurid prince Iskandar Sultan for his cousin Baysunghur. Apart from the link with the patron's name, the gift of the work for the education of the young prince highlights the importance of Iskandar as a role model for kingship. The picture, which is badly abraded, is located in the text between the end of the reign of Dara and the start of Iskandar's, that is, at precisely the same point where the illustration is inserted in the Freer Bal'ami, the text of which it follows very closely.[44]

The second painting of the same subject occurs in the *Tarikh-i Abu'l-Khair Khani*, composed by Mas'ud b. 'Uthman Kuhistani (mid-sixteenth century), a universal chronicle for the Shaibanid Uzbek chief, Abu'l-Khair (†1468).[45] The small square picture is placed in the bottom right hand corner of the page, at the point where Iskandar promises to carry out the three dying wishes of Dara; but instead of the Persian king lying mortally wounded, he is sitting on a rug next to Iskandar, very much alive and in conversation. The author expands the usual version of the text, as in other cases, adding verses apparently of his own composition. This work contains one other picture from the life of Iskandar of an episode that is yet to be identified.[46]

---

41   BL Add 2768, fol. 27ᵛ.

42   Blair (1995: 24–27).

43   Berlin Petermann I 386, fol. 27ʳ; Stchoukine et al. (1971: 17–18, pl. 13).

44   Juzjani, *Tabaqat*, 148; neither text nor manuscript here states that Iskandar put Dara in a coffin (cf. above, n. 27). The image is online at: https://digital.staatsbibliothek-berlin.de/ werkansicht?PPN=PPN740833111&PHYSID=PHYS_0059&DMDID=DMDLOG_0003.

45   Tashkent, al-Biruni Institute, no. 9989, fol. 65ᵛ.

46   No. 9989, fol. 66ᵛ. The story involves Khizr and seems to describe driving a passage through a mountain to release a river, but the poor image of the text available to us is barely legible.

4   Conclusion

With the exception of the painting last mentioned, the repertoire of pictures of Iskandar so far identified in Persian historical texts is limited to a mere seven examples of two subjects across a handful of works. It has to be said, furthermore, that with one exception (the Rashid al-Din manuscript in Edinburg), none of these paintings is of high artistic quality. These are first, five pictures of the fantasy operatic swansong of the dying Dara, all created in secular histories either copied or written in the Turko-Mongol era (thirteenth to fifteenth centuries), which served a clear political and ideological purpose in justifying Iskandar's conquests, legitimising his rule and advancing the continuity of Persian traditions. Passages, or works, that present a hostile view of Alexander's destruction of the Persian Empire and attacks on Zoroastrianism, were not illustrated. The second subject, Iskandar entering the northern darkness, is connected textually with the episode of Gog and Magog that follows, but no visual association is made; it occurs in two copies of the same work. And that's it: a striking contrast with over a thousand paintings of these and numerous other scenes derived principally from the Alexander Romance— which remains the common source for much of this material—that exist in Persian narrative and mystical poetry.

This may be due to several factors, among them first, that historical texts are in general much less frequently illustrated than other Persian literary works, reflecting the latter's greater popularity and perhaps the audience at which illustrations are directed. Secondly, although the writing of universal histories continued throughout the manuscript age, those that were illustrated at their peak in the sixteenth–seventeenth centuries came to focus more on early Islamic history and the lives of the Prophets (notably of course Muhammad) and Imams than on the secular dynasties. A corollary of this was the growth of the different genre of the lives of the prophets, which could include the by now 'saintly' Iskandar; furthermore, the continuing illustration of *Shahnama* manuscripts—generally regarded as 'history'—was no doubt sufficient to cater for the appetite for illustrated books.[47] While the image of Iskandar as an exemplary figure, found already in the poetic circles of Firdausi's eleventh-century Ghazna, continued to resonate in mirrors for princes and Muslim *adab* ('polite') literature (and as a topos in historical writing), such passages of text were not illustrated, leaving us with an impoverished vision of Alexander in Persian historical literature.

---

47   Melville (2011: 171, 180–184).

Bibliography

Primary Sources—Manuscripts
Berlin
Staatsbibliothek zu Berlin
   Petermann I 368

Edinburgh
University Library
   Or. MS 20

Istanbul
Topkapi Palace Museum Library
   H. (Hazine) 1653
   H. (Hazine)1654

New York
Metropolitan Museum of Art
   52.20.3

Tashkent
Abu Reyhan al-Biruni Institute of Oriental Studies
   No. 9989

Washington D.C.
Freer Gallery of Art
   F1957.16

Primary Sources—Editions
Bal'ami, Abu 'Ali. *Tarikhnama-yi Tabari.* Ed. Mohammad Raushan, Tehran: Soroush, 1999.
Firdausi, Abu'l-Qasim. *Shahnama.* Vol. V. Ed. Dj. Khaleghi-Motlagh, New York: Bibliotheca Persica, 1997; vol. VI. Ed. Dj. Khaleghi-Motlagh and M. Omidsalar. New York: Bibliotheca Persica, 2005.
Juzjani, Minhaj b. Siraj. *Tabaqat-i Nasiri.* Ed. 'Abd al-Hayy Habibi. 2nd ed. Kabul: History Society of Afghanistan, 1962.

Secondary Sources
Abdullaeva, Firuza (2010). 'Kingly Flight: Nimrūd, Kay Kāvūs, Alexander, or Why the Angel has the Fish.' *Persica* 23: 1–29.

Abdullaeva, Firuza (2012). 'A flying King'. In Stoneman, Erickson, and Netton, 405–409.

Abdullaeva, Firuza (2017). 'Alexander as Muslim Iskandar in Persian Literature: From Usurper to Saint and Prophet.' Unpublished paper, Medieval Chronicle conference in Lisbon (12 July 2017).

Abdullaeva, Firuza, and Charles Melville (2021). 'Iskandar and the Water of Life: A Note on Nizami's Impact on Later Manuscript Production.' In Elbakidze and Amirkhanashvili (2021). 377–392.

Allegranzi, Viola, and Valentina Laviola, eds. (2020). *Texts and Contexts. Ongoing Researches on the Eastern Iranian World (Ninth-Fifteenth C.)*. Rome: Istituto per l'Oriente C.A. Nallino.

van den Berg, Gabrielle (2011). 'Descriptions and Images. Remarks on Gog and Magog in Nizāmī's *Iskandar Nāma*, Firdawsī's *Shāh Nāma* and Amīr Khusraw's *Ā'īna-yi Iskandarī.*' In Bürgel and van Ruymbeke (2011). 77–93.

van den Berg, Gabrielle (2020). 'The Wall and Beyond: Some Notes on Text, Context, and Visual Representations of Iskandar, Ya'ğūğ and Ma'ğūğ in the Pre-Modern Persianate World.' In Allegranzi and Laviola (2020). 15–52.

Bertel's, Evgeniy (1948). *Roman ob Aleksandre*. Moscow-Leningrad: Izdatelstvo akademii nauk.

Blair, Sheila S. (1995). *A Compendium of Chronicles: Rashid al-Din's Illustrated History of the World*. Nasser D. Khalili Collection of Islamic Art, vol. 27. London: Nour Foundation.

Brend, Barbara (2003). *Perspectives on Persian Painting. Illustrations to Amir Khusrau's Khamsah*. London and New York: Routledge Curzon.

Bürgel, Johann-Christoph, and Christine van Ruymbeke, eds. (2011). *A Key to the Treasury of the Hakim. Artistic and Humanistic Aspects of Nizami Ganjavi's Khamsa*. Leiden: University Press.

Casagrande-Kim, Roberta, Samuel Thrope, and Raquel Ukeles (2018). *Romance and Reason. Islamic Transformations of the Classical Past*. New York: Institute for the Study of the Ancient World.

Dodkhudoeva, Larisa (1985). *Poemy Nizami v srednevekovoy miniatyurnoy zhivopisi*. Moscow: Nauka.

Elbakidze, Maka, and Ivane Amirkhanashvili, eds. (2021). *Intercultural Space. Rustaveli and Nizami*. Tbilisi: Shota Rustaveli Institute of Georgian Literature.

Fitzherbert, Teresa (2006). 'Religious Diversity under Ilkhanid Rule c. 1300 as Reflected in the Freer Bal'amī.' In Komaroff (2006). 390–406.

Gaullier-Bougassas, Catherine, ed. (2011). *L'historiographie medieval d'Alexandre*. Turnhout: Brepols.

Gaullier-Bougassas, Catherine, ed. (2015). *Alexandre le Grand à la lumière des manuscrits et des premiers imprimés en Europe (XIIe–XVIe siècle)*. Turnhout: Brepols.

Ghiasian, Mohamad Reza (2018). *Lives of the Prophets. The Illustrations to Hafiz-i Abru's "Assembly of Chronicles"*. Leiden: Brill.

Ghiasian, Mohamad Reza (2023). 'Text and Image of the Pishdadian in Rashid al-Din's *Jami' al-tawarikh* and Hafiz-i Abru's *Majma' al-tawarikh*.' In Melville (2023). In press.

Grabar, Oleg, and Sheila Blair (1980). *Epic Images and Contemporary History, the Illustrations of the Great Mongol Shahnama*. Chicago: University Press.

Hämeen-Anttila, Jaakko (2018). Khwadāynāmag. *The Middle Persian Book of Kings*. Leiden: Brill.

Hanaway, William L. (1994). 'Dārāb-nāma'. *Encyclopaedia Iranica* VII, fasc. 1: 8–9.

Hanaway, William L. (1998). 'Eskandar-nāma'. *Encyclopaedia Iranica* VIII, fasc. 6: 609–613.

Hillenbrand, Robert (2002). 'The Arts of the Book in Ilkhanid Iran.' In Komaroff and Carboni (2002). 134–167.

Kamola, Stefan (2019). *Making Mongol History. Rashid al-Din and the* Jami' al-Tawarikh. Edinburgh: University Press.

Komaroff, Linda, ed. (2006). *Beyond the Legacy of Genghis Khan*. Leiden: Brill.

Komaroff, Linda, and Stefano Carboni, eds. (2002). *The Legacy of Genghis Khan. Courtly Art and Culture in Western Asia, 1256–1353*. New York: Metropolitan Museum of Art.

Koroleva, Elena (2015). 'Texte et image dans la vie d'Alexandre de la *Chronique enluminée d'Ivan le Terrible*.' In Gaullier-Bougassas (2015). 389–407.

Koroleva, Elena (2019). 'Alexander the Great and Julius Caesar: Narratives of Kingship in several Manuscripts of the *Chronique dite de Baudouin d'Avesnes*.' *Iran* LVII.I: 3–11.

Manteghi, Haila (2018). *Alexander the Great in Persian Tradition: History, Myth and Legend in Medieval Iran*. London: I.B. Tauris.

Melville, Charles (2011). 'The Illustration of History in Safavid Manuscript Painting.' In Mitchell (2011). 163–197.

Melville, Charles (2016). 'Rashīd al-Dīn and the Shāhnāmeh.' *Journal of the Royal Asiatic Society* 26 (1–2): 201–214.

Melville, Charles, ed. (2023). *Illustrating History in Medieval Manuscripts*. Manuscript Cultures 21. Hamburg: Centre for the Study of Manuscript Cultures. In press.

Mitchell, Colin, ed. (2011). *New Perspectives on Safavid Iran. Empire and Society*. London and New York: Routledge.

Milstein, Rachel, Karin Rührdanz and Barbara Schmitz (1999). *Stories of the Prophets. Illustrated Manuscripts of* Qiṣaṣ al-Anbiyā'. Costa Mesa, CA: Mazda.

Milstein, Rachel (2018). 'Picturing the Archetypal King: Iskandar in Islamic Painting.' In Casagrande-Kim, Thrope, and Ukeles (2018). 48–63.

Nöldeke, Theodore (1890). Beitrage zur Geschichte der Aleksanderromans, Wien: in commission bei F. Tempsky. Buchhändler der Kaiser Akademie der Wissenschaften.

Raby, Julian, and Teresa Fitzherbert, eds. (1996). *The Court of the Il-khans 1290–1340*. Oxford Studies in Islamic Art XII. Oxford: University Press.

Rubanovich, Julia (2015). 'Why so Many Stories? Untangling the Versions of Iskandar's Birth and Upbringing.' In Rubanovich (2015): 202–240.

Rubanovich. Julia, ed. (2015). *Orality and Textuality in the Iranian World. Patterns of Interaction across the Centuries.* Leiden: Brill.

Rubanovich, Julia (2018). 'The Alexander Romance.' In Casagrande-Kim, Thrope, and Ukeles (2018). 26–47.

Simpson, Marianna Shreve (1997). *Sultan Ibrahim Mirza's* Haft Awrang. *A Princely Manuscript from Sixteenth-century Iran.* New Haven and London: Freer Gallery of Art, Yale University Press.

Stchoukine, Ivan, Barbara Fleming, Paul Luft and Hanna Sohrweide (1971). *Verzeichnis der Orientalischen Handschriften in Deutschland.* Vol. 16. Wiesbaden: Franz Steiner.

Stoneman, Richard, Kyle Erickson, Ian Netton, eds (2012). *The Alexander Romance in Persia and the East*, Groningen: Barkhuis Publishing and Groningen University Library.

Stoneman, Richard, ed. (2022). *Alexander the Great: The Making of a Myth.* London: British Library Publishing.

Stones, Alison (2019). 'Changing Perceptions of Alexander in French Chronicles.' *Iran* LVII.I: 12–30.

Soudavar, Abolala. 'The Saga of Abu-Saʻid Bahādor Khān. The Abu-Saʻidnāmé.' In Raby and Fitzherbert (1996). 95–218.

Suleimanova, Fazila (1985). *Miniatures, Illuminations of Nisami's "Hamsah".* Tashkent: Fann.

Venetis, Evangelos, trans. (2017). *The Persian Alexander. The first complete English translation of the Iskandarnāma.* London: IB Tauris.

19

Painted History in Chinon

Martine Meuwese

Abstract

This article presents a case study of an exceptional twelfth-century Plantagenet-related wall painting in a chapel devoted to St Radegund (patron saint of prisoners) in Chinon, showing a royal cortege with five riders. It probably depicts a contemporary event related to the 1173–1174 rebellion against King Henry II of England, but scholars still disagree on who are represented. Was the mural painting commissioned by Queen Eleanor of Aquitaine after her release from prison, commemorating her being led into captivity by her husband Henry II, or was it commissioned by Henry II as a memorial of the reconciliation with his four sons after their revolt? By means of the art-historical method of iconography, it is possible to conclude that all the riders are male and that the painting conveys a political message by Henry II. This case study aims to demonstrate that visual sources and art-historical methods can provide relevant information for chronicle studies.

1   King Henry II Plantagenet and His Rebellious Sons

There is nothing surprising about a king turning to popular authors to commission a history of his ancestors in order to glorify both his dynasty and himself. King Henry II (1133–1189) was no exception: he commissioned the Anglo-Norman author Wace to write a history of the Norman dukes of England, but Wace's project ran into trouble and around 1173 the king withdrew the commission. Wace was replaced by Benoît de Sainte-Maure, who was more favourable to King Henry's interest. Wace then undertook his own version of the history of the Normans, also at the king's request.[1] Roger of Howden was also active in royal service for some thirty years. He adopted the traditional chronicle format for his *Gesta Henrici et Ricardi* and *Chronica Magistri Rogeri de Hovedene*. The latter contains an account of English affairs from the early 1170s to

---

1   Gillingham (2006: 28) mentions that Henry showed little or no interest in historical writing of any sort if it was in Latin.

1201. However, there is no sign that these texts were intended to be presented or dedicated to the king.[2]

It is remarkable that no official history of Henry's family was written in the second half of his reign, perhaps as a result of the revolt of his four sons in 1173–1174, and later again in 1183 and 1187–1189. Young Henry had been crowned king by his father in 1170, but he was frustrated that his father had not given him a realm to rule. In late 1172, King Louis of France began to suggest to Young Henry that he should demand from his father either England or Normandy. In the spring of 1173 Eleanor of Aquitaine sent her sons Richard (the Lionheart) and Geoffrey to join Young Henry in France. This resulted in the first revolt of 1173–1174, led by Young Henry. The biggest loser in this conflict was Eleanor, who was imprisoned for fifteen years by her husband after the revolt, for the rest of his life.

Gerald of Wales was in royal service from 1184 onwards. In *De principis instructione* Gerald attacks Henry for the assault on Thomas Becket, saying that his sons' rebellions were divine vengeance for the murder. Book 3, Chapter XXVI prefaces the death of Henry II with an account of a painted chamber in the royal palace at Winchester. Gerald tells how Henry II had ordered that a space on the wall should be left blank in order to fill it with a painting of an eagle pecked at by its four young: one sitting on each wing and a third on the kidneys, tearing the parent with beaks and claws, while a fourth sat on its neck, waiting for a chance to tear out the eyes of its parent. When Henry was asked by his household what this painting meant, he answered that it referred to the mutiny of his four sons.[3] The youngest eagle represents John (Lackland), his favourite, who would hurt him more painfully than the other sons. It was to be concluded from this wall painting that no king was safe even in his own house. It is true that Henry did not expect his sons to rebel and the description by Gerald of the mural at Winchester castle and Henry's explanation show how much the treachery hurt.

The composition of this mural was probably based upon bestiary representations of the bird 'epopus' (hoopoe), pecked by its chicks. According to bestiary tradition, young hoopoes treat their parents tenderly in their old age: They pluck out their parents' old feathers, lick their dimmed eyes, warm them

---

2 See Gillingham (2006) and Staunton (2017: 194–195).

3 Gerald of Wales, *Instruction for a ruler*, 678–681. According to Henderson (1961: 175) Henry referred to the second rebellion of his sons, as in 1174 John 'was only six years old, too young to be the subject of bitter comment'. By the time of the second revolt John was fifteen, and Henry's favourite son.

beneath their wings and nourish them.[4] Unlike the hoopoe who cherishes its parents as a loving child, quite the opposite would apply to Henry's mural with the eagle young. The Winchester mural might also refer to Eleanor as 'the eagle of the broken treaty', as foretold in Geoffrey of Monmouth's *Prophecies of Merlin* in *Historia Regum Brittanniae*, Book VII, Chapter III: 'The eagle of the broken treaty will gild the bridle and rejoice in a third nesting'.[5]

Did the Winchester mural of the eagle pecked at by the four young really exist, or is it merely an allegorical invention by Gerald of Wales to make another reference to Henry's problems with his sons?[6] We cannot know for sure, but Gerald's description demonstrates that works of art can be used to make a political point. Images and their intended meanings can thus be of equal importance as textual information.

2   The Chinon Mural and Its Interpretations

In the summer of 1964, Albert Héron discovered a secular wall painting in a chapel devoted to St Radegund in Chinon. It depicts five people on horseback, riding from left to right (Figure 1). The riders are usually identified as members of Henry's family, but there is still no agreement among scholars 'who is who' and why this scene is represented in this chapel, instead of the royal castle nearby.[7]

The wall painting in the chapel at Chinon (2.15 m. long × 1.15 m. high) is generally dated to the last quarter of the twelfth century. Héron labeled the painting's topic 'chasse royale des Plantagenets' (royal hunt of the Plantagenets). Henry's favourite residence in France was the castle of Chinon; he turned

4   See Henderson (1961:176–178); Hassig (1995: 93 + figs.) and Binski (2011: 151 n. 109).
5   Geoffrey of Monmouth, *History of the Kings of Britain*, VII.III, 148–149. Roger of Howden in *Gesta Henrici II* (c. 1172–1192) and Ralph of Coggeshall speak of Eleanor as 'the eagle of the broken covenant who shall spread her wings over two kingdoms', and of her sons as the 'lion cubs who shall awake and roar loud'. Binski (2001: 151 n. 109) mentions that an allusion to Eleanor of Aquitaine in the Winchester mural seems just as likely.
6   See Aurell (2016: 38) and Henderson (1961: 176): 'The story is not, therefore, a first-hand report, and it has rather the appearance of a literary device'. Gerald was familiar with the text of *Physiologus*.
7   Cockerill (no date): 'Upon its discovery Héron identified the first rider as a king, the second figure as a lady, the third as a young man wearing a crown, and the last two riders as young men. Hence he hypothesized that the scene represents the abduction of Isabella of Angoulême from Hugh of Lusignan by Henry II and his youngest son John. He later changed his mind and identified the third rider as a young lady, thus excluding an identification as Queen Eleanor.' Also see Nilgen (2004: 61).

FIGURE 19.1   Mural painting with five Plantagenet riders on horseback in the chapel of St
                Radegund, near Chinon, late twelfth century
                PHOTO: THE AUTHOR

it into a massive fortress and the centre of power of Plantagenet France. We
know that Henry II enjoyed hunting in the forests of Chinon, but is this merely
a hunting scene? A representation of just a royal pastime would be exceptional
in a sacred space.

The first rider is a red-headed and bearded middle-aged man who points forward with the index finger of his right hand. He wears a crown and a mantle
lined with fur. The third figure is also crowned and wears a similar mantle.
There is no reason to assume that the cloak-linings of these two figures have
heraldic significance; its preciousness just indicates their rank. This second
royal person looks backwards, stretching the right arm towards the fourth rider,
who has a (damaged) hunting bird on the gloved hand of his outstretched
left arm. Most of the identification debate centres on the question of whether
Queen Eleanor can be identified as the second crowned figure. This detail of
the mural was reproduced on the covers of several books on Eleanor, such as
the biographies of Régine Pernoud and D.D.R. Owens, which helped strengthen
this interpretation.[8]

Art historian Nurith Kenaan-Kedar published several articles on the Chinon
painting. In her 1998 article she suggested that the mural might show Eleanor
being led into captivity by Henry II after the family revolt in 1174. The queen
would then be accompanied by her daughter Joanna, as the second rider, and

---

8   See Kenaan-Kedar (1998: 319) and Cockerill (no date).

two of her sons: Richard (with hunting bird) and Young Henry.[9] She suggested that Richard gives a falcon to his mother, but later scholars 'reversed' the
act represented here: Eleanor then handed Richard a falcon, explained as the
symbol of the Duchy of Aquitaine, which Eleanor ceded to Richard in 1172. The
bird is sometimes connected to the bird Eleanor holds on her seal, but there is
no record of a bird of prey as an emblem for Aquitaine.[10] It is unlikely that the
third rider handed the bird to Richard because that hand wears no glove.

Eleanor played an important part in her sons' rebellion, for which Henry
had her seized and imprisoned, but why should that unfavourable act be recorded by the king on a mural in a chapel, even outside her dominion?[11] As St
Radegund was the patron saint of prisoners, Eleanor could have commissioned
the wall painting for this chapel to celebrate her renewed freedom. In that case
she commissioned it after her liberation from prison after the death of Henry II
in 1189 or perhaps the early 1190s.

For reasons of space, I focus only on the main discussion points.[12] In order to
provide a decisive answer to the important question whether Queen Eleanor
is represented on the mural, it is crucial to take a closer look at the third figure in the cortege. Art historian Ursula Nilgen has convincingly argued that
there is no doubt that the third figure is a man: the male clothes with a mantle
clasp on the shoulder and without a girdle or any other female ornament, the
absence of long hair pulled back or braided and without any sort of veil under
the crown, all confirm that the third figure is a man. It is surprising that Nilgen's convincing methodological argument to look at all details of the painting
and the costume first before identifying the gender and identity of a person
represented, has not been taken more seriously by the scholars who particip-

---

9   The other option Kenaan-Kedar (1998) mentions is King John with Eleanor and Isabella
        of Angoulême, which would date the painting after 1200.

10   The falcon was considered a pun on the name Fulco (of Anjou), but would not explain its
        heraldic use for Aquitaine. Both the arms of Eleanor and Poitiers carry a lion. Brown (2003:
        22–23) interprets the bird on the seal as a dove, since a dove appears on sceptres from the
        eleventh century (Edward the Confessor); only in the fourteenth century Edward III takes
        a falcon as badge. Kenaan-Kedar (1998: 322) refers to London, BL, Additional 15216, fol. 11ᵛ
        (Tournai, late twelfth century) where two nobles laughing at St Martin dividing his mantle
        are represented with birds of prey on their hands.

11   Weir (1999: 315): 'Henry had dealt so discreetly with Eleanor after her capture that we do
        not even know where she was imprisoned during the years before her transfer to England.
        It is hardly likely that either he or his son Richard would commission a mural commem-
        orating her disloyalty and disgrace.'

12   Overviews of how the discussion developed can be found in Nilgen (2004) and Cockerill
        (no date).

ated in the debate, as this is one of the basic principles of art history.[13] One might object that Gervase of Canterbury in his *Chronica* described the flight of Eleanor in 1173: somewhere between Poitiers and Rouen, in spite of her disguise in men's clothes, she was caught and imprisoned.[14] This crossdressing is a nice historical detail that shows Eleanor's intelligence, but it makes no difference to the 'rules of representation' in medieval art, according to which someone's 'true' identity is always shown to the beholder of an image, even when (s)he is in disguise in the eyes of the characters in the story.

Thus we can conclude that this completely male cortege, including two kings, must represent King Henry and his four sons, and that the mantle linings of the two royal figures and the hunting bird of the fourth man should not be explained as genealogical or political references to the Plantagenet family, but just as generic status symbols. Henry II, the oldest man, rides in front, followed by John (the youngest son that was so dear to him), Young Henry (the second king), Richard (with the bird of prey) and Geoffrey at the end. Therefore we should also question Héron's identification as a hunting party, as there are no other hunting birds, trees, stags, dogs, rabbits, servants with horns that one would expect in a hunting scene.

Kenaan-Kedar mentioned the similar-looking iconographic motif of the journey of the three Magi on horseback, where often one of the kings points to the Bethlehem star, which is sculpted on the frieze of the Saint Michel portal of Poitiers cathedral (dated to 1163–1173).[15] This sculpture also shows a king turning around with an outstretched arm, which she does not mention. It is very likely that the iconographic motif of the Magi on horseback served as a source of inspiration for the Chinon mural, as I have found more compositional parallels in contemporary enamelled caskets from Limoges, on which the motif of the three Magi was very popular.[16]

---

13   See Nilgen (2004) for Kenaan-Kedar ignoring her arguments. Other participants in the discussion were often historians, who probably are less familiar with art historical conventions and arguments. It is surprising that there is still debate on the presence of Eleanor in the cortege, and that new interpretations of the figures are put forward; e.g. see Cockerill (2019) and Silva (2021).

14   See Kleinmann (2004: 55) and (Aurell 2017: 764).

15   Kenaan-Kedar (2004: 46).

16   For the three Magi on horseback with one king pointing forwards and another with an arm outstretched, e.g. see these Limoges caskets from the last quarter of the twelfth century: Paris, Musée de Cluny, CL. 23822; New York, Metropolitan Museum, 2019.423a.b. Also compare the composition of a cortege in an early thirteenth-century Bible miniature showing Zechariah's vision in Amiens, Bibliothèque Municipale, 21, fol. 168ʳ; the first rider points forwards and another holds a bird of prey on his fist.

As Henry and his sons ride towards the altar, the main purpose of the mural must be devotional. The Chinon painting was then most likely commissioned by Henry II, probably soon after 1174 (the end of the first rebellion) and not later than 1182.[17] The renewed rebellion started in 1183 and on 11 July 1183 Young Henry died of dysentery. The Plantagenet mural would then show that Henry II has forgiven his four sons after the revolt, thus turning the wall painting into a visual memorial of the reconciliation with his sons and heirs of his realms, placed under heavenly protection in a chapel near his French castle.[18] Hence the atmosphere of the mural is that of powerful (male) family unanimity combined with piety, completely ignoring the imprisoned Queen Eleanor.

3   Representing the Plantagenet Family

There are a few contemporary representations of the Plantagenet family in French art. The most important is the stained-glass window in the cathedral of Poitiers showing King Henry and Queen Eleanor, accompanied by their four young sons, in the act of humbly dedicating the window. Eleanor is clearly recognizable as a woman by the veil under her crown. The window is generally dated between December 1166 (the birth of John) and December 1170 (the murder of Thomas Becket, soon followed by the first rebellion).[19] It is not clear whether Henry or Eleanor was primarily responsible for the gift of this window, but the purpose is clearly to beg the church for mercy for the royal family.

A few decades later, the monastery of Fontevraud was chosen as the burial site for the Plantagenet family. The three effigies of Henry II, Richard and Eleanor were made by the same stone carver c. 1200, probably as commissions of Eleanor.[20] On her effigy she is shown with a crown on her veil, contemplating with a book in her hands; apparently the image of herself she wished to be remembered.[21] In 2016 Jesús Rodriguez Viejo identified the image of a woman

---

17   After a stylistic analysis Nilgen (2004: 62–63) dates the style of the Chinon mural to the 1170s.
18   This proposition was first made by Nilgen (2004: 66).
19   Eleanor and Henry married in Poitiers cathedral in 1152, when the building was still completely romanesque. For the dating of the royal window, see Nilgen (2004: 63) and Aurell (2016: 36–38). Brown (2003: 27) comments: 'Given the tenseness of the couple's relations after 1166, their appearance together as donors of the glass is curious'.
20   See Nolan (2003).
21   Kleinmann (2004: 52).

in prayer on the Beatus page of the Fécamp Psalter (The Hague, Royal Library, 76 F 13, fol. 28ᵛ), made 1180–1185, with Eleanor, relying in part on the scholarship relating to the Chinon mural, but that identification is not certain.[22]

There are no illustrations of Eleanor in English manuscripts. Chronicles and genealogies tend to focus on the males in the family, as in the Chinon mural. It can be assumed from both texts and images that red hair was dominant in the Plantagenet family. Geoffrey Plantagenet, Henry's father, was described as red-headed as is also obvious from his enamel effigy at Le Mans, c. 1155. Their red hair is often mentioned in descriptions of their constitution in English chronicles.

Around 1188 Gerald of Wales dedicated his *Topographia Hibernica* to Henry II. At the end of the first book of his sequel to the *Topographia*, the *Expugnatio Hibernica*—which Gerald claims was written at the behest of Henry II, but which was dedicated to his son Richard—gives a vivid description of Henry II. Gerald begins with a physical description: Henry's fiery hair, large round head, grey eyes that could flame with rage, voice, powerful body with a large belly and restless energy. The description gradually becomes more critical, exposing Henry's adulteries and his neglect of devotion to religion.[23] The physical appearance of Young Henry at his coronation in 1170 is described as very handsome: 'tall but well proportioned, broad-shouldered with a long and elegant neck, pale and freckled skin, bright and wide blue eyes, and a thick mop of the reddish-gold hair'. Richard was red-haired as well. A manuscript of the *Expugnatio Hibernica* (Dublin, National Library of Ireland, NLIMS 700, p. 147), illustrated c. 1200, contains a rare early portrait of the enthroned Henry II, shown with red hair and beard.[24]

Descriptions of the physiognomy of Henry II and his sons were later provided in Gerald's *De principis instructione*. The descriptions do not just list physical and character traits based on observation; they also echo a literary tradition of how to present a king, not only expressing what Henry was like, but also what a king should be like.[25] In later English chronicles and gene-

---

22 One of the arguments of Viejo (2016: 16) is the fur lining of the mantle, which can be dismissed for a Plantagenet connotation. The represented woman clearly is rich and noble; she wears a double wreath, but no crown. Hence there is no solid proof for an identification as Eleanor, who was still imprisoned (most of the time in England) at the time of manufacture in Normandy.

23 *Expugnatio Hibernica* I, 46; *Principis instructione* II, 29; and Staunton (2017: 156–160).

24 This manuscript can be consulted online: https://catalogue.nli.ie/Record/vtls000505800.

25 See *De principis Instructione* Book 3, ch. 28. Walter Map describes Henry at the end of *De Nugis curialium*, perhaps imitating Gerald. See Staunton (2017: 154) and Gillingham (2006:

alogies concerning the Plantagenet family that were illustrated in the thirteenth and fourteenth century, visual devices of Henry and his sons usually
refer to rank, common royal activities and the patronage of building works.
Hence these later 'portraits' of Henry and his sons are generic and interchange-
able.[26]

We can conclude that Eleanor is not present in this 'family picture' on the
wall of the Chinon chapel. As both chronicle texts and images not only presented a dynastic genealogy but also demonstrated 'what a good ruler should be
like', the Chinon mural probably aims to present to posterity a propaganda picture of the powerful Plantagenet father and his sons, riding peacefully together
towards the altar of the chapel near the French royal castle, in commem-
oration of their (re)union and to find heavenly blessing. Unfortunately, the
peace did not last long. The sons would soon make war on their father again,
with dramatic consequences, as—according to Gerald—was shown in the
painting of four young eagles attacking their parent on a wall of Winchester
castle.

Bibliography

Primary Sources—Manuscripts
Amiens
Bibliothèque Municipale
   21, fol. 168ʳ

---

41): 'His nickname, Curtmantle, should remind us of the fashionably and elegantly dressed
young man, the king "whose power", in Walter Map's words, "almost the whole world fears
and who is always robed in precious stuffs, as is right ('ut decet')."'

26   For *Effigies ad Regem Angliae* miniatures (BL, Cotton, Vitellius A.XIII, c. 1280–1300) and
other genealogies of British kings, see Collard (2007). Henry's predecessor Stephen
(d. 1154) is represented with a falcon; Henry and his sons are shown as generic kings.
Generic Plantagenet ruler 'portraits' were also inserted in a manuscript of *Peter Langtoft's
chronicle* (London, BL, Royal 20 A II, c. 1307–1327), Wace's *Brut* (Oxford, Bodleian Library,
Rawlinson D 329, second quarter of the fourteenth century). In the fourteenth-century
Abingdon Chronicle Henry II, enthroned, holds a bird of prey on his hand (Cambridge,
Trinity R.17.7, fol. 15ʳ). *Flores Historiarum* manuscripts also show genealogies of kings. A
genealogical roll of the English kings (London, BL, Royal 14 B VI, early fourteenth century)
shows 'busts' of Henry's children, including the girls.

Cambridge

Trinity College
R.17.7, fol. 15ʳ

Dublin

National Library of Ireland
NLIMS 700, p. 147

The Hague

Koninklijke Bibliotheek
KW 76 F 13, fol. 28ᵛ

London

British Library
Additional 15219, fol. 11ᵛ
Cotton Vitellius A.XIII, fol. 4ᵛ
Royal 20 A II, fols 7ᵛ–8ᵛ

Oxford

Bodleian Library
Rawlinson D 329

Primary Sources—Editions

Geoffrey of Monmouth. *The History of the Kings of Britain. An edition and translation of De Gestis Britonum* [*Historia regum Brittanniae*]. Eds. and trans. Reeve, Michael D. and Neil Wright (2007). Woodbridge, Boydell Press.

Gerald of Wales. *Instruction for a ruler* (*De Principis Instructione*). Bartlett, Robert ed. and trans. (2018). Oxford: Oxford University Press.

Giraldus Cambrensis. *Expugnatio Hibernica: The conquest of Ireland.* Scott, A.B. and F.X. Martin eds. (1978). Dublin: Royal Irish Academy.

Secondary Sources

Arrignon, Claude, Marie-Hélène Debiès, Claudio Galdersi and Éric Palazzo, eds. (2004). *Cinquante années d'études médiévales. À la confluence de nos disciplines. Actes du Colloque organisé à l'occasion du Cinquantenaire du CESCM Poitiers, 1er–4 septembre 2003* Turnhout: Brepols.

Aurell, Martin (2016). 'L'art comme propaganda royale? Henri II d'Angleterre, Aliénor d'Aquitaine et leurs enfants (1154–1204).' *Hortus Artium Medievalium. Journal of the International Research Center for Late Antiquity and Middle Ages* 21: 22–40.

Aurell, Martin (2017). 'Political Culture and Medieval Historiography: The Revolt against King Henry II, 1173–1174.' *History. The Journal of the Historical Association.* 751–771.

Binski, Paul (2011). 'The painted chamber at Westminster. The fall of tyrants and the English literary model of governance.' *Journal of the Warburg and Courtauld Institutes* 74: 121–154.

Brown, Elizabeth A.R. (2003), 'Eleanor of Aquitaine reconsidered.' In Wheeler and Parsons (2003). 1–54.

Cockerill, Sara (2019). *Eleanor of Aquitaine. Queen of France and England. Mother of empires.* Gloucestershire: Amberley Publishing.

Cockerill, Sara (no date; published as a PDF on Academia as an appendix to her book). *Two reputed representations of Eleanor of Aquitaine from her lifetime—a reevaluation.*

Collard, Judith (2007), '"Effigies ad Regem Angliae" and the Representation of Kingship in Thirteenth-Century English Royal Culture.' *Electronic British Library Journal.* 1–26.

Gillingham, John, 'The cultivation of history, legend, and courtesy at the court of Henry II.' In Kennedy and Meecham-Jones (2006). 25–52.

Hassig, Debra (1995). *Medieval Bestiaries. Text, image, ideology.* Cambridge: Cambridge University Press.

Henderson, George (1961). 'Giraldus Cambrensis. A note on his account of a painting in the King's chamber at Winchester.' *Archaeological Journal* 118: 175–179.

Kenaan-Kedar, Nurith (1998). 'Aliénor d'Aquitaine conduit en captivité. Les peintures murales commémoratives de Sainte-Radegonde de Chinon.' *Cahiers de civilisation médiévale* 41: 317–330.

Kenaan-Kedar, Nurith (2004). 'The wall painting in the Chapel of Sainte-Radegonde at Chinon in the Historical Context.' In Arrignon et al. (2004). 43–49.

Kennedy, Ruth, and Simon Meecham-Jones, eds. (2006). *Writers of the reign of Henry II. Twelve essays.* New York: Palgrave Macmillan.

Kleinmann, Dorothée (2004). 'La peinture de Sainte-Radegonde dans son contexte historique.' In Arrignon et al. (2004). 51–58.

Nilgen, Ursula (2004). 'The wall-painting in the Chapel of Sainte-Radegonde at Chinon in the Historical Context.' In Arrignon et al. (2004). 61–67.

Nolan, Kathleen (2003). 'The Queen's choice: Eleanor of Aquitaine and the tombs at Fontevraud.' In Wheeler and Parsons (2003). 377–405.

Silva, Aurzelle da (2021). 'La Chasse royale—l'image en mouvement et sonore: la peinture murale énigmatique de la chapelle Sainte-Radegonde à Chinon—an Essay.' *Cahiers de civilisation médiévale* no. 255: 223–238.

Staunton, Michael (2017). *The Historians of Angevin England.* Oxford: Oxford University Press.

Viejo, Jesús Rodriguez (2016). 'Royal Manuscript Patronage in late Ducal Normandy: A

Context for the Female Patron portrait of the Fécamp Psalter (c. 1180).' *Cerae. An Australasian Journal of Medieval and Early Modern Studies* 3: 1–23.

Weir, Alison (1999). *Eleanor of Aquitaine. By the wrath of God, Queen of England.* London: Jonathan Cape ltd.

Wheeler, Bonnie, and John Carmi Parsons, eds. (2003). *Eleanor of Aquitaine. Lord and lady.* New York: Palgrave Macmillan.

20

Divining the Past in London, Wellcome Library MS 8004: A Study and Edition of the Historical Notes in a Fifteenth-Century English Compendium

Sarah L. Peverley

Abstract

This paper introduces and provides an edition of the hitherto unpublished set of historical notes found in the mid-fifteenth-century compendium of Middle English texts extant in London, Wellcome MS 8004. It considers the contents of the notes, which include a brief epitome of universal and English history to 1415 and a synopsis of battles from 1066 to 1424, and highlights their affinity with a small group of short Middle English Chronicles and king lists, particularly the *Folger Brief History* written in 1442. The study concludes with a reflection on the function of historical material in what is predominantly a medical, astronomical and prognostic manuscript, and cautiously suggests that in addition to teaching readers the main facts of history the notes may have provided a practical digest of historical data to test the prognostic methods outlined elsewhere in the volume. The edition that follows is supplied with full textual and explanatory notes outlining likely sources, such as Ranulph Higden's *Polychronicon* and a version of the *Prose Brut*.

1   Introduction

Wellcome MS 8004 is a mid-fifteenth-century parchment compendium produced in the East of England and self-dated to 1454. Written in a professional anglicana hand, it contains a calendar, various astrological, astronomical, medical and prognostic texts—with accompanying tables and diagrams of Phlebotomy Man (fol. 18^r), lunar eclipses (fol. 29^r), Zodiac Man (fol. 40^r) and urine flasks (fols 58^v–61^r)—historical notes and a pilgrimage tract.[1] Except for the calendar and several of the tables, which are in Latin, all of the texts are in Middle English and are dialectally consistent with the East of England, particularly the

---

1   For the full contents of the manuscript see Voigts and Kurtz (2019).

Lincolnshire region.[2] Further evidence of the manuscript's East England origin is provided by the calendar, which contains the Feast and Translation of St
Hugh, Bishop of Lincoln, and the illumination, which is stylistically and decor-
atively identical to that produced by a group of artists responsible for at least
eight other manuscripts decorated in this area.[3]

The scribe originally included the name, profession and location of the first
owner, 'Richard', but this information has been erased and is only partially
recoverable under ultraviolet light.[4] In the eighteenth century the manuscript
was owned by Thomas Hill (1760–1840), who may have obtained it from
Thomas Park (1759–1834). It was at Clumber Park, Nottinghamshire, until 1938
and was subsequently owned by Alan Lubbock. Christies auctioned the manuscript on 29 November 1999 (Lot 9) and The Wellcome Library purchased it in
June 2002 from Sam Fogg Rare Books.

The historical notes (fols 42^r–44^v) are in two parts, the first being a brief epitome of universal and English history from the birth of Cain to the Battle of
Agincourt (1415), with a summary of England's demographic divisions taken
from Ranulph Higden's *Polychronicon*. Although the epitome begins with a
universal focus on biblical figures and religious matters of the twelfth and thirteenth centuries, it moves swiftly to fourteenth- and fifteenth-century affairs,
exhibiting a distinct interest in the dates, battles and casualties of the First and
Second Wars of Scottish Independence (1296–1328 and 1332–1357) and the Hundred Years War (1337–1453). Space is likewise given to natural phenomena, such
as plagues, weather and famine. The second part of the historical notes offers
a synopsis of key battles from Stanford Bridge (1066) to Verneuil (1424), repeating some of the information recorded in the epitome along with new material.
Like the first part, this section is attentive to conflicts fought in the North of
England or Scotland, with more than half of the battles recorded occurring
in those regions. Such an emphasis complements the manuscript's probable
Lincolnshire origin and may speak to the original owner's interest in Northern
history and Anglo-Scottish affairs. Equally, the emphasis may derive from the
sources informing the historical notes, elements of which have an affinity with

---

2 The linguistic profile undertaken for this edition showed a propensity for Northern forms,
   especially those attested in Benskin et al (see 2013: Linguistic Profiles 16, 30, 69, 210, 422 and
   587, all Lincolnshire).

3 Saint Hugh's Feast (17 November) and Translation (6 October) appear on fols 14^v, 15^v. For the
   artists of Wellcome 8004 see Simpson and Peverley (2015: 17–20).

4 The erasure reads: 'Richard etaly[?] the[?] H___ of þe Conte [or Cite?] of H_d_n [or
   Ly_d_n]' (f. 5^r). The final word has a suspension symbol at the end. Christies' sale catalogue
   suggests the 'City of Lincoln', which fits with the manuscript's probable locale but not with
   the visible letters.

material found in Higden's *Polychronicon* (a Northern composition) and *The Brut* (which records the Wars of Scottish Independence in some detail).[5]

Whether the emphasis on Northern affairs was intentional or not, the historical notes in Wellcome MS 8004 belong with the small number of brief Middle English chronicles and king lists described by Edward Donald Kennedy and Lister M. Matheson. They have the greatest correspondence with the structure and content of the *Folger Brief History* and likely share a common ancestor with this text.[6] Kennedy's observation that such concise histories were 'probably intended to offer a rapid survey of English history and to teach the main facts to the uneducated through recitation or memorization' (1989: 2622) holds true for the Wellcome notes, but in this particular compendium they may have had an additional function, which is best understood in the context of Wellcome MS 8004's overarching focus on observing, calculating and understanding the seen and unseen influences at work on humanity.

It is well known that medieval chroniclers viewed history as providential, revealing the will of God through the rise and fall of kings and kingdoms and the appearance of portents like comets, earthquakes and plagues. Yet the Wellcome notes bring this into sharp relief by recording important names, dates, births, deaths, natural disasters and socio-political events, and putting them in dialogue with the broader cosmological framework of the created world, as represented and interrogated by the other texts in the compendium. In this respect the notes complement the various computational tables and astronomical texts used for diagnosing and forecasting the influences of heavenly bodies, inauspicious days and weather, and provide a practical digest of historical data that can be used to test some of the prognostic methods articulated in the volume, such as *The Sphere of Pythagoras* (fols 18^v–19^r) and *The Victorious and the Vanquished* (fols 70^v–72^v). These two onomantic texts fre-

---

5   I refer simply to *The Brut*, rather than to any of the specific linguistic iterations of this text, because the Wars of Independence appear in the Anglo-Norman, Middle English and Latin *Bruts*. It is likely, but by no means certain, that a Middle English version of the text furnished some of the information. Unless otherwise stated, all comparative references to *The Brut* in this study are supplied from Brie's edition (1906, 1908).

6   See Kennedy (1989: 2637, 2666, 2833 and 2881) and Matheson (1998: 318–322, 347–348). The *Folger Brief History* is discussed by Kennedy (1989: 2666, 2881) and edited by Lipscomb (1996). It occurs in Folger Shakespeare Library MS v.a.198, fols 5^r–6^r, and is self-dated to 1442. The present edition follows Kennedy's title, *Folger Brief History* rather than Lipscomb's longer *Middle English Epitome of World and English History. A Tretis Compiled out of Diverse Cronicles* (self-dated to 1440) also shares some content with the Wellcome notes and *Folger Brief History*. Of further interest is the fact that the *Tretis* was once part of a miscellany copied by scribes working in the South-East Midlands who appear to have used Northern exemplars for their texts (Peverley 2019: 247).

quently appear in volumes like Wellcome MS 8004, instructing readers how to divine the outcome of battles, sickness, marriages and voyages through the numerical value of names.[7] A table is used to convert individual letters into a number, which is then pitted against another number to predict an outcome. The *Victorious and the Vanquished* even assigns the success of Alexander the Great's military campaigns to his use of the text.[8]

When viewed in conjunction with these other items, the Wellcome historical notes furnish relevant examples of past lives and events to illustrate that they are subject to the same forces and divinatory principals explored in the rest of the volume. Early readers wishing to practise their new-found divinatory skills, with a view to forecasting future events, could, in some cases, apply the prognostic methods outlined in the manuscript to the historical data to gain better insights into the affairs that had shaped their present. For example, when the information provided about the Battle of Northallerton (22 August 1138), is subjected to the process described in *The Victorious and the Vanquished*, it successfully predicts the outcome of the battle: that Thurstan, archbishop of York, 'ourcomyne and scomfett' [overcame and defeated] David, king of Scotland. Using the numerical equivalents for the alphabet defined by *The Victorious and the Vanquished* (fol. 71^v) and converting the letters of the protagonists' names as they are spelt in the historical notes—'Thurstane' and 'Dauid'—gives a total of ninety-four for Thurstane and fifty-one for Dauid. When each sum is then divided by nine, as instructed by the text, the results are ten with a remainder of four for Thurstan and five with a remainder of six for David. As the rules for the prognostication explain, the remainders are pitted against each other and with 'fowr and 6 qwo-so has 4 sall ourcome' [four and six, whosoever has 4 shall overcome] (fol. 71^r). Thurstan is therefore predicted to be the victor of the battle, confirming what the historical notes already record.[9]

While this example serves to demonstrate how the original owner of Wellcome MS 8004 could have tested one element of the manuscript's prognostic methods on the historical notes, it is nonetheless impossible to determine whether every aspect of the data could have been used in this way. A high degree of ambiguity is introduced into the prognostic method by the fact that it is not known how a medieval reader would have spelt a name: Would they follow the text? Would they use a different spelling? Would they switch

7   See Burnett (1988) and Edge, who notes examples of the *Sphere* appearing elsewhere alongside information about historic duels (2015: 131–143).

8   For the traditional association of Alexander with the *Victorious and the Vanquished* see Burnett (1988: 146–150).

9   The letter values of Thurstane's name are 8, 6, 5, 13, 11, 8, 3, 15, 25. Dauid's are 14, 3, 5, 15, 14.

from English to Latin or French to get the desired outcome?[10] Equally, for all the importance attached to names, dates and locations in the notes, some of the events recorded do not furnish enough detail to work reliably with the onomantic method demonstrated. Several notes, like that for the Battle of Crécy (26 August 1346), need supplementing with information lacking in the compendium, which may or may not have been known by, or accessible to, the original owner. Moreover, to test the predictions offered by *The Sphere of Pythagoras* on the fate of a journey, historical conflict or individual, one would first need to calculate the numerical value of the weekday and lunar day the event occurred on. In some instances, enough information is provided to work this out retrospectively using the other formulae and astronomical tools provided in the manuscript, such as the Lunar Tables (fols 23^v–31^r), the notes on inauspicious days (fols 65^r–68^v), or *Storie Lune* (fols 84^r–97^r). In other instances, the information is absent.

Further speculation and testing of the possible relationship between the prognostic materials and the historical notes lies beyond the scope of this little edition, but it goes out into the world with the hope that a future study of historical notes in diagnostic and prognostic compendia like Wellcome MS 8004 will better illuminate the connections medieval readers saw between texts that prompted them to look to the past and texts that helped them to look to the future. Doubtless these brief notes have a much bigger story to tell about the role historical writing played in the medieval world view and how those commissioning volumes like this one utilized the texts within them.

2   Editorial Practice

Capitalization, word division and punctuation have been modernized. Common scribal abbreviations and suspensions have been silently expanded. The scribe occasionally adds a bar across -*ll*, which may or may not denote -*lle*; however, as there is little consistency in the use of a bar in the commonly occurring word *batell*, barred -*ll* has been treated as otiose. Initial *ff*– has been changed to *F*. Textual and explanatory notes have been provided in footnotes.

---

10   There is no reliable answer to this question, but the potential confusion thrown up by late medieval England's trilingual culture is addressed in a similar compendium including onomantic texts in Edinburgh, National Library of Scotland Advocates MS 23.7.11 A-H. This manuscript contains fragments of seven or eight medical texts, many of which are in Middle English, and in one fragment the author warns readers to pay attention to how names are spelt ('be ware of spellyng of lettres', fol. 40^r). He explains that the names used for divination 'moste be record in laten' and 'nought in englyche' (must be recorded in Latin and not in English, fol. 40^r).

3   Edition

The Historical Notes in Wellcome MS 8004

In þe 15 ȝere of þe warld wasse Caym borne. And in þe 30 ȝer wasse Abel   fol. 41ʳ
borne. And in þe 130 ȝer Caym slewe Abel. And in þe 930 ȝer died Adam.
And in þe 230 wase Seth borne. And in þe 948 ȝer wasse Ennoke translate.
And in þe 2656 wasse Noye floyd.[11] And þe ȝer of our lord 49 wasse our lady
5   assumpte and borne into heuynne.[12] And in þe ȝer of our lord 69 wasse Petyr
and Paul martyrd.[13] And in þe ȝer of our lord 1210 wasse Iues expulsed and
pute owt of Ingland.[14] And þe same ȝer wase entyrdytyd Ingland and Wals
and duryd 6 ȝer.[15] And in þe ȝer 1107 wasse Saynte Thomas of Cantyrbery
martyryd.[16] And in þe ȝer 1319 wasse Sant Thomas of Lancastyr martyrd.[17]
10   And in þe ȝer of our lord 1346 wasse þe batyll of Crecy, and þe kynge of
Fraunce wasse ouyrcomyne.[18] And þe same | ȝere wasse þe batell of Durham   fol. 41ᵛ
and þere wasse takyn þe kynge of Skottys.[19] And in þe ȝer of our lord 1356

---

1 The first sentence is rubricated. The initial letter is gold on a red and blue ground with white
decoration. Six daisy sprays spring from the initial. Each subsequent sentence has a small blue
initial.   5 MS *assumpte*] *assupte* (missing the abbreviation for *m*).

---

11   With the exception of the year assigned to Enoch's translation, the chronology provided down to the year of the deluge corresponds with the information provided in
Higden's *Polychronicon* and its English translations by John Trevisa and the anonymous author of British Library, Harley 2261 (*Polychronicon*, II, 220–221, 236–237). Genesis
5 is the ultimate source of some of the information given here, as is Josephus's *Antiquities of the Jews*, which gives the year of Seth's birth as 230 and calculates the year of the
flood as 2656 (I, ii–iii). I have been unable to find another source dating Enoch's translation to the year 948 after creation, but there must be one. *The Folger Brief History*
in Folger MS V.a.198 lists similar details but differs in the years assigned to Adam and
Noah's flood (Lipscomb [1996: 23]).

12   *Polychronicon*, IV, 388–389.

13   Cambridge University Library Ff.1.6, fol. 110ʳ, also places the martyrdom of Saints Peter
and Paul in 69 CE. The *Polychronicon* dates the event to the last year of Nero's reign (IV,
412–413).

14   Edward I expelled the Jews from England in 1290. Cf. *Folger Brief History* (24), where
the year is 1289.

15   Pope Innocent III placed an interdict on England and Wales between 23 March 1208
and 2 July 1214.

16   Thomas Becket, archbishop of Canterbury, was martyred in 1170. The scribe (or his
source) has reversed the final two digits of the year. *Folger Brief History* (24) and Cambridge University Library Ff.1.6 (fol. 110ᵛ) also provide incorrect years, 1171 and 1210
respectively.

17   Thomas of Lancaster (c. 1278–1322) was executed on 22 March 1322.

18   The Battle of Crécy (26 August 1346). *Folger Brief History* places it in 1348 (24).

19   David II (1324–1371), king of Scots, was captured at the Battle of Neville's Cross (17 October 1346). Cf *Polychronicon*, VIII, 342–343 and *Folger Brief History* (24).

wasse þe battell of Payter and þer wasse takyne þe kynge of Fraunce.[20] And
in þe ȝer of our lord 1357 wasse þe batyll of Spayne and þer wasse takyne þe
bastard.[21] And þe ȝer 1315 wasse grete hungur in Ingland.[22] And þe ȝere 1349
wasse þe first pestylaunce in Ingland.[23] And in þe ȝer 1333 wasse þe grete
tempeste in Ingland.[24] And in þe ȝer 1361 wasse þe secund pestelaunce in   5
Ingland. And in þe ȝere 1369 wasse þe þird pestelaunce.[25] And in þe ȝer 1381
rose þe comyns of Kynt agayne þe grete menne and slewe þe archbysschop
of Cantyrbery and þe prior of Clerkenwell and odyr moo.[26] And in þe ȝer of
our lord 1415 Kynge Henri þe 5 wanne Harflw and in þe same ȝere wasse þe
batell of Agyngcourte, wher many Fraunch menne wer takyne and slayne.[27]   10

Ther ar in Ingland 46 ml and c parich kyrkys; and townys 52 ml cc and 20;
knyghtys feys 40 ml cc 15, of þe qwylke relegyus menne haue 18 m 40; countys
35; byschoppeprikys 17; cyttes 30.[28]

---

6 MS *in þe ȝere*] *in ȝere.*   11 MS *townys*] *towrys.*

---

20   The Battle of Poitiers (19 September 1356), during which Edward III's son, Edward, the
      Black Prince, captured John II of France. *Folger Brief History* records the French king's
      capture under the year 1358 (24).

21   A reference to the Castilian Civil War (1351–1369), during which Peter I of Castile and
      Henry of Trastámara, his illegitimate brother, fought for the throne. The conflict refer-
      enced appears to be the Battle of Nájera (3 April 1367), but the information provided
      is incorrect.

22   A reference to The Great Famine of 1315–1317, which affected Northern Europe. The
      Folger Brief History (24) mentions famine under the year 1370.

23   The Black Death reached England in 1348–1349. Cf. *Folger Brief History* (24).

24   England experienced various storms, floods and droughts in the late 1320s and early
      1330s; see Stone 2014: 435–462. *Folger Brief History* (24) records the "grete wynde" on
      Saint Maurus's Day in 1362.

25   The second and third significant recurrences of the Black Death in England were in
      1361–1362 and 1369. Cf. *Folger Brief History* (24).

26   A reference to the Peasants' Revolt of 1381, during which Simon Sudbury, archbishop
      of Canterbury, and Sir Robert Hales, Prior of St John of Jerusalem in Clerkenwell and
      Treasurer of England, were executed at Tower Hill. *Folger Brief History* (24) mentions
      the revolt but does not give the casualties.

27   The Siege of Harfleur (17 August 1415 to 22 September 1415) and the Battle of Agincourt
      (25 October 1415). Both appear in *Folger Brief History* (24).

28   This information is repeated on fol. 50^r, in a section concerning measurements. Its ulti-
      mate source is *Polychronicon*, II, 88–90, which records 45,002 parish churches, 52,080
      towns, 60,015 knights' fees, of which 28,015 are religious. The information is included
      (with varying figures) in a Latin geography preceding *Folger Brief History* in Folger
      Shakespeare Library, v.a.198, and a Latin note in British Library Sloane 3285, fol. 85^r,
      another fifteenth-century medical miscellany (See Lipscomb [1996: 20, 23]; Scott [1904:
      179]; and Loen-Marshall [2005: 112]).

Her may menne her of mayny gret batells. Bott þe fyrste wasse done befor
þe conqueste 4 myle frome Beuyrley, þat wasse in þe ȝer of our lorde 1066,
betweyne Harald of Ingland and anodyr kynge Harald, þe kynge of Dan-
marke, and þer wasse a grete oste of Danys kyllyd and dystrued.[29] The batell
5 of Alertoun wasse done in þe ȝer of our lord xi hundyrth and xviij and þen
Dauid, kynge of Scottys, with þe helpe of þe | archbysschoppe of ȝorke, þat   fol. 42ʳ
tyme called Thurstane, wasse ourcomyne and scomfett.[30] The batell of Aln-
wyk wase þe ȝer of our lord ml c iijˣˣ and xiij in þe qwilke wasse takyne Kynge
William of Scottes þat gaffe for hysse raunsone Northumbirland, Westmor-
10 land, and Cumbirland, qwyke wer haldyne with Scottys and Peghtes fro þe
fyrste commynge of Danysse vnto þat tyme.[31]

   The batell of Lews in Southsex wasse in þe ȝer of our lord ml cc iijˣˣ and iij
þat wasse between Kynge Henri þe third and Symond Mountford, þat tyme
erle of Lecytur, and oder barons with hyme and in þat batell wasse tane þe
15 same kynge Henri and Edward hys eldyste sone and holdyne in presone.[32]
The batelle of Euesame wasse in þe ȝer of our lord ml cc iijˣˣ and v in þe
moneth of Auguste and þer wasse kyllyd þe sayd Symond with xij barons
qwik had tane þe kynge before.[33]

   The batyll of Fawkyrke in Scotland wasse done in þe ȝer of our lord
20 ml cc iijˣˣ and xviij, wher þe lederse of þe Scotys on William Waleys and
odyr lordys of Scotland lefte þer oste withoutyne captayne and þerfor wasse
all þe ost sone perichte.[34] The dyscumfetur of Dunbar in Scotland was þe
ȝer of our lord ml cc and x and þer wasse kyllyd x thowsand of Scottys
and þe towne ȝeldyne.[35] The dysconfitur of Styrlyne in Scottland wasse þe

---

1 This sentence is rubricated.

---

29   The Battle of Stamford Bridge (25 September 1066). Stamford Bridge is approximately
     27 miles from Beverley.
30   Thurstan, archbishop of York, defeated David I of Scotland at the Battle of Northaller-
     ton, also known as the Battle of the Standard (22 August 1138).
31   William I of Scotland was captured at the Battle of Alnwick (13 July 1174). To obtain his
     freedom, he signed the Treaty of Falaise (1174), acknowledging English hegemony over
     Scotland.
32   Henry III and his son, Edward, fought against Simon de Montfort, earl of Leicester, at
     The Battle of Lewes (14 May 1264). The battle was part of the civil conflict known as
     the Second Barons' War. The year given in the historical notes is incorrect.
33   Simon de Montfort died at the Battle of Evesham (4 August 1265). The twelve barons
     who perished at the same time were Henry, de Montfort's son; Peter de Montfort; Hugh
     Despenser; William de Mandeville; Ralph Basset; Walter de Crespigny; William York;
     Robert Tregor; Thomas Hostelea; John Beauchamp; Guy Balliol; and Roger de Rouleo.
34   The Battle of Falkirk occurred on 22 July 1298, not in 1278. The Scots army, led by Wil-
     liam Wallace, was defeated by Edward I.
35   The year of the Battle of Dunbar (27 April 1296) is incorrect.

nexste ȝer aftyr and þer wasse our Inglysch mene dyscomfytt and many

kyllyd throuȝe a trayne of þe | Scottes.[36] The batell of Banekburne in Scot-
teland wasse in þe ȝer of our lord ml iijᶜ and xvij and þer our menne war
kyllyd xx thowsand for þe Scottys had mad many pyttfals and grete holys in
þe erth befor qwer þe batell wasse done.[37] The dyscumfytur of Myton was þe   5
ȝer of our lord ml iijᶜ xix wher þe lederse of our menne wasse clerkys and þe
ost cytysyns and burges þerfor wer þai sone dyscomfytt.[38] The dyscomfitur
of Byland Banke was in þe ȝer of our lord nexste folowynge aftyr þat and
þer our ost wasse lefte withoutyne any cabdene[39] or lord and þerfor it wasse
sone ourecomynen.[40] The batyll of Gladmor wasse in þe ȝer of our lord ml   10
iijᶜ xxxij and þer wasse mad a hyll of Scottys xx fott on hyght.[41] The batyll of
Halydoun Hyll faste besyd Berwyke wasse þe nexte ȝer aftyr and þer wasse
kyllyd of Scottys x thowsand and þe towne of Barwylk ȝeldyd to our kynge.[42]

The batell of Scluse in Flandyrs betweyne our mene and Fraunche menne
was þe ȝer of our lord ml iijᶜ xlvj in þe kalend of Septembre þer þe Fraunsch   15
men wer kyllyd and þe schyppys tane.[43] The batell of Crecy wasse in þe ȝer of
our lord ml iijᶜ xlvj in þe moneth of Septembre and þer þe kynge of Fraunch
wasse putt to flyght and þe kynge of Beme kyllyd and many odyr lordys with
hyme.[44] The batell of Doram was þe same ȝer and þer was tayne Kynge Dauid

---

8 MS *folowynge*] *foloynge*.   11 MS *hyght*] *hyrght*.

---

36   The Battle of Stirling Bridge (11 September 1297).

37   The English suffered heavy casualties at the Battle of Bannockburn (24 June 1314), due
      in part to the pits and ditches the Scots had prepared.

38   *The Brut* (I, 211), *The Lanercost Chronicle* (239) and Barbour's *The Bruce* (II, 426–428),
      also mention the high number of clerics and citizens slain at the Battle of Myton
      (20 September 1319). The English were led by William Melton, archbishop of York, John
      Hotham, bishop of Ely, and Nicholas Fleming, mayor of York.

39   This variation of captain is not recorded in the *Middle English Dictionary* (s.v. *capitain*,
      n.), but it appears as an irregular Scots variation of *captane* (n.) (see *A Dictionary of
      Older Scottish Tongue* via Skretowicz and Rennie 2004, s.v. *cabdan*, n.).

40   A reference to the Battle of Old Byland (14 October 1322), during which the leader of the
      English force, John of Brittany, earl of Richmond, was captured. Compare with *Poly-
      chronicon* (VIII, 317) and *The Brut* (I, 226) but neither recounts the encounter in the
      same way as this.

41   Many chronicles, including *The Brut* (I, 278–279), refer to the heap of Scottish dead at
      the Battle of Dupplin Moor (11 August 1332), also called 'Gladmore' or 'Gaskemore'.

42   The Battle of Halidon Hill (19 July 1333).

43   The naval battle at Sluys (24 June 1340) is incorrectly dated. The error may derive
      from eye-skip (authorial or scribal), as the incorrect month and year—September and
      1346—occur in the next sentence recording the Battle of Crécy. They were presumably
      copied by mistake.

44   As with the previous sentence, an error has crept into the dating of the Battle of Crécy

of Scottes and many erlys and barons wyth hyme and | many fled away and   fol. 43ʳ
it was done in þe kalend of Nouembre.⁴⁵ And in þe ȝer of our lord ml iiijᶜ xlvij
Kynge Edward wane þe towne of Calyse, bott fyrste he lad a sege þerto þat
lastyd a ȝer and mor.⁴⁶ The batell of Payters in Gyane was þe ȝer of our lord
5   ml ccc xlvj and þer by Edward þe oldyste sone of Kynge Edward wasse tayne
Ion þat callyd hymeselfe kynge of Fraunce and with hyme many odyr lordys
takyne and slane.⁴⁷ The batell of Spayne wase þe ȝer of our lord ml ccc iijˣˣ
xxxj and þer þe bastard of Spayne wasse scomfett and fled away.⁴⁸

And in þe ȝer of our lord ml ccc lxxxj þe commons of Kente and Esex rose
10 agayn some lordys for þe customs and bondage þat wasse begune emonge
þe sayme comons, and þen onn Iake Straw wasse þe captane, and qwene þai
come to Londone onn Symon archbyschoppe of Cantyrbery and a knyȝte of
þe Rodes and þe prior of Clerkynwell war takyne and onn þe Tour Hyll þe
same comons smott of þer hedys, and a fair place callyd Sauoy þai brynte it
15 all to colls. Bott att þe laste, with helpe of Lundon, þat same Iak Strawe wasse
slayne and þen hys company fled away, bott many wer takyne and putt to
ded.⁴⁹

The dyscomfytur of Homyldon Hyll wasse in þe ȝer of our lord ml iiijᶜ ij
and it was done on Holy Rod day in herueste and þer þe Scottys wasse oft
20 scomfett and many takyne: | þat is to say Erle Douglasse, þe erle of Fyffe, and   fol. 43ᵛ
many odyr lordys of Scottland with hyme.⁵⁰ The batell of Schrowsberye was
in þe ȝer of our lord ml iiijᶜ ij onn Mary Maudleyne day euynen and þer Syr

9 MS *lord*] lod. ‖ MS *ml ccc lxxxj*] ccc inserted above the line with a caret.   10 MS *agayn*]
inserted above the line.   14 MS *fair*] *far*.   15 MS *þat*] *þe þat*.   22 MS *of*] inserted above
the line.

(26 August 1346). The phrase 'kalend of Septembre', which appears (incorrectly) in the
previous sentence, offers a more accurate description of the date of the battle. It is
unclear whether the mistake is authorial, scribal, or carried over from a source. The
'kynge of Beme' is John the Blind (1296–1346), king of Bohemia.

45   Another reference to the Battle of Neville's Cross (17 October 1346).
46   Edward III's siege of Calais lasted from September 1346 to August 1347.
47   Despite getting the year of the Battle of Poitiers right earlier (19 September 1356), it is
      incorrectly given as 1346 here.
48   Another incorrectly dated reference to the Battle of Nájera (3 April 1367).
49   In addition to repeating the information given earlier, this second, longer reference to
      the Peasant's Revolt of 1381, includes the burning of Savoy Palace. Sir Robert Hales, one
      of the men executed by the rebels, is referred to as two separate people: the 'knyȝte of
      þe Rodes' and the Prior of Clerkenwell.
50   The Battle of Homildon Hill was fought on 14 September 1402 (the Feast of the Cross,
      or Holy Rood Day). Notable captives included Archibald, earl of Douglas and Murdoch
      Stewart, earl of Fife.

Henri Percy, þe eldyste sone of þe erle of Northumbirland, was kyllyd and
many a nobyll manne with hyme. And þen Syr Thomas Percy, þat tyme erle
of Worseter, aftyr þe battell was done, was tayne and sone aftyr putt to ded.[51]
The batell of Agyngcourte in Fraunce was þe ȝer of our lord ml iiijᶜ xxvij
and þer our kynge, with a fewe of our Inglysche menne, kyllyd a grete oste   5
of Fraunsche men and þat same tyme tuke þe duke of Orlyaunce, þe duk of
Burgone, þe erle of Ewe, þe erle of Endew, and þe steward of Fraunce callyd
Syr Bursegawd.[52] The batell of Vernell on Perch was þe ȝer of our lord m iiijᶜ
xx and þer was a grete oste of Franschmen and iiij ml Scottys slayne, þat is
to say þe erle Dowglasse, þe erle of Marre, and þe erle of Bughan wasse þer   10
ded, and many a prowd Scott with þem, on our lady euynen assumpcioun as
it fell þat ȝer, þerfore say we 'deo gracias'.[53]

---

6 MS *tyme*] inserted above the line.   8 MS *was*] inserted above the line. ‖ MS *m*] inserted
above the line.

---

51   The Battle of Shrewsbury took place on 21 July 1403, the eve of the Feast of Mary Mag-
      dalene. Sir Henry 'Hotspur' Percy, son of Henry Percy, earl of Northumberland, was
      killed, and Hotspur's uncle, Thomas Percy, earl of Worcester was executed two days
      later.

52   The Battle of Agincourt took place on 25 October 1415 (not 1427). The captives men-
      tioned are Charles (1394–1465), third duke of Orleans; Charles of Artois (1394–1472),
      count of Eu; Louis of Bourbon (1376–1446), count of Vendôme ('Endew'); and John II
      le Maingre (1366–1421), Marshal of France (known as Boucicaut). The inclusion of the
      'duk of Burgone' (i.e. duke of Burgundy) is an error: John the Fearless, duke of Bur-
      gundy, was not at the battle. It may be a mistake for John (1318–1434), duke of Bourbon,
      who appears between Charles of Orléans and Charles of Artois in other lists of the
      French casualties and captives (see, for example, the first version of John Hardyng's
      Chronicle in British Library Lansdowne 204, fol. 211ʳ, and *The Brut* extant in British
      Library Egerton MS 650, fol. 107ᵛ). As the list deals with captives, it is unlikely to be a
      mistake for one of the sons of Philip, second duke of Burgundy, who died at the battle:
      Anthony (1384–1415), duke of Brabant, Lothier and Limburg, and Philip II (1389–1415),
      count of Nevers.

53   The Battle of Verneuil (17 August 1424) was a decisive English victory over the French
      and Scots, whose forces were decimated. The dating of the battle to the eve of the
      Feast of the Assumption of Mary incorrectly places it on 14 August, the feast day
      being on 15 August. The year is also incorrect. Significant casualties included Archibald
      (†1424), earl of Douglas; and John Stewart (†1424), earl of Buchan. The earl of Mar
      did not die at Verneuil, but this is an error that occurs in other chronicles: see, for
      example, *The Brut*, II, 441, 498; and *An English Chronicle* (58). Of particular interest
      is the Latin Chronicle in London, College of Arms, Arundel 5, which includes the same
      names and the phrase 'Deo Gratias' (see Gairdner [1880: 164–165] and Kingsford [1913:
      321]).

Bibliography

Primary Sources—Manuscripts
Cambridge
Cambridge University Library
Ff.1.6

Edinburgh
National Library of Scotland
Advocates 23.7.11 A–H

London
College of Arms
Arundel 5
British Library
Egerton 650
Lansdowne 204
Sloane 3285
Wellcome Library
8004

Washington
Folger Shakespeare Library
V.a.198

Primary Sources—Editions
An English Chronicle 1377–1461. Ed. William Marx. Medieval Chronicles 3. Woodbridge:
   The Boydell Press, 2003.
'A Tretis Compiled out of Diverse Cronicles (1440): a Study and Edition of the Short
   English Prose Chronicle Extant in London, British Library, MS Additional 34,764'.
   Ed. Sarah L. Peverley. *The Medieval Chronicle* 12 (2019): 238–277.
[Barbour, John] *The Bruce*. Ed. Walter W. Skeat. EETS ES 21. London: 1870–1877.
The Brut of The Chronicles of England. 2 vols. Ed. Friederick W.D. Brie. EETS OS 131, 176.
   London, 1906, 1908.
Chronicon de Lanercost MCCI–MCCCXLVI. Ed. Joseph Stevenson. Edinburgh, 1839.
Flavius Josephus: Translation and Commentary, Volume 3, Judean Antiquities 1–4. Ed.
   Steve Mason and Louis H. Feldman. Leiden: Brill, 1999.
[*Folger Brief History*] 'A Latin Geography and a Middle English Epitome of World and
   English History'. Ed. Lan Lipscomb. *Manuscripta* 40 (1996): 19–28.
[Hardyng, John] *John Hardyng Chronicle: Edited from British Library Lansdowne 204*.

Ed. James Simpson, and Sarah L. Peverley. Kalamazoo, MI: Medieval Institute Publications, 2015.

[Higden, Ranulph] *Polychronicon Ranulphi Higden, Monachi Cestrensis*. 9 Vols. Ed. C. Babington and J.R. Lumby. Rolls Series 41. London, 1879–1886.

Three Fifteenth-Century Chronicles. Ed. James Gairdner. Camden Society, NS 28. Westminster, 1880.

Secondary Sources

Burnett, Charles S. (1988). 'The Eadwine Psalter and the Western Tradition of the Onomancy in Pseudo-Aristotle's Secret of Secrets.' *Archives d'histoire doctrinale et littéraire du moyen âge* 55: 143–167.

Skretowicz, Victor and Susan Rennie. *Dictionary of the Scots Language*. 2004 https://www.dsl.ac.uk/entry/dost/cabdan (accessed June 2021).

Edge, Joanne T. (2015). 'Nomen Omen: "The Sphere of Life and Death" in England, c. 1300–c. 1500.' Unpublished PhD thesis: Royal Holloway, University of London.

Kennedy, Edward Donald (1989). *Chronicles and Other Historical Writing*. Vol. 8 of *A Manual of The Writings in Middle English, 1050–1500*. Gen. ed. Albert E. Hartung. New Haven: Connecticut Academy of Arts and Sciences.

Kingsford, Charles L. (1913). *English Historical Literature in the Fifteenth Century*. Oxford.

Loen-Marshall, Maria Helena (2005). 'An Edition of the English Texts in British Library MS Sloane 3285: Practical Medicine, Sussex Dialect and the London Associations of a Fifteenth-Century Book'. Unpublished PhD. University of Glasgow.

Matheson. Lister M. (1998). *The Prose Brut: The Development of a Middle English Chronicle*. Tempe, AZ: Medieval and Renaissance Texts and Studies.

McIntosh, Angus, M.L. Samuels, Michael Benskin, Margaret Laing and Keith Williamson (2013). *An Electronic Version of A Linguistic Atlas of Late Mediaeval English*. http://www.lel.ed.ac.uk/ihd/elalme/elalme.html (accessed June 2021).

Stone, David (2014). 'The Impact of drought in Early Fourteenth-Century England.' *Economic History Review* 67:2: 435–462.

Voigts, Linda Ehrsam and Patricia Deery Kurtz (2019). *Scientific and Medical Writings in Old and Middle English: An Electronic Reference*. Ann Arbor: 2000, CD. Revised Online version at https://cctr1.umkc.edu/cgi-bin/search (accessed June 2021).

21

Expanding the Family: Royal Genealogical Rolls and the Prose *Brut* Chronicle

Jaclyn Rajsic

Abstract

This essay takes inspiration from Erik Kooper's study of a Latin Prose *Brut* chronicle found in Longleat House MS 55 and an Anglo-Norman genealogical roll from Brutus to Edward I (The Hague, Koninklijke Bibliotheek, 75 A 2/2). In an essay published on both sources, Erik proposed that we approach the Prose *Brut* chronicle as a genre rather than a distinctive text. This approach invites consideration of a group of continental French histories (fifteenth-century), disseminated in rolls and codices, which derive their abbreviated accounts of British, early English and post-Norman Conquest kings from the Anglo-Norman Prose *Brut* chronicle. This essay explores three insular versions of that history, all rolls (two are written in French and one in English), arguing that they fall under the umbrella of the Prose *Brut* genre. With a focus on the insular French rolls, it demonstrates some of the ways in which the authors adapt their continental sources to reflect English geographical, historiographical and literary interests, for example by adding references to insular legendary heroes and material drawn from chronicles and romances. Ultimately, the essay encourages further study of the Prose *Brut* chronicle's continental relatives, which invite us to test the limits of the Prose *Brut* genre.

From 2013 to 2015, I had the great pleasure and honour of working with Erik Kooper (together with our colleague Dominique Hoche) to co-edit a collection of essays in memory of Lister M. Matheson. I have fond memories of our collaboration; Erik made the project even more of a joy than it already was. In his essay for the collection (a study of an Anglo-Norman genealogical roll from Brutus to Edward I and a Latin Prose *Brut* chronicle), Erik asked what defines a Prose *Brut* chronicle.[1] He concluded that the Prose *Brut* is 'a genre, not a specific text', 'whose ultimate textual basis should be, or can be traced

---

1 I capitalize 'Prose *Brut*' throughout to distinguish it from 'prose *Brut*', which I use to mean any *Brut* chronicle written in prose.

to, the Oldest Version of the Anglo-Norman Prose *Brut*.[2] By this definition, two manuscripts—both royal genealogical rolls—would qualify as Prose *Brut* chronicles, albeit highly abbreviated ones: London, British Library, Add. 27342 (French) and Add. 29503 (English). Both manuscripts date to the fifteenth century, probably around the middle of that century. They, and another roll closely related to Add. 27342—Oxford, Bodleian Library, Bodley Rolls 2—are the subject of this essay.[3]

The short chronicles in Add. 27342 and Add. 29503 represent insular versions of a continental French history of England's rulers which I have called *Les Croniques d'Engleterre Abrégiées* (hereafter LCEA).[4] This short history flourished in fifteenth-century France, where it was disseminated (in rolls and codices) with a history of French rulers known as *A tous nobles* (hereafter ATN); together, ATN and LCEA were often situated alongside accounts of popes and emperors as abbreviated universal chronicles. The key point for this study is that LCEA is based on a copy of the Anglo-Norman Prose *Brut* chronicle, probably the Long Version.[5] In Add. 29503, LCEA was translated from French into English; in Add. 27342 it was adapted for an insular audience. Remarkably in comparison to the other known manuscripts (which are mainly continental), their histories of England's rulers stand alone: they are not paired with ATN or embedded within a larger history, and so their narratives are the only ones for readers to follow. Were their relationship to LCEA unknown, then we might have called them short Prose *Brut* chronicles. The question is can we still?

In an earlier essay (in which I first drew attention to the Additional rolls), I stressed the Anglo-Norman Prose *Brut*'s *influence* on LCEA: the Prose *Brut* 'shaped a whole group of short chronicles composed and copied on the Continent, and those abbreviated histories in turn contributed to the reception of the Prose *Brut*'s history in England', in both French (e.g. Add. 27342, Bodley Rolls 2) and English (Add. 29503).[6] Implicit in this remark was the view that LCEA should be considered part of the Prose *Brut* genre, or 'family' as I also like to

---

2   Kooper (2016: 89, 93).

3   On this relationship, and dates, see Rajsic (2016: 134, 145–147).

4   For the purposes of clarity, I refer to insular versions because the added 'English' material points to an intended insular audience. However, the manuscripts might have been produced in English-occupied areas of north-western France and then brought to England.

5   On LCEA see Rajsic (2016). In her study of Version H of ATN (i.e. the version that survives in the most manuscripts), Davis (2014: 20, 35–38) also found the French Prose *Brut* to be the source of the 'English' history, but she does not mention any particular version of the chronicle. For ATN, see most recently Norbye (2020).

6   Rajsic (2016: 149).

think about it. I was delighted, therefore, to see Julia Marvin do just that in her superb study of the Anglo-Norman Prose *Brut*. Marvin tallies 'fifty-two to fifty-seven' manuscripts, 'depending on how one considers short extracts, composite manuscripts, and manuscripts that draw only on *Brut* prologues or continuations'. She adds that 'this count does not include the Continental texts derived from the ANPB', from which the insular Add. 27342 and Add. 29503 are themselves derived.[7] If these continental texts were to be counted, then the top end of Marvin's range would nearly double.

We might look to Matheson's category of 'Peculiar Texts and Versions' of the Middle English Prose *Brut*. This category includes, among other things, 'reworked texts and versions of all or part of a *Brut* text, sometimes abbreviated or expanded by interpolations from other works', and 'very brief works that have used the *Brut* as a primary source'.[8] Could we have a similar category— one that invites shorter and 'reworked' texts—for the Anglo-Norman Prose *Brut*? I am hesitant to over-characterize, and as categories become more complex it becomes increasingly difficult to draw their defining lines, which must always be flexible. But it seems important both to recognize *LCEA*'s distinctiveness, which allows for focused study of its different versions and its many manuscripts, *and* to acknowledge its close relationship to the Anglo-Norman Prose *Brut*. In part, to do so spotlights continental receptions of the Prose *Brut*'s history. One might think of continental and insular versions of *LCEA* as direct descendants of the Oldest Version, not as closely related to it as the Long Version but still valued members of the family. Here I want to begin to better understand the insular family members.

I focus on Add. 27342 and Bodley Rolls 2, but I keep my eye on Add. 29503. In Bodley Rolls 2, *LCEA* sits in parallel with *ATN*, which receives a distinctly English spin. All three rolls descend from the shorter of two branches of *LECA* manuscripts, in which England's history begins with British king Lud rather than Aeneas and Brutus. (Add. 29503 ends with a roundel for King Henry IV; the other two manuscripts end with Henry VI.) Bodley Rolls 2 and Add. 27342 fill in some of the historiographical gap by supplying short accounts of Albina's and Brutus's arrivals on Albion; they then jump from Brutus to Lud. Either Add. 27342 was copied from Bodley or, more likely (I think), both rolls share a common source.[9] The scribes responsible for Add. 27342 and Bodley Rolls 2 present their 'English' histories in different ways, but both rolls share distinct-

---

7   Marvin (2017: 7–8 n. 20).
8   Matheson (1997: 256).
9   *LCEA* is more extensive in Bodley than in Add. 27342, owing partly to the Additional roll's layout. All text appears *within* (not beside) the roundels for England's rulers, their children and

ive features that make them stand out from the *LCEA* crowd. In what follows, I consider examples from their British and early English histories.

First, Add. 27342 and Bodley Rolls 2 make space for insular romance heroes who do not appear in the Prose *Brut* chronicle or in continental versions of *LCEA*. As I note briefly elsewhere, both summarize Guy of Warwick's defeat of Coldbrond in their account of King Athelstan. This was common in England's chronicles. The match takes place at ('dauant') Winchester.[10] At this point, the Additional roll takes the opportunity to connect another legendary figure—'Hauelok le roy de Danemerche'—with Winchester.[11] It is tempting to entertain the possibility that our author was familiar with the English romance *Havelok the Dane*, which places Havelok firmly in a period of pre-Norman Conquest English dominion, whereas in the Prose *Brut* and its source (Geffrei Gaimar's *Estoire des Engleis*) Haveloc is a sixth-century, regional ruler during the time of the British king Constantine, successor of King Arthur. In *Havelok*, Goldeboru's father, King Athelwold, rules from Winchester, the royal seat of West Saxon kings.[12] But both references—to Guy and Havelok—could come from chronicles instead. *Bruts* could follow the *Havelok* poet's lead by tying the Danish hero to early England, though never explicitly to Winchester.[13] In *Le Petit Bruit* (1309), Rauf de Boun mentions the 'noble chevaller' Guy of Warwick in relation to Thoraud, the youngest surviving son of King Havelok. Guy's and Havelok's names sit near to each another in the text, but Guy's fight with Coldbrond ('a Wincestre') does not appear until Athelstan's reign.[14] Add. 27342 might be unique in tying Guy and Havelok together via Winchester, however briefly and vaguely.

---

other figures (e.g. Norman dukes from Rollo to William the Conqueror). The results are large roundels and a large amount of empty space throughout the roll. In this space, notes naming cities, scenes and heraldic shields reveal that an impressive programme of illustrations was planned but never completed.

10   Rajsic (2016: 146).

11   Add. 27342: 'Guy de Wast*erick* desconfit Collobront le geant dauant Wy[n]cestre, *que* Hauelok le roy de Danemerche y auoit amené'. Both insular and continental versions of *LCEA* have the Anglo-Norman Prose *Brut*'s Curan (with Athelbright, Argentille, Edelfi and Orwenne), though he is not named as Havelok.

　　　In all quotations from manuscripts, modern capitalization and punctuation are used, i/j are normalized, and é is used to designate the past participle. All translations are mine unless otherwise indicated.

12   *Havelok*, line 158.

13   For Guy, see, e.g., Spence (2013: 85–86) and Wiggins (2007). For *Havelok*, see *Lay of* Haveloc, 149–209, which brings together 'shorter accounts of the Haveloc legend' (Burgess and Brook [2015: 1]).

14   *Petit Bruit*, 15, 17. Spence (2013: 90 and n. 73) discusses the episodes. With them, Rauf ties

More excitingly, Bevis of Hampton makes an appearance in Add. 27342 too (but not in Bodley). The reference again revolves around a specific location, here Bevis's founding of Arundel Castle. According to the Middle English romance, Bevis names the castle in honour of his horse, Arundel, following Arundel's victory in a horserace (Bevis is racing against two knights who are two miles ahead):

'Arondel,' queth Beves tho,
'For me love go bet, go,
And I schel do faire and wel
For thee love reren a castel!'
Whan Arondel herde what he spak,
Before the twei knightes he rak,
That he com rather to the tresore,
Than hii be half and more.
Beves of his palfrai alighte
And tok the tresore anon righte:
With that and with mor catel
He made the castel of Arondel.[15]

Add. 27342 fixes this foundation (regrettably without the horserace) to the reign of King Edgar the Peaceful, nephew of Athelstan: '[...] en son temps Beuez, conte de Suthaumpton, fist fere le chastel d'Arondel, le quel auoit espousé Dame Josiane la fille du Roy d'Ermonie, la quelle deuint Christienne pour l'amour de lui. Et regna cestui roy xvij ans, et fut coronné a Kyngeston' ('In Edgar's time Bevis, earl of Southampton, built the castle of Arundel. Bevis married Lady Josiane, daughter of the king of Armenia, who became Christian out of love for him. And this king ruled for seventeen years and was crowned at Kingston').[16] Add. 27342 is not alone in aligning the romance's fictional King Edgar with the historical ruler,[17] but to my knowledge its mentions of both Arundel Castle and

---

Guy's defeat of Coldbrond to a long-held alliance between the peoples of Norway and Denmark against any challengers. The alliance begins in Thoraud's time; it is ended by Guy's victory against the giant.

15 *Bevis*, lines 3531–3542. The episode also occurs in the Anglo-Norman *Boeve de Haumtone*.
16 I would tentatively suggest that the author had the English romance in mind based on the spelling of 'Bevez', as opposed to the Anglo-Norman 'Boeve'.
17 See, for example, the account in the Anglo-Norman *Brut Abregé*, which stresses Bevis's exile by Edward: *Metrical Chronicle*, 103 lines 429–434; discussed by Spence (2013: 86–87).

the conversion of the Muslim princess Josiane are exceptional.[18] The details suggest a special interest in romance material, and not necessarily in the episodes we might expect.

Bodley Rolls 2 uniquely features a different 'legendary' castle, in its account of Uther Pendragon. In this roll, Uther 'fist faire en pais de North ung chastel et le nomma le Chastel Uther' ('built a castle in a county in the North and called it Uther's Castle').[19] This would seem to refer to the now-ruined Pendragon Castle in Mallerstang, Cumbria. The castle was built in the twelfth century, probably by Sir Hugh de Morville (d. 1173/4), lord of Westmorland and one of the four knights involved in the murder of Thomas Becket. John Hardyng provides a fuller description in his chronicle, linking the castle to the Clifford family (the Cliffords 'had close familial ties with the Percies, whom Hardyng once served'):[20]

> Afore his dethe a castelle yit he made
> Upon the marche of Scotlond stronge and fayre
> Pendragoun hight in whiche he dwelte and bade
> In that contré whan that he wolde repayre.
> Of whiche place now the Clifford is his hayre
> And lorde in fe of alle the shyre aboute
> And shiriff als of Westmerlonde thurghoute.[21]

The two castles might point to the individual interests of the rolls' patrons (or the patrons of their shared source), but since neither genealogical tree diagram includes the Fitzalans, earls of Arundel, or the Cliffords or Percies it is difficult to be sure. What *is* clear is that these examples (and there are others)[22] begin to demonstrate that the author laying behind Add. 27342 and Bodley Rolls 2, and apparently the scribes of the rolls themselves, added to their continental French source to reflect English geographical, historiographical and literary interests.

---

18   Other *Bruts* that incorporate Bevis include *Castleford's Chronicle*, ii, lines 28690–700, which places Bevis during the reign of 'Kyng Adelbert' (i.e. the Kentish king Æthelberht) and makes him 'Westesex kynges son'.

19   Bodley Rolls 2.

20   *Hardyng*, n. to lines 2220–2226.

21   *Hardyng*, lines 2220–2226. Uther 'lete castels sone arere' in the Auchinleck version of the *Short English Metrical Chronicle*, though none are named: *Metrical Chronicle*, 67 line 991.

22   For example, Bodley Rolls 2 notes that Arthur's Round Table is held in the Great Hall at Winchester, while Additional has Albina and her sisters land at Totnes.

Their additions extended to their tree diagrams, which expand the Lancastrian genealogy in the rolls' contemporary sections. In their British sections, moreover, again unlike continental versions of *LCEA* (and Add. 29503), Add. 27342 and Bodley Rolls 2 show (from Uther Pendragon) the issue of King Arthur's sister (unnamed) by King Lot of Orkney (I quote from Add. 27342): 'Ceste fille fut femme au Loth de Orkanye'. Four roundels for the Orkney children name 'Gourmont | Mordred le traitre',[23] 'Gauuayn le Courtois' (Gawain), 'Agraueins' (Agravaine) and 'Generet' (Gareth).[24] The genealogy here reveals another romance influence, since early French romances were the first to name Lot's five sons by Arthur's sister Morgause, who replaces Anna (Gaheris is missing from our rolls). I have not come across comparable roundels in England's royal genealogical rolls. A few have a roundel for Mordred (as do many continental *LCEA* manuscripts), but, to my knowledge, not for his romance-derived brothers.[25] In many ways, therefore, Add. 27342 and Bodley Rolls 2 are exceptional among royal genealogical rolls composed in both England and France.

Not all their adaptations to *LCEA* point in an insular direction, however. One example jumps out to me that sheds light on the rolls' relationship to *ATN* manuscripts. It appears in their accounts of British king Constantine. Add. 29503 provides a typical example of *LCEA*'s account:

> [T]his Constantyne was kyng of Bretayne and aftur Emperowre of Rome, and went to dwell there and led hys moder wyth hym, wich fonde the Very Crosse in the Holy Londe. And whane he went to Rome he betoke the londe of Bretayne to the erle of Cornewayle that hyght Octouyen, wich made hym[self] kyng whan he sawe hys tyme and gouernyd the londe full nobilly as longe as he levyd. And [Octavian] ordeynyd that hys nevewe schulde be kyng, Conain Meriadok. But the Emperowre of Rome sent hys nevewe into Bretayne that hyght Maximeen.[26]

Strikingly in contrast, Add. 27342 and Bodley Rolls 2 relate Constantine's naming of Constantinople, division of the Roman Empire and death in Nicomedia (I quote from the Additional roll):

---

23 A horizontal line splits the roundel in two.

24 The mysterious Gourmont does not appear in Bodley Rolls 2, where the positions of Mordred's and Gawain's roundels are reversed. *LCEA* manuscripts usually label Mordred a traitor ('þe traytour' in Add. 29503).

25 For example, London, British Library, Cotton Roll xv 3, a roll with a short, Latin prose *Brut* chronicle and genealogical diagram, has a roundel for 'Rex Mordredus, nepos Artur' between the roundels for Arthur and Constantin.

26 Compare *Oldest*, 118–120.

[*Text in Constantine's roundel:*] Constantin le Gra[n]t fut roy de Bretaigne apres son pere l'an iij^C et viij. Et puis fut empereur l'an iij^C et onze, et bailla la terre de Bretaigne pour garder a Ottoman comte de Cornouaille, qui apres se fist roy. Cestui empereur fist moult d'onneur au pape Saint Siluestre, et nomma la cite de Bysance Constantinopole, et y ordonna le Sieige de l'Empereur. Et ausi fut diuisé premierment l'Empire en deux empires, cestass*auer* l'Empire de Rome et l'Empire de Constantinopole. Et fut victorian contre ses ennemis et morut en la cite de Nychomede, et eut trois filz, cestass*sauer* Constance, Constantin et Constant. Et regna xxx ans, x mois et xj jours.

[*Text in the roundels for Constantine's sons:*] Constance impera a Rome; Constantin a Constantinopole; Constant fut prince de Antyoche.

('Constantine the Great was king of Britain after his father in the year 308. And then he became emperor in the year 311 and entrusted the land of Britain to the care of Octavian, earl of Cornwall, who afterwards made himself king. This emperor did much honour to pope Saint Sylvester, renamed the city of Byzantium Constantinople, and there established the Emperor's Seat. He also first divided the [Roman] Empire into two empires, that is the Empire of Rome and the Empire of Constantinople. And he was victorious against his enemies, and died in the city of Nicomedia, and had three sons, called Constance, Constantine and Constant. Constantine ruled for thirty years, ten months and eleven days.')

('Constance ruled in Rome, Constantine in Constantinople, and Constant was prince of Antioch.')

There are traces of Latin in our insular French rolls, which would seem to suggest a Latin source. In Add. 27342, Constantine has 'victorian' (an error for 'victoriam') instead of 'victoire'; and each son (in his roundel in the Additional roll, in the Constantine paragraph in Bodley) 'impera' not 'regna' in Rome or Constantinople.[27] Although the brevity of the account could make its source difficult to pin down—universal chronicles such as the *Polychronicon* (c. 1327) are logical places to start—it turns out that the source *can* be identified. It is none other than a universal chronicle version of *LCEA*:

Constantin le grant premier de ce nom commenca **lan iiic et x** et **impera xxx ans x mois xi iours** et vint a **sevestre** pour estre nettoie de mesellerie

---

27   Bodley Rolls 2 does not have 'victoriam'. Constant, prince of Antioch (i.e. the historical Constantius Gallus), appears in Additional only.

et fut baptisie et guery. Et apres donna au pape dignitez et richesses. Cestui constantin mua le nom dune cite de grece qui ot nom visante et lappella **constantinoble** et la peuplia moult **et y ordonna le siege de lempire de romme** [et des lors en advent fut tenu la. **Et fut lempire de rome**] **du tout devise en deux parties dempires. Ce fut adire** deux sie-iges **dempereurs lempereur de romme et de constantinoble.**[28]

The paragraphs are not an exact match, but there is enough evidence here (including traces of Latin) to show that our insular author combined *LCEA*'s usual account of the British Constantine with a short universal chronicle's paragraph about Emperor Constantine the Great.

This finding is confirmed by some of Bodley's and Add. 27342's roundels, tellingly by a feature found in only a handful of *ATN* manuscripts. In their *LCEA* sections, these manuscripts depict, during the time of British king Conan Meriadok, a circular 'map' of Brittany naming its nine regions.[29] Bodley Rolls 2, Add. 27342 and Add. 29503 all have the Brittany map (but they arrange the names differently). In all likelihood, our three insular rolls descend from a short universal chronicle with versions C, G or Y of *ATN* (a total of four surviving manuscripts).[30] A Version Y roll—Manchester, John Rylands Library, Fr. 54—crossed the Channel from France to England and was reworked by English scribes 'some time between 1429 and 1448'.[31] For example, the scribes added illustrations and extended the English tree diagram in various places. Nine small city images even appear within the roll's Brittany diagram, but they are part of the original, continental history. Such images also appear in the other Version Y manuscript, another roll (New Haven, Yale University Beinecke Library, Marston 180), and in the only known copy of *ATN* Version C (London, British library, Cotton Roll XIII 33). Our insular rolls leave spaces for nine cit-

---

28　*Chronique Anonyme Universelle*, 262, 264. This quotation comes from a long universal chronicle roll with Version H of *ATN*, but accounts in short universal chronicle versions are comparable.

29　All are short universal chronicle versions of *ATN* (C, G and Y). Short universal chronicles without this diagram are Versions F (one manuscript, a roll), L (three manuscripts) and 2 (one manuscript, a codex) of *ATN*. A digitised Version L roll—New York, Columbia University Library, Plimpton MS 286—is available via the Digital Scriptorum. The Version 2 codex—Paris, Bibliothèque Nationale de France, MS fr. 23019, fols. 13r–34v—is available online via Gallica. This manuscript has a different diagrammatic history of England's kings in place of *LCEA* (on fols. 14r–33r): see Rajsic (2016: 1333 n. 32).

30　For the most up-to-date list of *ATN* versions and their manuscripts, see Norbye (2020: 254–259).

31　Norbye (2007: 130).

ies, but the drawings were never executed. Perhaps the illustrations were absent from their authors' exemplars. In any case, a short universal chronicle version of *ATN* with the Brittany map was certainly available in England. Whether JR Fr. 54 or a different manuscript was the source for the one from which Bodley Rolls 2, Add. 27342 or the English-language Add. 29503 derive requires further study.[32] But the above demonstrates that our insular French author had access to a short universal chronicle version of *ATN* and drew on its wider (i.e. non-insular) material, but extracted the 'national' histories from their larger context. Add. 27342 went furthest in this regard by omitting *ATN*; the author of Add. 29503 had a complementary project. And all the while, Add. 27342, Bodley Rolls 2 and their source infused *LCEA* with material about English history and geography, derived from a range of chronicles and (directly or indirectly) from romances. As we see with history writing throughout the Middle Ages, the abbreviation process is also one of compilation, adaptation and invention.

All things considered, Add. 27342 and Bodley Rolls 2 are less like the Anglo-Norman Prose *Brut* chronicle than their continental cousins (or parents)—Add. 29503 adheres more closely to these European relatives—but both are undeniably related to the Prose *Brut*, and ultimately to the Oldest Version. The Prose *Brut*, via continental versions of *LCEA*, provides the core narrative (and genealogy) for all three insular rolls, despite Add. 27342's and Bodley Rolls 2's many revisions.[33] So, are these rolls Prose *Brut* chronicles, or aren't they? To what extent does a manuscript's inclusion of *ATN* (e.g. Bodley Rolls 2) or accounts of popes and emperors affect our ability to think about these genealogical histories as short Prose *Bruts*? If the strand of early printed editions of *The Chronicles of England* that combines the Prose *Brut* with material from the *Fasciculus temporum* (including roundels and tree diagrams) can be counted as a 'type' of English Prose *Brut* text, then why not universal chronicle versions of *LCEA*?[34] Or are the latter more simply abbreviated Prose *Bruts* that

---

32   Version Y manuscripts and London, College of Arms, Numerical Schedules 9/48, which I identified in 2015 (Norbye has since named its *ATN* text Version G), conclude *LCEA* by noting the marriage in 1406 between Isabelle of France, King Richard II's widow, to Charles d'Orléans. Add. 29503 translates this paragraph into English verbatim, which suggests that its author was working from a Version Y or G manuscript.

33   The Prose *Brut*'s influence on Add. 27342 and Bodley Rolls 2 has limits, however. From around the time of the Norman Conquest, the original author compiles material from other sources; the Prose *Brut*'s narrative is much less recognisable from this point.

34   See Matheson (1997: 339–348). The Middle Dutch *Brut*, published by Jan Veldener in 1480 as part of a larger series of chronicles, is worth consideration here too. Sjoerd Levelt has shown the Prose *Brut* to be the source for much of this short chronicle's material; but, like continental versions of *LCEA*, the Dutch text is embedded within an illustrated universal

appear alongside other short histories? The more the Prose *Brut* genre or family expands (and genres do evolve and overlap), the more difficult it becomes to
account for the many shapes its history takes. Yet, that development is precisely
what makes this body of texts and manuscripts so fascinating and rewarding
to study. The concept of a family of texts, rather than the notion of 'a specific
text',[35] more accurately captures the Prose *Brut*'s flexibility. It enables us to look
simultaneously at the history's characteristic features (which family members
may share to different extents) and to the revisions and continuations (in different languages, periods and places) that reflect its lasting appeal.[36] This in
turn means rethinking some of the ways the Prose *Brut* has been characterized, for example as a national history—its European reception also shows a
multi-national interest. In full awareness that I am about to have my cake and
eat it too, I propose that we think of Bodley Rolls 2, Add. 27342, Add. 29503
and continental versions of *LCEA* as Prose *Brut relatives*, not quite 'versions' of
the history but instead short Prose *Brut* chronicles derived from continental
adaptations of the Anglo-Norman Long Version. They *are* Prose *Bruts*, but they
are also *not* Prose *Bruts* and more than the Prose *Brut*, especially when sur-
rounded by or infused with other material. By approaching the Prose *Brut* as
a genre or family, we are able better to recognise their debt to Anglo-Norman
versions of the chronicle and focus our attention on their reshapings, and continental receptions, of the Prose *Brut*'s material. I would love to know what Erik
thinks.

Bibliography

Primary Sources—Manuscripts
London
British Library
   Additional 27342
   Additional 29503
   Cotton Roll xv 3
   Cotton Roll XIII 33

---

chronicle. We might think about the Middle Dutch *Brut* as another continental relative of
the Prose *Brut* chronicle.

35   Kooper (2016: 89).
36   Compare Helen Cooper's family resemblance theory about the romance genre: Cooper
(2004: 26). Peculiar Versions of the English Prose *Brut* come to mind again here, since
some incorporate universal chronicle and romance material: Matheson (1997: 256–334).

College of Arms
   Numerical Schedules 9/48

Manchester
John Rylands Library
   Fr. 54
   Fr. 99

New Haven
Yale University, Beinecke Library
   Marston 180

New York
Columbia University Library
   Plimpton 286

Oxford
Bodleian Library
   Bodley Rolls 2

Paris
Bibliothèque Nationale de France
   Fr. 23019

Wiltshire
Longleat House
   55

Primary Sources—Editions

EETS OS—Early English Text Society, Original Series

[Anonymous] *The Anglo-Norman Lay of* Haveloc: *Text and Translation*. Ed. and trans. Glyn S. Burgess and Leslie C. Brook. Gallica 37. Cambridge: D.S. Brewer, 2015.

[Anonymous] *An Anonymous Short English Metrical Chronicle*. Ed. Ewald Zettl. EETS OS 196. London: Oxford University Press, 1935.

[Anonymous] 'Bevis of Hampton', in *Four Romances of England: King Horn, Havelok the Dane, Bevis of Hampton, Athelston*. Eds. Graham Drake, Eve Salisbury and Ronald B. Herzman. Middle English Texts Series. Kalamazoo: Medieval Institute Publications, 1999, 200–321.

[Castleford, Thomas] *Castleford's Chronicle, or, The Boke of Brut*. Ed. Caroline D. Eckhardt. 2 vols. EETS OS 305, 306. Oxford: Oxford University Press, 1996–1998.

[Anonymous] *La Chronique Anonyme Universelle: Reading and Writing History in Fif-teenth-Century France*. Ed. and trans. Lisa Fagin Davis. London: Harvey Miller Publishers, 2014.

[Hardyng, John] *Hardyng's Chronicle: Edited from British Library MS Lansdowne 204*. Eds. James Simpson and Sarah Peverley. Middle English Texts Series. Kalamazoo: Medieval Institute Publications, 2015.

[Anonymous] 'Havelok the Dane', in *Four Romances of England*. In Drake, Salisbury and Herzman, eds. (1999). 85–159.

[Anonymous] *The Oldest Anglo-Norman Prose* Brut *Chronicle: An Edition and Translation*. Ed. and trans. Julia Marvin. Medieval Chronicles 4. Woodbridge: The Boydell Press, 2006.

[Rauf de Boun] *Rauf de Boun: Le Petit Bruit*. Ed. Diana B. Tyson. Plain Texts Series 4. London: Anglo-Norman Text Society, 1987.

[Veldener, Jan] *The Middle Dutch* Brut: *and Translation*. Ed. and trans. Sjoerd Levelt. Liverpool: Liverpool University Press, 2021.

Secondary Sources

Burgess, Glyn S., and Leslie C. Brook, ed. and trans. (2015). 'Introduction'. See [Anonymous] *The Anglo-Norman Lay of* Haveloc.

Cooper, Helen. (2004.) *The English Romance in Time: Transforming Motifs from Geoffrey of Monmouth to the Death of Shakespeare*. Oxford: Oxford University Press.

Davis, Lisa Fagin, ed. and trans. (2014). 'Introduction.' See [Anonymous] *La Chronique Anonyme Universelle*.

Kooper, Erik. (2016). 'Longleat House MS 55: An Unacknowledged *Brut* Manuscript?' In Jaclyn Rajsic, Erik Kooper and Dominique Hoche, eds. *The Prose* Brut *and Other Late Medieval Chronicles: Books Have Their Histories*. York: York Medieval Press. 75–93.

Marvin, Julia. (2017). *The Construction of Vernacular History in the Anglo-Norman Prose* Brut *Chronicle: The Manuscript Culture of Late Medieval England*. York: York Medieval Press.

Matheson, Lister M. (1998). *The Prose* Brut: *The Development of a Middle English Chronicle*. Tempe AZ: Medieval & Renaissance Texts & Studies.

Norbye, Marigold Anne. (2020). 'Roll or Codex for 'A tous nobles'? The Physical Expressions of a French Genealogical Chronicle'. In Stefan G. Holz, Jörg Peltzer and Maree Shirota, eds. *The Roll in England and France in the Late Middle Ages: Form and Content*. De Gruyte. 217–262.

Norbye, Marigold Anne. (2007). 'A Popular Example of "National Literature" in the Hundred Years War: *A tous nobles qui aiment beaux faits et bonnes histoires*'. *Nottingham Medieval Studies* 51: 121–142.

Rajsic, Jaclyn. (2016). '"Cestuy roy dit que la couronne de Ffraunce luy appartenoit": Reshaping the Prose *Brut* Chronicle in Fifteenth-Century France'. In Peter Crooks,

David Green and W. Mark Ormrod, eds. *The Plantagenet Empire, 1259–1453: Proceedings of the 2014 Harlaxton Medieval Symposium*. Donington: Shaun Tyas. 128–149.

Spence, John. (2013). *Reimagining History in Anglo-Norman Prose Chronicles*. Woodbridge: York Medieval Press.

Wiggins, Alison, and Rosalind Field, eds. (2007). *Guy of Warwick: Icon and Ancestor*. Studies in Medieval Romance. Cambridge: D.S. Brewer.

22

(Re)Deeming the *Historia Croylandensis* as Historical Fiction

Lisa M. Ruch

Abstract

The chronicle of Crowland Abbey is typically viewed as having two parts: the Ingulf or pseudo-Ingulf chronicle, running to 1089 C.E., and the subsequent continuations. The earlier portion has long been seen as a propagandistic forgery, and has been derided as infamous, naïve, and fantastical. Consequently, the latter, more historically verifiable portions have garnered more scholarly attention. This article focuses on the Ingulf portion of the chronicle, analyzing it for its literary qualities. A close reading of the chronicle's narrative structure, characterizations, and elevated diction helps to showcase the text as a fictionalized, heroic depiction of the abbey's foundation and early history, fashioned to portray not just its legitimacy but also its destiny as a religious centre. The *Historia Croylandensis* provides an example of a chronicle as a literary enterprise: a thoughtfully crafted narrative intended to both engage and motivate its audience.

While the foundation of Crowland Abbey can be dated to the latter half of the tenth century, the opening portion of its chronicle, the *Historia Croylandensis*, sometimes called *Ingulf's Chronicle*, depicts a monastery that had heroic origins and a long, illustrious history, dating back to the seventh century.[1] This first portion is a frame narrative, seemingly written by Ingulf, abbot of the house from 1086 to 1109. The narrative persona of Ingulf leverages his sources for the coverage before his time and adds first-person detail to what is contemporaneous, displaying a focused, ongoing commitment to recording the monastery's rights and place in history. The text garnered early attention from scholars, with editions appearing in 1596 and 1684. In their enthusiastic search for data on the history of pre-Norman England, antiquarians scoured the chronicle, ignoring anachronisms and inconsistencies. It was not until the nineteenth century that

---

1　The spelling of Crowland/Croyland has varied over time. I will use Crowland, but when quoting others, preserve the spelling in the original.

scholars began to question the text's historicity. Once that questioning began, however, the pendulum swung, and majority opinion deemed the *Historia Croylandensis* a fifteenth-century fraud. Sir Francis Palgrave labelled the first portion of the chronicle 'little more than an historical novel—a mere monkish invention.'[2] Having translated the text, Henry Riley derided its authors, saying, 'their purpose was selfish, and their conduct, oppressive and mendacious.'[3] Joseph Stevenson, another translator, was more reserved in his assessment, calling the Ingulf text 'interesting as a work of fiction, but on the whole valueless as an historical document.'[4] Thomas Duffus Hardy labelled it 'undoubtedly a monkish forgery,'[5] while Antonia Gransden damned the text's authors with faint praise, opining that 'the monks of Crowland excelled even those of Glastonbury in the art of fabrication.'[6] Nicholas Pronay and John Cox attributed this fabrication to an inferiority complex on the part of the monks at Crowland, a monastery with neither a famous resident, advantageous location, nor great donor; thus, the chronicle was 'a product of that collective chip on the shoulder.'[7]

More recently, a few scholars have seen merit in the *Historia Croylandensis*. David Roffe noted the chronicle's 'handiwork in an elaborate and historical conceit.'[8] In his study of medieval forgeries, Alfred Hiatt called the text 'engaging and ingenious,'[9] lauding its 'creative, at times flamboyant, form of pastiche.'[10] Those scholars who have noted the Ingulf chronicle's narrative power make a compelling argument—when readers immerse themselves in the prose, it becomes an entertaining account, replete with heroics, suspense, loss, and redemption. Thus, it should be read not as it purports to be—a true history—but as an extended origin tale, with folkloric and literary qualities. Viewed through this lens, the chronicle can and should be celebrated for its narrative integrity and artistry.

This judging of the chronicle in light of what category it may or may not fall under—history or fiction—is a modern concern, born of the disciplinary labelling of academic fields and the categorization of subjects. Historical fiction has, as a genre, occupied an uneasy middle ground in this debate. As

---

2   *Historia Croylandensis*, trans. Riley, xii.
3   Riley (1862: 133).
4   *Historia Croylandensis*, trans. Stevenson, xxi.
5   Hardy (1966: 61).
6   Gransden (1982: 400).
7   Pronay & Cox (1986: 2).
8   Roffe (1995: 108).
9   Hiatt (2004: 37).
10   Hiatt (2004: 45).

Jerome de Groot observes, readers of historical fiction are 'consciously engaging with a text that is actively, explicitly lying to us while simultaneously claiming that it is somehow historically accurate and truthful.'[11] However, fictions such as these serve not merely as entertainment; they can have rhetorical impacts to make as well, 'provid[ing] a space for political intervention and reclamation.'[12] The recent popularity of Hilary Mantel's *Wolf Hall* trilogy is a case in point. Whether her writings are pigeonholed as historical fiction or fictionalized history,[13] Mantel got people talking about Thomas Cromwell: 'It is for that reason that Mantel can achieve acclaim for a sympathetic portrayal of a subject few people would have wanted to read only a few years ago. There can be few better testimonies to the value of well-written historical fiction.'[14] Much as Mantel's books redress and humanize the character of Cromwell, so too does the opening portion of the *Historia Croylandensis* shine a light on Crowland Abbey as, in its medieval denizens' eyes, a venerable, celebrated institution in which to be proud. The following close reading of the chronicle's narrative will highlight these literary qualities and strategies.

A storied monastery needs a storied origin, and Crowland had that in St Guthlac. Guthlac's life story was written around 730 or 740 and relates his desire to become a hermit. Told of a desolate spot in the fens, he took himself there, and fought off the indigenous demons to prove his endurance and sanctity. The connection of Guthlac to the foundation of Crowland Abbey was put into writing by Ordericus Vitalis in the twelfth century, when Ordericus spent five weeks as a guest at the abbey, studying its archives and consulting with its brothers. In his *Ecclesiastical History*, he explains that Ethelbald gifted land to Guthlac and ordained the building of the monastery. The *Historia Croylandensis* adds detail to this, relating that Ethelbald came to Guthlac in distress, having been banished from his kingdom. Guthlac advised him to have faith and prophesized a successful reign. A while later, Guthlac died and Ethelbald journeyed to his hermitage to mourn. As he was praying, the deceased Guthlac appeared to him, assuring him that he would regain his kingship within the year. From this point, 'signa virtutum ac sanitatum per invocationem intercessionis illius coruscare frequenter coeperunt' ('miracles of power and healing began con-

---

11   de Groot (2009: 57).
12   de Groot (2010: 140).
13   See Rex (2020) and Reimer (2020) for opposing views on Mantel's trilogy and its categorization and Kenny (2022) for discussion on how Mantel's writing effectively contextualizes and fleshes out Cromwell for readers.
14   Wilson (2012: 3).

tinually to shine forth')[15] to those who invoked the help of Guthlac, and in his
memory, Ethelbald granted the island of Crowland so that the religious house
could be built.

This auspicious beginning inspired subsequent Mercian rulers, who variously confirmed and extended the rights of Crowland Abbey. King Withlaf, the
chronicle relates, visited the shrine of St Guthlac at least once a year, always
bringing the gift of 'aliquod pretiosum notabileque jocale' ('some precious valuable jewel').[16] He was especially moved by the tomb of St Etheldritha, also of
Crowland, opting to inter his son and his wife on either side of her. He was succeeded by his brother Bertulph, who seized the jewels to pay for soldiers to fight
the Danish invaders who were ravaging London. Concurrent with this threat,
sickness began to overshadow the land in a literal sense, as a mass paralysis
spread across all England. A spontaneous cure was effected at an ecclesiastical council when the Archbishop of Canterbury was healed while discussing
matters related to Crowland. Other clerics followed his lead, and word spread,
resulting in a nationwide pilgrimage to the abbey. Initially a place of solitude,
Crowland becomes, by the end of this section of the narrative, a nexus of sacred
power, sought out by all of England.

This time of great honour for Crowland was overshadowed by the spectre
of the Danish incursions, which increased in severity in the 860's. In 870, as
the narrative relates, 'cumque ibidem per totam illam aestatum terram ad
cineres refadissent ferro flammaque devorantes' ('the whole of the summer was
spent in reducing the land to ashes, and devouring it with fire and sword').[17]
This began a period of struggle and privation for Crowland. Abbot Theodore
ordered that the abbey's treasures be hidden or taken away for safekeeping,
and, while celebrating Mass, was killed at the altar by the invaders, along with
the prior and sub-prior. A ten-year-old resident, Tugarius, described as having
'facie corporisque forma venustissimus' ('an elegant form and a beautiful countenance'),[18] begged to be killed as well, but was disguised by a Danish earl and
was the sole survivor at the abbey, taken as prisoner. Adding to the pathos was
the desecration of the holy graves and the incineration of the saints' relics. As
the Danes left with their booty, two of their chariots were mired in the fens, and
in the ensuing confusion, young Tugarius made his escape. Returning to Crowland, he was reunited with those monks who had left prior to the massacre, and
together, they picked through the ruins, finding the tortured and mutilated bod-

---

15   *Historia Croylandensis*, ed. Fulman, 10; trans. Stevenson, 569.
16   *Historia Croylandensis*, ed. Fulman, 11; trans. Stevenson, 581.
17   *Historia Croylandensis*, ed. Fulman, 20 [misprinted as 14]; trans. Stevenson, 595.
18   *Historia Croylandensis*, ed. Fulman, 22; trans. Stevenson, 597.

ies of their brethren. Most pitiful, the chronicle relates, were those of Grimketul and Agamund, 'qui ambo centum aetatis annos exegerant, gladiis in Claustro transfossi' ('both of whom were more than a hundred years of age, and had been transfixed with swords in the cloister').[19]

At this point in history, religious houses became extinct across England. With the exception of Saint-Augustine's, Canterbury, 'the unbroken existence of a community observing the monastic life can nowhere be proved or even suggested with any real degree of probability.'[20] However, the Crowland chron-icler sets up a scenario where continuity was maintained. According to the account, despite its having been being pillaged and taxed to almost nothing, Abbot Godric took steps to preserve the abbey, sending some of the surviving monks to friends and supporters, and remaining with the rest at Crowland. These few stalwarts 'vitam suam cum summa inopia protrahebant' ('passed their lives in the midst of deep indigence').[21] Meanwhile, England was even-tually restored to peace with the repulsion of the Danes and the reigns of kings Alfred and Edward the Elder. By the reign of Athelstan, says the chronicle, Abbot Godric, 'sed longo senio gravatum' ('though weighed down by old age'),[22] still held sway at Crowland, along with some fellow monks. As part of his reli-gious patronage, Athelstan vowed to rebuild the abbey, but died before he could do so. His successor, Edmund, also promised to restore Crowland, but was killed before he could do so. During Edmund's reign, the narrative explains, Abbot Godric died, seventy years after the decimation of the abbey by the Danes. In despair, some of the surviving monks left for other religious houses, leaving just three brothers behind—styled by the text as 'sancta trinitas' ('the holy trin-ity').[23]

Into this rather desperate strait stepped the savior of Crowland Abbey, the chancellor Turketul, described in appropriately heroic terms as 'virum quippe prudentissinium, ac omnis honestatis ac aequitatis sectatorem' ('a man of the greatest prudence, and a follower of all virtue and equity').[24] Passing by Crow-land on his travels, Turketul met the three monks there; they took him in overnight, shared with him their meagre food, and told him of their survival and privations. Turketul was greatly impressed, and as the chronicle relates,

---

19   *Historia Croylandensis*, ed. Fulman, 23; trans. Stevenson, 599.
20   Knowles & Hadcock (1971: 11).
21   *Historia Croylandensis*, ed. Fulman, 27; trans. Stevenson, 604.
22   *Historia Croylandensis*, ed. Fulman, 29; trans. Stevenson, 607.
23   *Historia Croylandensis*, ed. Fulman, 29; trans. Stevenson, 607.
24   *Historia Croylandensis*, ed. Fulman, 30; trans. Stevenson, 608.

Ab illo namque die [ac deinceps] animus ejus dictis senibus, ac Croylan-
densi Monasterio tam intimo ac individuo amore conglutinatus eft, ut
per totam viam suam quotidie quibuscunque occurrentibus, tam in diver-
soriis quam in viis, Croyiandensium senum humanitatem exponeret,
ianctitatem extolleret, caritatem praedicaret, calamitatemque deplora-
ret. Ab ipsoque tunc primitus processit, quod Croyland Curteys cogno-
men accepit.

> *Historia Croylandensis*, ed. Fulman, 30.

(from that day forward his mind was united to these old men and the monastery of Croyland with such intimate and undivided affection, that he
daily related to whomsoever he happened to meet through the whole of
his journey, whether at the inns or in the highways, the courtesy of the
old men of Croyland; he extolled their sanctity, proclaimed their charity,
and deplored their calamities. And from him it first arose that Croyland
received the surname Curteys.)

> *Historia Croylandensis*, trans. Stevenson, 609.

Turketul not only vowed to rebuild the abbey, but to re-invent himself as a holy
man, taking the cowl and joining the community there as monk and abbot.

At this juncture, the narrative steps back in time over twenty-five years
to incorporate Turketul's backstory. The prologue to his life cites 'secundum
Chronicorum fidem' ('the authority of chronicles'),[25] although no other extant
text even mentions his existence. However, according to the *Historia Croylandensis*, he was an exemplary man in multiple walks of life, and responsible for
the rebirth of Crowland Abbey as a spiritual centre. The text says that Turketul
served as a central advisor to Edward the Elder, all the time shunning hon-
ours offered to him; indeed, he 'tanquam tendiculas Sathanae ad animas sub-
vertendas, omnibus vitae suae temporibus penitus abhorrebat' ('shrank from
them during the whole of his life as if they were snares of Satan for subverting
souls').[26] He then aided Athelstan, joining him at the Battle of Brunanburh and
playing a pivotal role in the fighting. Afterwards, the chronicle relates, 'In tam
duro certamine saepius se gloriabatur a Domino conservatam Turketulus, &
se foelicissimum & fortunatum quod nunquam hominem occiderit, neminem
mutilaverit, cum pugnare pro patria, & maxime contra Paganos, licite quisque
possit' ('Turketul used often to boast that the Lord preserved him in so severe

---

25   *Historia Croylandensis*, ed. Fulman, 36; trans. Stevenson, 616.
26   *Historia Croylandensis*, ed. Fulman, 36; trans. Stevenson, 616.

a conflict, and that he was most happy and fortunate in not having either slain or mutilated a single man, though any one might fight lawfully for his country, and above all against Pagans').[27] Remaining in his post as chancellor as Edmund took the throne, Turketul, who was starting to lean toward a religious life, visited Crowland and shared with the three surviving monks his intention to take the cowl. Doing so, he helped restore Crowland's ancient landholdings, bringing the abbey back to its former glory. A charismatic and heroic figure, he was followed by 'multi literati viri' ('many men of letters'),[28] some of whom joined him in the religious life, and others of whom remained laymen, unwilling to part ways with him.

Clearly wishing to memorialize Crowland's continuity as an ancient house, Turketul took time to converse with those monks who had remained there through the troubled times, as well as two others who had returned, ensuring that their reminiscences were recorded in writing, thus preserving, as the chronicle explains, 'historiam istam, continentem majora memoranda domus nostrae, cum paucis incidentiis Regni Merciorum, & Westsaxonum, a nostra prima fundatione per Ethelbaldum Regem, usque ad decimum quartum annum regni inclyti Regis Edgari' ('a history containing the principal events of our house, with a few incidents regarding the kingdom of the Mercians and the West Saxons from our first foundation, by king Ethelbald, to the fourteenth year of the renowned king Edgar').[29] This bit of metafiction returns the chronology of the text back to where it needs to be after the biographical digression. Having served their role as custodians and memory keepers for Crowland, the veteran monks died, ranging from 115 to 168 years old. Unable to attain such a venerable age, Turketul died at 68. His dedication to Crowland extended to the end of his life, as, on his deathbed, he exhorted his brothers 'quasi prophetice' ('as in a prophetic manner')[30] to guard their fire with care. At this point in time, the abbey was again secure and solvent, as a full ring of bells was cast and additional buildings were constructed—out of wood, as vividly described in the text, in a moment of literary foreshadowing.

This idyllic period cycled to another time of struggles, as famine and pestilence spread, followed by another wave of Danish invasions. Building the literary tension, the narrative voice forewarns, 'Sed haec nuncia sunt malorum' ('But these things were the beginnings of evils').[31] Crowland was heavily taxed,

---

27   *Historia Croylandensis*, ed. Fulman, 37; trans. Stevenson, 618–619.
28   *Historia Croylandensis*, ed. Fulman, 40; trans. Stevenson, 622.
29   *Historia Croylandensis*, ed. Fulman, 48; trans. Stevenson, 634.
30   *Historia Croylandensis*, ed. Fulman, 52; trans. Stevenson, 639.
31   *Historia Croylandensis*, ed. Fulman, 56; trans. Stevenson, 646.

both in a financial and a logistical sense, as it served as a refuge for the multitudes fleeing the destruction of the land. Danish invaders were followed by the Normans, adding, it seems, insult to injury. Hereward the Wake is celebrated in the chronicle as a rebel hero. The detail is added that his mother-in-law came to England, where she chose to give up the secular life and adopt 'sanctimonialem habitum' ('the monastic habit') at Crowland, where she 'vix aestate quarta jam transacta, in nostro sepulta monasterio requiescat' ('professed a religious life for a length of time with great sanctity').[32] Hereward, meanwhile, continued his resistance to the Normans, coming face to face with Yvo Talbois, who plays the role of arch-nemesis of Crowland through the remainder of Ingulf's chronicle.

Talbois, as is appropriate for a literary villain, is introduced into the text in hyperbolic terms:

> Contra vero monasterium nostrum, ac omnes Croylandenses diabolico instinctu tanto furore efferayus eft, ut varie Croylandensium animalia in mariscis cum canibus suis infectans, longius effugaret, lacubus immergeret, nonnulla caudis, auribus mutilaret, & crebro spinis ac tibiis jumentorum fractis, penitus inutilia redderet. Dominum etiam Vlketulum praedecessorem meum tunc Abbatem pro viribus destruere jugiter incursans, & injurians deterreret.
>
> *Historia Croylandensis*, ed. Fulman, 71.

> (As for our monastery, he was excited against it by an instinct of diabolical fury: throughout Croyland he hunted with his dogs the animals in the fens, drove them to a distance, drowned them in the lakes, cut off their tails and ears, and not infrequently rendered the beasts of burden perfectly useless by breaking their backs and legs. Above all, he never ceased with might and main to attempt the destruction of the then abbot, my predecessor the lord Ulketul, or to seek to terrify him by his violence.)
>
> *Historia Croylandensis*, trans. Stevenson, 668.

An agent of the Normans, Talbois collaborates with them in harassing Crowland, impounding assets, bringing in monks from Anjou to occupy the abbey, and defaming it through lies. The Norman conspirators are described in Biblical terms with allusions from the Book of Job: 'velut in corpore Behemoth sqama sqamae conjuncta suisset, veritatis omne spiraculum refutant' ('as in the body

---

32   *Historia Croylandensis*, ed. Fulman, 67, 68; trans. Stevenson, 663.

of the Behemoth scale is closely joined to scale, so these persons with a thousand excuses defended each other in their wickedness').[33] Capping off these atrocities was the beheading of Earl Waltheof, who became Crowland's next protector saint. As the abbot Ulketul preached about Waltheof's martyrdom, he was accused by Yvo Talbois of idolatry, and stripped of his office.

The next abbot was Ingulf, the purported author of this portion of the *Historia Croylandensis*. Here, the text transitions to first-person voice, as Ingulf relates his life story. He frames himself as a bit of a hero. He attained a classical education at Oxford, boasting that 'in Aristotele arripiendo supra multos coaetaneos meos profecissem, etiam Rhetoricam Tullii primam, & secundam, talo tenus induebam' ('in the apprehension of Aristotle I acquired a proficiency beyond many of my own age, and became thoroughly imbued with the knowledge of the first and second books of Tully').[34] This is all the more remarkable, given that it places him at Oxford before any teaching there is known to have occurred. Both devout and adventurous, Ingulf then travelled to the Holy Land and Rome in his role as secretary to the then duke William of Normandy. As a monk, he rose through the administrative ranks, eventually becoming abbot at Crowland. According to his account, his destiny there was foretold when he was visited in a dream by an abbot, two bishops, and a retinue of saints; among them were Saints Guthlac and Waltheof.

Ingulf then relates the tale of Asford, who tried to seize Crowland's assets unjustly and met with divine revenge in the form of a fatal fall from his horse and the subsequent defilement of his corpse as it was swept from its coffin into the mire by a sudden downpour 'quod utique fluentibus aquis dies Noetica credebatur' ('that the flowing waters resembled the deluge of Noah').[35] Crowland's prosperity seemed assured as this story spread; as Ingulf explains, 'non erat, qui deinceps Dominum defensorem nostrum auderet in aliquo offendere, necqui sanctum Guthlacum de cetero praesumeret ad iracundiam provocare' ('Henceforward there was no one bold enough to offend in any respect the Lord our defender, or presumptuous enough to provoke St Guthlac to anger').[36] When a harsh winter led to famine in the area, Ingulf sat in vigil at Guthlac's tomb, during which an angelic voice was heard, and sacks of grain miraculously appeared in the cemetery.

The tone of the narrative shifts as Ingulf comments, 'Prosperitatis iter gaudens hucusque cucurri: jam labor & luctus funera tanta strepunt' ('Hitherto I

33   *Historia Croylandensis*, ed. Fulman, 72; trans. Stevenson, 669.
34   *Historia Croylandensis*, ed. Fulman, 73; trans. Stevenson, 670.
35   *Historia Croylandensis*, ed. Fulman, 77, trans; Stevenson, 677.
36   *Historia Croylandensis*, ed. Fulman, 77; trans. Stevenson, 677.

have run my journey in prosperity and rejoicing: now the harsh notes of labour, and sorrow, and death, clash around me').[37] The instigator of this turn in fortune is the nemesis, Yvo Talbois, who renewed his vendetta against Crowland, where, Ingulf laments, 'omnem malitiam suam in Domum nostrum evomuit' ('he vomited forth all his malice against our house').[38] At this point in the narrative, the late Turketul's prophetic deathbed admonition about fire is recalled in hindsight, as a devastating blaze destroyed nearly all of the abbey. Ingulf describes the conflagration in graphic detail, but takes comfort in recalling his shifting of many charters and documents from the library years before; shielded from the fire, they survived to provide witness to the abbey's history and assets. Ingulf spent his remaining active years overseeing the second rebuilding of Crowland and ends his portion of the chronicle with the noting of the banishment of his antagonist Yvo Talbois from England.

Viewed as a discrete text, the opening, Ingulf portion of the *Historia Croylandensis* is an engaging piece of literature, with its heroic characters, the ongoing conflict of good versus evil, and the highs and lows of cyclical fortune. Crowland's setting in the once demon-infested fens is symbolically significant; as Justin Noetzel explains, 'The spatial transformation that Guthlac enacts through his strength and faith elevates the land beneath him into the realm of the sacred, and the spiritual foundation that he builds becomes the literal foundation of the church and monastery that are built in Crowland.'[39] We come to root for the abbey and its denizens as protagonists who face repeated challenges. The many inconsistencies in linear time and historically verifiable facts fade into the background when the chronicle is looked at as an example of historical fiction, a genre which often toys with actual timelines for dramatic effect. The text shows other literary qualities as well: classical references, alliteration, elevated diction, and theatrical emplotment.

That the author or authors of the *Historia Croylandensis* had literary inclinations should not come as a surprise. Manuscripts known to have been produced or held at Crowland Abbey reveal such a tendency. The Guthlac Roll[40] is a pictorial biography of the saint, showing vignettes of his life, perhaps intended as a model for stained glass. Douai Public Library MS 852 incorporates narratives of Guthlac, Waltheof, and others, blending in elements of saga literature.[41] In the midst of these texts is a brief history of the abbots of Crowland.

---

37   *Historia Croylandensis*, ed. Fulman, 94; trans. Stevenson, 705.
38   *Historia Croylandensis*, ed. Fulman, 95; trans. Stevenson, 706.
39   Noetzel (2014: 127–128).
40   London, BL Harley Roll Y 6.
41   See Colgrave (1956: 39–42) for details on this MS.

Eleanor Parker opines that this manuscript reveals an ongoing literary tradition at the abbey, melding Scandinavian and English influences.[42] A lengthy Latin chronicle from Crowland,[43] dating from the thirteenth century, contains later medieval marginalia that indicates readers' interest in the abbey's traditions; notes on Guthlac's life and death, the foundation of Crowland Abbey by Ethelbald, and the martyrdom of Waltheof parallel main points of the *Historia Croylandensis*. Carl Watkins points out that 'Crowland's saintly patrons were integrated into the process of guaranteeing the economic and political viability of the monastery.'[44] Our critical reading of writings from Crowland, both those now labelled history and fiction, helps us form a wider, more complete perspective on this undertaking.

Those who study medieval historiography have long been familiar with the overlap between these genres, a hybrid 'type of imaginative romantic fiction that ran alongside the development of the severer form of history.'[45] Chronicle narratives that are patently legendary, or that present history in an unambiguously fictional light, need not be dismissed as somehow less worthy than verifiable historical accounts. As Suzanne Fleischman reminds us,

> Were we to compile a medieval dictionary, history would no doubt have to be redefined as 'familiar,' 'legendary,' 'what was held to be true.' This definition might provoke discomfort in certain quarters inasmuch as legendary has since come to be synonymous with false. But the issue at the time was not objective truth as distinct from subjective belief. For the Middle Ages and even well beyond, historical truth was anything that belonged to a widely accepted tradition.
>
> 1983: 305

As Beverley Southgate adds, 'History's ability to make us feel good—to make sense of events, and leave an impression of meaning and purpose—indicates one of its most important functions; but it fulfils that function by itself proving to be a hybrid mixture of fact and "fabulation".'[46] Accordingly, Justin Lake sees 'benefits in an approach that combines meticulous historical scholarship with an appreciation of the literary features of narrative historiography.'[47] The first

---

42   See Parker (2014) for examples and discussion.
43   London, BL Additional MS 35168.
44   Watkins (1996: 109).
45   Southgate (2009: 4).
46   Southgate (2009: 153–154).
47   Lake (2014: 353).

portion of the *Historia Croylandensis* is a prime case in point. Ingulf's chronicle should be celebrated for its power as a gripping tale, crafted for the purpose of identity formation and legitimization at Crowland Abbey. Discussing the chronicle, Cristian Ispir has warned that 'Caution is required not to throw the historical baby out with the historiographical bathwater.'[48] This admonition might well be applied to other chronicles also; their stories are worth the read.

Bibliography

Primary Sources

[*Historia Croylandensis.*] Ed. W. Fulman. *Rerum Anglicarum Scriptorum Veterum*, vol. 1. Oxford: 1684. 1–132 & 449–593.

[*Historia Croylandensis.*] Trans. Henry T. Riley. *Ingulph's Chronicle of the Abbey of Croyland*. London: Bohn, 1854.

[*Historia Croylandensis.*] Trans. Joseph Stevenson. *The History of Ingulf. Church Historians of England*, vol. 2, part 2. London: Seeley's, 1854. 565–725.

Ordericus Vitalis. *The Ecclesiastical History of England and Normandy*, vol. II. Trans. Thomas Forester. London: Bohn, 1854.

Secondary Sources

Colgrave, Bertram (1956). *Felix's Life of Saint Guthlac*. Cambridge: Cambridge University Press.

de Groot, Jerome (2009). 'Beyond the Bodice-Ripper.' *History Today* 59.10: 57.

de Groot, Jerome (2010). *The Historical Novel*. London & New York: Routledge.

Fleischman, Suzanne (1983). 'On the Representation of History and Fiction in the Middle Ages.' *History and Theory* 22.3: 278–310.

Gransden, Antonia (1982). *Historical Writing in England II*. London: Routledge.

Hardy, Thomas Duffus (1966). *Descriptive Catalogue of Materials Relating to the History of Great Britain and Ireland*, vol. II. London: Kraus Reprint.

Hiatt, Alfred (2004). *The Making of Medieval Forgeries: False Documents in Fifteenth-Century England*. London and Toronto: British Library & University of Toronto Press.

Ispir, Cristian (2020). 'History Writing in the Cloister: *The Crowland Chronicle*.' In *Guthlac: Crowland's Saint*, eds. Jane Roberts and Alan Thacker. Donington, Lincolnshire: Shaun Tyas. 426–447.

Kenny, David (2022). 'The Human Pared Away: Hilary Mantel's Thomas Cromwell as an Archetype of Legal Pragmatism.' *Law and Literature* 34.1: 109–139.

---

48   Ispir (2020: 436).

Knowles, David & R. Neville Hadcock (1971). *Medieval Religious Houses: England and Wales*, second edition. Harlow, Essex: Longman.

Lake, Justin (2014). 'Authorial Intention in Medieval Historiography.' *History Compass* 12.4: 344–360.

Noetzel, Justin T. (2014). 'Monster, Demon, Warrior: St. Guthlac and the Cultural Landscape of the Anglo-Saxon Fens.' *Comitatus* 45: 105–131.

Parker, Eleanor (2014). 'Siward the Dragon-Slayer: Mythmaking in Anglo-Scandinavian England.' *Neophilologus* 98: 481–493.

Pronay, Nicholas & John Cox (1986). *The Crowland Chronicle Continuations: 1459–1486*. London: Richard III and Yorkist Trust.

Reimer, Jonathan (2020). 'History and Fiction.' *First Things: A Monthly Journal of Religion & Public Life*, November: 3–4.

Rex, Richard (2020). 'The Mirrors and the Smoke.' *First Things: A Monthly Journal of Religion & Public Life*, August: 1–7.

Riley, Henry Thomas (1862). 'The History and Charters of Ingulfus Considered.' *Archaeological Journal* 19: 32–49 & 114–133.

Roffe, David (1995). 'The Historia Croylandensis: A Plea for Reassessment.' *English Historical Review* 110.435: 93–108.

Southgate, Beverley (2009). *History Meets Fiction*. Harlow, England: Pearson.

Watkins, Carl (1996). 'The Cult of Earl Waltheof at Crowland.' *Hagiographica* 3: 95–111.

Wilson, Derek (2012). 'Brewer's Boy Made Good.' *History Today* 62.12: 3.

23

Dating the Past in Wace's *Roman de Rou*

Françoise Le Saux

Abstract

Wace's *Roman de Rou*, composed between 1160 and 1174, is an ambitious work charting the history of the dukes of Normandy from the Viking Rollo to Duke Robert Curthose, who ended his life in prison under his brother Henry I of England. A study of the chronological references in the work reveals a clear reluctance to use dates by year from the Incarnation, preferring to chart the progression of time through internal landmarks, in particular the length of ducal or royal rules. The key points chosen in this way in the final part of the *Rou* suggest that the historiographer used them to support an indirect comment on the recent history of his homeland.

The *Roman de Rou* has a special place in the development of French vernacular historiography. Composed and revised at various points between 1160 and 1174, it presented its author, the Norman poet, hagiographer and historian Wace, with some thorny challenges, one of which was that he had to satisfy very different audiences. His account had to be authoritative and recognized as such by his Latinate clerical peers; at the same time, it needed to be shaped to the expectations of a mixed lay audience, which would have included the descendants of the protagonists of the events recounted. One of these descendants was of course the King of England himself, but the pressure of less exalted Norman families in Wace's immediate social and professional circle in Bayeux and Caen would also have been considerable.[1] To this, one may add the fact that there was no established template for historiography in the vernacular dealing with events still in living memory.

The *Rou*, like the *Roman de Brut*, has as its foundation narrative one key Latin history, the *Gesta Normannorum ducum* of William of Jumièges, supplemented and reshaped in the light of other authoritative accounts.[2] Unlike the *Roman de Brut*, however, the main source of the *Rou* did not provide a neat narrat-

---

1   See van Houts (2004: esp. xlv–xlvii).
2   See Le Saux (2005: 153–160).

ive like Geoffrey of Monmouth's *Historia regum Britannie*, neither did it cover the entirety of the period under consideration.[3] For the last 2000 lines of the *Rou*, Wace had to construct his own account of the difficult relations between the Conqueror's sons, drawing upon monastic annals, legal documents, various chronicles and eyewitness accounts, both oral and written. Another, crucial difference with the *Roman de Brut* is an inevitable degree of emotional involvement of the writer in the recent history of his Norman homeland. The prefaces to Wace's two histories reveal a marked difference in tone and programme. The *Roman de Brut* announces in neutral terms a reliable, chronological account of the successive kings of England:[4]

> Ki vult oïr e vult saveir
> De rei en rei e d'eir en eir
> Ki cil furent e dunt il vindrent
> Ki Engleterre primes tindrent,
> Quels reis i ad en ordre eü,
> E qui anceis e ki puis fu,
> Maistre Wace l'ad translaté
> Ki en conte la vérité.
>> *Roman de Brut*, 1–8.

(Whoever wishes to hear and to know about the successive kings and their heirs who once upon a time were the rulers of England—who they were, whence they came, what was their sequence, who came earlier and who later—Master Wace has translated it and tells it truthfully.)
>> WEISS (1999: 2–3).

By contrast, the programme announced in the opening lines of the 'Chronique ascendante' of the *Roman de Rou*, an ascending genealogy from Henry II down to Rollo that serves as introduction to the work as a whole, is altogether more pointed, and indeed personal:[5]

> Mil chent et soisante anz out de temps et d'espace
> Puiz que Dex en la Virge descendi par sa grace,
> Quant un clerc de Caen, qui out non Mestre Vace,
> S'entremist de l'estoire de Rou et de s'estrace,

---

3 On this difference between Wace's two histories, see Blacker (2006: 55–62).
4 Text and translation of the *Roman de Brut* are from Weiss ed. and transl. (1999).
5 The *Roman de Rou* is quoted from Holden ed. (1970–1973); translation by Burgess (2004).

Qui conquist Normendie, qui qu'en poist ne qui place,
Contre l'orgueil de France, qui encore les menasce,
Que nostre roi Henri la congnoissë et sace.

> *Rou*, 'Chronique ascendante', 1–7.

(One thousand, one hundred and sixty years in time and space had
elapsed since God in His grace came down in the Virgin, when a cleric
from Caen by the name of Master Wace undertook the story of Rou [i.e.,
Rollo] and his race; he conquered Normandy, like it or not, against the
arrogance of France which still threatens them—may our King Henry
recognise and be aware of this.)

> BURGESS (2004: 13).

Wace is openly claiming ownership of this 'estoire', announcing a specific
agenda: it is a warning to Henry II not to trust France, presented as Normandy's
hereditary enemy. The implication is that Henry himself, the son of a duke of
Anjou married to a onetime French queen, might not be familiar with the history of his Norman ancestors. The choice of an ascending genealogy to open the
Rou, as well as being an elegant way of introducing the founder of the House of
Normandy, could therefore be seen as a pointed reminder to the King of England that he is a descendant of Rollo's. There is a sense of political urgency
in this Preface that is absent from the *Roman de Brut*, the history of a foreign
people whose days of power were long gone.

The *Roman de Rou* has three parts, clearly distinguished by their metre and
the narrator's persona. The first part (hereafter *Rou* I; 750 lines long), draws
heavily on the first Book of Dudo of St Quentin's *De moribus et actis primorum
Normanniae ducum* and relates the depredations of the Viking Hasting, a precursor of Rollo's.[6] The 'Seconde partie' (hereafter, *Rou* II; 4425 lines long) is the
beginning of the subject matter proper; it opens with the adventures of Rollo
and its companions and ends with Duke Richard I securing a lasting peace
with Lothar, the king of France. Finally, the third and final part ('Troisième
Partie'; hereafter *Rou* III) gives a lively account of the deeds of Duke Richard
and his successors, up to Duke Robert Curthose's defeat at Tinchebray against

---

6   This first part has been viewed by earlier scholars as a discarded first draft and is published
    in an Appendix in Holden's reference edition and Burgess's translation of the *Roman de Rou*.
    This is problematic from a purely narrative point of view, however, as *Rou* II is clearly a con-
    tinuation in terms of content, even though the verse form is different. See Le Saux, (2005:
    162–169).

his brother, King Henry I of England. It is the longest of the three parts, with 11440 lines including preface and epilogue.

The first and third parts of the *Rou* open with very similar prefaces, corresponding almost word for word and both of them signalling a serious scholarly intent: 'Pour remembrer des ancesours / les fez et les diz et les mours, / doit on les livres et les gestes / et les estoires lire as festes, / les felonies des felons / et les barnages des barons' ('To remember the deeds, words and ways of our ancestors, books, chronicles and histories should be read out at festivals, and also to remember the wicked deeds of wicked men and the brave deeds of brave men.')[7] These lines announce a programme of what may be described as authoritative celebratory memorialization. The *Rou* thus marks its intended distance from Dudo's extravagant panegyric, promising a fair and truthful account of a shared ancestral past. The balancing act between the demands of historical accuracy and the positive stance required by Wace's patron (the king or otherwise), not to mention his friends, family and colleagues in Normandy, becomes particularly delicate in *Rou* III, with the hot potatoes of the English Conquest and its aftermath of conflict within the ruling family—all within living memory. The question of the relative importance to grant to England in a history of the Normans would also have been an issue for the historiographer. I propose to explore here an apparently marginal tool used by Wace in attempting to resolve these difficulties: his chronological markers.

It is conventional in historiography to attach events to the year in which they occurred. In addition to their function of anchoring these events to a specific time, dates add to the sense of reliability by hinting at indebtedness to written sources such as annals or legal documents. It is striking, therefore, that so few precise dates appear in the *Roman de Rou*.[8] In the 'Chronique ascendante', only two events are dated by year: 1160, the year Wace started to work on the *Rou* (1) and 1066, the year of William of Normandy's conquest of England (179–180). These landmarks divide history in two: a 'modern' period extending to the time of writing, marked by the increasing importance of England, and an arguably more heroic period, with at its heart Normandy and the Norman people led by the ducal house. At the same time, years counted from the Nativity of Christ implicitly place the events recounted within a universal perspective, that of the Redemption of mankind. In addition to these two year dates, Wace provides

---

7   *Rou* I: 1–6; Burgess (2004: 223). The first six lines of *Rou* III are almost identical to those of *Rou* I: 'Pur remembrer des ancesurs / Les feiz e les diz e les murs, / Les felunies des feluns/ E les barnages des baruns / Deit l'um les livres e les gestes E les estoires lire a festes.'

8   For a detailed comparative analysis of the dating styles of Dudo, Benoît de Sainte-Maure and Wace, see Mathey-Maille (2007: 21–53).

internal dating information in the form of the duration of successive rules. We are thus told that King Stephen reigned for 19 years (135) and King Henry I for 36 years and a half years (146); William (the Conqueror) was in his twelfth year of rule when he was victorious at the battle of Val-ès-Dunes (155), was duke of Normandy for 32 years, then both duke and king for a further 21 years (186–187); Robert the Magnificent was duke of Normandy for 7 years (221); Duke Richard II died in the thirtieth year of his rule (234); Richard I governed Normandy for 53 years, a detail mentioned twice (267 and 281); and William Longsword was duke for 25 years (301).

This list is noteworthy for what is missing—there is no mention of the length of the brief rule of Duke Richard III, or even of the very name of Duke Robert Curthose. Only the direct ancestors of Henry II have been foregrounded, while the rule of William the Conqueror is given special prominence, twice with reference to Normandy rather than England. In the 'Chronique ascendante', the chronological anchoring of the dukes prior to the Conquest is self-referential rather than universal, and the achievements chosen for celebration are closely linked with the Norman religious houses founded or supported by Rollo's descendants, in particular Cerisy, Fécamp, St Vandrille en Caux, Mont Saint-Michel or Jumièges. Anecdotes relating to the period following William the Conqueror's obtaining the crown of England, by contrast, are mostly located in England. Place is as significant as time, perhaps even more so.

Rou I stands alone in that the events narrated are located mostly outside of Normandy and have as main protagonist an anti-hero unrelated to the Norman dukes other than through his Scandinavian origins. It features no specific dates at all, but is placed at the time of the dismembering of the Carolingian empire, under 'King Louis', that is, Louis the Pious, son of Charlemagne (*Rou* I, 283–316). We are therefore within the world of the 'matière de France', associated with Charlemagne and his successors; the internecine fighting that allows Hasting to devastate France provides confirmation of the degeneracy of the French memorably denounced in the 'Chronique ascendante' (50): 'forslignié sont dont l'en souloit chanter', ('they have degenerated, those of whom songs were once sung'). *Rou* I functions as a justification of the narrator's anti-French stance in the 'Chronique ascendente', but equally provides a foil for Hasting's younger compatriot Rollo, particularly with regard to his attitude towards Christianity. It is no coincidence that the account of Hasting's sacrilegious behaviour at Luni takes over a third of this part of the *Rou*.

Rou II, by contrast, is punctuated by chronological references, with three years explicitly mentioned: 866, the year Rollo arrives in Normandy (393); 912, when Rollo's baptism fully makes him a worthy ruler (1171); and 966, the murder of Rollo's pious son, William Longsword (2012–2013), who died before he was allowed to act on his vocation for monastic life.[9] From the outset, these two rulers are associated with relics and religious houses, particularly Jumièges (400–402; 1701–1702). The longer anecdotes in this part of the work are concentrated at the end of the rule of the dukes, following a pattern of coming to power—overcoming opposition—achievements—offspring—death and burial place. The final element in this sequence, the tomb of the duke, allows the narrator to affirm the Christian credentials of his protagonists: both Rollo and his son William are buried in the church of Our Lady in Rouen and their tombs provide tangible authority to the information given. Wace makes a point of telling us that their epitaphs are still legible (1312–1313 and 2015–2016). *Rou* II ends with the account of the difficult youthful years of William Longsword's son, Richard I, which cover well over half of this part of the *Rou*, a full 2408 lines out of a total of 4425. There are no explicit chronological markers in this section, but it is rich in colourful vignettes and culminates in battle scenes narrated with epic verve as Richard fights off the French with the help of his (pagan) Scandinavian allies.[10]

Rou III is of especial interest from the viewpoint of the construction of an authoritative vernacular narrative in the latter half of the twelfth century. Despite Wace's well-established use of local written archival material which would have enabled him to add precise year references to his main sources, he does not do so. Moreover, he also omits the dates by year found in his main source of such significant events as the years of death of Dukes Richard II, Richard III or Robert I.[11] In the entire 11,440 lines of this final part of the *Rou*, we find only two dates: 996, when Richard II becomes Duke of Normandy at the death of his father Richard I (*Rou* III: 767) and 1066, when Duke William II becomes King of England (*Rou* III: 8985). Moreover, in the following line, the narrator puts a question mark over the very validity of the date of 1066, in what appears to be the tongue-in-cheek proviso of 'se li clerc ont conté par dreit' (literally: 'if the scholars got it right'). A surprising comment considering the importance of an event that was both celebrated and well-recorded. The recourse to multiple sources that did not always agree is of course the hallmark of *Rou* III, and on a certain level this a perfectly reasonable remark in a culture where the New Year did not necessarily start on 1 January. Made in relation to the last year date

---

9   These dates should have read 876, 912 and 945, as in Wace's sources.

10   Duke Richard I is very much depicted in *Rou* II in the mould of the rebelling barons of the 'epic of revolt'; the contrast with *Rou* III suggests that Wace was having to deal with strongly conflicting accounts. See Philip E. Bennett (2006: 41–54).

11   These dates (1026, 1028 and 1035 respectively), are mentioned in the *Gesta Normannorum ducum*, ed. van Houts, Book 2, v.17, vi.2 and vi.12.

to be quoted in the *Roman de Rou*, however, Wace's distancing himself in this way suggests a more programmatic reason for his scepticism, one which could be linked to the desire to retain a strong focus on Normandy at a point where England becomes more central to the concerns of the Norman dukes.

Chronological references in *Rou* III, as in the 'Chronique ascendante', are predominantly made in relation to the length of ducal rules: Richard I dies after 29 years of rule (*Rou* III: 2237), Richard II rules for two years (*Rou* III: 2281), Robert I for eight years (*Rou* III: 3239). The rule of William II, however, stands out for the severity of the obstacles he had to overcome, due to his young age and illegitimate birth. The Battle of Val-ès-Dunes, marking his victory over the Norman opposition, is a turning point in William's rule, and is explicitly placed twelve years after he succeeded his father (*Rou* III: 3588). It is a break with the past, in that the young duke only manages to subdue his barons and close relatives by appealing to the King of France for support, whereas his predecessors—in particular Richard I—are regularly depicted as having to fight against the treacherous kings of France. At the same time, France itself has undergone changes. The death of Lothar, at the time of Duke Richard I, marks the end of the glorious lineage of Charlemagne, an aspect stressed in *Rou* III: 659–664:

> En Lohier faili la ligniee
> Qui longement fu bien prisiee
> Par tut le mund, de Charlemaigne,
> Qui tint Seisuine e Alemaine
> E Rome e France e Lumbardie
> E d'Espaine mult grant partie.

> (With Lothar, the lineage which had been admired for a long time throughout the world came to an end; it was the lineage of Charlemagne, who held Saxony, Germany, Rome, France, Lombardy and a very large part of Spain.)
>
> BURGESS (2004: 98).

These lines implicitly pick up the theme of the degeneracy of the French present in the 'Chronique ascendante'—the Capetians do not have the prestige or pedigree of the Carolingians—and encourage the reader to view events through an epic prism. The paucity of chronological landmarks is accompanied, particularly in the rules of dukes Richard I and Robert I, by strings of striking anecdotes arguably even more memorable than those recounted in relation to the Conquest of England. Richard I is depicted in these anecdotes as a wise

Christian ruler whose Normandy is peopled by mysterious maidens and strange knights. The duke has night vision, defeats an undead man in an isolated chapel at night and acts as intermediary between the devil and an angel fighting over the soul of the sinful sacristan. This is the stuff of legend.[12] The more tangible reality of the duke's rule is attested by his building new churches and monasteries and improving existing ones in Fécamp (705–716), the Mont St Michel (697–700) and Rouen (691–696, 701–704). A chapel is built over his burial place (765–766). Wace's depiction of Duke Robert I is no less colourful. Flamboyant and generous to excess (a trait illustrated by three anecdotes), this Duke dies of poisoning on the way back from a pilgrimage to Jerusalem via Byzantium (giving rise to five lively anecdotes). His tomb in Nicea, we are told, is still standing (3219–3220) and his chamberlain donates the relics obtained in the Holy Land to the abbey of Cerisy.[13]

The larger-than-life quality of these dukes is tempered by the two rules that separate them, which are altogether darker in tone. This is the logical consequence of the historical events that took place at that time: under Richard II, Normandy goes to war against England, the English commit a horrendous massacre of the Danes living in England and Brittany is ravaged by Viking raids. This is also when the seeds of the Conquest are sown, with Alfred and Edward, the young English princes, fostered in Normandy, and Emma, the sister of Duke Richard II, marrying two successive kings of England. Richard III is poisoned after just two years in power, while embroiled in conflict with his brother (and eventual successor) Robert. Wace appears to have exploited the grimness of this period to spell out the strengths and weaknesses of the ducal house, providing a point of comparison for future events. The anecdotes of Richard I and Robert II function as a form of light (though not meaningless!) relief between the near-constant succession of treason, rebellion, conflict and murder that each Norman duke has to confront.

Not all of the anecdotes of *Rou* III are to be found in Wace's written sources. This raises the question of credibility, particularly in a section with so few chronological landmarks. Wace addresses this by emphasising his credentials: he has personally known the three kings Henry of England (*Rou* III: 177–184), is well educated, experienced in writing in the vernacular and a respectable Bayeux prebendary (*Rou* III: 5306–5316). He was an eyewitness to certain events, and can draw upon the accounts of close family members, some of

---

12   A special issue of *Annales de Normandie* (2014) is devoted to Richard I, who entered legend as Richard the Fearless. Wace's anecdotes in this part of the *Rou* are analysed by Blacker (2014: 131–144), Le Saux (2014: 145–160) and Laurent (2014: 161–172).

13   On Wace's anecdotes relating to Robert the Magnificent, see Mathey-Maille (2011: 73–84).

whom appear to have been very close to the dukes themselves.[14] This personal as well as scholarly credibility counterbalances the haziness of anecdotal time.

The rule of William II was obviously of major significance, both for Normandy and for England. A close reading of the account of the run-up to the Conquest and its aftermath suggests a degree of ambivalence on Wace's part, but ostensibly the Duke is given a positive, heroic treatment. His conception and early childhood is the subject of two anecdotes (placed before Robert the Magnificent's departure for Holy Land) that endow him with a quasi-mythical aura, with portents of future grandeur. William the Conqueror's rule fittingly extends over half of the narrative and pride of place is given to the battle of Hastings. The anecdotes in the section prior to the Conquest, however, fall seriously short of the glamour of those relating to his father and great-grandfather; the emphasis is predominantly on the duke's enemies, his various conflicts and his attempts to secure allies. The Conquest of England marks a turning point, signalled inter alia by the unusual wealth of chronological information regarding the Conqueror's death: he was ill for six weeks (*Rou* III: 9163) and died at the age of 64 on 8 November (*Rou* III: 9233), having become Duke of Normandy at the age of seven (*Rou* III: 9235). The rule of William the Conqueror also marks a break in the history of Normandy. Even though Robert Curthose was long dead by the time Wace was penning his history, the length of his rule is not noted. The only regnal length in the final 2000 lines of the *Rou* is that of Henry I, at the very end of the work (*Rou* III: 11,418), where we are told that he reigned for 37 years as King of England. No mention is made of his having also ruled Normandy, which has in this sense been subsumed under England.

The hero of the final section of the *Rou* appears to be Henry I of England, with a sympathetic and entertaining account of the challenges he faced during his youth, but there appears to be little doubt that Wace saw Robert's betrayal by the Normans as a sign of degeneracy on the part of a people who until then had been portrayed as the worthy successors of Charlemagne. The anecdote of the garden of Rouen that never again bore fruit after treason was fomented there (*Rou* III: 11,297–11,308) carries dark warnings that transcend the immediate context. The near-disappearance of chronological references rooted in

---

14   Wace thus states that he was present when the remains of Duke Richard II were ceremoniously removed from his grave in Fécamp (*Rou* III: 2241–2246) and quotes his father's memory of the departure of the Norman vessels for England even though it conflicts with information in his written sources (*Rou* III: 6423–6432). He also appears to claim that Turstin the chamberlain of Robert the Magnificent, was his grandfather on his mother's side (*Rou* III: 3225).

Normandy itself corresponds to the fading of Normandy as a political and cultural power; the only time indication directly relating to the Norman soil is the mention that the war between Henry I and his brother William Curthose lasted six years (*Rou* III: 11, 144). Regnal lengths now refer to those of the kings of England: William Rufus's rule of thirteen years (*Rou* III: 10,034–10,036) and—in the very last lines of the work before the epilogue—Henry I's 37 years as King of England (*Rou* III: 11,417–11,418). None of these important events are dated by year.

In conclusion, it would seem that Wace chose the style of his time references with some care, charting the history of Normandy according to local, internal landmarks, more specifically the regnal length of its dukes. The eschatological dimension implicit in dating by year from the Nativity of Christ is transferred to Norman geography, in particular its churches and religious houses, which themselves are closely connected to Rollo and his successors. After the rule of William the Conqueror, Normandy appears to descend into a temporal limbo, with the frame of reference now focused on the Crown of England. With the Conquest starts a process of *translatio* of Norman prowess to the English kingdom, and as Normandy loses political power, so does she recede from chronological history.

Bibliography

Primary Sources

The Gesta Normannorum ducum of William of Jumièges, Orderic Vitalis and Robert de Torigni. Ed. and trans. Elisabeth M.C. van Houts, Oxford: Clarendon Press, 1992–1995.

[Wace] *Wace's Roman de Brut. A History of the British*. Ed. and trans. Judith Weiss, Exeter: University of Exeter Press, 1999.

[Wace] *Le Roman de Rou de Wace*. Ed. A.J. Holden. Société des anciens textes français. Paris: Picard, 1970–1973.

[Wace] *The History of the Norman People. Wace's Roman de Rou*. Trans. Glyn S. Burgess. Woodbridge: Boydell and Brewer, 2004.

Secondary Sources

Bennett, Matthew (2006). 'The Uses and Abuses of Wace's *Roman de Rou*.' In Burgess and Weiss (2006). 31–40.

Bennett, Philip E. (2006). 'The Reign of Duke Richard in the *Roman de Rou*.' In Burgess and Weiss (2006). 41–54.

Blacker, Jean. (2014). '"Si que jel vi e jeo i ere": témoignages de Wace sur Richard sans Peur.' In Mathey-Maille and Gaucher-Rémond (2014), 131–144.

Blacker, Jean. (2006). 'Narrative Decisions and Revisions in the *Roman de Rou*.' In Burgess and Weiss (2006). 55–71.

Burgess, Glyn S. and Judith Weiss eds. (2006). *Maistre Wace. A Celebration.* Proceedings of the International Colloquium held in Jersey 10–12 September 2004. St Helier: Société Jersiaise.

Laurent, Françoise. (2014). 'Intention didactique ou tentation romanesque? Les anecdotes de la vie de Richard Ier dans le *Roman de Rou* de Wace.' In Mathey-Maille and Gaucher-Rémond (2014). 161–172.

Le Saux, Françoise. (2014). 'Richard le Scandinave? Héroïsme et métissage culturel dans le *Roman de Rou* de Wace.' In Mathey-Maille and Gaucher-Rémond (2014). 145–160.

Le Saux Françoise H.M. (2005). *A Companion to Wace.* Cambridge: D.S. Brewer.

Mathey-Maille, Laurence, and Élisabeth Gaucher-Rémond, eds. (2014). *Richard sans Peur, duc de Normandie entre histoire et légende.* Actes du colloque qui s'est tenu à l'Université du Havre les 29 et 30 mars 2012. *Annales de Normandie. Revue semestrielle d'études regionales* 64.1.

Mathey-Maille, Laurence, and Huguette Legros, eds. (2011). *La Légende de Robert le Diable du Moyen Âge au XXe siècle.* Actes du colloque de Caen des 17 et 18 septembre 2009. Rouen: Édition Paradigme.

Mathey-Maille, Laurence (2011). 'De la chronique à la légende: le portrait de Robert le Magnifique chez Wace et Benoît de Sainte-Maure.' In Mathey-Maille and Legros (2011). 73–84.

Mathey-Maille, Laurence (2007). *Écritures du passé. Histoires des ducs de Normandie.* Paris: Honoré Champion.

24

1095 and All That: Brief Reflections on Social Memory and the 'Non-Canonical' Texts of the First Crusade

Carol Sweetenham

Abstract

The First Crusade is arguably one of the most thoroughly chronicled events in medieval history, with a number of texts devoted entirely or in large part to its events. These texts have been much studied, forming what might be described as the 'canonical texts' of the crusade. This paper looks at depictions and reminiscences of the crusade through a different lens: sources whose primary focus was not the crusade but which preserve some material relating to it. The paper looks at a selection of sources in which we find such material, spanning the twelfth to the fourteenth centuries and with a wide geographical range across Europe. It assesses the extent to which these sources give us additional information about the events of the crusade, and concludes that they are of some value. Arguably however they are of more value in helping us understand the social memory and perceptions of the crusade: what did people remember, and what still mattered enough to recount decades after the events themselves?

• • •

'... a Memorable History [of the First Crusade] comprising all the parts you can remember ...'[1]

• •
•

The First Crusade was one of the most chronicled events of the Middle Ages, seen as literally miraculous: 'hoc enim non fuit humanum opus, sed divinum'

---

1 With apologies to Sellar and Yeatman's *1066 and All That*.

('This was not the work of men: it was the work of God').[2] It was recounted by both eyewitness participants (Raymond of Aguilers, Fulcher of Chartres, the *Gesta Francorum* and Peter Tudebode) and authors in the decade or so which followed (Ralph of Caen, Albert of Aachen, Gilo of Paris and the three reworkings of the *Gesta Francorum* by Baldric of Bourgueil, Guibert of Nogent and Robert the Monk). These have been styled with some justice the 'canonical' texts of the crusade.

However, the crusade had a much wider narrative presence in other histories, texts and chronicles not focused exclusively on the crusade. This paper examines a selection of these sources: these might be characterized as non-canonical accounts. It makes no claim to be a comprehensive survey; the sources have been chosen to reflect a deliberately wide period from the twelfth to the fourteenth century and a geographical range across Europe in order to illuminate how widespread—and consistent—the memory of the events of the Crusade was. It assesses how far they give us additional information and where their authors might have found it. It argues that, whilst these sources are not without value, their importance lies rather in what they tell us about the social memory of the crusade: what did people remember, what still mattered enough to recount and how had the story changed in the telling?

1   The Importance of the First Crusade

The number of texts recounting the crusade and the emphasis on the miraculous nature of its success should not obscure a simple fact: not all authors felt the need to give a detailed account of the events. At one end of the scale, authors such as Orderic Vitalis, William of Malmesbury, Henry of Huntingdon and later Matthew Paris devote considerable space to it. Orderic for example gives a full account spanning two books based on the account of Baldric of Bourgueil.[3] Interestingly some of these comment that the crusade was such an important event that it deserves to be inserted as a digression from the main narrative: 'ob cuius rei magnitudinem digrediendi veniam a lectore postulo' ('On account of the magnitude of this event I beg the reader's indulgence for a digression').[4] Conversely other texts are happy to rely on accounts in other authors: the Imperial Chronicle comments for example that, since others have

---

2   Robert, *Prologus*, 4.
3   Orderic books IX and X.
4   Henry 423, Greenway's translation.

already produced elegant accounts of the crusade, it feels no need to do likewise; and the early thirteenth-century Hugh of Lerchenfeld gives up part way through, reducing the crusade to a whirlwind list of names and signposting his readers to Robert the Monk's *Historia Iherosolimitana* instead.[5]

In other texts interest in the events surrounding the crusade is limited to its local impact. Sicard of Cremona refers to the crusade, for example, in a sentence referring to crusaders passing through Cremona on their way to the Holy Land.[6] Local interest tends to be centred around two aspects in particular: the preaching tour of Urban in 1095 and the role of local crusaders. Geoffrey of Vigeois for example describes Pope Urban's visit to the Limousin, the churches visited and dedicated and the prelates who attended; his preaching of the crusade is alluded to in a sentence, 'exhortabatur de Jerosolymitano itinere' ('he exhorted them to undertake the journey to Jerusalem').[7] Similarly, the *Gesta Andegavensium peregrinorum* ascribed to Fulk le Réchin concentrates on Urban's visit to Anjou and in particular on acts relating to Fulk's family: the translation of his uncle Godfrey's remains to the church of St Nicholas, and the Pope presenting a golden flower to Fulk as a token of exceptional esteem.[8] The second aspect, the role of local crusaders, has been much studied in recent years, with the crusade closely linked to the construction of aristocratic and family identity. Hence we see local leaders included amongst the leaders of the crusade as in Geoffrey of Vigeois, who includes Raymond of Turenne and Golfier of Las Tours. We also see their experiences highlighted: thus Fulk's description of the crusade focuses almost entirely on the local lords Hugh of Chaumont and Ralph of Beaugency.[9]

Many of the texts extend the story of the crusade to the disastrous follow-on expedition of 1101 and beyond, as indeed do Fulcher, Guibert, Albert and Ralph. What we see in the non-canonical accounts, however, is that expedition presented as a follow-on to and even an inevitable result of the crusade. Geoffrey of Châlard, for example, in a short notice preserved in his anonymous *Vita* describes Urban's preaching followed immediately by William IX taking the Cross for the 1101 crusade. This marks a move away from the initial overwhelming amazement at the success of the crusade to a more distanced appreciation of its role in the course of events.

---

5 *Chronicles of the Investiture Contest*, 188; Hugh of Lerchenfeld chapter VI.
6 Sicard 161–162.
7 Geoffrey 427.
8 Fulk chapter I, 345. For significance O'Farrell Rowe (1931).
9 Paul (2005).

2   The Historical Value of the Non-canonical Texts

With the partial exception of Fulk and Geoffrey, who heard Urban's preaching though not at Clermont, none of these authors were eyewitness participants of the crusade. Some had access to eyewitness sources. Most, however, even in the years soon after the crusade relied largely or entirely on written sources. The early twelfth-century anonymous *Narratio Floriacensis* for example comments 'prodigia ostendit Salvator ... quae nos, quoniam aliorum scriptis tenentur, omisimus' ('the Redeemer manifested prodigies ... which we have omitted since they can be found in the writings of others').[10]

What is striking is the diversity of sources used. Some texts mention Alexius seeking help from the West; the early twelfth-century Hugh of St-Fleury quotes from his apocryphal letter to Robert of Flanders, also referred to by Hugh of Lerchenfeld.[11] Robert's work is specifically referred to by Hugh of Lerchenfeld under the name *Historia Gotefridi*. Fulcher of Chartres is widely used, particularly for events after 1099. To some extent we can track textual relationships: the anonymous account from Fleury is near-identical with that of Sigebert of Gembloux, and Sigebert in turn forms the basis for the account of Otto of Freising. All these quote near-verbatim parts of the letter sent from Daimbert to the West in September 1100: the low price of provisions early on in the crusade, the numbers of combattants and details of Saracen casualties at the battle of Ascalon, and the description of the crusade as a succession of six battles. Frutolf likewise draws extensively on the letter.[12] In some texts, conversely, it is impossible to discern a particular or indeed any source: the thirteenth century *Estoire de Jérusalem et d'Antioche* pursues a course largely of its own until 1099, when it adopts a narrative recognisably that of Fulcher of Chartres. What this tells us is that these sources were widely available at an early stage and continued to be available into the thirteenth century. It also tells us that there was no one obvious source to follow.

Many of the texts also contain unique information about the crusade. The anonymous chronicle from Fleury adds a story about the nephew of Baldwin being sawn in half 'in modum ligni' ('just like a block of wood') when captured by Saracens.[13] The *Narratio* contains extensive detail on the siege of Jerusalem and the crusade of 1101 not found elsewhere.[14] We might, however, want to draw

---

10   *Narratio* chapter V, 357.
11   Hugh of St-Fleury chapter I 363; Hugh of Lerchenfeld chapter 2. Text of letter in *Kreuzzugs-briefe*; translation and references in my translation of Robert the Monk.
12   *Chronicles*, 133–136.
13   *Anonymi* chapter XIV, 373.
14   *Narratio* chapters VIII–X, 358–360.

a tenuous line between information which adds to our knowledge and information which appears to dramatize familiar elements of the crusade. Thus the
Narratio contains a dramatic deathbed confession by Bohemond's brother Guy
about his treacherous relations with the Greeks: this is likely to tell us more
about the enduring theme of perceived Byzantine treachery during the crusade than an actual event.[15] The same text underlines the fact that Godfrey was
not king of Jerusalem by describing the other leaders pressurising him not to
adopt the title of king.[16] This information cannot be verified precisely because
it is unique; but it gives us at the least an insight into what contemporaries
believed to have happened.

There are reasons to treat the testimony in these texts with some caution.
Even texts written at or near the time of the crusade contain inaccuracies.
Fulk for example describes Eustace of Boulogne as Godfrey's father rather
than his brother, and sets the arrival of Corbaran three years rather than
three days after the taking of the city.[17] Authors betray a measure of uncertainty about key events or characters of the crusade: thus Fulk refers to Peter
the Hermit as 'heremita quidem, Petrus Acheriensis' ('a certain hermit, Peter
of Achères').[18] Some authors indeed comment on these difficulties: Otto of
Freising recounts in some detail the martyrdom of Thiemo of Salzburg, but
questions the veracity of the story on the grounds that Islam does not wor-
ship idols.[19] All this suggests that knowledge of the crusade was not necessarily easy to verify amongst those who had not been involved or close to the
events, and that even major events of the crusade were not necessarily well
known.

Similarly material may be presented reflecting popularly held conventions.
The martyrdom of Thiemo of Salzburg after the 1101 crusade is recorded in three
separate but closely related accounts, two claiming to be eyewitness. The archbishop refuses to repair a Saracen idol, is mocked by a devil inside an image of
Mohammed, and is martyred at very great and horrible length. This reflects two
intersecting sets of conventions. As martyr Thiemo refuses to betray his faith
no matter how appalling the consequences, and his suffering exalts his martyrdom. Islam meanwhile is presented in a hideously distorted fashion familiar
from the conventions of the *chanson de geste*.[20]

---

15   *Narratio* chapter XV, 362.
16   *Narratio* chapter X, 360.
17   Fulk chapter II, 346; chapter V, 347.
18   Fulk chapter II, 346.
19   Otto 411–412.
20   Tolan (2002: 108–109); Camille (1989: 129–164).

However we should not dismiss entirely the testimony of these accounts. Distance from the events does not preclude perceptive judgements, giving us an insight into how the events of the crusade were perceived outside the immediate circle of those involved. Thus Sigebert comments with acerbic accuracy that Antioch was handed over to Bohemond 'propter vitandum tedium et famem et maxime propter discordias principum' ('owing to the miseries of daily existence, hunger, and above all because of disagreements between the princes').[21] There is also some evidence of detailed knowledge of events, albeit preserved in a somewhat garbled form. The continuator of Frutolf of Michelsberg for example inserts an episode into material drawn from the letter of Daimbert of Pisa in which during the siege of Antioch the emir of Babylon (Cairo) borrows the best fighters from the Frankish force in order to intimidate Jerusalem into surrender by showing off the strength of his supposed allies: whether or not this happened, it reflects the actual conquest of Jerusalem from the Turks by the Egyptian Fatimids in 1098.[22]

3   The Creation of a Social Memory of the Crusade

None of these texts were written by eyewitnesses of the crusade. Neither, unlike many of the authors of the canonical texts, did their authors have a particular personal or political interest in the outcome. This does not mean that the authors do not approach the text from a specific standpoint: on the contrary they have particular reasons for describing the crusade in the way they do whether as of local interest or as an essential constituent of universal history. But because they are one step removed from the crusade they give us an insight into the social memory and hence construction of a crusade narrative.

It is possible to discern the outline of what one might call a popularly accepted version of crusade events: as Abbott comments on the construction of narratives over time, 'elements of the story persist even as they are subject to change'.[23] We see a similar process in these narratives: a focus on relatively few events of the crusade, the details of which differ across texts but which form a recognized narrative of highlights. It might seem a bit perverse to include in this list elements which are conspicuous by their lack of emphasis compared to the stress laid on them on the canonical accounts: but this in itself tells us

---

21   Sigebert cols. 226–227.
22   *Chronicles*, 156.
23   Abbott (2002: 24).

something about elements seen as important to the crusade by participants which were less important to later audiences, and therefore largely dropped out of social memory.

- The crusade begins with Urban's preaching in response to the humiliations suffered by Christianity in Jerusalem, 'derisiones in Christum dominum et in religionem nostram' ('the mocking indignities inflicted on the Lord Christ and on our religion').[24] In some texts Peter the Hermit is a key figure, Hugh of Fleury for example describing him as one of the leaders of the crusade; in others such as Geoffrey of Vigeois or the *Narratio Florinacensis* he is not even mentioned.[25] Some texts such as the *Narratio* mention celestial portents; these are described in great detail by the anonymous continuator of Frutolf.[26]
- There is an enormous wave of response. Many texts such as Hugh of Fleury, Geoffrey of Vigeois, Sigebert and the continuator of Frutolf lay stress on the range of crusaders.[27]
- A list of leaders is routinely given, generally including Adhemar, Godfrey and his brothers Eustace and Baldwin, Robert of Flanders, Hugh of Vermandois, Stephen of Blois, Raymond IV, Bohemond and Robert of Normandy. Geoffrey of Vigeois adds Anselm of Ribemont, Raymond of Turenne and Golfier of Lastours; Sigebert adds Baldwin of Mons.[28]
- Several texts refer to the massacres of the Jews in the Rhineland, and Geoffrey of Vigeois explicitly describes Folmarus 'comes Metensis' as one of the leaders of the crusade who takes the cross. The massacres are referred to by Geoffrey, Sigebert and the *Anonymi*, and both Frutolf and his continuator.[29]
- Greek treachery, a theme particularly emphasized in the *Narratio Floriacensis* and by Frutolf's continuator in his account of 1101.[30]
- Little emphasis on events at Nicaea and the battle of Dorylaeum; the former is passed over even in early texts such as the *Narratio Floriacensis* and Hugh of Fleury. The *Gesta Adhemari*, based on Raymond of Aguilers, gives more detail on both and Fulk refers to the battle though not by name.[31]
- Selected highlights of events at Antioch: we find consistent references to famine, the escape down ropes of some Christians, the surrender of the city

---

24 Hugh of Fleury chapter I, 363.
25 Hugh of Fleury chapter II, 364.
26 *Narratio* chapter I, 356.
27 Hugh of Fleury chapter I, 363; Geoffrey 427; SG col. 226; *Chronicles*, 146.
28 Geoffrey 428; SG col. 226.
29 Geoffrey 428; SG col 226; *Anonymi* chapter I, 371; *Chronicles*, 130–131, 151–153.
30 *Narratio* chapter III, 357; chapter XI, 361; chapter XIV, 362; *Chronicles*, 163–165.
31 *GA* chapter III, 354; Fulk chapter III, 346.

by treachery, the flight of Stephen of Blois and the discovery of the Holy Lance. There is relatively little emphasis on the battle of Antioch and less on intervention by the saints, who are mentioned by Hugh of St Fleury and Hugh of Lerchenfeld.[32]

- In a similar vein there is relatively little justification of Bohemond's possession of Antioch. Hugh of Fleury however talks in positive terms about this: 'tradita est conservanda Buiamundo, assensu totius populi et consilio procerum sapientium' ('[Antioch] was handed over to Bohemond for safe keeping with the agreement of the entire crusade and on the advice of the wise lords').[33] The arguments mattered intensely in the first years of the twelfth century, but their importance was to fade with the death of Bohemond.

- Some comment on the problems experienced during the autumn of 1098, but relatively little reference to cannibalism; this is found only in Sigebert and the *Anonymi*, who describe it both at Antioch and at Ma'arrat-an-Nu'man.[34] The Old French Crusade Cycle lays the responsibility entirely on the Tafurs, semi-outcasts in the Christian army. Unease about the episode clearly lingered.[35]

- Reference to the siege towers at Jerusalem and to walking barefoot round the walls. Many texts such as Hugh of Fleury and Sigebert refer to the amount of blood spilt at the Temple.[36]

- Limited reference to the battle of Ascalon other than in the tradition represented in Sigebert and based on Daimbert's letter.[37]

- General agreement that Godfrey was ruler, for example in Hugh of Fleury. The *Narratio* is clear however that Godfrey refused to be king under pressure from the other leaders.[38]

- Some discussion of the crusade of 1101: significant details in the *Narratio* and the anonymous continuator of Frutolf.[39]

This differs in several respects from what one might call the canonical narrative. Unsurprisingly, it places more emphasis on events in Europe at the start of the crusade and less on those in the Holy Land. There is less sense of the turning points which could have spelt disaster for the crusade—Dorylaeum, the battle of Antioch and the need to defend the newly conquered city in the battle of

---

32   Hugh of Fleury, chapter V, 365; Hugh of Lerchenfield chapter X, 384.
33   Hugh of Fleury, chapter VI p. 365.
34   *Anonymi* chapter V, 371; SG cols. 226–227.
35   For discussion and references see Sweetenham (2014).
36   Hugh of Fleury chapter VII, 366; SG col. 227.
37   SG cols. 227–228.
38   Hugh of Fleury chapter VIII, 367; *Narratio* Chapter X, 360.
39   *Narratio* chapter XI, 360–361; *Chronicles*, 162–171.

Ascalon. There is too less sense of the divinely ordained success of the crusade and more emphasis on the failure of 1101.

Two elements are particularly worth noting. The first is the large number of references to the massacres of the Jews in the Rhineland, something absent from the canonical texts bar Albert of Aachen who criticises these attacks.[40] Frutolf's continuator draws a contrast between those leading the massacres and the behaviour of Godfrey.[41] Arguably the massacres would have sat uncomfortably in an account of an enterprise blessed by God.

The second is the lack of emphasis on Bohemond's achievements. A longrunning debate in First Crusade scholarship is the extent to which Bohemond argued the legitimacy of his possession of Antioch in order to promote his personal agenda in the West.[42] However we see relatively little of this in these texts. Where Bohemond is mentioned specifically, there is consensus that the crusaders agreed to hand Antioch to him. However there is little if anything about his role in arranging the surrender of Antioch or his leadership in the subsequent battle, and relatively little about the battle itself or the saints implied as intervening to help the Normans. This suggests that, if Bohemond's aim was to use his crusade experiences as propaganda, it did not meet with universal or long-lasting recognition.

The construction of a social memory needs, by definition, to be memorable: 'to be remembered at all, the facts must be preserved in images, arranged in stories'.[43] What we see in this collective account is a nucleus of scenes and images which constitute a remembered story of the crusade. This gives us some insight into how the crusade was generally perceived in Western Europe as opposed to the narrative created by those in Outremer (Fulcher, Ralph, William of Tyre) or those seeking to retrofit a theological narrative (Robert, Guibert, Baldric).

4   The Evolution of Social Memory

With increasing distance from the events of the crusade, the social memory evolved further away from the events of 1095–1099. This is not to suggest that authors did not continue to produce detailed accounts of the crusade, as Matthew Paris did in his *Chronica Maiora*. And the received story of the crusade

---

40   Albert book I chapter 26–27.
41   *Chronicles*, 151–153.
42   Russo, 'Il viaggio'.
43   Fentress and Wickham (1992: 73).

continues to be recognisable even in the more fanciful accounts. The thirteenth century account included in the universal history of Alberto Milioli follows the familiar narrative arc of Peter the Hermit—Urban—Antioch—Jerusalem—Ascalon. Whilst some of the details have been confused, with for example the Turk who betrays Antioch encouraged by St George described in terms familiar from the *Gesta Francorum*, the author clearly had access to Fulcher of Chartres and quotes hexameters from his work.[44]

In parallel we see refractions of the crusade where fictional elements increasingly seep into perceived reality. 'The social meaning of memory .... is little affected by its truth; all that matters is that it be believed'; social memories might combine the fictional and the factual.[45] One version of this lies in what expanded into an entire poetic fictional universe of the crusade, taking events from the Crucifixion up to just before the loss of Jerusalem in 1187.[46] The Old French Crusade Cycle developed out from the original nucleus focused on the crusade itself (the *Chanson d'Antioche*, *Chanson des Chétifs* and *Chanson de Jérusalem*), acquiring a long prequel about the ancestry of Godfrey of Bouillon and an equally long sequel covering the events of the twelfth century, and eventually transforming the events of 1095–1099 into a fantasy world where the arch-adversary Kerbogha converts to Christianity and crusaders consort with the King of the Fairies. This fictional version became welded together with more factual material in some of the later non-canonical accounts. The thirteenth-century universal chronicle of Alberic Trium Fontium, for example, quotes the entirely fanciful events of the *Chanson des Chétifs* from the cycle as fact, referring to Harpin of Bourges and Richard of Chaumont.[47]

Other accounts continued to be produced alongside these fictional versions. The thirteenth-century *Estoire de Jérusalem et d'Antioche* gives us some insight into quite how far such a narrative could evolve.[48] The account begins with the siege of Jerusalem and the pilgrimage there by Charlemagne.[49] Peter the Hermit then goes to Jerusalem with Robert le Diable, a journey which happened in 1034 although dated by the text to 1099.[50] Peter goes to Constantinople; however the unidentified but Bad Abbot of St Genepuire influences the emperor's mind against him, based on his personal experience of

---

44   *Alberti liber*; for St George 630 and GF 69; hexameters 629 and Fulcher I.23, 631 and
      Fulcher I.30.
45   Fentress and Wickham (1992: xi).
46   Cycle (1977–2003); Crist and Cook (1972).
47   Albericus 807; *Chétifs* laisses 1–40.
48   Dating by Meyer (1894).
49   *Estoire* 623.
50   *Estoire* 623–624.

poisoning Robert Guiscard to save the Byzantine empire, and suggests that the emperor should encourage Soliman to attack the hermit. This Soliman does at Nicaea with help from Salahi (Saladin?), deciding inexplicably however to spare Peter. Peter now meets Urban and receives a mandate to preach the crusade.[51] At Clermont William of Poitiers is the first to take the cross, accompanied by such luminaries as Robert de St-Rémi (the author of the *Historia Iherosolimitana* in a new guise?), Lamberc king of Hungary and Godfrey's (non-existent) brother Ralph.[52] On reaching Constantinople Bohemond has to give his (non-existent) son to the emperor as a hostage at the suggestion of the (non-existent but ever-helpful) abbot of St Genepuire.[53] Events continue in this fashion to the despair of the editors of the *Recueil* until Godfrey is elected king in preference to William of Poitiers, Robert of Normandy and Robert of Flanders and the crusade comes to a Full Stop.[54] Thereafter the text follows Fulcher of Chartres with some measure of fidelity.

It is easy to poke fun at such an account. We might wonder (fruitlessly) why an author who clearly had access to Fulcher's account, recounting for example the episode of the drowned pilgrims found to have crosses on them from Fulcher, did not make more use of it.[55] But what it shows us is that interest in the crusade remained strong enough in the thirteenth century for stories to be circulating, albeit by now in distinctly garbled form, and to be worth writing down. And that in turn tells us something about the tenacity of the social memory around the crusade. Rather than despair over the inaccuracies of the *Estoire* as a source we should meet such a text on its own terms: a valuable if somewhat offbeat witness to the fact that the social memory of the crusade was alive and well more than a century after it happened.

Bibliography

Abbreviations

MGH, SS   Monumenta Germaniae Historica, Scriptores
PL   *Patrologiae cursus completus*. Series Latina, J.P. Migne
RHC.Occ   *Recueil des Historiens des Croisades, Historiens Occidentaux*, Académie des Inscriptions et Belles-Lettres, Paris 1841–1906, 16 vols.

---

51   *Estoire* 624–625.
52   *Estoire* 625–626.
53   *Estoire* 628.
54   *Estoire* 639.
55   *Estoire* 628; Fulcher I.8.

Primary Sources—Editions

[Alexius, letter of.] For the letter see *Kreuzzugsbriefe* 129–136; for translation and references see my translation of Robert the Monk, *Robert the Monk's History of the First Crusade: Historia Iherosolimitana*. Aldershot: Ashgate, 2005. 219–222.

Albericus Trium-fontium monachus: *Chronica a monacho Novi-monasterii Hoiensis interpolata circa 1241*. MGH SS 23, 1874. 674–950; 803–813.

Albert of Aachen, *Historia Ierosolimitana: History of the Journey to Jerusalem*, ed. and trans. Susan B. Edgington. Oxford: OUP, 2007. Referred to as Albert.

[Albertus Miliolus].*Alberti Milioli Notarii Regini Liber de Temporibus*, ed. Oswald Holder Egger, MGH SS 31. 1903. 336–539; 29–31.

Anonymi Florinensis Brevis Narratio Belli Sacri, RHC Occ. vol. 5. 371–373. Referred to as *Anonymi*.

Baldric of Bourgueil: *Historia Jerosolimitana* ed. Steven Biddlecombe. Woodbridge: Boydell and Brewer, 2014.

Chronicles of the Investiture Contest: Frutolf of Michelsberg and his continuators, trans. T.J.H. McCarthy. Manchester: MUP, 2014. Referred to as *Chronicles*.

[Daimbert, letter of.] Hagenmeyer, *Kreuzzugsbriefe* 167–174.

Li Estoire de Jérusalem et d'Antioche, RHC. Occ V. 621–648. Referred to as *Estoire*.

Fulcher of Chartres, *Historia Hierosolymitana (1095–1127)*, ed. Heinrich Hagenmeyer (Heidelberg: Carl Winter, 1913). Referred to as Fulcher.

Gesta Adhemari, Episcopi Podiensis, Hierosolymitana, RHC.Occ. vol. 5. 354–355.

Gesta Andegavensium Peregrinorum, RHC Occ. vol. 5. 345–347 Also edited by Louis Halphen and René Poupardin, *Chronique des contes d'Anjou et des seigneurs d'Amboise*. Paris: Picard, 1913. 232–239. Referred to as Fulk.

Gesta Francorum et aliorum Hierosolimitanorum, ed. Roger A.B. Mynors, trans. Rosalind Hill. London: Nelson, 1962. Referred to as GF.

Vita Gaufredi Castaliensis, ed. Auguste Bosvieux, *Mémoires de la Société des Sciences naturelles et archéologiques de la Creuse* III (1862) 75–119. 90–92.

[Geoffrey of Vigeois]. *Ex chronico Gaufredi coenobitae, Recueil des Historiens des Gaules et de la France*, Martin Bouquet, vol. 12. Paris, 1781. 421–451. 427–428. The new edition by Pierre Botineau and Jean-Loup Lemaître, trans. Bernadette Barrière. Paris: Editions de Boccard, 2021 was not available at time of writing. Referred to as Geoffrey.

Gilo of Paris, *Historia Vie Hierosolimitanae*, ed. and trans. Chris W. Grocock and J. Elizabeth Siberry. Oxford: OUP, 1997.

Guibert of Nogent, *Dei Gesta per Francos et cinq autres textes*, ed. Robert B.C. Huygens, CCCM 127A. Turnhout: Brepols, 1996.

Henry of Huntingdon, *Historia Anglorum: the History of the English People*, ed. and trans. Diana Greenway. Oxford: Clarendon Press, 1996. 423–443. Referred to as Henry.

Hugh of Lerchenfeld, *Ratisponensis Canonici Breviarium Passagii in Terram Sanctam*, RHC.Occ. vol, 5. 380–384. Referred to as Hugh of Lerchenfeld.

Hugh of Fleury, *Modernorum regum Francorum actus*, MGH SS 9, 376–395, ed. Georg Waitz. 1851. Cited from the excerpt in RHC.Occ vol. 5. 363–367, *Hugonis de Sancta Maria Itineris Hierosolymitani compendium*. Referred to as Hugh of Fleury.

Kreuzzgsbriefe: Heinrich Hagenmeyer, *Die Kreuzzugsbriefe aus den Jahren 1088–1100*. Innsbrück: Verlag der Wagner'schen Universitätsbuchhandlung, 1901.

Matthew Paris, *Chronica Maiora* ed. Henry R. Luard, 6 vols. London: Rolls, 1872–1882. Vol. 2 43–110

Narratio Floriacensis de captis Antiochia et Hierosolyma et obsesso Dyrrachio, RHC OCC vol. 5. 356–362. Referred to as *Narratio*.

The Old French Crusade Cycle ed. Jan A. Nelson and Emanuel J. Mickel (1977–2003). 10 vols. Tuscaloosa: University of Alabama. Vol. 4, *La Chanson d'Antioche*, ed. Jan A. Nelson (2003); vol. 5 *La Chanson des Chétifs* ed. Geoffrey M. Myers, (1981); vol. 6 *La Chanson de Jérusalem* ed. Nigel Thorp (1992).

[Orderic Vitalis]. *The Ecclesiastical History of Orderic Vitalis*, ed. and trans. Marjorie Chibnall, 6 vols. Oxford: Clarendon Press, 1969–1980. Books IX and X in vol., v.

[Otto of Freising]. *The Two Cities: a Chronicle of Universal History to the year 1146 AD by Otto, bishop of Freising*, translated Charles C. Mierow. New York: Columbia University Press, 1928. 405–410. Referred to as Otto.

Passiones beati Thiemonis, RHC.Occ vol. 5. 357–381.

[Ralph of Caen]. *Radulphi Cadomensis Tancredus*, ed. Edoardo d'Angelo. Turnhout: Brepols, 2011.

[Raymond of Aguilers]. *Le 'liber' de Raymond d'Aguilers*, ed. John H. and Laurita L. Hill. Paris: Paul Geuthner, 1969.

[Robert the Monk]. *The Historia Iherosolimitana of Robert the Monk*, ed. Damien Kempf and Marcus Bull. Woodbridge: Boydell and Brewer, 2013.

[Sicard of Cremona]. *Sicardi episcopi Cremonensis Cronica—1213*, ed. Oswald Holder Egger, MGH.SS 31. 1903. 22–181

Sigebert of Gembloux. *Chronica* PL vol. 160 9–546, cols. 225–228. Referred to as SG.

[Tudebode]. *Historia de Hierosolymitano Itinere*, ed. John H. and Laurita L. Hill. Paris: Paul Geuthner, 1977.

William of Malmesbury, *Gesta Regum Anglorum* ed. and trans. Roger A.B. Mynors, 2 vols. Oxford: Clarendon Press, 1998–1999. Book IV, chapters 343–371;

Secondary Sources

Abbott, H. Porter (2002; third edition 2021) *The Cambridge Introduction to Narrative*. Cambridge: Cambridge University Press.

Camille, Michel (1989). *The Gothic Idol: Ideology and Image-Making in Medieval Art*. Cambridge: Cambridge University Press.

Cook, Robert and Larry Crist (1972): *Le deuxième cycle de la croisade: deux études sur son développement*. Geneva: Droz.

Fentress, James and Chris Wickham (1992). *Social Memory*. Oxford: Blackwell.

Meyer, Paul (1894). 'Notice sur un manuscrit de la Bibliothèque Sainte-Geneviève ren-
fermant des extraits de Maurice de Sully.' *Romania* 23: 497–507.

Paul, Nicholas (2006). 'The Chronicle of Fulk le Réchin: a reassessment.' *Haskins Society
Journal* 18: 19–35.

Paul, Nicholas (2005). 'Crusade, memory and regional politics in twelfth-century
Amboise.' *Journal of Medieval History* 31.2: 127–141.

Rowe, J. O'Farrell (1931): 'The Pope's Golden Rose'. *Irish Monthly* 59.697: 454–457.

Russo, Luigi (2005). 'Il viaggio di Boamondo d'Altavilla in Francia (1106): un riesame.'
Archivo Storico Italiano 163: 3–42.

Sweetenham, Carol (2014). 'The Count and the Cannibals: the Old French Crusade
Cycle as a Drama of Salvation'. *Jerusalem the Golden: the Origins and impact of the
First Crusade*, ed. Susan B. Edgington and Luis García-Guijarro. Turnhout: Brepols.
307–328.

Tolan, John (2002). *Saracens: Islam in the medieval European imagination*. New York:
Columbia University Press.

25

Between Material Reality and Literary *Topos*: 'Towns' in the *Anglo-Saxon Chronicle*

Letty ten Harkel

Abstract

This paper discusses the role of 'towns' in the *Anglo-Saxon Chronicle* from an interdisciplinary perspective, drawing on insights from the discipline of archaeology. How did the *Chronicle* depict these places? Can we discern changes over time? Through an analysis of the *Chronicle* texts as a living set of documents, the paper comments both on the role of 'towns' in early medieval England and on the function of the *Chronicle* in contemporary society. It concludes that 'towns' in the *Anglo-Saxon Chronicle* existed between material reality and literary topos: their physicality carried as much symbolism as their literary depictions.

1 Introduction

I first encountered early medieval England in 1996, during an introductory course in Old English taught by Erik. I do not know whether it was Erik's enthusiasm, or the fact that Old English was more 'my' kind of thing than other introductory topics, or (most likely) a combination of both, but the early medieval world felt real, exciting, and alive. More than two and a half decades later, I predominantly study the first-millennium inhabitants of the North Sea world through archaeological evidence. In this short contribution, I revisit my favourite set of chronicles—a group of closely related manuscripts jointly referred to as the *Anglo-Saxon Chronicle*—to discuss the role of 'towns' in early medieval society from an interdisciplinary perspective. How did the *Chronicle* depict these places, and how does that compare to their material 'realities' as deducted from archaeological investigations? Were they merely a backdrop for action, or did they serve a narrative function? Can we discern changes over time in the way(s) they were depicted, and how does that compare to their development as complex settlements in the real world?

The *Anglo-Saxon Chronicle* describes a densely named landscape, frequently referencing places that we might recognize as the populated 'towns' of the later period. Their mentions are often devoid of descriptive detail, but—partially thanks to decades of archaeological research—it is clear that they encompassed a variety of places, including fortified centres and the deserted ruins of abandoned Roman towns. The question of what we mean by the word 'town' has been subject to extensive academic debate.[1] During the twentieth century, their economic and demographic aspects stood central.[2] In the last 20 years, however, their ideological dimensions have received more attention, as reminders of the past splendour of the Roman Empire and/or references to the heavenly Jerusalem as the ultimate idea of *civitas*.[3] In this view, the distinction between 'towns' and ecclesiastical settlements such as minsters and abbeys—sharing the same symbolic significance—becomes blurred.

Choosing criteria for inclusion in this paper was no easy feat considering the difficulties of definition and the huge transformations that took place in the settlement landscape of England between the eighth and eleventh centuries. Placename evidence can shed some light on the perception of places by their inhabitants and contemporaries, although categories are overlapping. Relevant suffixes include (variations of) -*burg*, denoting 'fortification' and later 'borough' or 'market town'; -*ceaster*, usually referring to former Roman cities and towns; and those instances of -*wic* that refer to undefended coastal and riverine trading places—often considered 'proto-urban'—but not where they denote places used for specialized production, especially dairy farming.[4] The placename element -*tun* is largely excluded: although etymologically related to present-day 'town', it apparently did not obtain this meaning until the Middle English period, before which it was used for 'village', 'hamlet', 'manor' or 'vill'.[5]

This is not the first discussion of 'towns' in the Old English literary corpus. Bintley's detailed overview of settlements and strongholds in Old English and Anglo-Latin written sources—which also draws on historical and archaeological insights but excludes detailed discussion of the *Anglo-Saxon Chronicle*—distinguishes four phases, starting with an emphasis on 'ruin mythologies'.[6] From the seventh century, the Church makes a major impact, followed—in the Alfredian period—by a symbolic metamorphosis that transformed former

---

1   E.g., Ten Harkel (2013: 157–159).
2   E.g., Astill (2009).
3   E.g., Blair (2006: 247–251); Bintley (2020: 19); Carver (2011: 932–933); Ten Harkel (2013: 157–159).
4   Smith (1970a: 58–62; 85–87; 1970b: 257–263); Swanton (2000: xxxiii).
5   Smith (1970b: 188–198); Swanton (2000: xxxiii).
6   Bintley (2020: 29–73).

Church enclaves into 'places for community and prosperity', paving the way for the 'spiritual strongholds' of later pre-Conquest England.[7]

Bintley's phases reflect the material reality of the developing urban landscape in post-Roman Britain. Before the eighth century, there were no places that we would recognize as 'towns', although the stone-built ruins of Roman cities were tangible reminders of a past urban civilization. The fate of British towns was different to that of their counterparts in areas of the former Roman Empire where the Church retained a stronger grip on society. There, evidence for 'continuity' of urban functionality can be ascribed, at least in part, to the presence of powerful (arch)bishops. From the seventh century, many former Roman towns in Britain were also reoccupied as bishoprics or minsters and— at least among the educated population—imbued with *civitas* symbolism.[8] Archaeological evidence from most former Roman cities in Britain is largely restricted to ecclesiastical activity until the tenth century: as Blair states, these places did not need 'trade, industry, or specialized occupations' to be considered '*civitates*'.[9]

The later ninth and tenth centuries, corresponding to Bintley's Alfredian metamorphosis, saw investment in the refurbishment of old (Iron Age and Roman) and the construction of new fortifications as part of a defensive network against Viking invaders.[10] This was paralleled in the Viking-controlled north and east, with substantial investment in places like York and Lincoln.[11] Some of these (especially those that also fulfilled an ecclesiastical role) grew into complex and multi-functional settlements. In the north, sustained economic and demographic growth followed their defensive/military phase almost immediately, while in the south, this did not happen until the later tenth or eleventh centuries.[12]

Current archaeological understanding of the urbanization of pre-Conquest Britain also has some points of divergence from Bintley's four phases. The eighth century was the heyday of a new settlement form: the aforementioned *wics* or *emporia*—places with relatively large populations specialising in manufacturing and trade—including well-known examples such as York (*Eoforwic*), London (*Lundenwic*), Ipswich (*Gipeswic*) and Southampton (*Hamwic*) in England, and *Quentovic* and *Dorestad* in Francia. Although twentieth-century

---

7   Bintley (2020: 75–185).
8   Blair (2006: 247–248).
9   Blair (2006: 248).
10   Baker and Brookes (2013).
11   E.g., Ten Harkel (2013).
12   Astill (1991).

scholars commonly regarded these as 'proto-urban' settlements—a first step towards the high medieval urbanized landscape—they have made a notably low impact on the surviving textual corpus.[13]

What a close reading of the *Chronicle* can add to this discussion results from the specific characteristics of the genre. In 2002, David Dumville defined a chronicle as a 'living text', stating that 'it was part of the function of a chronicle to be altered', often involving a succession of different authors, later additions or corrections, and new recensions.[14] From the multiple versions, adaptations and reworkings of the *Anglo-Saxon Chronicle*, the focus of this paper will rest on the oldest of the surviving manuscripts—version A—in comparison to the other main versions in Old English (B–E).

Manuscript A (Cambridge, Corpus Christi College MS 173, ff. 1^v–32^r) was written in a single hand until the annal for 891 (corresponding to Bintley's Alfredian reinvention). The period 892–924 is covered by a series of detailed annals representing a contemporary account of the Viking invasions. The later tenth- and eleventh-century entries are largely unique to MS A. In c. 1011, it was transferred from Wessex to Canterbury.[15] It ends after the annal for 1070.[16]

The other surviving versions under consideration here are all later. Manuscript B (British Library MS Cotton Tiberius Avi, ff. 1–34) covers the period up to AD 977 and was written by a single scribe in the later 970s. Manuscripts C (British Library MS Cotton Tiberius Bi, ff. 115^v–64) and D (British Library MS Cotton Tiberius Biv, ff. 3–86), with a hiatus for the period 189–693, were both composed in the mid-eleventh century, adding information from different local sources; C ends in 1066 and D in 1079.[17] Manuscript E (Oxford, Bodleian Library MS Laud 636) is the most recent of the surviving manuscripts, largely copied out in c. 1120 and maintained as a contemporary account until the 1150s.[18] In this paper, only the annals up to 1070 (where version A stops) are considered. All versions discussed here, as well as several other related sources, can be traced back to a now-lost, ninth-century original. The earlier parts of D and E are likely copied from a now-lost manuscript that originated in the north, drawing on Bede's *Ecclesiastical History* and a set of northern annals.[19]

---

13   E.g., Biddle (1976) and Hodges (1982).
14   Dumville (2002: 18, 21).
15   Swanton (2000: xxi–xxii).
16   Swanton (2000: 206).
17   Swanton (2000: xxiii–xxvi).
18   Swanton (2000: xxvi–xxvii).
19   Swanton (2000: xviii, xxix).

If we consider the different parts of the *Chronicle* as products of the times when they were written, version A provides an opportunity to chart any changes in the perceived significance of 'towns' during a key period in the process of urbanization, between the ninth and eleventh centuries. Comparison with the other versions can provide further insights, although the textual relationships between the manuscripts imply that it is mainly in the differences between texts that we should expect to see later voices filter through. Reference to archaeological insights furthermore allows for comparison between the literary and the material worlds of southern Britain between the ninth and twelfth centuries.

This paper is structured into three parts, each corresponding to a group of annals in manuscript A. The first covers the period up to 891, the second 892–924, and the third 924–1070. Key passages are highlighted, differences between the manuscripts are discussed, and placed in the context of archaeological knowledge. The discussion is necessarily brief, but it will hopefully provide an interesting perspective on the role of 'towns' and the significance of the *Anglo-Saxon Chronicle* in ninth- to twelfth-century society.

2 The Period up to AD 891

The first set of annals under consideration provides an insight into the perception of 'towns' in the late ninth century. This was a time when many former Roman cities and forts had long been transformed into important bishoprics or minsters (but had not yet accumulated the full economic and demographic characteristics that *we* might expect a 'town' to have), and when the heyday of the *emporia* was already waning, possibly at least partly as a result of disruptions caused by Viking raids.

Starting with version A, former Roman cities dominate the selection of 'towns' that are mentioned in the annals to AD 891. They consistently have the placename element *-ceastre* (e.g., 'Hrofesceastre', Rochester; 'Wintaceastre', Winchester) to emphasize their Roman origin, except London and Canterbury, which are usually variations of 'Lundenburg' and 'Cantwaraburg'.[20] References are largely devoid of detail. Their role in the narrative mainly falls into two categories: as places of ecclesiastical significance and as military targets (and

---

20   Throughout this paper, all the Old English is taken from Thorpe (2013) and all modern English translations from Swanton (2000). Years, including corrections in brackets, follow Swanton (2000).

here, their role is shared by much lower numbers of other types of places, especially in the ninth-century entries, including newly constructed fortifications).

Both aspects emphasize their symbolic significance. This is aptly illustrated through a brief reference to Asser's *Life of Alfred*, likely written in 893 and a product of the same milieu as the original version of the *Chronicle*. Asser employs the widely used literary *topos* of the capture and/or restoration of a city—often following destruction, commonly by fire—by exemplary rulers on two occasions.[21] In chapter 83 he states that in the year 886, 'Aelfred ... post incendia urbium stragesque populorum, Lundoniam civitatem honorifice restauravit et habitabilem fecit' ('Alfred ... restored the city of London splendidly—after so many towns had been burned and so many people slaughtered—and made it habitable again').[22] In chapter 91, he states that Alfred invested in 'civitatibus et urbibus renovandis et aliis, ubi nunquam ante fuerant, construendis' ('cities and towns to be rebuilt and ... others to be constructed where previously there were none').[23]

Asser uses the words *civitas*, a term that was preserved for the ruins of stone-built Roman towns, and *urbs*, which was used more commonly in Anglo-Latin for places enclosed by earthen ramparts.[24] The *civitates* were the places that, since the arrival of the Augustinian mission in Kent towards the end of the sixth century, had seen the foundation of episcopal sees and minsters in an attempt by the Church to regain spiritual control over a lost province.[25] By linking Alfred explicitly to this process as a restorer of *civitas*, set against the backdrop of city-burning, Asser placed his king in the same tradition, as a restorer of both *civitas* and *Romanitas*.[26]

Turning to the *Chronicle*, if all 78 annals in this section of A that include a mention to any 'town' are considered together, it is notable that the most commonly named 'town' is Rome ('Rome'). It occurs in 19 annals (approximately ¼)—including once to state that 'there was none who travelled to Rome' (889)—followed by London and Rochester (8 annals each) and Winchester (7 annals). Rome's prominence in the *Chronicle* illustrates its importance—as a concept—in the early English mindset.

---

21   E.g., Baghos 2021; Kraus (1994: 270).

22   Keynes and Lapidge (1983: 97–98); Latin from https://www.thelatinlibrary.com/asserius .html.

23   Keynes and Lapidge (1983: 101); Latin from https://www.thelatinlibrary.com/asserius.html.

24   Blair (2005: 248–249).

25   Blair (2005: 249); also see Bintley (2020: 75–76).

26   Blair (2005: 249).

Often the only reason that former Roman towns are mentioned is because they are (arch)bishoprics. For example, the annal for 633 states that 'Paulinus ... occupied the bishop's seat in Rochester'. In other cases, they serve as the location of the baptisms or burials of important individuals, such as the baptisms of Cynegils, Cwichelm and Cuthred at Dorchester in 635, 636 and 639 respectively, or the burials of Eadberht and Egbert in York, mentioned in 738.

The annal for 867 (866) seems to confirm that the former Roman towns were not densely populated places: that year, the raiding-army occupied York city ('Eoforwic ceastre'), seemingly without any resistance, and it is only then that the Northumbrians under Ælla 'gathered a great army and sought out the raiding-army at York city and broke into the city ('ceastre')'. The rendering of York as 'Eoforwic ceastre'—the *ceastre* associated with the *wic*—is consistent in the annals up to 891 in version A. Only the annal for 189 renders the placename as 'Euerwic', but this is a later addition. Given the archaeological evidence for a ninth-century extra-mural settlement at York in the Fishergate area, commonly held to be the *-wic* site, this reinforces the preoccupation of the chronicler with former Roman 'towns' at the expense of the relatively densely-occupied, economically-significant *emporia*.[27]

Comparison with the later manuscripts reveals a less consistent use of language. Most passages that occur in all five versions (e.g., AD 738, 869) retain the *-ceaster* element, but several annals mentioning York are unique to 'northern' versions D–E, and these invariably drop the *-ceaster* element. They include references to (arch)bishops (and, once, a king) of 'Eoferwic' (e.g., AD 744, 766, 777 (779)), thus separating the direct association between (arch)episcopal sees and their Roman heritage. D–E also omit the *-ceaster* element in the annal for 189 (the passage is absent in B–C).

References to London in the different manuscripts of the *Anglo-Saxon Chronicle* provide a parallel. In version A, London is consistently referred to as 'Lundenburg'. The annal for 604 refers to a bishop's seat in 'Lundenwic' (commonly held to indicate the extra-mural settlement that existed in the area where now the Royal Opera House is located, with evidence for specialist manufacturing activity and long-distance trade), but this is a later addition.[28] The passage is absent from versions B–D, but E also renders the name as 'Lundenwic'.[29] Only the annal for 839 (842) gives the name as *Lundenne* (in all versions). References to London that do not occur in version A but do occur in later

---

27   Mainman (2019).
28   Blackmore et al. (2012).
29   This is similar to the entry for 616, which is a later addition in version A, absent from B–D and included in E.

manuscripts drop the -*burg* element almost without fail, as can be seen in the
annals for 656 and 675 (only present in E), 731 (present in D and E) and 883
(present in B–E).

The annal for 886 (885)—the last entry to mention an English 'town' in this
group of annals, present in all versions, and recounting the same events as those
described by Asser (above)—serves a clear narrative function. The chronicler
states that 'King Alfred occupied London fort ('Lundenburg') and all the English race ('all Angelcyn') turned to him'. The -*burg* element (paralleling Asser's
civitas, in this case) is shared by several English fortifications (e.g., *Wihtgaras
byrg* (Wihtgar's stronghold) in 530 and 544, or *Bebbanburh* (Bambury) in 547),
but, interestingly, none of the Viking raiding army's fortifications have the suffix
-*burg*.

To understand the full significance of the passage, the annals up to 891 must
be considered as a whole. Especially the annal for 409 (410) is important, which
states that 'the Goths destroyed the stronghold of Rome ('Romeburg'), and
afterwards the Romans never ruled in Britain'. The third reference to Rome in A,
it uniquely renders the name as 'Romeburg' instead of the usual 'Rome'. More
explicitly than Asser, the chronicler creates a direct link between the loss of
Rome, accompanied by a loss of Roman political power, and the restoration of
London, intrinsically related to political success.

The passage is shared by versions B–C and falls within the hiatus in D, but
in E, A's 'Romeburg' ('the stronghold of Rome') is changed subtly into 'Romana
burh' ('the stronghold of the Romans'), explicitly linking the 'town' to its population in a way that does not occur in earlier versions. It suggests a twelfth-
century understanding of 'towns' as populated places that was somewhat anachronistic. This idea is strengthened by a passage in the annal for 616 in E,
absent from the other manuscripts. Referring to a period before the heyday of
the *emporia*, when archaeological evidence suggests the former Roman towns
were predominantly ecclesiastical enclaves, it states that 'þa wurdon Lunden-
ware heðene' ('at that time the inhabitants of London [lit. 'London-dwellers']
... were heathen').

3   The Period 892–924

In this set of annals, the narrative in A (and B–D) is dense and several differences with the previous section exist (coverage in E is sparse and not included
here). Rome is not mentioned at all: instead, the narrative focuses on the
movements of the English and Viking armies. This was the period—Bintley's
Alfredian reinvention—when old fortifications were refurbished and new ones

constructed as part of a defensive strategy against the Vikings, some of which grew out to become towns.[30] Archaeological evidence for the functioning of these places in ways that we would recognize as 'urban' remains absent for this period, although the text of the *Chronicle* suggests that the strategic and administrative potential of fortified places was increasingly realized.

The literary *topos* of successful kingship linked to the construction/restoration of 'towns' is mainly apparent in A's contemporary account. The last three entries in this section—unique to A—discuss Edward's fortification building, stating that he ordered them to be 'gebetan ٦ gesettan' ('improved and occupied') (922 (918)), 'gesettan ٦ gemannian' ('occupied and manned') and 'gebetan ٦ gemannian' ('improved and manned') (923 (919)) and 'gemannian' ('manned') (924 (920)). In two of the annals, this is paired explicitly with references to the subjugation of groups of people to Edward's rule as king.

In all manuscripts, 'towns' are frequently depicted as populated, although perhaps least clearly in the eleventh-century D-version. The annal for 896 (895) in A–C refers to 'þa men of Lundenbyrig' ('the men of London town'). D changes 'þa men *of* Lundenbyrig' to 'þa men *on* Lundenbyrig' [my emphasis], thus rendering the association between people and *burg* somewhat vaguer. A–C also contain a reference to 'þa men' of Hereford, Gloucester and 'þam niehstum burgum' ('the nearest strongholds') in 918 (914), whereas D omits the phrase 'þa men', but this may be a scribal error.

'Burgware' ('fortification-dwellers') are mentioned for London ('Lundenbyrg') in 894 (893)—although D omits the phrase—and 896 (895), and for Chichester in 895 (894). Swanton translates this term as 'inhabitants' for London (894 (893)) and 'the garrison' for Chichester (895 (894)). Given the use of the same word in two consecutive annals, however, it is more likely that the same meaning was intended and that a clear dichotomy between military and non-military occupation is anachronistic.[31]

The relationship between ecclesiastical authority and 'towns' remains clear, but there is also evidence for secular identities connected to these places. The entry for 897 (896), present in A–D, only identifies ecclesiastical magnates by the 'town' to which they belong (e.g., 'Swiðulf biscop on Hrofesceastre'), while secular ones are identified by regions (e.g., 'Ceolmund ealdorman on Cent'). However, there are now multiple references to generic people 'dwelling' (*buan*) in or 'belonging' (*hieran*) to a *burg*. Examples include the entry for 919 (915) (unique to A), which mentions 'þa burgware þe hie ær budon' ('the

30   Baker and Brookes (2013); Bintley (2020: 119–155).
31   Swanton (2000: 86, 88; also see xxxiii, 147, n. 10).

burgware who had earlier dwelt there' (i.e., in Bedford)). The entry for 918 (914) includes a reference to 'þa ieldstan men ealle mæste þe to Bedanforde hierdon ⁊ eac monige þara þe to Hamtune hierdon' ('almost all the principal men who belonged to Bedford, and also many of those who belonged to Northampton').[32]

The adjective 'ieldstan' indicates a degree of social stratification, also suggested by the first references to (town-)reeves: the Winchester 'wicgefera' (A–D, 897 (896)) and the 'gerefa' of Bath (A–C, 906 (905)), which version D renders as 'tunegerefa'. The element *wic* in 'wicgefera' possibly suggests economic significance. The *tun* element in the eleventh-century D version represents an early example where its meaning had shifted from 'village', 'hamlet', 'manor' or 'vill' to its present meaning of 'town', highlighting the increasing administrative importance of places like Winchester.[33]

4   The Period 925–1070

From the later tenth and eleventh centuries, archaeological evidence points to demographic growth and socio-economic complexity. The narratives in the different *Chronicle* manuscripts diverge increasingly. Coverage in A is thin, but includes several alliterative poems, two of which are considered here. Although the symbolic significance of towns continues to figure prominently, evidence for the greater diversity of 'urban' form and status, and the presence of urban populations, also shines through.

'The Capture of the Five Boroughs' (942) employs the literary *topos* of the capture of a city by a strong king (Edmund) resulting in the liberation of the people, reinforcing the connection of 'towns' to people. The 'cities' in question here are 'burga fife / Ligereceaster / ⁊ Lincylene / ⁊ Snotingaham / swylce Stanford eac / Deoraby' ('five boroughs: Leicester and Lincoln, and Nottingham, likewise Stamford also and Derby'), places with diverse origins as Roman towns and Mercian estate centres.

It is worth noting that the placename Lincoln—despite its Roman origins—does not have the -*ceaster* element, while elsewhere references to London (959, 962) drop the -*burg* element. Different types of economic 'town' now also appear more frequently in A. For example, in 993, the Vikings 'overran' 'Sandwic' ('Sandwich') and 'Gipeswic' ('Ipswich'), while the entry for 1031 describes

---

32   B omits the reference to Northampton. Also see 921 (917): 'Tæmeseforda (Tempsford) ... ⁊ hit budon ⁊ bytledon', and 'se here þe to Hamtune (Northampton) hierde'.

33   See above and Smith (1970b: 188–198); Swanton (2000: xxxiii).

how Canterbury Christ Church receives 'the harbour at Sandwich ('þa hæfenan on Sandwic'), and all the rights that arise there'. This trend becomes more apparent in the eleventh-century entries in versions C–E, when the use of the word 'port' ('market town') appears (e.g., 1010, the 'port' of Northampton (C–E); 1055, the 'port' of Hereford (C–D, but E: 'burh'); 1068, 'þa portmen' ('the men of the market-town') of York (E, but D: 'burhmenn').

'The Capture of the Five Boroughs' is also included in B–D, but absent from E. Later annals in C–D also refer to 'þæt folc into Fifburhingum' ('the people in the Five Boroughs') (C, 1013), which E subtly changes into 'þet folc *of* Fifburhingan' [my emphasis]. By the eleventh century, there was clearly a territorial unit that had derived its name from this group of 'towns'. Versions C–E all state that 'ferde se æþeling ... in to Fif burgum' ('the prince rode ... into the Five Boroughs') (C, 1015).[34] Given the fact that 'The Capture of the Five Boroughs' is absent from E, it is likely that this territory had become a commonly understood entity by the twelfth century at the latest.

The second alliterative poem under consideration here is the annal for 973, present in A–C. It describes the setting for Edgar's coronation as 'ðære ealdan byrig / Acemannes ceastre / eac hi igbuend / oðre worde / beornas Baðan nemnað' ('the ancient town of Ache-man's city—the warriors dwelling in the island also call it by the other term Baths'), using both 'byrig' and 'ceastre' but also referencing its name in common parlance. It is absent from D–E, which place the coronation (in prose) 'æt Hatabaðum', without including any descriptive elements underlining the symbolic significance of the location.

This is not to say that town-symbolism has left the narrative in the eleventh- and twelfth-century versions of the *Chronicle*. Descriptions of the destruction and wholesale burning of 'towns' (for which, on the whole, no archaeological evidence exists) emphasize the direness of the situation in the eleventh-century annals in C–E (e.g., 1003 (Exeter, Wilton), 1004 (Norwich, Thetford), 1006 (Sandwich, Wallingford). This is contrasted with London's resilience: in 994, the Vikings intend to set fire to London but 'suffered more harm and injury than they ever imagined that any town-dwellers ('buruhwaru') would do to them'. In 1009, 'they [the Vikings] often attacked London town ('þa buruh Lundene'), but praise be to God that it still stands sound, and they always fared badly there'. Immediately afterwards in the narrative, the raiding army travels to Oxford and 'burned down the town' ('þa buruh')).[35]

---

34   The same entry also includes a reference to 'Seofon bur(h)gum' ('seven boroughs'); Williams (2013) for a discussion of their likely identification and significance.
35   Old English from C.

Finally, the eleventh-century entries in C–E commonly include references to townspeople as actors. In 1013, the 'buruhwaru' of Oxford and Winchester submit to the raiding army and give them hostages. In 1016 and 1018, the 'Lundenwaru' and 'burhwaru' buy peace from the raiding army.[36] In 1048 (1051), the king gets very angry with the 'burhware' of Dover (only in E). Most interesting, perhaps, is the annal for 1006, which—in the middle of a lengthy description of the destruction caused by the raiding army—states that the 'Wincester leode' ('people of Winchester') are able to 'see' the raiding army, in a passive role that serves to emphasize the imminent threat of the situation.[37]

5   Discussion

Although the evidence from the *Chronicle* lacks descriptive detail, 'every text … has something to tell us, and its own language in which this is communicated'.[38] In some ways, the lack of detail is what makes it so interesting. It reminds us that the (educated) readership for whom the *Chronicle* was intended did not need to have explained the symbolic meanings that pervaded their material reality and its literary depictions.

The symbolic significance of towns (in all their forms) is evident throughout the *Chronicle*, but it is perhaps clearest in the annals up to 924 in A. Also in later sections, however, 'towns' were more than a backdrop for action: their capture or destruction reinforced the relative success of the various rulers who were in power at the time. London occupied a special place, starting with the juxtaposition of the destruction of 'Romeburg'/loss of political power and the capture of 'Lundenburg'/political success, and ending with its resilience in the face of persistent Viking attacks.

The main changes over time—although the evidence is by no means entirely straightforward, nor should we expect it to be—include increasing diversity of urban form and status, and a growing emphasis on towns*people*. In the early tenth century, there are references to royal orders for towns to be 'gesettan' and 'gemannian'. Was this Bintley's symbolic metamorphosis, transforming former Church enclaves into 'places for community and prosperity', in action?[39] Archaeological evidence for sizeable populations is still scarce for this period, but the *Chronicle*—like other near-contemporary written sources and

---

36   Old English from C.
37   Old English from C.
38   Bintley (2020: 195).
39   Bintley (2020: 119).

as a product of the West-Saxon educated environment—'may have played an active role in refashioning the perception of settlements and strongholds' until they became the populated places of the Anglo-Norman period.[40]

All in all, this brief analysis of 'towns' in the *Anglo-Saxon Chronicle* underlines another lesson I first learnt from Erik's lectures: the importance of interdisciplinarity. The 'towns' in the *Anglo-Saxon Chronicle* were real places built of earth and stone, but their materiality was imbued with symbolism as much as their literary depictions, making it impossible to understand either without reference to the other. Even when their economic and demographic dimensions developed, this merely added to the complexity of the meanings they held. As such, they bridged the divide between material reality and literary *topos* in complex ways that this brief paper cannot possibly do full justice to. I hope that it will nevertheless inspire others to investigate this topic further.

Bibliography

Primary Source

The Anglo-Saxon Chronicle: According to the Several Original Authorities. Ed. B. Thorpe. Cambridge: Cambridge University Press, 2012.

Secondary Sources

Astill, G.G. (1991). 'Towns and Town Hierarchies in Saxon England.' *Oxford Journal of Archaeology* 10 (1): 95–117.

Astill, G. (2009). 'Medieval Towns and Urbanization.' In R. Gilchrist and A. Reynolds (eds), *Reflections: 50 Years of Medieval Archaeology 1957–2007*, 255–270. Leeds: Maney.

Baghos, M. (2021). *From the Ancient Near East to Christian Byzantium: Kings, Symbols, and Cities*. Cambridge: Cambridge Scholars Publishing.

Biddle, M. (1976). 'Towns.' In D.M. Wilson (ed.), *The Archaeology of Anglo-Saxon England*, 99–150. London: Methuen and Co.

Bintley, M.D.J. (2020). *Settlements and Strongholds in Early Medieval England: Texts, Landscapes, and Material Culture*. Turnhout: Brepols.

Blackmore, L., R. Cowie and A. Davis (2012). *Lundenwic: Excavations in Middle Saxon London 1987–2000*. London: Museum of London Archaeology.

Blair, J. (2006). *The Church in Anglo-Saxon Society*. Oxford: Oxford University Press.

---

40   Bintley (2020: 154).

Baker, J. and S. Brookes (2013). *Beyond the Burghal Hidage: Anglo-Saxon Civil Defence in the Viking Age*. Leiden: Brill.

Carver, M.O.H. (2011). 'What Were They Thinking? Intellectual Territories in Anglo-Saxon England.' In H. Hamerow, D.A. Hinton and S. Crawford (eds), *The Oxford Handbook of Anglo-Saxon Archaeology*, 914–947. Oxford: Oxford University Press.

Dumville, D. (2002). 'What Is a Chronicle?' *The Medieval Chronicle* 2: 1–27.

Hodges, R. (1982). *Dark-Age Economics: The Origins of Towns and Trade AD 600–1000*. London: Duckworth.

Keynes, S. and M. Lapidge (1983). *Alfred the Great: Asser's Life of Alfred and Other Contemporary Sources*. London: Penguin.

Kraus, C.S. (1994). '"No Second Troy": Topoi and Refoundation in Livy, Book V'. *Transactions of the American Philological Association* 124: 267–289.

Mainman, A. (2019). *Anglian York*. Pickering: Blackthorn.

Smith, A.H. (1970a). *English Place-Name Elements Part 1*. Cambridge: Cambridge University Press.

Smith, A.H. (1970b). *English Place-Name Elements Part 2*. Cambridge: Cambridge University Press.

Swanton, M. (2000). *The Anglo-Saxon Chronicles*. London: Phoenix Press.

Ten Harkel, L. (2012). 'Urban identity and material culture: a case-study of Viking-Age Lincoln, c. AD 850–1000.' *Anglo-Saxon Studies in Archaeology and History* 18: 157–173.

Williams, G. (2013). 'Towns and identities in Viking England'. In D.M. Hadley and L. Ten Harkel (eds), *Everyday Life in Viking-Age Towns: Social Approaches to Towns in England and Ireland, c. 800–1100*, 14–34. Oxford: Oxbow.

26

Die Kritik des einen Autors entspricht dem Lob des Anderen

Das Bild König Stephans von England in der Historia Novella *und den* Gesta Stephani *(12. Jahrhundert)*

Grischa Vercamer

Zusammenfassung

Chroniclers often arrange their works around the deeds of famous nobles: great deeds are praised, demerits are concealed or completely erased. If the chronicles reflect on (military) conflicts, it is normally recognizable on which side the chronicler stands: ‚good guys‘ against ‚bad guys‘, often congruent with the historical winners and losers. This raises the question whether there are tangible narrative patterns that allowed medieval chroniclers to stage good and bad reigns in a comprehensible way for their readers. This article will explore the question on the basis of two chronicles written in England during the civil war of 1135–1153. The ‚Anarchy‘ overshadowed the entire reign of Stephen of Blois as English king. Rarely do medievalists have two completely opposite, but contemporary chronicles available on the same historical event. This is the case with the *Historia Novella* by William of Malmesbury and the anonymous *Gesta Stephani*. Thus, as a second goal of the article, there is the chance to find out whether the two chroniclers were unambiguously only on one side by completely demonising the other side. Precisely put: does William only take the position of his ‚heroes‘ Matilda, Earl Robert of Gloucester and the later King Henry II (1154–1189)? And is the anonymous author of the *Gesta* unequivocally only on the side of Stephen I? As it turns out, that was not the case. But when an author reports bad things about his hero, the question arises: why he did so? The answer seems simple for the *Gesta Stephani*: the author was aware that he could not conceal certain negatively connoted deeds of King Stephen, since they were known in the circles of the English elite anyway. However, he smartly modified them so that what were actually negative actions were supposedly interpreted by him positively. In the case of the *Historia Novella*, it seems more difficult: when William of Malmesbury criticises Mathilda twice severely for her behaviour, a certain misogyny seems to resonate here. Earl Robert von Gloucester as her highest supporter and representative is depicted on the other side always in a positive way.

1   Einleitung

Die zentrale Frage des folgenden Texts lautet: Wie gingen hochmittelalterliche Historiographen vor, um ‚gute' oder ‚schlechte' Herrschaft zu inszenieren? Dafür werden zwei ausführliche historiographische Texte herangezogen: Die *Historia Novella* von Wilhelm von Malmesbury († 1143) und die *Gesta Stephani* eines anonymen Autors. Beide Werke können als Zeitgeschichte bezeichnet werden; der Betrachtungsgegenstand ist der sogenannte Englischen Bürgerkrieg (‚The Anarchy') in den Jahren 1135–1153.[1] Wilhelm von Malmesbury schrieb diesbezüglich eindeutig zugunsten der Tochter des englischen Königs Heinrich I., Mathilde und ihres minderjährigen Sohns Heinrich II. (später englischer König: 1154–1189) – der Auftraggeber des Werks war Robert, Earl von Gloucester (1100–1147, ein unehelicher Sohn Heinrichs I.). Der anonyme Autor wiederum schrieb für Stephan von Blois (englischer König: 1135–1154), den politischen Gegner Mathildes. Für die Forschung ergibt sich somit die seltene und günstige Situation, dass genau verfolgt werden kann, wie politische oder militärische Handlungen der eigenen und der gegnerischen Parteien von beiden Seiten narrativ inszeniert wurden. Wenn die gleichen Handlungen verarbeitet wurden, kann sogar eine direkte Gegenüberstellung vorgenommen werden.

Diese Gegenüberstellung der beiden Werke und die damit verbundene Problematik kann in dem hier gesetzten Rahmen nicht erschöpfend behandelt werden, da schlicht der Platz fehlt. Eine umfangreiche diesbezügliche Abhandlung ist in Arbeit, sie soll mit diesem Text korrespondieren.[2] Für die Festschrift galt die Vorgabe, eine moderne Forschungsproblematik aus dem Bereich der mittelalterlichen Chronistik vorzustellen, die man gerne mit dem Jubilar diskutieren würde. Daher wird in einem ersten Schritt die methodische Grundproblematik erläutert, während in einem zweiten Schritt die Wirksamkeit der Theorie an ausgewählten Beispielen in den besagten Werken illustriert wird.

2   Methodische Einleitung

Mediävisten müssen, wenn sie Charakter und politisches Handeln hochmittelalterlicher Herrscher einordnen wollen, im Wesentlichen auf zwei Quellengattungen zurückgreifen: Urkunden und narrative Quellen in Form von Historien, Chroniken und Viten. Bei beiden Gruppen handelt es sich im Sinne von Ernst

---

1   Cf. King (1984: 133–153).
2   Sie soll *The Medieval Chronicle* in absehbarer Zeit als längerer Artikel angeboten werden.

Bernheim um Überlieferungen, die ‚Traditionsanspruch' für sich in Anspruch nehmen können, sie wurden also intentionell für die Nachwelt geschaffen. Urkunden transportieren über ihre Arengen, Narrationes, Siegel/Bullen und ihr generelles Aussehen ein direkt kommuniziertes politisches Programm des jeweiligen Fürsten. Die richtige Einordnung der politischen Aussagen von Urkunden ist seit Langem Aufgabe der historischen Diplomatik und Sphragistik. Rückschlüsse auf Charakter und politisches Wirken der jeweiligen Herrscher können jedoch allenfalls Stückwerk bleiben, man bekommt keinesfalls ein umfassendes Bild präsentiert, dafür ist die Information einfach zu spärlich. Narrative Quellen andererseits transportieren wesentlich breitere politische Vorstellungen und Wahrnehmungen der zeitgenössischen Autoren.[3] Dieses geschah nicht von ungefähr: Die Historiographen waren in ihren Texten regelrecht dazu gezwungen, eine flüssige Erzählung vom politischen Handeln der beschriebenen Fürsten zu komponieren.[4] Wenn sie dabei über zeitgenössische Fürsten berichteten und zudem als gut informiert einzustufen sind (z. B. durch Herrschernähe),[5] muss die Forschung davon ausgehen, dass die Autoren bei ihrer Textkonstruktion, nachdem sie sich einen zeitlichen Rahmen gesetzt hatten (zum Beispiel die Herrschaftsjahre eines bestimmten Fürsten), sorgsam selektierten: Welche Ereignisse sollten erwähnt und welche besser durch Schweigen übergangen werden? Allein aufgrund dieser Auswahl konnten Historiographen positive oder auch negative Impulse für das Wirken eines Fürsten geben.

Stand die Auswahl der Ereignisse für das anvisierte Werk einmal, mussten sich die Historiographen weiterhin überlegen, welche Ereignisse sie in ihrer Chronik in besonderer Weise hervorheben wollten, indem sie diese mit verschiedenen stilistischen Werkzeugen ausschmückten (z. B. durch direkte Rede, Insertion von Urkunden oder auch lyrische Gedichteinschübe). Bestimmte Erzählstränge konnten auch einfach sehr lang ausfallen, wodurch automatisch die Aufmerksamkeit des Lesers gelenkt wurde. Verschiedene Überlegungen werden die damaligen Autoren angetrieben haben: die eigene Schreibintention (*causa scribendi*) sowie die Vorgaben des Auftraggebers, das Zielpublikum

---

3 Goetz (2007: 3–18).

4 Schmid (2008: 251).

5 Schmale (1985: 149) hat zudem eine Einteilung in den Berichtszeitraum vorgenommen: 1) Vergangenheitsgeschichte, 2) Gegenwartsgeschichte (Zeitgeschichte). Dabei ist zu beachten, dass gegenwartsgeschichtliche Werke häufig wesentlich geringer verbreitet waren (oftmals besitzen wir nur den Autographen) als die erste Gruppe. Das lag wohl daran, dass man oftmals doch nur für die eigene Institution schrieb (also ein Kloster) oder sogar nur für sich (privater Charakter).

(Hof, Kloster usw.), der angestrebte Erziehungs- oder Unterhaltungswert (*educare et delectare* – Stichwort: serious entertainments), die Länge des Werks sowie die damit verbundenen Produktionskosten. Nicht zuletzt war die Frage nach dem eigenen Wahrheitsanspruch zentral: Historiographische Werke sind narrativ aufgebaut, berichten daher selten theoretisch über zugrundeliegende politische Strukturen, stellen aber dennoch ganz eindeutig und fast immer herrschaftliches Handeln ins Zentrum ihres Interesses.[6] Mittelalterliche Herrscher handelten wie heutige Politiker nicht immer klug, machten Fehler, hatten charakterliche Dispositionen, die den Zeitgenossen unangenehm auffielen. Der Historiograph musste sich fragen, welche Kritik am zeitgenössischen Fürsten generell legitim war. Was war also ‚sagbar'? Ferner: Erlaubte ihm sein eigener sozialer Status (z. B. als Abt oder Bischof) eine Äußerung von Kritik, die über die allgemein anerkannten Konventionen hinausging?

Fast immer galt dabei die Faustregel: ‚Gute Herrschaft' ließ sich leichter vermitteln.[7] Positives zu sagen oder Lob auszusprechen, kostete nicht viel und konnte Vorteile in Form von Auszeichnungen oder sogar Ämtererwerb einbringen. Otto von Freising brachte es im Prolog der *Gesta Friderici* (Mitte des 12. Jahrhundert) gut auf den Punkt:

> ‚Die Absicht aller, die vor uns Geschichte geschrieben haben, war es, so meine ich, die glänzenden Taten tapferer Männer zu preisen, um die Menschen zur Tatkraft anzuspornen, die verborgenen Handlungen der Feiglinge dagegen entweder zu verschweigen, oder, wenn sie ans Licht gezogen werden, nur zu erwähnen, um die gleichen Sterblichen abzuschrecken.'[8]

Mittelalterliche Herrscherkritik als Forschungsfeld ist noch recht jung, bedarf weiterer Studien.[9] Hier ist nicht der Platz, um das ausgiebig zu besprechen, soviel ist jedoch aus den bisherigen Studien klar: In frühmittelalterlichen Zeiten wurde – so suggerieren es bisherige Arbeiten z. B. von Matthias Becher oder Marita Blattmann, die einen längeren Zeitraum überblicken – offener kriti-

---

6 Goetz (1999: 415).

7 ‚Herrscherkritik oder gar königsfeindliche Auslassungen wurden seltener schriftlich fixiert als Lobsprüche – und wenn sie niedergeschrieben wurden, dann hatten sie eine geringere Überlieferungschance als positive Äußerungen.', Blattmann (2003: 9).

8 ‚Omnium qui ante nos res gestas scripserunt hec, ut arbitror, fuit intentio virorum fortium clara facta ob movendos hominum ad virtutem animos extollere, ignavorum vero obscura facta vel silentio subprimere vel, si ad lucem trahantur, ad terrendas eorumdem mortalium mentes promendo ponere.' – Gesta Friderici, Prol., 114–115.

9 Vgl. Kellermann/Plassmann/Schwermann (2019: 11–32); Vercamer (2020: 275–342).

siert (z. B. Gregor von Tours), sukzessive nahm dies jedoch zum Hochmittelalter ab.[10] Oftmals wurde Kritik im Hochmittelalter ‚zwischen den Zeilen‘ oder auch implizit geäußert.[11] Um die Authentizität der Kritik zu überprüfen, ist man auf weitere, zeitgleich geschriebene Werke angewiesen. In der Regel verfügt die moderne Forschung zur hochmittelalterlichen Historiographie für das politische Handeln eines bestimmten Fürsten in einer bestimmten Zeit und in einem bestimmten Raum meist nur über einen zentralen Text (wie die oben angeführte *Gesta Friderici*).[12] Waren weitere vorhanden, komplementierten sie meist den ersten Text, standen diesem jedenfalls nicht komplett gegensätzlich gegenüber.

3   **Die *Historia Novella* und die *Gesta Stephani* – unterschiedliche Wertungen der politischen und militärischen Handlungen König Stephans**

Es handelt sich daher, im Anschluss an das zuvor Gesagte, um eine glückliche Ausnahme, dass die Forschung für den sogenannten Englischen Bürgerkrieg (‚The Anarchy‘) im 12. Jahrhundert über zwei ausführliche historiographische Texte verfügt, die sehr deutlich zwei unterschiedlichen politischen Lagern entstammten:[13] Die *Historia Novella* von Wilhelm von Malmesbury († 1143) und der *Gesta Stephani* eines anonymen Autoren. Den historischen Hintergrund bilden die englischen Unruhen, die insgesamt 18 Jahre andauerten (1135–1153) und die

---

10   Becher (2009: 70–71) zieht das Fazit, dass zur Merowinger-Zeit viel und harte Kritik an den Königen geübt werden konnte und wurde, während man in der Karolinger-Zeit dazu überging, die Könige/Kaiser nicht mehr direkt zu kritisieren, sondern meist über die Verfehlungen der Ehefrauen oder Töchter zu treffen. Wenn ein Mann – so das Denken dahinter – nicht den eigenen Haushalt kontrollieren konnte, war er ebenfalls als Herrscher ungeeignet. Bei den Ottonen und Saliern wurden diese Vorwürfe immer stärker ausgeblendet – es gab nur noch versteckte Hinweise (so z. B. für Agnes, die Mutter von Heinrich IV., der man wegen ihres allzu vertraulichen Umgangs mit Bischof Heinrich II. von Augsburg ein Verhältnis nachsagte – Becher, 68). Das Motiv, dass der König unmittelbar für das Unglück des Volks verantwortlich gemacht werden kann, bricht laut Blattmann (2003: 21) mit Kaiser Heinrich IV. (2. Hälfte des 11. Jahrhunderts) ab. Es kommt später nicht mehr vor.

11   Vercamer (2020: 348, 469, 506–507).

12   Görich (2011: 22–23) betont, dass die Gesta (bis 1160 reichend) durch andere zeitgenössische Werke ‚ergänzt‘ werden.

13   Die gesamte Periode von Heinrich I., Mathilde und Stephan kann als eine äußerst fruchtbare Zeit für die englische Geschichtsschreibung bezeichnet werden, aber bezüglich der Zeitgeschichtsschreibung ragen die beiden genannten Werke heraus – Gransden (1974: 136–218).

gesamte Regierungszeit Stephans von Blois als englischen Königs (1135–1154) überschatteten. Wie erwähnt, beide Autoren standen sich in ihrer politischen Bewertung der Ereignisse eindeutig gegenüber: Wilhelm von Malmesbury vertrat die Position Mathildes, der Tochter Heinrichs I., sowie ihres Sohnes Heinrichs (II.), während sich der anonyme Autor der Gesta auf Seiten Stephans von Blois befand.

Beide Texte sind der Forschung wohlbekannt und es existieren für beide Texte moderne Editionen – sie sollen hier lediglich mit ihrer jeweiligen Schreibintention kurz vorgestellt werden:

Wilhelm von Malmesbury (1090–1143)[14] kam bereits als Waise in das Benediktinerkloster von Malmesbury und wurde dort zum Gehilfen des Abts Gottfried bei der Errichtung der Bibliothek. Nach dessen Tod wurde Wilhelm selbst Bibliothekar des Klosters. Obgleich ein Großteil seiner Bildung auf das unmittelbare Umfeld des Klosters Malmesbury zurückgeht, ist Wilhelm auch viel gereist, um Recherche zu betreiben oder sich mit Intellektuellen seiner Zeit auseinanderzusetzen. Bereits als Dreißigjähriger hatte er zwei umfassende Werke, die Geschichte der englischen Könige und die Geschichte der englischen Bischöfe (*Gesta Regum Anglorum* und die *Gesta Pontificum Anglorum*), beendet. An die Königsgeschichten schloss schließlich die *Historia Novella* an, die man als sein ‚Alterswerk‘ (er war ca. 50 Jahre alt) bezeichnen kann. Da das Buch von Robert von Gloucester, dem unehelichen Sohn Heinrichs I. und Bruder Mathildes, in Auftrag gegeben wurde, muss es trotz der vielfach beteuerten Objektivität Wilhelms in seinem Werk als tendenziös gesehen werden. Es umfasst die Jahre 1126 bis 1142, stellt also gänzlich Zeitgeschichte dar. Buch 1 und 2 sind zeitlich zusammenhängend entstanden (wohl im Jahr 1140), während Buch 3 erst nach der Schlacht von Lincoln (Feb 1141) beendet wurde, also im Jahr 1142/43. Das Werk blieb unvollendet, Wilhelm verwies sehr klar darauf, dass er von der Flucht Mathildes aus Oxford (1142) noch ausführlicher berichten wolle, da er noch einiges dafür in Erfahrung bringen müsse – dazu kam es jedoch nicht mehr. Im Prolog schrieb Wilhelm an Robert von Gloucester, dass er die Geschichte der Könige bis Heinrich I. bereits aufgeschrieben habe (also die *Gesta Regum Anglorum*), aber dem Wunsch des Earls gerne entspreche, die englischen Geschehnisse moderner Zeiten niederzuschreiben: ‚Quid enim plus ad honestatis spectat commodum, quid magis conducit aequitati, quam diuinam agnoscere circa bonos indulgentiam, et erga peruersos uindictam.‘ (‚Denn was wäre mehr von Vorteil für die Tugend, was eher der Gerechtigkeit zuträg-

---

14   Gransden (1974: 166–185); Lisa Ruch, William of Malmesbury, in: The Encyclopedia of the medieval chronicle (2010: 1511–1512).

lich, als die göttliche Gunst für die Guten sowie die göttliche Strafe für die Schlechten kennenzulernen.' [Übers. GV])[15] Die Intention des Autors ist eindeutig: Die Sache des Earls und seiner kaiserlichen Halbschwester Mathilde sollte unterstützt werden.

Der unbekannte Autor der *Gesta Stephani*[16] wurde von der Forschung mit mehreren potentiellen Personen in Zusammenhang gebracht: Viele Details in dem Werk sprechen für den Bischof von Bath, Robert von Lewes[17] – allerdings schlug Edmund King 2006 alternativ einen Kanoniker im Londoner Umfeld vor.[18] Vom Schreibstil stand der Anonymus anderen gebildeten Historiographen seiner Zeit nicht nach. Die Tatenbeschreibung beginnt mit der Krönung Stephans (1135) und endet mit der Krönung Heinrichs II. (1154), behandelt also ebenfalls rein zeitgenössische Geschichte. Das Werk ist durchgehend erzählend aufgebaut, nennt keine Daten und hat nur eine Unterteilung in zwei Bücher. Die politische Geschichte Englands wird jedoch kaum reflektiert – die wichtigen Konzile und Treffen dieser Periode werden lediglich erwähnt.[19] Angefangen wurden die *Gesta* in den späten 1140er Jahren, jedoch wurde der letzte Teil wohl erst nach 1153 zu Ende geführt.[20] Der früheren Annahme eines komplett einseitigen Bildes – hier König Stephan, dort die Partei um Mathilde – wurde in neueren Studien widersprochen. Der Autor beschäftigte sich durchaus mit dem Anspruch Mathildes auf den englischen Thron, nahm ihn also schon ernst, wies ihn aber in seinem Werk schlussendlich zurück. Vermeintlichen Gegnern Stephans wird jedoch Höfischheit und Ritterlichkeit attestiert – so kann man dem Urteil Kings folgen, der von einer ,world of consensus, of *conventiones*' spricht, die einem aus den GS entgegentreten.[21] Der Autor der GS schrieb keinen Prolog, startete aber wie in der HN mit einem klaren Schwarzweißbild von ,gut' und ,schlecht': ,Vbi nam, eo regnante [Heinrich I.], iudicii caput, [...]. Anglia siquidem, iustitiae prius sedes, pacis habitaculum, pietatis apex, religiosis speculum, [...].' (,Dort nämlich, während er regierte [Heinrichs I.], Quelle der Gerechtigkeit [...]. Da ja England früher Sitz des Rechtes, Wohnung des Friedens, Spitze der Frömmigkeit, Spiegel des Religiösen [war]'

---

15   HN, Prol., 2.
16   William Smith, Gesta Stephani, in: The Encyclopedia of the Medieval Chronicle (2010: 700–701).
17   Ausführlich dazu der Editor der GS: Mynors, Introd., GS, XXIX–XXXVIII.
18   King (2006: 206).
19   King (2006: 201).
20   Frühere Vermutungen über eine zeitliche Aufteilung vor 1147 und danach werden von King (2006: 202–203) recht kritisch gesehen.
21   King (2006: 205).

[Übers. GV]).[22] Nach dem Tode Heinrichs I. verkehrte sich diese Situation komplett: ‚[...] peruersitatis postea locus, dissensionis recessus, inquietudinis disci-
plina omnisque rebellii effecta est magistra.' (‚[...] später [ist England] zu einem
Ort der Verderbtheit, einem Rückfall in Streit, einer Verfassung der Unruhe,
einer Lehrerin aller Rebellion gemacht worden.' [Übers. GV]).[23] Ein neuer Herrscher musste, in dieser Logik bleibend, schnell her und nur eine Seite weiter
im Manuskript liest man: ‚Stephanus Bulonicensis comes, uir praeclara nobi-
litatus prosapia, Angliam cum paucis applicuit' (‚Stephan von Blois, ein durch
sein berühmtes Geschlecht adeliger Mann, landete mit nur wenigen [Gefolgs-
leuten] in England.' [Übers. GV])[24] Er war der *nepotum solus carissimus* (‚der
allerliebste der Neffen') des verstorbenen Königs Heinrich I. Er wird in diesem
Zuge durchweg positiv charakterisiert: ‚Fuit siquidem, quod in nostri tempo-
ris diuitibus constat esse rarissimum, diues et humilis, munificus et affabi-
lis; sed et in omni militari congressione, siue in hostium qualibet obsidione,
audax et fortis, discretus et longanimis.' (‚Er war nämlich, was unter den Rei-
chen unserer Zeit wirklich selten war, gleichzeitig reich und demütig, mild-
tätig und leutselig, sowohl in allen militärischen Konflikten wie in jeglicher
Bedrängnis durch Feinde mutig und stark, besonnen und geduldig' [Übers.
GV]).[25]

Beide Autoren, sowohl in der HN als auch in den GS, steckten also anfangs
deutlich ihre Ziele ab. Wilhelm schrieb zusätzlich, dass die Guten (*boni*) und
die Schlechten (*perversi*) klar voneinander unterscheidbar seien. Es geht ihm
(wie sicherlich dem anonymen Autoren auch) darum aufzuzeigen, wer sich
göttlicher Gunst erfreuen konnte. Das impliziert jedoch, dass die Guten eigentlich nicht schlecht und die Schlechten nicht gut handeln konnten. Stimmt das
so? Kommen keine Zwischentöne zum Tragen?

Doch! – Generell kann man für beide Werke, HN und GS, recht gut heraus-
arbeiten, wo ‚gute Herrschaft' und wo ‚schlechte Herrschaft' dargestellt wird
(vgl. Tab. 26.1).[26] Es lassen sich aber eben auch Stellen finden, die man als Zwischentöne bezeichnen kann, also ‚Gute Herrschaft im schlechten Licht' und
‚Schlechte Herrschaft im guten Licht'. Diese Stellen werden alle in der ein-
gangs genannten Studie, die mit diesem Text korrespondieren soll, analysiert.
Dort werden die unterschiedlichen Darstellungen von Kaiserin Mathilde, Earl

---

22   GS, cap. 1, 2.
23   GS, cap. 1, 2.
24   GS, cap. 2, 4.
25   GS, cap. 2, 4.
26   Zur Erfassung dieser Stellen vgl. Vercamer (2020: 45) – zu kurze Stellen (in der Narratolo-
        gie ‚Zustandsveränderungen' genannt) eignen sich für die Auswertung nicht.

TABELLE 26.1   Darstellung von guter und schlechter Herrschaftsausübung

	Historia Novella	Gesta Stephani
Gute Herrschaft	18	27
Gute Herrschaft im schlechten Licht	2	6
Schlechte Herrschaft	18 (15 von König Stephan)	4
Schlechte Herrschaft im guten Licht	2	(1)

Robert von Gloucester und König Stephan von Blois, sowohl im Positiven als auch im Negativen, in aller Ausführlichkeit besprochen.

Ein in sich geschlossener Bereich betrifft die kritischen Ausführungen Wilhelms von Malmesbury in der HN über verschiedenen politischen und militärischen Handlungen Stephans von Blois sowie die dem gegenüberstehenden Darstellungen des zweiten, anonymen Autors – hier können direkte Vergleiche vorgenommen werden.

Es gibt dahingehend in der HN insgesamt 18 Stellen (vgl. Tab. 26.1), in denen von schlechter Herrschaft (meist König Stephan, 15 Stellen) berichtet wird. Diese sind tabellarisch in Regestenform vollständig erfasst (vgl. Tab. 26.2, im Anhang), wobei für den Vergleich auf der rechten Seite auch die Darstellungen derselben Ereignisse in den GS genannt werden (jeweils mit Quellenstellen), wenn diese dort ebenfalls behandelt wurden. Wenn das in den HN aufgeführte Ereignis in den GS nicht aufgeführt wurde, so wird meist eine Stelle in den GS angeführt, die einen ähnlichen Aussagewert hat.

Da diese Tabelle für sich genommen sehr aussagekräftig ist, müssen die einzelnen Szenen hier im Fließtext nicht alle ausgiebig besprochen werden, sondern es kann auf generelle Aspekte eingegangen werden. Zunächst ist festzuhalten, dass ein relativ trockener narrativer Stil in beiden Werken bei den besprochenen Stellen vorherrscht. Bei Wilhelm wird an einer Stelle eine komplette Urkunde zitiert, aber ansonsten kommt es in beiden Werken nicht zu großen Einschüben – hier und da erfolgt direkte Rede. Die Erzählperspektive ist in beiden Werken meist auktorial und es wird dabei häufig und gerne vom Autor kommentiert. Bei Wilhelm wechselt der auktoriale Erzähler bisweilen zum Ich-Erzähler, wenn Wilhelm selbst bei einem Ereignis anwesend war.

Wir schauen uns zunächst Wilhelms Kritik (in der HN) an Stephan und die Gegendarstellung des Anonymus der GS etwas genauer an (mit Verweis auf die durchnummerierten Stellen in der Tabelle 2, im Anhang): HN: Stephan, so Wilhelm, soll den englischen Staatsschatz sehr schnell nach seiner Krönung verschwendet haben – ein klarer Vorwurf also. Die GS behaupten wiederum, dass

Mathilde Teile des väterlichen Schatzes an sich genommen habe und offenbar für falsche Dinge verwendete – der Autor kommentierte, dass der Schatz besser Bedürftigen hätte zukommen sollen (Nr. 1). Beiden Autoren war also durchaus bewusst, dass der Schatz des alten Königs Heinrichs I. schnell verausgabt wurde, die Schuld dafür suchten sie aber jeweils beim politischen Gegner.

Weiter: HN: Stephan habe auf dem Konzil von Westminster (1136) versprochen, die englische Kirche und deren Güter zu achten, wurde aber dann sehr schnell wortbrüchig (Vorwürfe sind Nepotismus, Plünderung etc.) – als klarer Beweis wurde in der HN eine Königsurkunde inseriert. Hier wird deutlich, dass Stephan, den der Autor noch als Grafen von Blois hochgeschätzt hatte, als König und durch die königlichen Berater charakterlich korrumpiert wurde. GS: Der Anonymus betont zur selben Angelegenheit, dass Stephan der englischen Kirche das zurückgab, was sie unter Heinrich I. verloren hatte: Freiheit und Respekt. Weiterhin sieht auch dieser Autor, dass die königlichen Versprechen gegenüber der englischen Kirche nicht gehalten wurden, schiebt es aber auf die schlechten Berater (,consiliatores peruersi') (Nr. 2, 3). Die Wortbrüchigkeit Stephans als Königs stand also beiden Autoren vor Augen, nur: Der Anonymus versucht mit einem altbekannten Mittel von der Schuld Stephans abzulenken, indem er auf die schlechten Berater verwies.

Die nächste wichtige Situation: HN: Stephan verübte 1137 einen nicht gelungenen Mordanschlag auf den Earl Robert von Gloucester (den Halbbruder der Kaiserin), was er später bereute – über eine kurze direkte Rede Stephans wird deutlich, dass Neid auf die Regierungsqualitäten des Konkurrenten ihn angetrieben habe. Dieses Ereignis findet jedoch überhaupt keinen Widerhall in den GS (Nr. 4), wird mit Schweigen übergangen.

HN: 1138 sei Stephans schlechte Herrschaft immer deutlicher geworden, er könne sich gegen viele englische Hochadelige nicht durchsetzen, die ihrerseits immer mehr Königsgüter und Privilegien entfremden würden. Robert von Gloucester sagte dem König folglich öffentlich die Gefolgschaft auf. GS: Der Anonymus kehrt das in der HN geäußerte Argument geradezu um: Stephan verhalte sich beim Kampf gegen verschiedene Adelsrebellionen wie ein zweiter Herkules, er versuche allem gerecht zu werden, was fast unmöglich sei (Nr. 5). Wieder finden wir die Situation vor, dass die Spannung der Regierung Stephans beiden Autoren bewusst ist, aber exakt gegenteilig ausgedeutet wird.

HN: Stephans Angst vor Sympathisanten für Mathildes Sache im englischen Adel habe ihn 1139 dazu angetrieben, nun auch Bischöfe und deren Güter (Burgen) zu belangen – namentlich die Bischöfe Alexander von Lincoln und Roger von Salisbury. GS: Die beiden genannten Bischöfe hätten ihre Ämter aufs Schlimmste missbraucht, indem sie illegitim weltliche Macht ausübten. Das Vorgehen Stephans gegen die Bischöfe sei damit gerechtfertigt, doch auch für diesen Autor nicht ganz entschuldbar. Auch bezüglich dieser Situation führt der Autor jedoch, wie schon oben bemerkt, v. a. den schädlichen Einfluss der Berater an (Nr. 6, 7).

HN: Auf dem Konzil von Winchester (am 29. August 1139) habe Bischof Heinrich von Winchester, der einerseits päpstlicher Legat und andererseits der jüngere Bruder Stephans war, den König gerügt: Der ältere Bruder habe zu keinem Zeitpunkt seine Sünden gegenüber den beiden oben genannten Bischöfen und dem Bischof von Ely bereut. Später habe sich Heinrich von Winchester sogar gemeinsam mit dem Erzbischof von Rouen mit der Bitte zu Stephans Füßen geworfen (also ein sehr starker Erniedrigungsgestus, der eigentlich vom König nicht übergangen werden konnte), die englische Kirche nicht weiter zu plündern. Das Anliegen wurde jedoch weitestgehend vom König ignoriert. GS: Die Beschreibungen dieses Konzils stehen in einem sehr klaren Gegensatz zur HN. Alle bischöflichen ‚Schlupfwinkel' des Krieges (es geht um die Burgen) seien vom König konfisziert worden, was grundsätzlich völlig richtig gewesen sei. Allein der Fakt jedoch, dass es sich um geistliche Güter gehandelt hat, machte Stephan auch in den Augen des Anonymus schuldig. Daher habe sich Stephan jedoch richtigerweise äußerst demütig gegenüber den Konzilsteilnehmern in Winchester benommen, wie der Autor unterstreicht. Heinrich von Winchester (also der jüngere Bruder) wird in den GS wiederum sehr ambivalent gesehen, da er u. a. Robert von Gloucester eine Rückkehr nach England ermöglicht habe. So etwas sollte ein Bruder seinem Bruder (dem König) nicht antun, kommentierte der Autor (Nr. 8, 9).[27] Dadurch sollte wohl die Integrität des Legaten intentional herabgewürdigt werden; seine anderweitig verzeichneten Handlungen, z. B. der geschilderte Fußfall bei Wilhelm (der in den GS nicht genannt wird), mussten für den Leser der GS in einem ganz anderen Licht erscheinen.

HN: England sei unter der Herrschaft von Stephan sehr unsicher geworden, dabei wird Stephans Regierungsstil (schlecht) direkt dem von König Heinrich I. (gut) und Roberts von Gloucester (gut) gegenübergestellt. Earl Robert bemühe sich um Umsicht und Ausgleich, während Stephan eigens die Wirtschafts- und Münzpolitik verschlechtert habe, um Robert zu schaden. Stephan stelle also sein individuelles Wohl über das englische Allgemeinwohl, so der Vorwurf. GS: Hier ist vielleicht die überhaupt deutlichste Alternativdarstellung zur HN zu sehen: Der Anonymus stellt Stephan nämlich als Friedensgaranten *par exellence* dar, während hingegen der *populus Anglorum* über alle Maßen gelebt haben soll bzw. sündig geworden sei und somit den göttlichen Zorn

---

27 Bewusst wird von Wilhelm beiseite gelassen, dass Stephan erst sechs Monate zuvor päpstliche Rückendeckung auf dem zweiten Laterankonzil für seine Politik bekam – Vercamer (2020: 85).

auf sich geladen habe. Vor diesem Hintergrund seien weder die vielen Kon-
flikte in England noch die gelungene Landung Mathildes und Roberts in England weiter verwunderlich (Nr. 10, 11) – in jedem Falle nicht die Schuld Stephans. Analytisch interessant daran ist, dass die Schuldzuweisung geradezu
diametral unterschiedlich ausfällt, da bei Wilhelm der Herrscher am Unglück
seines Volkes schuld ist, während in den GS das Volk selbst dafür angeführt
wird.

HN: Stephan habe – mehrmals wird das bei Wilhelm von Malmesbury
betont – ausländische Ritter, v.a. aus der Bretagne und Flandern, nach England eingeladen, denen es jedoch meist nur um Beute und Plünderung gehen
würde, die England also schwer geschadet haben. Diesen räuberischen Rit-
tern stehe der König völlig machtlos gegenüber – konkret wird der flämische
Ritter Robert Fitz Hubert genannt, der schließlich von einem Parteigänger
Roberts von Gloucester gefasst wurde. König Stephan könne – so der Vorwurf –
also generell den Frieden im Land nicht garantieren. GS: Auch der Anonymus
beschreibt Robert Fitz Hubert als äußerst brutal und grausam, nur sei dieser
zum Zeitpunkt der Gefangennahme eigentlich Parteigänger von Earl Robert
und nicht vom König gewesen – dabei verschwieg der Anonymus jedoch, dass
es Stephan war, der den flämischen Ritter ursprünglich nach England eingeladen hatte (Nr. 12).

HN: Stephans Innen- und Außenpolitik wird als desaströs angeprangert –
selbst der jüngere Bruder, päpstlicher Legat und Bischof Heinrich von Winchester, würde sich von diplomatischen Aufgaben zurückziehen (z.B. bei Ver-
handlungen mit dem französischen König), da König Stephan unprofessionell
vorgehe und ihm offenbar an einem wirklichen Friedensprozess nichts läge.
Dieses Ereignis wird von den GS nicht erwähnt (Nr. 13), also mit Schweigen
übergangen.

HN: Ein wirkliches Sakrileg habe Stephan begangen, als er im Konflikt mit
der Partei Mathildes 1140 die Marienkirche von Bristol entweiht habe, indem
er sie zu einer Burg umfunktioniert habe. GS: Auch der Anonymus kam nicht
umhin, diese Handlung als äußerst problematisch anzusehen und kommentierte, dass ‚nullus peccatus impunitus‘ (‚keine Sünde ungesühnt‘) bleibe – die
Niederlage von Lincoln 1141 wird hier also prophetisch vorausgesehen bzw.
sinnvoll integriert (Nr. 14).

HN: 1140 zu Weihnachten habe der König einen eigenen Parteigänger ange-
griffen, den Earl von Chester, was ohne Ankündigung oder Lösung des Treue-
eides zwischen beiden geschah. Wilhelm kommentierte, dass dem König geradezu jegliches Instrument recht sei, um seine Macht zu vergrößern. GS: Der
Anonymus ließ die Stelle nicht aus, sah jedoch die Schuld für das königliche
Vorgehen beim Earl von Chester, der einerseits nicht ausreichend loyal gegen-

über dem König gewesen sei und andererseits die Einwohner seines Earldoms unterdrückt habe. Das königliche Eingreifen ist daher richtig und gerechtfertigt (Nr. 15).

Erstaunlicherweise wird Stephan im weiteren chronologischen Verlauf der HN von Wilhelm von Malmesbury nicht mehr kritisiert, obgleich noch mehr als ein Drittel des gesamten Werkes (in der Edition die Seiten 85–132) folgt. Das wird vermutlich daran liegen, dass Mathilde nach der Schlacht von Lincoln (1141) die Macht übernahm (Stephan war gefangengenommen worden) und ihre Herrschaft, laut Wilhelm, letztlich nicht zufriedenstellend ausfüllte. Dafür konnte Stephan natürlich nichts. Es scheint recht deutlich, dass aus Wilhelm hier eine gewisse Form der Misogynie spricht. Erwähnenswert ist jedenfalls, dass die oben (Tab. 26.1) genannten beiden Stellen, wo ‚Gute Herrschaft im schlechten Licht' geschildert wird, sich jeweils klar auf Mathilde beziehen. Andererseits beziehen sich die 18 Stellen, wo ‚gute Herrschaft' geschildert wird, interessanterweise fast durchgehend auf Robert, den Earl von Gloucester – Mathilde selbst wird damit also nur mittelbar in Zusammengang gebracht, da der Earl für Mathilde wirkte und kämpfte. Das kann hier jedoch leider nicht weiter ausgeführt werden.[28]

4   Fazit

Aufgrund der oben analysierten Beispiele und der Tab. 26.2 (Anhang) können folgende generelle Feststellungen gemacht werden: Wilhelm von Malmesbury kritisierte König Stephan in der HN als inkompetenten, korrupten König, der eigentlich vor nichts zurückschreckte (genannt werden Mordanschlag, Kirchenentweihung, Konfiszierung geistlicher Güter). Der Anonymus der GS seinerseits überging diese Vorwürfe an Stephan erstaunlicherweise nicht, sah aber die meisten historischen Situationen im anderen Lichte bzw. die Schuld dafür bei anderen (schlechte königliche Berater, illoyale Parteigänger Stephans, anhaltende Adelsrebellionen, das sündige englische Volk). Er entschuldigte das königliche Handeln Stephans somit sehr deutlich. Jedoch: Sowohl die Kirchenentweihung in Bristol als auch die Behandlung der Bischöfe von Salisbury, Lincoln und Ely sah er aber auch selbst sehr kritisch. Er gebrauchte diese offenbar nicht kaschierbaren negativen Handlungen Stephans jedoch geschickt, um diese mit dem zeitweiligen Verlust des Königtums durch Stephan während sei-

---

28   Verwiesen sei auf Vercamer (2020: 86). Zur Kritik von Mathilde durch Wilhelm ebd. (2020: 199–200) und die angekündigte Abhandlung.

ner Gefangenschaft 1141 in Zusammenhang zu bringen (im übertragenen Sinne: ‚jede Sünde wird Konsequenzen haben'). Damit suggerierte er dem Leser, dass Stephan für seine (wenigen) Sünden bereits 1141 bezahlt habe, ihm diese für seine künftige Regierung also nicht mehr vorgeworfen werden können.

Die Schilderungen, bei denen der König negativ abschneidet, haben eines gemeinsam: Es handelt sich um politische Affären, die englandweit bekannt gewesen sein dürften. Der Anonymus konnte diese also nicht einfach durch Schweigen übergehen und benannte sie daher lieber direkt beim Namen – fast um Stephan dabei in Schutz zu nehmen. Die beiden Stellen jedenfalls, die der Anonymus überging, die aber in der HN von Wilhelm breit behandelt wurden, betrafen den Mordanschlag Stephans auf Robert von Gloucester und die schlechte königliche Diplomatie in Frankreich. Vielleicht, so könnte man mutmaßen, waren diese Ereignisse unter dem englischen Adel weniger bekannt.

Generell kann man sagen, dass im 12. Jahrhundert – etwas im Gegensatz zu den oben vorgestellten Thesen von Martina Blattmann und Matthias Becher – durchaus offen am Herrscher Kritik geübt wurde und er für das Unglück seines Volkes verantwortlich gemacht wurde. Vielleicht ein Spezifikum der englischen Chronistik? Hier bedarf es sicherlich weiterer Forschung. Auf der anderen Seite konnte festgestellt werden, dass es einem zweiten Autor (GS) durchaus leicht fallen konnte, die geäußerte Kritik des ersten Autors (HN) zu relativieren, teils sogar problemlos in Lob umzuwandeln. Zu wenig konnte die Kritik in der HN mit eindeutigen Beispielen (auch durch Zahlen belegt) untermauert werden, zu vieles blieb im Ungefähren, konnte daher umstandslos von der anderen Seite relativiert oder eben umgekehrt werden. Die Tatsache, dass auch die heutige Forschung Probleme damit hat, das gezeichnete Bild der einen oder der anderen Seite eindeutig zu bestätigen (da letztlich nicht genug anderweitige Quellen vorhanden sind),[29] muss zu denken geben. Damit kann ein abschließendes modernes Urteil über die Herrschaft Stephans eigentlich nicht gefällt werden. Das Beispiel führt (einmal mehr) deutlich vor Augen, dass die moderne Forschung stets sehr vorsichtig mit dem Urteil einzelner mittelalterlicher Historiographen umgehen muss.

---

29   Crouch (2000: 340–343) zeigt gut auf, dass das Bild Stephans als Herrscher in der anglo-amerikanischen Forschung bis in die 1970er Jahre ein desaströses war (gerade im Vergleich zu Heinrich I. und Heinrich II.). Dieses hat sich in den letzten Jahrzehnten stark gewandelt, aber auch Crouch tut sich mit einem abschließenden Urteil Stephans Herrschaft während des Bürgerkriegs (‚Anarchy') nicht leicht, betont vor allem die limitierten Herrschaftskompetenzen Stephans (im Vergleich zu Heinrich I.). Eventuell doch letztlich durch Wilhelm von Malmesburys Urteil inspiriert?

Anhang

TABELLE 26.2   Kritische Darstellung König Stephans anhand einzelner Textpassagen in den HN sowie die (relativierende) Darstellung derselben historischen Begebenheiten in den GS

Kritik an der Herrschaftsführung von König Stephan in der *Historia Novella*	Darstellung ebendieser historischen Ereignisse in den *Gesta Stephani* oder Alternativdarstellung bei Nichterwähnung des konkreten Ereignisses
1. 1135: Stephan bekommt Heinrichs I. Schatz (ca. 100.000 Pfund) in seine Gewalt und verschwendet ihn anschließend. Wilhelm schreibt, dass dieses Verhalten merkwürdig sei, da Stephan als Graf von Blois noch sehr demütig gewesen sei. (HN 17, 30–33)	1. Heinrichs Schatz wird erwähnt – der Übergang auf Stephan wird dabei als unproblematisch dargestellt. Der Schatzmeister William de Pont de l'Arche übergibt die Burg Winchester mitsamt des Schatzes sofort nach Stephans Krönung (GS 4, 8). Später (22, 46) wird beschrieben, dass Mathilde Teile des väterlichen Schatzes an sich genommen habe, obgleich es gerechter und besser für die Seele Heinrichs I. gewesen wäre, diesen Teil den Bedürftigen zu spenden.
2. 1136: Konzil von Westminster: Stephan gibt vor, die englischen Kirchengesetze und -güter zu achten. Wilhelm inseriert diesbezüglich als Nachweis eine königliche Urkunde. Die Urkunde wird später vom König gebrochen. (HN 18, 32–37)	2. König Stephan gibt der Kirche das zurück, was sie unter Heinrich I. verloren hat (letzterer hat die Kirche unterdrückt): Freiheit und Respekt. (GS 13, 24–28)
3. 1136: Die zitierte Urkunde wird sehr schnell von Stephan gebrochen: Bischöfe werden gefangen genommen, Kirchen geplündert, nicht geeignete Personen in hohen Kirchenämtern eingesetzt etc. Wilhelm schiebt das alles zwar auf die ‚schlechten königlichen Berater‘, aber Stephans Charakter wurde dadurch korrumpiert. (HN 19, 36–37)	3. Der Autor kommentiert, dass Stephen seine Versprechen gegenüber der englischen Kirche beachtet hätte, wenn er nicht *consiliatores peruersi* gehabt hätte. (GS 13, 26–28)
4. 1137: Stephan verübt einen Mordanschlag auf Robert von Gloucester. Stephan gibt dieses sogar zu und beteuert, so etwas nie wieder zu tun. Stephans Neid auf die Macht des Earls wird thematisiert, Stephan wird dabei wörtlich zitiert: ‚Cum me in regem elegerint, cur me destituunt? Per nascentiam Dei, numquam rex deiectus appellabor.‘ (‚Wenn sie mich zum König gewählt haben, warum verlassen sie mich nun? Bei der Geburt Gottes, ich werde niemals König ohne Thron genannt.‘) (Übers. GV) (HN 20, 37–41)	4. Ereignis wird nicht erwähnt.

TABELLE 26.2   Kritische Darstellung König Stephans (*fortges.*)

Kritik an der Herrschaftsführung von König Stephan in der *Historia Novella*	Darstellung ebendieser historischen Ereignisse in den *Gesta Stephani* oder Alternativdarstellung bei Nichterwähnung des konkreten Ereignisses
5. 1138: König Stephans schlechte Herrschaft wurde immer offensichtlicher. Er kann sich gegen die englischen Adeligen nicht durchsetzen, die ihm immer mehr Privilegien und Königsgüter entreißen – er stellt sich als völlig unfähig im Königsamt heraus. Earl Robert widerruft daraufhin legitimerweise seine Treue ('more maiorum amicitiam et fidem interdixit'). Stephan habe sich das Königreich *illicite* angeeignet und seine früheren Treueschwüre gebrochen. (HN 21, 40–43)	5. Der Kampf Stephans gegen einzelne englischen Adeligen wie Robert de Brampton, Eustace Fitz John, Geoffrey de Talbot oder Gilbert de Lacy wird beschrieben. Es wird deutlich, dass Stephan von seiner Seite alles unternimmt, um allem gerecht zu werden. Die militärischen Aufgaben Stephans, der versucht das Land zu befrieden, werden von dem Autoren als Herkulesaufgabe dargestellt. Die Kriege Sauls und anderer biblischer Könige seien im Vergleich mit den Lasten Stephans zu vernachlässigen (GS 32, 68). Der Überfall auf den Bischof von Bath Robert von Lewes, wird wiederum als Schande der königsfeindlichen Partei in Bristol gebrandmarkt. (GS 28, 60)
6. 1139: Stephan fürchtet sich vor den Sympathisanten Mathildes und lässt englische Adelige beim kleinsten Verdacht einsperren. Der Neid weltlicher Adeliger bezüglich der Besitzungen der Bischöfe Alexander von Lincoln und Roger von Salisbury wird geschildert. Sie verlangen vom König, dass die Bischöfe enteignet werden sollten. Wiederholt wird Stephan als ein König dargestellt, der sich durch die Forderungen Anderer führen ließ. Er macht einerseits Versprechungen an die Kirche, nicht gegen diese zu agieren, hält sich dann aber nicht an sein eigenes Wort. (HN 22, 44–47)	6. Das königliche Vorgehen gegen die beiden Bischöfe von Lincoln und Salisbury wird gerechtfertigt. Beide Bischöfe hätten ihre kirchlichen Ämter auf das Schlimmste missbraucht, indem sie illegitim weltliche Macht ausübten. Stephans Berater (u. a. namentlich der Graf Walram von Meulan) raten dem König zum schnellen Eingreifen, da diese Bischöfe mit Mathilde paktierten. Der Autor macht auf die Zerrissenheit Stephans aufmerksam (GS 34, 74–76), der sich schließlich aber doch für seine Berater entscheidet. Das entschuldigt der Autor zwar irgendwie aufgrund des Drucks der Berater, aber er geißelt die Tat deutlich. (GS 34, 76)
7. 1139: Konzil in Oxford: Der König greift zu einer List, um sich die Güter und Burgen des Bischofs von Salisbury anzueignen (HN 23, 46–49): Die Vasallen (*homines*) des Herzogs der Bretagne beginnen einen Streit mit den Vasallen des Bischofs von Salisbury am königlichen Hof, der blutig endet. Der König verlangt anschließend als Genugtuung für die königliche Beleidigung die Schlüssel für die bischöflichen Burgen. diese werden ihm unter Zwang übergeben.	7. In den GS kommt es bei Hof direkt zu einem Streit der bischöflichen und königlichen Ritter (*milites*), den der königliche Berater Walram von Meulan angestachelt hat. Anschließend werden die Bischöfe von Salisbury und Lincoln gefangen genommen, als ob sie 'regiae maiestatis transgressores' wären (also gegen Stephan vorsätzlich vorgegangen wären) – hier ist auch die GS sehr kritisch (GS 35, 76). Dennoch findet der Autor es mit Verweis auf die Bibel, Mark 12, 17 ('Redde Caesari quae sunt Caesaris') richtig, dass die Burgen Stephan anschließend unter Zwang übergeben mussten werden.

TABELLE 26.2   Kritische Darstellung König Stephans (*fortges.*)

Kritik an der Herrschaftsführung von König Stephan in der *Historia Novella*	Darstellung ebendieser historischen Ereignisse in den *Gesta Stephani* oder Alternativdarstellung bei Nichterwähnung des konkreten Ereignisses
8. 1139: Konzil von Winchester unter Vorsitz des päpstlichen Legaten Heinrich von Winchester (der Bruder des Königs): Der Legat rügt König Stephan öffentlich, dass er drei Bischöfe von England verfolgt und zwei festgesetzt hat (die Bischöfe von Salisbury, Lincoln und Ely) (HN 25, 50–53). Der König habe danach zu keinem Zeitpunkt seine Sünden bereut oder gebüßt.	8. Die Erzählung von dem Konzil steht im klaren Gegensatz zur HN: Nach den GS wird auf dem Konzil festgelegt, dass alle Schlupfwinkel (*receptacula*) des Tumultes und des Krieges von den Bischöfen an den König ausgeliefert werden müssen; gleichzeitig wird aber der König für sein hartes Vorgehen gerügt. Der König entschuldigt sich und fügte sich dem Urteil der Konzilsteilnehmer, indem er sein königliches Gewand abnahm und ‚demütig das Urteil hinnahm'. (*sententiam humiliter suscepit*) (36, 80)
9. 1139: Der päpstliche Legat/Bruder Stephans, Heinrich von Winchester, und der Erzbischof von Rouen, Hugues von Amiens, flehen Stephan an, indem sie ihm zu Füssen fallen, die englische Kirche nicht weiter zu plündern und ihr die verbrieften Rechte wieder herzustellen. Stephan, obgleich in dem Moment demütig und den Geistlichen zugeneigt, tut später – auf Anraten seiner Berater – nichts, um zum Frieden zurückzukehren und die Kirche zu schonen. (HN 30, 58)	9. 1139: Die Szene wird nicht erwähnt, dafür wird Bischof Heinrich von Winchester in seiner Rolle als Bruder Stephans stark kritisiert, da er Robert von Gloucester (der nunmehr ein Feind des Bruder war) erlaubt, England zu betreten und eine Rebellion anzustacheln (GS 41, 88). Derart, so der Autor, dürfe ein Bruder nicht auftreten. Die Integrität Heinrichs von Winchester wird dadurch deutlich herabgesetzt, was wiederum Stephans Handlungen aufwertet.
10. Stephans Herrschaft wird direkt mit der von Heinrich I. verglichen: ‚Erat ergo uidere calamitatem, Angliam, preclarissimam quondam pacis nutriculam, speciale domicilium quietis, ad hoc miseriae deuolutam esse, ut nec etiam episcopi nec monachi de uilla in uillam tuto possent progredi' ‚Derart war die Katastrophe sichtbar, dass England, einst die glänzendste Ernährerin des Friedens, ein besonderer Hort der Ruhe, in eine derartige Misere versunken war, da nicht einmal Bischöfe und Mönche sicher von einem Ort zum anderen reisen konnten.' [Übers. GV] (HN 36, 72) (HN 36, S. 70–73)	10. Stephan (GS 37–39, S. 80–84) wird als Friedensgarant gelobt, der viele (namentlich genannte) Opponenten des Königreichs erfolgreich bekämpft. Es ist hingegen der *populus Anglorum* (GS 40, 84), welcher durch Luxus und Müßiggang sowie andere Untugenden den Zorn Gottes hervorgerufen habe (besonders der Adel wird kritisiert). ‚Es war kein Wunder' (‚non fuit mirum'), dass England durch derart viele Kriege und Konflikte gequält wurde. Der Zustand Englands wird in den GS ähnlich wie in der HN gesehen, aber die Schuld dafür wird dem englischen Volk und nicht dem König gegeben.

TABELLE 26.2   Kritische Darstellung König Stephans (*fortges.*)

Kritik an der Herrschaftsführung von König Stephan in der *Historia Novella*	Darstellung ebendieser historischen Ereignisse in den *Gesta Stephani* oder Alternativdarstellung bei Nichterwähnung des konkreten Ereignisses
11. Stephans Herrschaft wird mit Roberts Regierungsstil verglichen (der vorhergehende Vergleich mit Heinrichs I. Regierung kam also nicht von ungefähr): Robert bemüht sich um Umsicht und Ausgleich während Stephan die Wirtschafts- und Münzpolitik nur verschlechtert, um Robert überall zu schaden. Stephan stellt somit sein Wohl über das englische Allgemeinwohl. (HN 37, 72–75)	11. Der Autor der GS stellt es als göttliche Vorhersehung (*providentia dei*) dar, dass Robert und Mathilde überhaupt in England landen können. Die dahingehenden Vorsichtsmaßnahmen Stephans seien eigentlich gut gewesen. Die Schuld träfe eben das englische Volk (siehe oben), König Stephan kann mit allen seinen Bemühungen nichts dagegen tun, dass England im Chaos versinkt. (GS 40, 86)
12. Die Machtlosigkeit König Stephans gegenüber räuberischen Rittern, die er zuvor selbst aus der Bretagne und Flandern gerufen hat, wird unterstrichen – konkret erscheint Robert Fitz Hubert als barbarisch (‚immanis et barbarus‘). Dieser wird schließlich von einem Gefolgsmann (John Fitz Gilbert) von Robert von Gloucester getötet – der König selbst scheint völlig hilflos und überfordert. (HN 39, 74–77)	12. Alle Adeligen fallen hinterhältig von König Stephan ab, obgleich sie ihm vorher den Lehenseid geschworen hatten (41, 90). In diesem Zuge wird Robert Fitz Hubert auch von der GS als sehr schlecht und gewalttätig dargestellt (‚viro crudelissimo‘) (GS 43, 92). Er wird später als Anhänger Roberts von Gloucester (GS 50, 104) genannt. Als dieser sich gegenüber dem Earl als untreu erwies, wird er – wie in der HN – von John Fitz Gilbert gefangen und später gehängt (GS 52, 108). Es besteht also kaum ein Unterschied zur HN, nur das verschwiegen wird, dass Stephan ihn nach England eingeladen hatte. Dafür wird betont, dass er zunächst aufseiten Roberts von Gloucester gewirkt habe.
13. 1140: Die verfehlten Friedensbemühungen Stephans in seiner Innen- und Außenpolitik werden geschildert: Selbst der päpstliche Legat, der Bischof von Winchester, zieht sich schließlich zurück, da Stephan unumstößliche diplomatische Gesetze nicht eingehalten habe: Wenn der König seinem Bruder (also dem Legat) Verhandlungsvollmachten gibt bzw. diesen verhandeln lasse und dann schließlich alle Beteiligten – außer eben Stephan – zustimmen (der französische König; Mathilde und Robert von Gloucester werden genannt), dann torpediere der König auf eine sehr unprofessionelle Weise den angestrebten Friedensprozess und man müsse davon ausgehen, dass ihm daran nichts liege. (HN 40, S. 76–79)	13. Dieses Ereignis wird von den GS übergangen.

TABELLE 26.2   Kritische Darstellung König Stephans (*fortges.*)

Kritik an der Herrschaftsführung von König Stephan in der *Historia Novella*	Darstellung ebendieser historischen Ereignisse in den *Gesta Stephani* oder Alternativdarstellung bei Nichterwähnung des konkreten Ereignisses
14. 1140: König Stephan entweiht die St Marienkirche von Bristol und funktioniert sie zur Burg um (HN 42, 82–85) – ein Sakrileg in Wilhelms Augen: ,Wäre es nicht besser zu sterben und glorreich im Kampf zu fallen als solch große Schande zu erleiden?' [Übers. GV] (,Nonne prestaret mori et gloriose occumbere, quam tam insignem contumeliam pati?')	14. Auch in den GS wird diese Tat aufs Schärfste kritisiert (GS 43, 94): Stephan habe damit Gott selbst beleidigt, da ein Gotteshaus zu eben dem Zweck des Betens (,domus orationis') konstruiert wurde und nicht als ,habitaculum bellantium' (,Behausung von Kriegern'). Der Autor weist dann darauf hin: ,nullum peccatum impunitum' (,keine Sünde bleibt ungesühnt'): Die desaströse Zukunft Stephans (die dem Autor ja bekannt war) hänge mit dieser Sünde zusammen (also das Jahr 1141).
15. 1140 [Eintrag unter 1142]: König Stephan betrügt in diesem Jahr seinen eigenen Anhänger, den Earl Ranulf II. von Chester, und dessen Bruder, indem er sie in Lincoln zu Weihnachten in der dortigen Burg belagert. Das scheint vielen unrecht, da der König den Earl nicht von seinem Treueeid ihm gegenüber befreit hat und ihn nun zum heiligen Hochfest einfach angriff. Wilhelm kommentiert, dass ,[...] er [Stephan] keine Gelegenheit auslassen wollte, um seine Macht zu vergrößern [...]', ,[...] qui nullam occasionem ampliandae potestatis omittere uellet [...].' Es wundert daher nicht, dass der Earl und sein Bruder von Stephan abfallen und ins Lager von Kaiserin Mathilde wechseln (HN 41, 80–83).	15. 1140: Auch die GS berichten darüber (GS 54, 110–112): Hier wird jedoch hervorgehoben, dass der Earl von Chester seiner Loyalität gegenüber dem König nicht mehr wie einst nachkam. Zudem unterdrückt er mit seiner Familie die Bürger von Lincoln und die Menschen in der Umgebung. Diese Bürger wenden sich heimlich mit der Bitte an den König, den Earl seines Amts zu entheben. Stephan zog also heran und belagerte die Burg Lincoln. Earl Ranulf hatte sich jedoch schon vorher mit Robert von Gloucester zusammengetan und kam nun seinerseits mit einem großen Truppenaufgebot an einem hohen Feiertag (Maria Lichtmess) nach Lincoln. Gleichzeitig wird beschrieben, wie Stephan bei der Messe seine Kerze ausgeht und auch noch in seiner Hand bricht – er kann die beiden Hälften jedoch wieder zusammenfügen und die Kerze wird wieder angezündet. Diese Szene wird vom Autor als Gotteszeichen dafür gesehen, dass Stephan für seine Sünden zeitweilig das Königreich verlieren werde, es aber wieder zurückgewinnen würde.

Bibliographie

Quellen

[Gesta Frederici:] *Bischof Otto von Freising und Rahewin. Die Taten Friedrichs oder richtiger Cronica (Gesta Frederici seu rectius cronica).* Transl. Adolf Schmidt, Ed. Franz-Josef Schmale. Freiherr-vom-Stein-Gedächtnisausgabe 17. Darmstadt: Wissenschaftliche Buchgesellschaft, 1965.

Gesta Stephani. Ed. and Transl. Kenneth Reginald Potter (with a new introduction and notes by R.H. Davis). Oxford Medieval Texts. Oxford: Clarendon Press, 1976. Referred to as: GS

William of Malmesbury. *Historia novella.* The contemporary history. Ed. Edmund King/ translated by K.R. Potter. Oxford Medieval Texts. Oxford: Clarendon Press, 1998. Referred to as: HN

Sekundärliteratur

Anderson, Carolyn (1999). ‚Narrating Matilda, ‚Lady of the English,' in the Historia Novella, the Gesta Stephani, and Wace's „Roan de Rou": the desire for land and order.' *Clio* 29: 47–67.

Becher, Matthias (2009). ‚Luxuria, libido und adulterium. Kritik am Herrscher und seiner Gemahlin im Spiegel der zeitgenössischen Historiographie (6. bis 11. Jahrhundert).' In *Heinrich IV.*, Ed. Gerd Althoff. Ostfildern: Thorbecke: S. 41–72.

Blattmann, Marita (2003). ‚ „Ein Unglück für sein Volk": Der Zusammenhang zwischen Fehlverhalten des Königs und Volkswohl in Quellen des 7. bis 12. Jahrhunderts.' In *Goslar im Mittelalter. Vorträge beim Geschichtsverein*, Ed. Hansgeorg Engelke. Bielefeld: Verlag für Regionalgeschichte, 9–28.

Chibnall, Marjorie (1993). *The Empress Matilda: queen consort, queen mother and lady of the English.* Oxford: Blackwell.

Creighton, Oliver Hamilton (2018). ‚Landscapes of War and Status: Siege Castles and the ‚Anarchy' of King Stephen's Reign'. In *L'environnement du château.* Ed. Peter Ettel et alii, Caen: Presses universitaires de Caen. 89–106.

Crouch, David (1999). *The reign of King Stephen, 1135–1154.* Harlow: Longman.

Dunphy, Raymond Graeme, ed. (2010). *The Encyclopedia of the medieval chronicle.* Leiden: Brill.

Görich, Knut (2011). *Friedrich Barbarossa. Eine Biographie*, München: C.H. Beck.

Goetz, Hans-Werner (1999). *Geschichtsschreibung und Geschichtsbewußtsein im hohen Mittelalter.* Berlin: Akademie Verlag.

Goetz, Hans-Werner (2007). ‚ „Vorstellungsgeschichte": Menschliche Vorstellungen und Meinungen als Dimension der Vergangenheit. Bemerkungen zu einem jüngeren Arbeitsfeld der Geschichtswissenschaft als Beitrag zu einer Methodik der Quellenauswertung.' In: *Vorstellungsgeschichte: gesammelte Schriften zu Wahrnehmungen,*

Deutungen und Vorstellungen im Mittelalter, Ed. Anna Aurast et alii. Bochum: Winkler. 3–18.

Gransden, Antonia (1974). *Historical writing in England c. 550 to c. 1307*. Ithaca, N.Y.: Cornell University Press.

Hanley, Catherine (2019). *Matilda: empress, queen, warrior*. New Haven, London: Yale University Press.

Kellermann, Karina, Alheydis Plassmann, and Christian Schwermann (2019). ‚Kritik am Herrscher – Möglichkeiten, Chancen, Methoden. Einleitung.‘ In *Criticising the Ruler in Pre-Modern Societies*, Ed. iidem., Göttingen: V&R unipress. 33–54.

Dalton, Paul, and G.J. White, eds. (2008). *King Stephen's reign: 1135–1154*. Woodbridge: Boydell Press.

King, Edmund J. ‚The Anarchy of King Stephen's Reign‘. *Transactions of the Royal Historical Society* 34 (1984): 133–153.

King, Edmund J. (1994). *The Anarchy of King Stephen's Reign*. Oxford: Clarendon Press.

King, Edmund J. (2006). ‚The Gesta Stephani‘. In *Writing medieval biography, 750–1250. Essays Frank Barlow*. Suffolk: Boydell & Brewer. 195–206.

King, Edmund J. (2010). *King Stephen*. New Haven, London: Yale University Press.

Schmale, Franz-Josef (1985). *Funktionen und Formen Mittelalterlicher Geschichtsschreibung. Eine Einführung*. Darmstadt: Wissenschaftliche Buchgesellschaft.

Schmid, Wolf (2008). *Elemente der Narratologie*, Berlin: De Gruyter.

Thomson, Rodney Malcolm, Emily Dolmans, and Emily A. Winkler, eds. (2017). *Discovering William of Malmesbury*. Woodbridge: Boydell & Brewer.

Vercamer, Grischa (2020). *Hochmittelalterliche Herrschaftspraxis im Spiegel der Geschichtsschreibung. Vorstellungen von „guter" und „schlechter" Herrschaft in England, Polen und dem Reich im 12./13. Jahrhundert*. Wiesbaden: Harrassowitz.

Weiler, Björn K.U. (2000). ‚Kingship, usurpation and propaganda in twelfth-century Europe: the case of Stephen‘ In: *Anglo-Norman Studies* 22: 299–326.

27

Lübeck Welthistorisch: Die Anfänge der Städtisch-Lübischen Geschichtsschreibung um 1300

Jürgen Wolf

Zusammenfassung

The present article outlines the development from simple detailed historical accounts to the universal-historical town chronicle. In the thirteenth century, Lübeck ascended to a significant metropolis of the Baltic Region, as is evident not least from a series of sumptuously decorated law books. A historical self-portrait was, however, yet to be penned. An interest in chronicles begins to develop around 1300 as smaller historical works emerge from the direct context of the City Council (Rat) and are entered into the city's most important books. This begins with situation-dependant accounts such as collections of annals, and culminates at the end of the fourteenth century in an extensive town chronicle with a universal-historical introduction, beginning with the Creation (Genesis). The aim of these historical works was ultimately to find Lübeck a place in universal sacred history.

1 Vorwort

Als historische Größe ist Lübeck in der klerikal-gelehrten lateinischen Geschichtsschreibung seit dem späten 12. Jahrhundert – implizit – präsent. Helmold von Bosau erwähnt die Stadt – ihre Geographie, einzelne Gebäude, einzelne Personen und Ereignisse, die Gründung, die große Brandkatastrophe – vielfach in seiner bis in seine Gegenwart (1170/1171) reichenden *Chronica Slavorum*.[1] Arnold von Lübeck führt in seiner *Chronica* nicht nur Helmold weiter, sondern rückt Lübeck stellenweise deutlicher in den historischen Blickpunkt.[2] Im Fokus stehen aber die Slawengeschichte, Reichsgeschichte sowie bei Arnold

---

1 Alle Stellen im Register unter *Lubeke* im Register der Ausgabe Helmold (1937: 257 f.); siehe kursorisch zu Helmold Berg (1981: 976–979) sowie zu Auftraggeberhintergrund und Intentio Goetz (2008: 392–395).

2 Arnold von Lübeck (1868); siehe kursorisch zu Arnold von Lübeck Berg/Worstbrock (1978/2004).

dann mehr denn je Herzog Heinrich der Löwe. In beiden lateinischen Chro-
nikwerken ist Lübeck nur ‚Geschehensort', wenn auch Augenzeugenberichte
unmittelbar in die Geschicke der Stadt und des Erzstifts hineinführen. Beide
Werke stehen explizit in der ‚Tradition der geistlichen Geschichtsschreibung'.[3]
Eine historiographische Idee der Stadt selbst oder eine irgendwie geartete
städtische Geschichtsschreibung repräsentieren sie gerade nicht; es gibt sie
schlicht noch nicht.

Im 13. Jahrhundert steigt Lübeck zur bedeutendsten Stadt des Ostseeraums
auf. Mit dem Aufstieg geht ein anfangs auf dem Latein und klerikaler Schriftex-
pertise beruhender, dann ab den 1260er Jahren aber auch auf der niederdeutschen Volkssprache und eigenständig-städtischer Schriftkompetenz basieren-
der, schnell unglaubliche Dynamik entwickelnder Verschriftlichungsprozess
einher: Um 1230 wird das Recht der Stadt zunächst schriftlich-lateinisch, ab
den 1260er Jahren auch und bald vorrangig in der niederdeutschen Volkssprache fixiert. Die städtische Schriftlichkeit ist dabei einerseits nach innen gerich-
tet (Kämmerei, Urteile, Erbsachen etc.), hat andererseits aber auch eine nach
außen gerichtete Komponente. So werden Lübische Rechtshandschriften und
damit Lübische Schriftlichkeit bald in den gesamten Ostseeraum exportiert.

Im Selbstverständnis wie in der Außenwirkung ist Lübeck nun Metropole.
Fassbar wird diese neue Idee der Stadt in eben dieser Rechtsüberlieferung: Seit
den 1260er Jahren entstehen in der städtischen Kanzlei Lübische Rechtsbücher
für den internen wie für den externen Gebrauch. Anfangs sind es einzelne Kodi-
zes, bald eine ganze Serie oftmals prachtvoller Handschriften.[4] Um 1300 haben
schließlich fast alle Städte des Ostseeraums ihr Recht bzw. ihr Rechtsbuch aus
Lübeck bekommen.[5] Das Skriptorium der Lübischen Kanzlei professionalisiert
sich dabei ab den 1280er Jahren soweit, dass entsprechende Rechtshandschriften in Serie und auf höchstem inhaltlichen wie äußerlichen Niveau hergestellt
werden können.[6] Chef der Kanzlei (*cancelere*) wird in diesen Jahren Albrecht
von Bardewik,[7] den man nach modernen Kriterien vielleicht als Innen- und
Außenminister der Stadt bezeichnen könnte.

---

3   Siehe Wriedt (1987: 401).
4   Einen grundlegenden Überblick bietet der gerade erschienene Forschungsband Bardewik
    (2021); zur Überlieferung der Rechtshandschriften vgl. zusammenfassend https://www.hands
    chriftencensus.de/werke/3051 (‚Lübisches Recht') und https://www.handschriftencensus.de/
    werke/481 (Albrecht von Bardewik: ‚Lübisches Recht' für Elbing).
5   Zur Verbreitung des Lübischen Rechts vgl. Cordes (2021c) und Wolf (2021b), sowie vor allem
    die Überblickskarte in Bardewik (2021): Bd. 1 (mit Erläuterung von Albrecht Cordes ebenda:
    19–34).
6   Dazu umfassend Wolf (2020) sowie Wolf (2021a) und Wolf (2021b).
7   Siehe Keil (1978) und besonders Lokers (2021: 315–340).

Seine Idee scheint eine schriftbasierte Organisation der Stadt, vielleicht sogar der Städte des gesamten südlichen und östlichen Ostseeraums, gewesen zu sein. So mag man die Rechtsbuchexporte und die nicht zuletzt damit verknüpften diplomatischen Initiativen interpretieren, wobei die diplomatischen Initiativen Lübecks über den Ostseeraum hinausreichen und unmittelbar in die Zentren der geistlichen wie weltlichen Macht zielen; exemplarisch angesprochen seien die Kontakte zu Kaisern und Königen sowie Bischöfen und Päpsten.

2   Die Chronik

‚Imme jare van Godes bort over dusent unde tvehundert in deme achten unde neghentychghesten jare' (Chronik 2, 1899: 301), also im Jahr 1298, lässt besagter Kanzleichef Albrecht von Bardewik ‚tho des rades unde der meynen stades nut' (Chronik 2, 1899: 301; Übers.: Zum Vorteil des Rates und meiner Stadt) ein umfangreiches Buch anlegen, dass alle Elemente dieses städtischen Aufstiegs sichern und dokumentieren soll. Dieser sogenannte *Copiarius* (Lübeck, AHL, Hs. 753)[8] enthält Abschriften vieler für die Stadt wichtiger Urkunden, Privilegien, Verträge, Briefe. Die gesamte lübische Vergangenheit wird in diesem einen Buch – das gleichsam per se eine Schatzkammer, aber auch so etwas wie das Grundgesetz Lübecks ist – ‚organisiert'. Doch die Idee dieses Buchs geht deutlich über das Bewahren, Sichern und Schonen der Originale hinaus, denn erstmals für die Lübecker Ratsschriftlichkeit wird eine völlig neue Textsorte in ein städtisch-lübisches Buch aufgenommen: Eine C h r o n i k.

Dieses rund 30 eng beschriebene Buchseiten umfassende Geschichtswerk (fols 335^r–350^r) erscheint für das neue Selbstverständnis Lübecks grundlegend, zumal nicht nur Ereignisse aus der näheren und ferneren Vergangenheit aufgezeichnet, sondern die Gesamtgeschichte in eine historische Narratio eingebunden wird. Sie zeigt in letzter Konsequenz Lübeck im Konzert der Großen der Zeit auf einer Stufe mit den Herrschern (Könige, Päpste, Bischöfe, Fürsten), d.h. den bis dato das historische Koordinatensystem im Sinn von Translatio imperii und Weltaltermodell bestimmenden Basiselementen.

---

8   Zur Handschrift vgl. umfassend Whitley (2021) sowie ergänzend Lokers (2021: Bd. 2, 328–340) und kursorisch https://www.handschriftencensus.de/7581. Die originalen Urkunden werden gleichzeitig in der Trese, etwa in der Funktion einer Schatzkammer, in der (städtischen!) Marienkirche aufbewahrt; siehe Graßmann (1974) und Albrecht (2010).

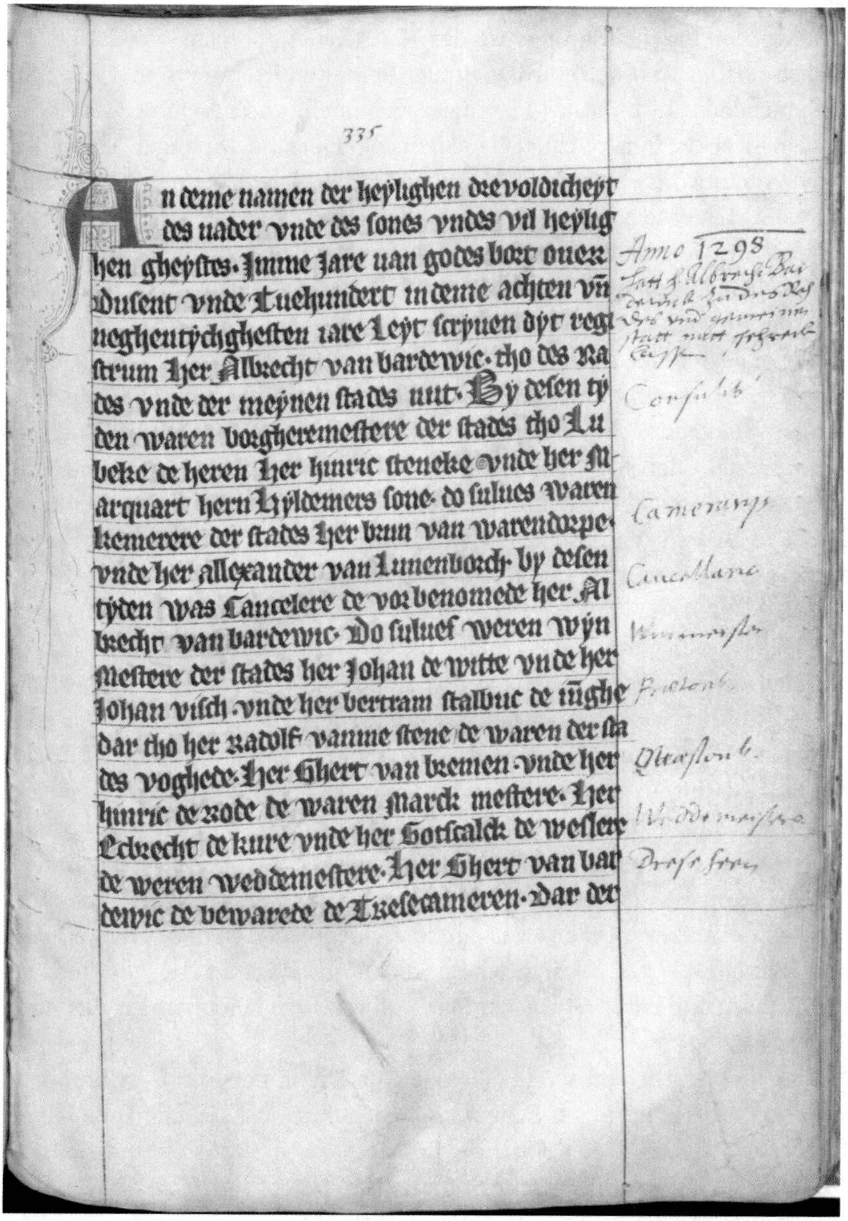

FIGURE 27.1 Lübeck, Stadtarchiv, Hs. 753 (Copiarius), fol. 335ʳ: Beginn der chronistischen Aufzeichnungen mit Datierung (‚Imme Jahre uan godes bort ouer Dusent vnde Tuehundert in deme achten vñ neghentýchghesten iare' = 1298), Auftraggeber (‚Albrecht van bardewic') und Intentio (‚tho des Rades vnde der meýnen stades nut')

2.1 *Auftrag und Idee: Lübeck am Rand der Weltgeschichte*

Auftraggeber für die Chronik ist der Kanzleichef Albrecht von Bardewik höchstselbst (s. Abb. 27.1). Er beauftragt die besten Experten seiner Kanzlei, entsprechendes historisches Material zu sammeln und zusammenzustellen. Für einen ersten Teil zeichnet der Stadtschreiber und Diplomat Alexander Huno[9] verantwortlich, für einen zweiten Teil der Kaplan (und spätere Stadtschreiber) Luder von Ramesloh.[10] ‚Im offiziellen Dienst der Stadt füttern sie die amtliche Geschichtsschreibung, die – ähnlich der Urkundenabschriften – der Ratsbefugnis untersteht, aber auch auf die Öffentlichkeit – „tho des Rades unde der meẏnen stades nut" – ausgerichtet ist.'[11]

Der erste Teil der Chronik nimmt die Gesta-Idee der klassischen lateinischen Geschichtsschreibung auf und erzählt von den Taten großer ‚Geschichtsheroen'. Stadtgeschichte erscheint dabei allenfalls als Hintergrundfolie. Im Zentrum steht der ‚here her Hinric von Mekelenborch', das ist Fürst Heinrich I. von Mecklenburg (Chronik 2, 1899: 302). Dass ein Fürst im Zentrum des Berichts steht, überrascht vor dem Hintergrund des beschriebenen Gesta-Modells der zeitgenössischen Geschichtsschreibung gerade nicht, zumal Heinrich als Kreuzfahrer bzw. Pilgerreisender (‚pelegrimaze') eingeführt wird und damit gleichsam automatisch Protagonist der Heilsgeschichte ist. Ganz in diesem heilsgeschichtlichen Sinne wird von den Kreuzzugsabenteuern des Herzogs ausführlich berichtet, wobei en passant weitere Zentralgestalten der Heilsgeschichte eingeführt werden: Sultan ‚Ladschin' (al-Malik al-Mansur Husam ad-Din Ladschin; 1297–1299) und Papst Bonifaz VIII. (1294–1303). Es folgen Berichte aus dem Umfeld der Könige Rudolf von Habsburg (1273–1291) und Albrecht von Österreich (1298–1308) – wohl nicht zufällig eingeleitet mit den Worten ‚eyn grot wunder in der cristenheit' (Chronik 2, 1899: 303). Die lübischen Chronisten verweilen also in heilsgeschichtlichen Dimensionen. In weiteren Berichten treten die Erzbischöfe von Köln, Mainz und Trier, die Herzöge von Sachsen und Bayern sowie der Markgraf von Brandenburg in Erscheinung (Chronik 2, 1899: 304).

Dass ‚by desen tyden scude och vele wonders in der werlde' (Chronik 2, 1899: 302; Übers.: in diesen Zeiten geschahen auch viele erstaunliche Dinge in der Welt), schreibt den Bericht expressis verbis in die Welt- und Heilsgeschichte ein. Das welthistorische Szenario ist damit entworfen – Lübeck tritt jedoch zunächst noch nicht als Akteur in Erscheinung. Aber, und da wird es nun für die Stadt interessant: Die genannten welthistorischen Protagonisten

---

9   Siehe kursorisch Keil (1983), Menke (1960: 116–120) und Wolf (2021b: Bd. 2, 387 f.).
10   Siehe kursorisch Parigger (1985), Wriedt (1987: 406) und Whitley (2021: 39, 93, 99).
11   Whitley (2021: 93); darin Textzitat nach der Handschrift korrigiert (s. Abb. 27.1).

stehen allesamt mit Lübeck in Kontakt. Sie verleihen Lübeck Rechte und Privilegien, stellen für Lübeck Urkunden aus, kommunizieren mit Lübeck, verhan-
deln mit der Stadt, schließen gemeinsame Bündnisse. Und die Stadt stellt für
sie Pferde ('mer den 30 ors ane andere perde'; Übers.: mehr als 30 Streitrosse
und andere Pferde), Ausrüstung und Sold für Söldnertruppen ('den gaf de stat
solt'; Übers.: denen gab die Stadt Sold) (Chronik 2, 1899: 302). Lübeck ist zwar
nicht selbst Akteur der Weltgeschichte, doch stets dabei – gleichsam implizit, schleichend, rückt die Stadt so in die Weltgeschichte hinein. Wenn dann
nach 26 Jahren Gefangenschaft beim Sultan der Kreuzfahrer Herzog Heinrich
von Mecklenburg bei seiner Rückkehr über Rom – einmal mehr selbstverständ-
lich – auch und gerade in Lübeck Station macht (Chronik 2, 1899: 306), scheinen Lübeck und Rom erstmals nicht mehr nur implizit symbolisch verbunden,
sondern faktisch auf einer Ebene. Und natürlich wird der Herzog in Lübeck
überschwänglich empfangen: 'se reden geghen ene myt scalle unde untfeng-
hen ene myt groten eren, unde se sanden eme tho willekome ryke presante. ...
aldus nymt de mere eyn ende' (Chronik 2, 1899: 306; Übers.: Sie ritten ihm entgegen mit Freudenlärm und empfingen ihn mit großen Ehren und sandten ihm
als Willkommensgruß kostbare Geschenke ... damit hat die Geschichte hier ein
Ende).

2.2   Lübeck als Akteur in der Weltgeschichte

Im zweiten Teil der Chronik stehen kriegerische Auseinandersetzung in 'Rygbe'
(Riga) (Chronik 2, 1899: 307) im Zentrum. Es geht um Auseinandersetzun-
gen der Bürger von Riga mit den 'broderen van deme Dudyschen hus', d.h.
dem Deutschen Orden.[12] Die Bürger der Stadt wollen, gegen das Vorrecht des
Ordens, an der Düna Brücken, Dämme und Mühlen anlegen. Als sie ohne
Erlaubnis mit den Arbeiten beginnen, kommt es zu kriegerischen Auseinan-
dersetzungen mit dem Orden. Auf Bitten der Bürger soll Erzbischof Johann III.
von Riga (der auch Graf von Schwerin war) den Streit schlichten. Als dies nicht
den erhofften Erfolg zeigt, wird sogar der Papst involviert. Trotzdem scheitern
die Schlichtungen, die Kriegshandlungen werden wieder aufgenommen.

Nachdem Erzbischof und Papst erfolglos waren, kommt Lübeck ins Spiel:
'Tho deseme daghe sanden de heren, de ratmanne, van Lubeke dor endrachty-
cheyt an beyden scyden ere ghoden boden, hern Johanne Keysere unde myt

---

12   Seit 1268 unterhielt der Deutsche Orden in Lübeck einen eigenen Hof. Die Beziehungen
      zwischen Orden und Stadt waren zunächst 'sachlich-neutral', später aber auch durch die
      Konkurrenz um Einflusssphären im Ostseeraum geprägt. So strebten einige Städte im
      Ostseeraum unter Ordenseinfluss zugunsten des Lübischen Rechts eine Lösung aus der
      Ordenshoheit an.

eme eren capellan hern Ludere, eynen prester, den her Bertram Mornwech nach Gotland' (Chronik 2, 1899: 308; Übers.: Zu diesem Termin sandten die Herren, die Ratmannen von Lübeck, für die Befriedung beider Seiten ihre ehrenhaften Boten, Herrn Johann Keyser und mit ihm ihren Kaplan, Herrn Luder, einen Priester, und den Herrn Bertram Mornwech, nach Gotland) und von dort nach Riga. ,Die städtischen Boten, besonders die aus Lübeck, werden als ungetrübte, unparteiische Schiedsrichter dargestellt, die wesentlich für die Friedensstiftung vor Ort agieren, „der heren boden van Lubeke unde de anderen stede karben hyr na tho hant tho lande unde scheden aldus van der stat tho der Ryge an ende unde schopen nicht, dat drapende was tho den vrede".'[13]

Bald darauf müssen sich die Rigaer der Überfälle der heidnischen Litauer erwehren, was dank des durch Lübeck und die anderen Städte gesicherten Friedens mit dem Orden gemeinsam mit diesem gelingt. Die Kausalkette – obwohl gerade nicht explizit formuliert – macht die Idee dieser Geschichte transparent:

- Krieg ist schädlich, besonders schädlich unter christlichen Streitparteien (Stadt Riga und der Orden).
- Schlichtung gelingt selbst den herausragendsten Protagonisten nicht (Erzbischof, Papst).
- Lübeck ist so integer und so ,uneigennützig', d. h. ,christlich-ideal', dass erst seine städtischen Diplomaten den Konflikt lösen können.
- Erst nach der Wiederherstellung des christlichen Friedens – des Gottesfriedens – kann man sich gegen die Heiden erwehren, denn dies verlangt das Zusammenspiel aller christlichen Kräfte.
- Quintessenz: Lübeck ist Garant des Gottesfriedens.

Anders als im ersten Teil der Chronik ist Lübeck nicht mehr nur passiv beobachtend und helfend dabei, Lübeck ist nun a k t i v e r Teil der Handlung und damit der Weltgeschichte, und zwar nicht nur gleichberechtigt, sondern letztlich sogar den althergebrachten heilsgeschichtlichen Instanzen: Orden, Bischof, Papst, übergeordnet, weil uneigennützig, rein der Sache verpflichtet, vernünftiger, letztlich christlich-ideal. Lübeck ist ,still und leise' in der Weltgeschichte angekommen.[14] Zu bedenken wäre in diesem Kontext allerdings, für wen diese Berichte gedacht waren und welche Funktion sie hatten. Das Buch, der *Copiarius*, gehörte jedenfalls zu den wichtigsten Büchern der Stadt überhaupt – doch wer konnte ihn einsehen? Menke ist ratlos und formuliert: ,Ein Publikum, das sie [die chronistischen Berichte] hätte lesen können, ist

---

13   Whitley (2021: 98).
14   Menke hebt die Unterschiede auch heraus, legt den Fokus beim zweiten Teil allerdings auf das „geschäftlich Wichtige" (1960: 119).

nicht recht vorstellbar. Es könnte höchstens ein kleiner Kreis von Ratsfreunden Bardewiks gewesen sein. Auch sind die Aufzeichnungen keinesfalls durch das eindeutige Interesse, den Anstoß eines festeren Öffentlichkeitskreises entstanden. Man wird sie also, was die Unentschiedenheit ihrer Form schon nahelegt, als V e r s u c h e unter der Leitung Bardewiks bezeichnen können.'[15] Mir scheinen sie allerdings weit mehr als ‚nur' Versuche – es ist die Bewusstwerdung der eigenen Geschichtlichkeit. Und gerade das sie transportierende Buch, der *Copiarius*, vermitteltet genau in diesem Sinn so etwas wie ein Statement, denn er ist eines der zentralen städtischen Bücher überhaupt: ‚Wir sind jetzt nicht nur über Urkunden und Akten, sondern auch über die Geschichte Teil der Heilsgeschichte.'

3   Von der Proto-Chronik zur Chroniktradition: Die Stadt Lübeck in der Weltgeschichte

Schon diese ersten chronistischen Versuche im Bardewikschen *Copiarius* aus dem Jahr 1298 hatten implizit über den Lübecker ‚Tellerrand' hinausgeblickt und mit Königen, Päpsten, dem Sultan als heidnischen Gegenspieler (jedoch hier sehr positiv gezeichnet), den Fürsten und Bischöfen sowie Kreuzzug und Heidenkriegen heilsgeschichtliche Dimensionen eröffnet. Es war allerdings eine gegenwartsbezogene Sichtweise. Lübeck selbst war nur ‚vorsichtig' ergänzend und erst im 2. Teil aktiv mitpräsent. Eine explizit formulierte chronologische Einordnung in die Weltalter bzw. die Heilsgeschichte fand nicht statt.

Die Proto-Chronik im *Copiarius* des Albrecht von Bardewik steht jedoch am Anfang einer über das Mittelalter hinausreichenden chronistischen Tradition Lübecks, deren Nucleus schließlich die überragende Stellung Lübecks in der Heilsgeschichte sein wird. Für die kommenden Jahrzehnte sind es zunächst weitere situative Aufzeichnungen eines Anonymus, nun im Bardewikschen Kodex des Lübischen Rechts (Jurjewetz, Museen der Stadt Jurjewetz, ЮКМ-2010; früher Lübeck, Stadtarchiv, Hs. 734, darin Fragm. 2). Keinesfalls zufällig handelt es sich wieder um eines der zentralen Bücher des Lübischen Selbstbewusstsein, dass man als ‚Behälter' für die Aufzeichnungen wählte: Die von Albrecht von Bardewik für den Rat initiierte herausragendste Prachthandschrift des *Lübischen Rechts*!

Auf einem eingelegten Blatt in dieser von der Stadt selbst 1294 in Auftrag gegebenen Prachthandschrift werden die Ereignisse der Jahre 1316–1320 ein-

---

15   Menke (1960:120).

getragen.[16] Im Zentrum stehen ‚pestilentz, hunger, hohee waßer vnd sturm‘ (Ganina 2021: 345) sowie eine allumfassende Hungerkatastrophe im gesamten nord- und ostseeischen Raum. ‚Auch die tragische Geschichte vom Gastmahl von Nyköping (‚Nyköpings gästabud‘) im Jahre 1317 (nicht 1316!), als der schwedische König Birger seine Brüder Erik und Waldemar zu einem Fest lud und in einem Turm verhungern ließ, ist seiner Aufmerksamkeit nicht entgangen.‘[17]

Noch ist alles kleinteilig, in der Regel gegenwartsbezogen und die heilsgeschichtliche Gesamtidee erscheint allenfalls vage zwischen den Zeilen, doch sehen wir ein wachsendes historisches Interesse. Albrecht von Bardewik, Alexander Huno und Luder von Ramesloh, d. h. Kanzler und Stadtschreiber, sammeln schon lange Historisches. Der entscheidende Schritt zur Stadtchronik ist damit vorbereitet, wird aber in der Ära des Kanzlers Albrecht von Bardewik – noch – nicht vollzogen. Vielleicht bedurfte es der großen Unwetter und Hungerkatastrophe, über die der Anonymus berichtet.

Wriedt[18] vermutet, dass im Bettelordensumfeld – er denkt speziell an die Franziskaner im Lübecker Katharinenkloster – eine solche größere Geschichtsidee ihre Wurzeln hat und stellt damit die alte These von Koppmann[19] in Frage, dass der bis 1349 belegte Lübecker Stadtschreiber Johannes Rode (‚Ruffus‘)[20] kurz vor der großen Pest eine erste Stadtchronik von 1105–1276 und dann eine Fortsetzung bis 1347 verfasst habe. Belegt ist eine entsprechende chronistische Arbeit des Stadtschreibers nicht, wohl aber das chronistische Projekt. Der die chronistischen Arbeiten ab 1385 fortführende Franziskaner Detmar berichtet in der Einleitung seiner Chronik nämlich, dass der ‚stades coroniken was nicht togeheschreven bi sos unde druttich jaren; ok was se brekastich der ding, de ghescheen weren an vele jaren unde an vele landen.‘ (Übers.: Die Stadtchronik war über 36 Jahre nicht weitergeschrieben worden. Auch war sie defizitär hinsichtlich der Dinge, die in vielen Jahren und in vielen Landen geschehen waren.) Und das ‚her Thomas Můrkerke unde heer Herman Langhe [...], desse coroniken vormiddest eyme ghestliken personen, en lesemester in sunte Franciscus orden, de sich nicht vil nomen, went he begheret God dar an to lovende, unde sich nicht‘, in Auftrag gegeben haben (Chronik 1, 1884: 195; Übers.: Herr Thomas Murkerke und Herr Hermann Lange ... [gaben in Auftrag] ... diese Chronik vermittels eines Geistlichen, und zwar einem Lesemeister im Fran-

---

16   Abdruck mit Übersetzung und Untersuchung Ganina (2021: 342–353); siehe ergänzend
        Menke (1960: 120).
17   Ganina (2021: 347).
18   Wriedt (1987: 401–426).
19   Koppmann (1897).
20   Wriedt (1992: 378 f.).

ziskanerorden, der es uneigennützlich auf sich nahm, weil er wünschte, Gott damit zu ehren und nicht sich selbst).

Halten wir also fest: Nach chronistischen Anfängen im *Copiarius* 1298, getragen von Kanzler und Führungspersonal der Kanzlei, führte ein Anonymus, vermutlich ein weiterer Kanzleimitarbeiter, wie der Überlieferungsort verrät, die chronistischen Arbeiten um 1320 weiter. Entgegen der Annahmen Wriedts, die 1349/50 abgebrochene *Stadeschronik* sei ‚das erste Werk der Lübecker Geschichtsschreibung [...], für das sich eine Beziehung zum Rat nachweisen läßt‘,[21] gibt es also schon ein halbes Jahrhundert früher eine vom Rat der Stadt initiierte Geschichtsschreibung.[22] Eine zusammenhängende Stadtchronik existierte aber noch nicht. Erst in den 1340er Jahren ging man im Auftrag der städtischen Führungselite daran, solche eine Stadtchronik zusammenzustellen – ob durch den Stadtschreiber Johannes Rode oder ‚externe Mitarbeiter‘ im Franziskanerkloster, bleibt offen. Diese Arbeit endete im Jahr 1349 abrupt – vermutlich durch den Tod. Die große Pestwelle hatte Lübeck erfasst. 36 Jahre später wird das Projekt ‚Stadtchronik‘ wieder aufgenommen. Im Auftrag der Lübecker Gerichtsherren Thomas Murkerke und Hermann Langhe arbeitet nun der Franziskaner Detmar[23] an einer großen Stadtchronik, die die älteren Arbeiten mit Berichten von 1105 bis 1347 aufnehmen und zunächst bis in seine Gegenwart ergänzen und dann kontinuierlich fortführen sollte. Die ersten Fortsetzungsberichte dürfte er noch selbst eingetragen haben.

Für unsere Frage sind aber nicht die Fortschreibungen dieser Stadtchronik von Interesse, sondern deren Beginn. Vielleicht schon Detmar selbst oder seine beiden städtischen Auftraggeber erkannten, dass das Geschichtsmodell aus Lübecker Perspektive eine entscheidende Lehrstelle hatte: Die lübische Geschichte begann nicht mit der Schöpfung, sondern erst ‚spät‘ im letzten Weltalter mit der Stadtgründung bzw. deren unmittelbarer Vorgeschichte. Dieses Manko wollte man beseitigen. Detmar oder ein Detmar-Kompilator zogen eine Universalchronik zu Rate: Eine *Sächsische Weltchronik*. Der mit dem Jahr 1105 beginnenden lübischen Stadtchronik wurde ein Exzerpt aus der *Sächsischen Weltchronik* vorangestellt, und ‚plötzlich‘ begann die Lübische Geschichte mit der Schöpfung. Der aus der Weltchronik entnommene Part über-

---

21   Wriedt (1987: 408 f.).

22   Wriedt (1987: 409) erwähnt „die kurzen Berichte über die Jahre 1297/98 und 1316 bis 1321 in den Rechtskodizes", billigt ihnen aber keine historiographische Dimension zu.

23   Von 1368–1380 ist Detmar als Lesemeister und bis 1394 generell als Mitglied des Franziskanerkonvents von St Katharinen in Lübeck nachweisbar; vgl. kursorisch Sandfuchs (1980: 68) und Wriedt (1987: 403 f.) sowie detaillierter zu Quellen und Entstehungshintergründen Menke (1960: 93–109).

nimmt deren Reimvorrede und setzt dann mit dem Schöpfungsbericht ein, reicht allerdings nur bis zu Alexander dem Großen.[24] Vordergründig bleibt also weiter eine große chronistische Lücke, nun von Alexanders Tod bis zum Jahr 1105. Unser Chronist weiß diese Lücke aber elegant zu schließen, wenn er ausführt: ‚Nach deme mal da wy myd desser kroneken sind komen over mer, so dencke ik van der stadt Lubeke antohevende unde vorder mer mede in to bringhende van pawesen, keyseren, vorsten, steden unde heren. Hyr betenget sik de croneke van Lubeke. De Mylde Christ Vader aller saligen de gheve uns na dessem levende sinen ewighen vrede, sunderliken jo den ghennen, dede der erbaren staed Lubeke unde dat meine gud myd buwen vorderen ...‘ (Chronik 1, 1884: 124; Übers.: Nachdem wir mit dieser Chronik nach Europa [‚over mer‘] gekommen sind, so gedenke ich von der Stadt Lübeck anzufangen zu berichten und mehr zu berichten von Päpsten, Kaisern, Fürsten, Städten und Herren. Hier beginnt die Chronik/Geschichte von Lübeck. Der milde Christus, Vater aller Seeligen, gebe uns nach diesem [irdischen] Leben seinen ewigen Frieden, und zwar besonders denjenigen, die die ehrbarer Stadt Lübeck und die Wirtschaft allgemein mit Bauen förderten ...). Mit Alexander kommt die Weltgeschichte also ‚over mer‘, d. h. sie kommt „zu uns", womit die ‚dudeschen herren‘ gemeint sind. Hier beginnt die Geschichte der Sachsen, und keinesfalls zufällig wird genau ein Sachsenherzog – Heinrich der Löwe – nach einer ersten ‚Vorgründung‘ durch die Wenden und einem weiteren Versuch durch Graf Adolf II. von Schauenburg schließlich der Hauptstadtgründer sein. Damit ist der weltgeschichtliche Kreis geschlossen, der nun mit der Schöpfung beginnend in der Reihe ‚van pawesen, keyseren, vorsten, steden unde heren‘ explizit die Stadt miteinschließt.

Überliefert ist diese um den heilsgeschichtlichen Part erweiterte Detmar-Kompilation in zwei in Lübeck entstandenen Handschriften des 15. Jahrhunderts: Der im Jahr 1842 in Hamburg verbrannten Handschrift der Bibl. der Patriotischen Gesellschaft und dem Mitte des 15. Jahrhunderts vollendeten Ms. Lub. 2° 4 der Lübecker Stadtbibliothek.[25] Der erste nachweisbare Besitzer dieses Kodex, Peter van Kollen, war wie alle späteren Besitzer in Lübeck ansässig.[26]

---

24   Sächsische Weltchronik (1877: 65,1–78,22).

25   Beschreibungen Wolf (1997: 97–99); vgl. https://handschriftencensus.de/3545 und https:// handschriftencensus.de/4868.

26   Vgl. zur weiteren Lübecker Geschichtsschreibung des Spätmittelalters z. B. die Überblicke bei Menke (1960) und Möbius (2011).

Bibliographie

Quellen – Handschriften

Jurjewetz

Kunsthist. Museum

ЮКМ-2010 [früher Lübeck, *Stadtarchiv*, Hs. 734]

Lübeck

Stadtarchiv

Hs. 753 (*Copiarius*)

Stadtbibliothek

Ms. Lub. 2° 4 (*Detmar-Chronik* mit Einleitung aus der *Sächsischen Weltchronik*)

Hamburg

Bibl. der Patriotischen Gesellschaft

Ms. im Jahr 1842 verbrannt (*Detmar-Chronik* mit Einleitung aus der *Sächsischen Weltchronik*)

Quellen – Gedruckte

Arnold von Lübeck (1868). *Arnoldi chronica Slavorum. Ex recensione I.M. Lappenbergii.* In *Scriptores rerum Germanicarum in usum scholarum ex Monumentis Germaniae Historicis* recudi fecit Georgius Heinricus Pertz. Hannover: Hahnsche Buchhandlung.

Chronik 1 (1884). *Die Chroniken der niedersächsischen Städte: Lübeck*, Bd. I. Hg. von Karl Koppmann, (Die Chroniken der deutschen Städte vom 14. bis ins 16. Jahrhundert 19). Leipzig: Vandenhoeck & Ruprecht.

Chronik 2 (1899). *Die Chroniken der niedersächsischen Städte: Lübeck*, Bd. II. Hg. von Karl Koppmann (Die Chroniken der deutschen Städte vom 14. bis ins 16. Jahrhundert 26). Leipzig: Vandenhoeck & Ruprecht (S. 287–316 Abdruck der Bardewik-Chronik von fols 335^r–350^r).

Helmold (1937). *Helmolds Slavenchronik* (*Helmoldi presbyteri Bozoviensis Cronica Slavorum*). In *Monumenta Germaniae Historica. Scriptores rerum Germanicarum in usum scholarum separatim editi* 32. Hg. von Bernhard Schmeidler. Hannover: Hahnsche Buchhandlung.

Sächsische Weltchronik (1877). *Sächsische Weltchronik.* In: MGH Deutsche Chroniken II. Hg. von Ludwig Weiland. Hannover: Hahnsche Buchhandlung: 1–384.

Urkundenbuch 1–3 (1843–1871). *Urkundenbuch der Stadt Lübeck* 1–3. Hg. vom Verein für Lübeckische Geschichte und Altherthumskunde. Lübeck: Grauthoff.

Sekundärliteratur

Albrecht, Thorsten (2010). ,Die Trese – die Schatzkammer des Rates der Hansestadt Lübeck in der Marienkirche.' *Jahrbuch für Hausforschung* 60: 363–369.

Bardewik (2021). *Der Bardewiksche Codex des Lübischen Rechts von 1294*. Bd. 1: Faksimile und Erläuterungen. Hg. von Natalija Ganina, Albrecht Cordes und Jan Lokers namens des Vereins für Lübeckische Geschichte und Altertumskunde. Edition: Nigel F. Palmer und Natalija Ganina. Übersetzung: Albrecht Cordes und Dorothea Heinig; Bd. 2: Edition, Textanalyse, Entstehung und Hintergründe. Hg. von Natalija Ganina, Albrecht Cordes und Jan Lokers. Oppenheim: Nünnerich-Asmus Verlag.

Berg, Dieter/Franz Josef Worstbrock (1978/2004). ,Arnold von Lübeck'. *Verfasserlexikon. Die deutsche Literatur des Mittelalters* 1: 472–476 + 11: 137.

Berg, Dieter (1981). ,Helmold von Bosau.' *Verfasserlexikon. Die deutsche Literatur des Mittelalters* 3: 976–979.

Bruns, Friedrich (1932). ,Der Verfasser der lübischen Stadeschronik.' *Zeitschrift des Vereins für lübeckische Geschichte und Altertum* 26: 247–276.

Bruns, Friedrich (1921). ,Der Verfasser der Lübecker Annalen.' *Lübische Forschungen. Jahrhundertgabe des Vereins für Lübeckische Geschichte und Altertumskunde*: 255–266.

Bruns, Friedrich (1903). ,Die Lübecker Stadtschreiber von 1350–1500.' *Hansische Geschichtsblätter* 31: 45–118.

Bruns, Friedrich (1951). ,Der Lübecker Rat. Zusammensetzung, Ergänzung und Geschäftsführung von den Anfängen bis ins 19. Jahrhundert.' *Zeitschrift des Vereins für Lübeckische Geschichte und Altertumskunde* 32: 1–69.

Cordes, Albrecht (2021a). ,Die Sprache der Statuten des lübischen Rechts (ca. 1224–1642).' *Zeitschrift für deutsches Altertum* 150: 84–102.

Cordes, Albrecht (2021b). ,Die Geschichte des Lübischen Rechts im Ostseeraum bis 1350. Zugleich eine Erläuterung der Karten zur Verbreitung des lübischen Rechts.' In *Bardewik* Bd. 1: 19–34.

Cordes, Albrecht (2021c). ,Das lübische Recht im Bardewikschen Codex von 1294.' In *Bardewik* Bd. 2: S. 286–303.

Fehling, Emil Ferdinand (1925/1978). *Lübeckische Ratslinie von den Anfängen bis auf die Gegenwart*. Veröffentlichungen zur Geschichte der Freien und Hansestadt Lübeck A 7, Heft 1. Lübeck: Schmidt Röhmhild (Nachdruck).

Ganina, Natalija (2021). ,Aufzeichnungen eines Lübecker Unbekannten über Ereignisse von 1316–1320.' In *Bardewik* Bd. 2: 342–353.

Goetz, Hans-Werner et al. (2008). *Geschichtsschreibung und Geschichtsbewusstsein im hohen Mittelalter*. Orbis mediaevalis. Vorstellungswelten des Mittelalters 1. 2. Ergänze Auflage. Berlin: Akademie Verlag.

Graßmann, Antjekathrin (1974). ,Von der Trese, der Schatzkammer des Lübeckischen Rats.' *Zeitschrift des Vereins für Lübeckische Geschichte und Altertumskunde* 54: 87–93.

Hoffmann, Erich (1988). ‚Lübeck im Hoch- und Spätmittelalter. Die große Zeit Lübecks.‘ In *Lübeckische Geschichte*, hg. von Antjekathrin Graßmann. Lübeck: Schmidt-Röhmhild: 79–328.

Keil, Gundolf (1978). ‚Albrecht von Bardewik.‘ *Verfasserlexikon. Die deutsche Literatur des Mittelalters* 1: 175.

Keil, Gundolf (1983). ‚Alexander Huno.‘ *Verfasserlexikon. Die deutsche Literatur des Mittelalters* 4: 311–312.

Koppmann, Karl (1897). ‚Die Lübische Stadeschronik und ihre Ableitungen.‘ *Hansische Geschichtsblätter* 25: 149–202.

Lokers, Jan (2021). ‚Lübeck um 1300.‘ *Bardewik* Bd. 2: 306–341.

Lutterbeck, Michael (2002). *Der Rat der Stadt Lübeck im 13. und 14. Jahrhundert. Politische, personale und wirtschaftliche Zusammenhänge in einer städtischen Führungsgruppe*. Veröffentlichungen zur Geschichte der Hansestadt Lübeck B 35. Lübeck: Schmidt-Röhmhild.

Malm, Mike (2014). ‚Albrecht von Bardewick.‘ *Deutsches Literatur-Lexikon. Das Mittelalter* 6: 611–614.

Menke, Johann Bernhard (1960). ‚Geschichtsschreibung und Politik in deutschen Städten des Spätmittelalters. Schluß – Lübeck.‘ *Jahrbuch des Kölnischen Geschichtsvereins* 34/35: 85–194.

Möbius, Sascha (2011). *Das Gedächtnis der Reichsstadt. Unruhen und Kriege in der lübeckischen Chronistik und Erinnerungskultur des späten Mittelalters und der frühen Neuzeit* (Formen der Erinnerung 47). Göttingen: Vandenhoeck & Ruprecht.

Parigger, Harald (1985). ‚Luder von Ramesloh.‘ *Verfasserlexikon. Die deutsche Literatur des Mittelalters* 5: 960–961.

Sandfuchs, Thomas (1980). ‚Thomas Sandfuchs, Detmar von Lübeck.‘ *Verfasserlexikon. Die deutsche Literatur des Mittelalters* 2: 68–69.

Schneider, Reinhard (2000). ‚Riga im Mittelalter. Eine Kaufmannsstadt im Schnittpunkt verschiedener Kulturen.‘ In *Grenzkultur – Mischkultur*, hg. von Roland Marti. Veröffentlichungen der Kommission für Saarländische Landesgeschichte und Volksforschung 35. Saarbrücken: SDV: 189–207.

Whitley, Robert (2021). *Pragmatische Literatur aus dem Lübischen Kanzleiskriptorium. Grundsätzliche Überlegungen anhand ausgewählter Beispiele*. Marburg: Mag. Masch.

Wolf, Jürgen (2021a). ‚Ein Blick in das Lübische Kanzleiskriptorium. 1250–1350.‘ In *Bardewik* Bd. 2: 354–369.

Wolf, Jürgen (2021b). ‚Lübische Rechtsbücher in Serie. Buchproduktion als Herrschaftsinstrument.‘ In *Bardewik* Bd. 2: 370–395.

Wolf, Jürgen (2020). ‚Frühe Handschriften des Lübischen Rechts. Identitätsstiftung via Buch- und Textgestalt?‘ In *Bücher und Identitäten. Literarische Reproduktionskulturen der Vormoderne*, hg. von Nicole Eichenberger u. a. Wiesbaden: Reichert: 105–120.

Wriedt, Klaus (1966). ‚Die Annales Lubicenses und ihre Stellung in der Lübecker Geschichtsschreibung des 14. Jahrhunderts.' *Deutsches Archiv für Erforschung des Mittelalters* 22: 556–586.

Wriedt, Klaus (1978). ‚Das gelehrte Personal in der Verwaltung und Diplomatie der Hansestädte.' *Hansische Geschichtsblätter* 96: 15–37.

Wriedt, Klaus (1987). ‚Geschichtsschreibung in den wendischen Hansestädten.' In *Geschichtsschreibung und Geschichtsbewußtsein im späten Mittelalter*, hg. von Hans Patze. Vorträge und Forschungen 31. Sigmaringen: Thorbecke: 401–426.

Wriedt, Klaus (1992). ‚Rufus-Chronik.' *Verfasserlexikon. Die deutsche Literatur des Mittelalters* 8: 378 f.

Bibliography of Publications by Erik Kooper Since 2007

This bibliography supplements the 'Select Bibliography of the Writings of Erik Kooper' in the volume of studies presented to Erik on the occasion of his sixty-fifth birthday and retirement from the University of Utrecht, *People and Texts: Relationships in Medieval Literature: Studies Presented to Erik Kooper*, ed. Thea Summerfield and Keith Busby (Leiden: Brill, 2007), 199–205.

2008

The Medieval Chronicle v, ed. Erik Kooper, Amsterdam and New York, 2008.

2009

The Medieval Chronicle vi, ed. Erik Kooper, Amsterdam and New York, 2009.

2010

'Het familiewapen: van kerkenningsteken tot statussymbool', in: *Madoc* 24, 2010, 66–74.

2011

'*Arthur*: A New Critical Edition of the Fifteenth-Century Middle English Verse Chronicle', Marije Pots and Erik Kooper, in: *The Medieval Chronicle* vii, ed. Juliana Dresvina and Nicholas Sparks, general ed. Erik Kooper, Amsterdam and New York, 2011, 239–266.

'Guests of the Court: An Unnoticed List of Arthurian Names (British Library, Add. 6113)', in: *"Li premerains vers", Essays in Honor of Keith Busby*, Faux Titre, Volume: 361, ed. Catherine M. Jones, Amsterdam, 2011.

The Medieval Chronicle vii, ed. Juliana Dresvina and Nicholas Sparks, general ed. Erik Kooper, Amsterdam and New York, 2011.

2012

'A Source for the Middle English Poem *Arthur*', in: Erik Kooper and Julia Marvin (eds.), *Arthuriana*, 22 (4), Special Issue in Honor of Edward Donald Kennedy, 2012, 25–45.

'Three twelfth-century kings and their successors in some Middle English chronicles', in: Karen Hodder & Brendan O'Connell (eds.), *Transmission and Generation in Medieval and Renaissance Literature: Essays in Honour of John Scattergood*, Portland, Or., 2012, 37–51.

'Van nieuwkomer tot letter-lijk. De droeve geschiedenis van de Oud-engelse letter genaamd wynn, "vreugde"', in: *Madoc* 26, 2012, 237–240.

2013

'Content Markers in the Manuscripts of Robert of Gloucester's Chronicle', in: *The Medieval Chronicle* VIII, ed. Erik Kooper and Sjoerd Levelt, Amsterdam and New York, 2013, 43–74.

'Laʒamon's Prosody: Caligula and Otho—Metres Apart', in: *Reading Laʒamon's* Brut: *Approaches and Explorations*, Studies in Literature, Volume 52, ed. Rosamund Allen, Jane Roberts, and Carole Weinberg, Amsterdam and New York, 2014, 419–441.

The Medieval Chronicle VIII, ed. Erik Kooper and Sjoerd Levelt, Amsterdam and New York, 2013.

2015

The Medieval Chronicle IX, ed. Erik Kooper and Sjoerd Levelt, Amsterdam and New York, 2015.

2016

'Longleat House MS 55: An Unacknowledged *Brut* Manuscript?', in: *The Prose* Brut *and Other Late Medieval Chronicles. Books have their Histories: Essays in Honour of Lister M. Matheson*, ed. Jaclyn Rajsic, Erik Kooper and Dominique Hoche, Woodbridge and Rochester, NY, 2016, 75–93.

The Medieval Chronicle X, ed. Ilya Afanasyev, Juliana Dresvina, and Erik S. Kooper, Leiden, 2016.

'The Middle English Life of St Teilo', Erik Kooper and David Callander, in: *The Mediaeval Journal* 6 (1), 2016, 29–72.

The Prose Brut *and Other Late Medieval Chronicles. Books have their Histories: Essays in Honour of Lister M. Matheson*, ed. Jaclyn Rajsic, Erik Kooper and Dominique Hoche, Woodbridge and Rochester, NY, 2016.

2018

'The Case of the Cutting Copyist: Or, How London, British Library, MS Sloane 2027 of Robert of Gloucester's *Chronicle* Lost 4000 Lines', in: *Editing and Interpretation of Middle English Texts: Essays in Honour of William Marx*, ed. Margaret Connolly and Raluca Radulescu, Turnhout, 2018. 109–131.
The Medieval Chronicle 11, ed. Erik Kooper and Sjoerd Levelt, Leiden and Boston, 2018.
'Telling Tales', in: European Literary History—an Introduction, ed. Maarten de Pourcq and Sophie Levie, New York, NY, 128–138.

2019

The Medieval Chronicle 12, ed. Erik Kooper and Sjoerd Levelt, Leiden and Boston, 2019.
'The Style and Authorship of the Kildare Poems', Erik Kooper and Annelies Kruijshoop, in: In Other Words: Transcultural Studies in Philology, Translation and Lexicology. Presented to Hans Meier on the Occasion of his 65th Birthday, ed. J. Lachlan Mackenzie and Richard Todd, Berlin and Boston, 2019, 45–56.

2020

The Medieval Chronicle 13, ed. Erik Kooper and Sjoerd Levelt, Leiden and Boston, 2020.

2021

The Medieval Chronicle 14, ed. Erik Kooper and Sjoerd Levelt, Leiden and Boston, 2021.

Index

Names have been normalized according to English custom, also for the contributions in French and German. All medieval and early modern persons have been alphabetised under their given name, and only modern authors under their surname. Works are listed under the name of their author when known. From the footnotes, only authors, works and manuscripts not mentioned in the text on the same page are indexed.